Rhode Island
General Court of Trials

1671 - 1704

---

transcribed by Jane Fletcher Fiske

Boxford, Massachusetts
1998

ISBN 0-9615790-2-1

TABLE OF CONTENTS

LIST OF COURTS AND TERMS

General Court of Trials at Newport
unless otherwise noted

** indicates a break in chronological order of entries*

LIST OF COURTS AND TERMS, *continued*

LIST OF COURTS AND TERMS, *continued*

GLOSSARY

The following definitions are drawn from Henry Campbell Black *et al.*, *Black's Law Dictionary*, abridged sixth ed. (St. Paul, Minn.: West Publishing Co., 1991) and the *Oxford English Dictionary* (CD-ROM version), selected for 17th and 18th century usage.

Bailiff: person acting in administerial capacity who has the custody and administration of lands or goods for the benefit of the owner, and is liable to render an account thereof.

Chance medley: a sudden affray (*chance medlée*); homicide by misadventure, or in self-defence. ". . . not done with foregoing malice, and so chance medley, because it has a present intent to kill."

Defendant: the party against whom relief or recovery is sought ... the person defending or denying.

Deponent: one who deposes, gives under oath testimony that is reduced to writing.

Deposition: the testimony of a witness taken upon oral question or written interrogation, *outside* of court, and put in writing, to be used as evidence in a court case.

Detinue: a form of action for recovery of personal chattels from one who acquired possession of them lawfully, but retained it without right, together with damages for the detention.

Execution: the carrying out of something, such as a judgment of the court. This often involved seizing and selling property of a defendant in order to satisfy a judgment against him.

Fee in tail: to be held by exclusive heirs (*entailed*), as directed by a will (as in primogeniture, when property passes to the eldest son).

Fee simple: to hold to a person or his heirs forever, absolutely, and simply.

GLOSSARY, *continued*

Mandamus: "We command." A judicial writ directed to an inferior court, an officer, etc., commanding some specified thing to be done.

Nihil dicit: "He says nothing." Name of a judgment which may be taken as of course against a defendent who omits to plead or answer plaintiff's declaration or complaints within time limits . . . judgment for want of a plea.

Non suit: a term broadly applied to a variety of terminations of an action which do not adjudicate issues on the merits of the case. In early use, the cessation of a suit resulting from the voluntary withdrawal of the plaintiff.

Oyer and Terminer: a half-French phrase applied in English to the assizes, directed to the judges and empowering them to "inquire, hear, and determine" treasons, felonies, and misdemeanors.

Plaintiff: a person who brings an action ... seeks remedial relief for an injury to rights; a complainant.

Seized or **seised** [of property]: from *seisin,* possession of real property, in *fee simple, q.v.* (thus *seised in fee simple* means to hold legal title to the land in question).

Trespass: unlawful interference with one's person, property, or rights.

Trover: action for the recovery of damages against a person who had found another's goods and wrongfully converted them to his own use.

Writ: a written judicial order for instituting an action. (The writ is usually the first document found in a case, giving the reason for the suit and sometimes ordering the arrest of the defendant.) There are many kinds of writs, such as **writ of execution**, which directs the sheriff to enforce the judgment of the court.

INTRODUCTION

The value of court records as a resource for both genealogists and historians is well understood. In Rhode Island this source is especially important, because of the damage and destruction (in 1779, during the British retreat to New York) of many of the records of Newport, which for many years was the most active town in the colony as well as the seat of government.

In 1640 circuit quarterly courts were established in Rhode Island, and records of these earliest courts are scattered in the manuscript volume, "Rhode Island Colony Records, 1646-1669," at the Rhode Island Archives. Records covering the years 1641 to 1646 were abstracted and included by Howard M. Chapin in the second volume of his *Documentary History of Rhode Island* (Providence, 1920). In 1647 the Code of Laws was adopted and the General Court of Trials established; at first the new court was also a circuit court, semi-annual and later quarterly. Most of the records of this court covering the period 1647 to 1670 are preserved in the manuscript volume just mentioned, and a transcription was published by the Rhode Island Historical Society in two very small books, *Rhode Island Court Records [:] Records of the Court of Trials of the Colony of Providence Plantations*, Volume I covering 1647 - 1662, and Volume II, 1663 - 1670 (Providence, 1920, 1922).

In 1671 the court began keeping its records in a separate book, which has long been known as "Book A" or "Newport Court Book A," and it is from this that the present transcription has been made. Book A has been traditionally kept with later Newport County Court Books (which begin with "Book B" and continue alphabetically), although it covers the entire colony, from 1671 to 1721, when the counties were established and with them county courts. At one time, therefore, it was at the Newport Court House, and it evidently traveled with the other Newport court records to the Veterans' Auditorium in Providence, then to Providence College Archives, the Superior Court Building in Providence, and finally to the Rhode Island Judicial Archives at One Hill Street in Pawtucket.

I began transcribing Book A about 1985, when it was at Providence College. The reaction of most people who saw me working on it was astonishment that anybody would want to do such a thing, but when J. Stephen Grimes was put in charge of the court records he suggested making good ledger-sized photocopies so that I could work on it more easily at home — an offer quickly accepted and accomplished. Unfortunately Steve was able to copy only half the book before the records were moved again, to a location where no large copier was available. Thus the present transcription ends in 1704. It will be noted, however, that around 1700 information entered became briefer and more concise, in contrast to the earlier records for which full transcription seems more valuable. Should someone feel inclined to do further work with the second half of Book A, abstraction and summarization of the cases might well suffice.

The twelve pages of records from the Court of Trials at Warwick 1659 - 1674 that appear as an appendix are copied directly from a transcription made by Helen Capwell and published originally in pamphlet form about 1922 by the Shepley Press. After I came across a copy at an antique book sale a couple of years ago, it seemed appropriate to include these records here in order to make them more widely available.

Most of the files — the documents entered as evidence for the cases such as depositions, deeds, wills, accounts, and notes — for the period of Book A have been lost. For later county court records, however, there are a great many surviving files, beginning around 1721. I have personally made 1,182 abstracts of case files and scattered material found in the Newport County Court Records, and have published this collection as *Gleanings From Newport Court Files 1659 - 1783* (1998). Material therein dated before 1721 consists primarily of copies of wills, deeds, and agreements from those years that were entered into evidence for cases heard later. Some represent original documents that were lost afterwards, in 1779 when disaster befell the Newport records.

My own work with the Rhode Island Court Records could be called a labor of self-indulgence. The handful of researchers who share my addiction for transcribing early records will understand. I hope that there are others who will benefit from the results, thus making this publication worthwhile.

Acknowledgements

An inquiry from Glenn LaFantasie, editor of the Roger Williams Papers, first set me on the hunt for Book A, in the early 1980s after it had been removed from Newport. The book was subsequently located at Providence College, where the Archives staff cheerfully allowed me to work with it and to make copies from it. I am especially grateful to J. Stephen Grimes, who took note of my efforts and produced for me the set of beautiful ledger-sized copies which made this transcription possible.

Jane Fletcher Fiske, F.A.S.G.

The Generall Court of Tryalls Held ffor his Maj[ties] Collony of Rhod Island &c. At Newport the 8th of May 1671

Mr Benedict Arnold Governor
Mr John Clarke Dept Govor
Captn John Cranston Asistant
Mr John Coggeshall Asistant
Mr James Barker Asistant
Mr William Carpenter Asistant
Mr Tho Harris Senr Asistant
Mr Roger Williams Asistant
Mr William Baulston Asistant
Lt John Albro Asistant
Captn John Greene Asistant
Mr Benja. Smith Asistant
John Sanford Recorder
James Rogers Genrl Serjant
Mr John Coggeshall Genrl Treasurer
Lt Joseph Torrey Genrl Aturney

The Grand Jurry Empanelled
Mr Richard Tew fforeman
Mr Edward Smith
Mr Edward Robinson
Mr John Gould
Mr Thomas Ward
Mr John Peckham senr
Mr Georg Lawton
Mr Jacob Mott
Mr Stukly Westcott
Mr Hugh Parsons
Mr Phillip Eeads
Mr Marmaduke Ward
Mr Samuell Hubbard:
Geo Gardner

Grand Jurry Returned six Bills May 8th
Returned ffower Bills May 9th

On the Rehearinge of an action of the case for non performance of a Bill of Loadinge Com[m]enced by Mr **Thomas Harte** Plaintiff against **Marke Ridley**, Defendt Dam. 40li sterll:

Jurry of Tryors:

Mr William Weeden fforeman
William Case
Tho Burge
Weston Clarke
Leonard Smith
Antho. Emry
Ralph Earll
Thomas Mancester Senr
Abia Carpenter
William Hiscox
John Reed
Steven Mumford

Grand Jurry Returned six Bills May 8th
Returned ffower Bills May 9th

The Jurrys Verditt: Wee finde for the plaintiff Damage Twenty pounds currant pay of this Collony and Cost of Court. The said verditt accepted by the Court and Judgment granted thereon.

Whereas Mr **John Coale** of Narragansett was Bound in a Bond of 50li to the good behavior and not to Exercize any of office by vertue of the Authorety of Conecticott and he beinge in Court Called apeared, and none apeareing to accuse him for breach of the said Bonds the Court doe acquitt him, and he is cleered by proclamation in open Court payinge ffees.

Whereas **John Pearce** of the Towne of Portsmouth senr was bound in a Bond of tenn pounds to the peace and good behavior and **Thomas Brooke** and **William Wood** beinge Sureties he the said John Pearce havein appeared in Court Desireing to be Releast of his said Bonds the Court haveinge Considered the matter doe see cause to Continew the said Pearce in his former Bonds untill the next Court of Tryalls in October next and doe acquitt his Sureties from beinge bound any Longer.

On the Rehearinge of an action of the case for nonperformance of Covinnant Com[m]enced by **John Sanford** plaintiff against Mr **Randall Houlden** Defend^{t}

The same Jurry above named only William Hiscox Exempted, Nicholas Easton Junr Aded

The Jurrys Verdict Wee finde for the Defend^{t} Cost of Court.

An action of Debt upon accompt Damage 1000^{li} Com[m]enced by **Sarah Reape** Widdow Plaintf against **Samuell Reape** Defendant which said action beinge called in Court, and and there haveinge been much adjetation about the said differrence and it beinge at length unanimously signefyed both by pltf and defend^{t} that they were willinge a Compossure might be made not only of the differrence concerninge the present action but of all other differences accounts Debts Demands dues and disputs whatever heretofore had, moved or dependinge; either betweene the said **Samuell Reape** and his Brother **William Reape** Dureinge the life of the said William Reape, or between the said Samuell Reape and the said Sarah Reape since the Decease of the said William Reape: And in order to Reach a Composure did in the present Court Nominate and Choose ffower persons for Arbitrators of all and singular the Matters, Differrences, accompts, Debts, Demands, dues and Disputes whatever above mentioned, which persons soe Named and chosen are **Captn Peleg Sanford, M^{r} ffrancis Brinley, Captn John Sanford** and **Mr Richard Baily**, And alsoe have unanimosly and joyntly Chosen the Hono^{d} **Benedict Arnold** Esqr. Govno^{r} of this his Maj^{ties} Collony for Umpier in the matters above premissed, to the Award of which said Arbitrators and Umpier and any fower or three of them the said plaintiff and Defend^{t} did declare they would submitt as a fynall end and Conclussion of all and every matters abovesaid provided that the said Award be as efectuall to all intents Constructions and purposes as a Verdict of Jurry and Judgment of Court thereon and given under the hand of the said Umpier and arbitrators and any fower or three of them, at or before the fower and Twentith day of June next Insueing this pressent Court: It is therefore Enacted and ordained by this pressent Court, by and with the Consent of the said plaintiff and defend^{t}. The Award of the said Arbitrators and Umpier or any fower or three of them and Concerninge the premisses given under their hands at or before the time above mentioned shall be as Efectuall to all intents Constructions and purposes whatsoever as a Verdict of Jurry and Judgment of Court theron, in which shall be noe Reveiw nor Rehneareinge: And that the said Award made in Manner and forme as aforesaid shall be a warrant unto the Recorder to Issue out an Exicution according to Law to Levie and distraine the sum ordered by the said Award to be awarded to pay or owe the same, which Exicution the said Recorder is not only Impowred but Required to Issue out according to Law, And in pursuance hereof It is ordered by the pressent Court by and with the Consent of the said parties and of the Umpier and Arbitrators above mentioned that the said Umpier and Arbitrators shall first meete at **Capt Morris house** in Newport upon Wedensday the ffowerteenth day of the aforesaid June before whome the plaintiff and defend^{t} Either in their proper persons or by their Aturnys are to appeere.

The above written was by plaintiff and Defend^{t} [*torn*]

Upon an action of the Case for Debt upon account Dama. 250^{li} sterll.

[2] Dated October the 11th 1670 Com[m]enced by Mr **Benedict Arnold** Senr Plaintiff against **Gershom Wodell** Defendt. May the 1st 1671 a Nihill dicett Entred by the pla. in the Recorders office. The said Case beinge in Court Called the Defendant nor any for him did not appeere to Answer.
The same Jurry of Tryall formerly named. The Jurris Verdict: Wee finde due to the Plaintiff Debt and Damages Upon the account of silver seventy one pownd: Upon the account of provissions pay Debt and Damage twelve pound in Currant pay of this Collony, and Cost of Court — Judgment Granted by the Court. Exicution Given forth thereon.

An action of the Case Debt and Damage 20li Com[m]enced by **Peter Talman** Plaintiff against **Rebecca Sadler** Defendt. The action beinge Called in Court The Plaintiff and Defendt did in this Court mutually agree and Referr their Differrences unto the judgment and Detirmination of the Honord Deputy Govor John Clarke and Captn John Cranston, to be heard and Issued by them before or on the 24th day of June next.

Upon an Indictment by the Genrl Aturney against **Lott Strainge** for ffenceing in a highway in the Towne of Portsmouth, the said Lott Strainge beinge Mandamassed and in Court Called appeered. Pleads Not Guilty and Referrs him selfe to the Cuntry for Tryall.
The Jurriors

William Weeden, forman	Ralph Earll
William Case	Tho Manchester senr
Thomas Burgis	Abiah Carpenter
Weston Clarke	John Reede
Leonard Smith	Steven Mumford
Antho. Emry	Nicholas Easton junr

The Jurries Verdictt (Nott Guilty): The Courts Judgment That he shall be Cleerd by proclama. payinge ffees: which proclamation was done in open Court.

Upon an Indictment by the Genrl Aturney against **John Harris** ffor Grand Larceny he beinge bound to this Court and in Court Called, pleads Not Guilty and Referrs him selfe for Tryall to god and the Cuntry: The same Jurry that were on Lott Straing his case abovesaid —
The Jurrys Verdict: (Guilty): The Courts Sentance is that the said John Harris shall be forthwith seveerly whipt with tenn stripes and also be kept in prisson untill he hath payd **Willia[m] Case** tenn shills. for the sheepe he stole from him and pay Court ffees. The Centance of whipping Exicuted according to the Senance.

Thomas Wilcky beinge bound in a Bond of tenn pownds to the good behavior and to appeere at this Court who beinge Called did appeere and is in Court Clered by proclamation paying ffees.

Upon An Indictment by the Genrl Aturney against **Peter Lee** ffor Grand Larceny: he being bound to this Court, and in Court Called appeered pleads not Guilty and Referrs him selfe for Tryall to god and the Cuntry: same Jurriors —
The Jurris Verdict (Guilty) The sentance of the Court is that Peter Lee shall be forthwith seveerly whipt with ten stripes, and keept in prisson till he pay tenn shills. to **William Case** for a sheepe he hath stole from him, and pay Court ffees. The Courts

sentance of whippinge Exicuted.

Upon an Indictment by the Gen^{rl} Aturney against **Elissabeth** the wife of **Peter Lee** for Grand Larceny she beinge in Court Called did not appeere: and two daies after beinge called did not appeere. And it beinge Eleaged that she is in a weake sickly Condition The Court doe order that her former bonds be Continewed untill the next Court of Tryalls in October.

Upon an Indictment by the Gen^{rl} Aturney against Mr **William Almy** for fenceing in a highway in the Towne of Portsmouth he beinge Mandamassed and in Court Called pleads not Guilty and Referrs him selfe for Tryall to god and the Cuntry, the said Almy putinge in some Exceptions that he beinge Indicted for ffenceinge in a high-way lyinge betweene the Lands of the said William Almy and **Phillip Shearman**; And It not beinge in the Indictment Expressed in what Towne: Upon the Debate of the Matter Mr William Almy doth Asent that the Indictment shall stand with this addition that is the high way ment in the Indictment lying in the Towne of Portsmouth and leadinge to a Springe betweene the Lands of the said Almy and Shearman where now their dwelling housis are scittuated.

The Jurrio^{rs}

Mr Will Weeden fforeman	John Reed
William Case	Steven Mumford
Tho Burgis	Nicholas Easton Junr
Weston Clarke	John Odlin
Leonard Smith	Emanuall Wooly
Abia Carpenter	Nathanill Dickins

The Jurrys Verdict (Guilty) The Court accept the Verdict and order it to be Recorded; a writt of Restitution granted fforth.

Robert Good servant to Mr **Willm Hiscox** beinge bound to the peace and good behavio^{r} and to appeere at this Court: beinge in Court Called did appeare, and none appearinge to charge him for breach of his said Bond the Court doe cleere him by proclamation payinge ffees.

Upon an Indictment by the Gen^{rl} Aturney against **William Thomas** prissoner for Burglary:

The prissoner being Cald for was brought into the Court and Answered, being askt whither Guilty or not Guilty pleads not Guilty and Refers him selfe for Tryall to God and the Cuntry.

The Jurriors

Mr William Weeden fforeman	Ralph Earll
William Case	Antho Emry
Thom Burgis	Thomas Manchester sen^{r}
Weston Clarke	Robert Stanton
John Reede	Edward Greenman
Steven Mumford	Richard Knight

The Jurris Verdict: Guilty. The Courts sentance is that the said **William Thomas** shall be hanged by the neck untill he be Dead Dead. Upon his Earnist peticons the Court doe see cause to suspend the Exicution of the said William Thomas untill the 9th day of June next.

Com[m]itted to the keepinge of the Gen^{rl} Treasurer Mr John Coggeshall untill they be Cald for one silver wine cupp unmarkt, one silver Bodkin marked M.B. two silver sawes spoones with forkes at the other ends which said plate was taken from **Mathew Boomers** wife which William Thomas owned he had stolne from Mr **Kemball** a Smith in Boston.

Upon Indictment by the Gen^{rl} Aturney against **ffrancis Usleten** (prissoner) for muthering **John John Cockrum alias Cockerill**: The said Usleten beinge brought into Court was Called forth to Answer, Beinge Askt whither Guilty or not Guilty, pleads not Guilty and Referrs himselfe for Tryall to God and the Cuntry.

[3] The Jurry of Tryalls on Usletons Indictm^{t}

Ralph Earll fforeman	Robert Stanton
Willia. Case	William Rogers
Tho. Burgis	Jeremiah Browne
Leon. Smith	John Horndell
Thomas Manchester Senr	Zachery Gant
Abiah Carpenter	Thomas Nicolls

The Jurries Verdict Not Guilty: The Courts sentance is that the said Usleton doe Remaine in prisson untill he hath paid his ffees: which shall be paid out of his Estate alredy sequestered, and then the Rest to be Returned to him: And that the said Usleton shall within tenn daies Depart Rhod Island and to be kept close prissoner untill he doe depart, and shall not Returne againe to Inhabitt in any Towne of this Collony without leave from the Majestrates in each Towne Upon his perrill.

John Peckham Senr and **Nicholas Cotterill** Senr both of Newport doe in this pressent Court severally and Joyntly Recognize unto his Maj^{tie} in the full sum[m] of one hundred pownds sterll. to be Levied on their or either of their Lands goods or Chattills That **Elinor** the wife of **Mathew Boomer** of Newport shall make her personall appeerance at the next Gen^{rl} Court of Tryalls to be held for this Collony in Octob^{r} next at Newport there to Answer to such chargis as shall be Eleaged against her and in the meanetime that the said Elinor shall be of a peaceable and good abearinge unto all his Majesties Leig people in this Collony.

Anthony Evernden and **John Angell** of the Towne of Providence beinge chossen by the said Towne to serve on the Grand Inquest and they not attending that service are fined twenty shill^{s} a peece.

Mr **Walter Todd** of the Towne of Warwick being chossen to serve on the Grand Inquest and not attending that service is fined Twenty shillings.

John Randall of the Towne of Westerly beinge chossen to serve on the Grand Inquest and not attending that service is fined Twenty shillings.

John Reed chossen by the Towne of Warwick to serve on the pettit Jurry and not Atendinge that service is fined Twenty shillings.

Jeffery Champlin beinge by the Towne of Westerly chossen to serve on the petty Jurry and not attendinge that service is fined Twenty shillings.

At an Especiall Court of Tryalls (by the Gen^{rl} Assembly sitting the 3^{d} May 1671) Ordered to Sitt and be Houlden at Newport
June the 15th 1671

Mr Benedict Arnold Governo^{r}
Mr John Clarke Dep^{t} Govr
Cap^{tn} John Cranston Assista-
Mr John Coggeshall Assis-
Mr James Barker Assista-
Mr William Carpenter Assista-
Mr Thomas Harris Assista-
Mr Roger Williams Assista-
Mr William Baulston Assista-
Lt John Albro Assista-
Captn John Greene Assista-
Mr Benja Smith Assista-
John Sanford Recorder
Mr James Rogers Gen^{rl} Serj^{t}
Lt Joseph Torrey Gen^{rl} Atur^{y}

Gran Jurrymen
Mr Richard Tew fforeman
Mr Edward Smith
Mr Robert Stanton
Mr Edward Greenman
Serj^{t} Clement Weaver
Mr James Man
Mr Henry Bull
Mr Edward ffisher
L^{t} ffrancis Brayton
Mr Willia[m] Wilbore
Mr Georg Lawton

Pettitt Jurrymen
Mr William Dyre foreman
William Hiscox
Thomas Nicolls
John Bliss
John Greene
John Peckham jun^{r}
John Spencer
Thomas Dungin
Ralph Earll
William Correy
Latham Clarke
Henry Brightman

Upon an Indictment by the Gen^{rl} Aturney against an Indian by the English called **John** by the Indians **Quashcome**, ffor offeringe very great abussis unto **Martha** the wife of **Edward Lay** by throwinge her downe in the high way way and actinge as if he would Ravish her &c

The said Indian beinge brought into Court, and his Indictm^{t} Red, and by our Honord Governo^{r} Interpreted unto him; The said Indians answer is that he doth not know whither he did any such act as charged withall, and if the English doe say he did, he will not say they ly for he doth not know whether he did such an act or not, for he saith he was Cockewa- And putts him selfe for Tryall to twelve men the Jurrey, and not to the Majestrates — The Jurris Verdict is Guilty.

The Verdict of Jurry upon the Indian called Quashcome, alias John beinge considered and weighed by the Court the major part of the Court did declare that although the acts com[m]itted by him were of very heinous nature and did deserve Exemplary punishment: yett they could not sentance him to death by vertue of that law provided against such as com[m]itt a Rape.

Wee Benedict Arnold Govr, John Cranston, William Carpenter, and John Green Asistants doe declare that whereas the Majo^{r} part of the Judges of the pressent court have passed their sentance that the prissoner Quashcome alias John, is not Guilty of the sentance of Death to be past upon him, Wee are fully satisfyed he is worthy of Death, and are ffree that Sentance of Death be past on the said prissoner, which if it be not, wee are cleere in our Judgments that there is noe other punishm[t] can by the Court be inflicted on him by Law since the Indictment brings not his fact under any other head, as breach of Law Except Rape, which if he be sentanced ffor Wee owne that the Gen[rl] Asembly may upon adress in that case made pardon him or Mittigate the punishment, but conclude it not ffitt to be considered by the Asembly, untill after the sentance aforesaid be past by this Court. This Wee give under our hands to be Entered in this present Court upon Record. Dated at a Court of Tryalls held at Newport pr order of the Gen[rl] Asembly June 15th *1671*

Benedict Arnold Gov[r]
John Cranston Asistant
William Carpenter, Asistant
John Greene Asistant.

[4] It is Ordered and agreed by the Majo[r] part of the Court that the Indian Quashcome shall not yett be cleered by proclamation, and the said Indian is ordered to be Remanded again to prisson till cald ffor.

Upon an Indictment by the Gen[rl] Aturny against **Wickhopash**, an Indian by the English called **Harry** for Gran Larceny, for ffellonious takeinge away goods from **Thomas Cornell** of Portsmouth.

The said Indian being brought into Court and Examined ownes him selfe Guilty of the Charge, only pleads that he was Drunk when he did it; the pertickulars stolne beinge one Rapier, and two yards of Tradeinge cloth, The Courts sentance is that the said Indian Wickhopash shall forthwith be sevearly whipt with therty stripes, and the said Indian shall pay unto M[r] Thomas Cornell (he haveinge Receivd his Rapier) the sum of ffower powdns and pay Court ffees which is one pownd seven shillings eight pence, which sum[m]s shall be paid within a Months time after this Court which if the said indian within that time doe not pay he shall according to law be sold for a slave.

June the 16[th] this court adjourned till tomorrow one of the clock after noone.

June 17[th]. This day the Court mett againe according to former order and fell upon the debate of the Verdict of the Jurry upon **Quashcome alies John**, upon whome although they could not (as is Exprest in a former order) pronounce the sentance of Death, because Neither the Bill did accuse him of Rape nor the Jurrys Verdict declare him to be guilty thereof Neither did the plaintiff charge him therewith but declared Expressly the contrary, yett forasmuch as they were unanimous as to the heinousnes of the crimes Com[m]itted by him, soe that he deserved severe punishment and thereupon had ordered him to prisson againe untill further cald for, and for as much as the Deputy Go[vr] with the rest of the Magestrates that were of that minde did move the Gen[rl] Asembly for their advice in that case, And the Asembly haveinge satt long and almost tired did desolve without afoardinge pressent Asistance therein: Therfore the court with joint consent came to this Result that the said Indian called Quashcome als John shall remaine in durance according to the said order, and that this pressent cause shall be againe presented to the next Gen[rl] Asembly for their advice therin, and in the meane time noe part of his chaines shall be removed from him.

Whereas **Sam[ll] Sanford** was appointed by the late Asembly to attend this Court as a Jurryman and he [stating] that the Reason of his beinge absent was, that his wife beinge with child and neare the time of her delivery and alsoe she liveinge remote from

Neighbours, he is by the Court Excussed.

Robert Hassard and **John Pinner** both of Portsmouth, being appointed to attend this Court as jurrymen and they not attending that service are fined twenty shillings a peece.

This Court desolved the 17th of June.

The Genrl Court of Tryalls Held ffor his Majties Collony at Newport the 18th day off October *1671*

Mr Benedict Arnold Governor
Mr John Clarke Dept Govor
Captn John Cranston Asistant
Mr John Coggeshall Asist-
Mr James Barker Asist-
Mr William Carpenter Asist-
Mr Roger Williams Asist-
Mr Thomas Harris Senr Asist-
Mr William Baulston Asist-
Lt John Albro Asist-
Captn John Greene Asist-
Mr Benja- Smith Asist-
John Sanford Recorder
Mr James Rogers Genrl Serjant
Lt Joseph Torrey Genrl Aturn-

Gran Jurry men
Mr Edward Smith fforeman
Mr Henry Bull
Mr Nathanill Johnson
Mr Joshua Coggeshall
Mr William Case
Mr Stephen Arnold
Mr John Salman
Mr Hugh Parsons
Mr Edward ffisher
Mr Icobod Potter
Mr Nathanell Dickins
Mr John Reed.

Mr **Edward Greenman** beinge Chossen a jurry man by the Towne of Newport and in obedience to Authorety apeerd and declared that he is both sick and lame, and cannot attend that service, is by the Court discharged.

Robert Stanton beinge chossen a Jurryman for this Court by the Towne of Newport, and he haveinge declared to the Govr and Mr John Coggeshall that by Reason of his Extraordinary lameness he is unable to attend that service the Court doe see cause to discharge him from that service.

John Pearce Senr of Portsmouth being continewed by the last Court of Tryalls of his former bonds unto this Court, and he haveinge presented himselfe unto this Court desireinge a discharge or a continewance of his said bonds The Court upon that his Request and inquirie into former proceeds doe see cause to Continew the said John Pearce in his fformer Bonds, and he ownes himselfe in Court herewith content.

In a Case of Reheareinge Entred by Mr **John Green**, Aturney to **Marke Ridly** in an action Com[m]enced by Mr **Thomas Harte** against the said Ridly, And **Edward Richmond** at the Last Court beinge admitted an Aturney in the Case, he apeeringe and beinge redy to answer the said Rehearing The Court doe declare and owne the power of the said Richmond as Aturney to be still vallid and stable. And the action beinge called and the said Mr John Greene as Aturney to Mark Ridley refussinge to prossicute the aforesaid Rehearinge — This Court doe Order and sentance that the verdict and [5] Judgment of the last Genrl Court of Tryalls held the 8th of May last shall stand and be performed by Exicution to be Issued forth by the Recorder. Alsoe Mrs **Harte** Widow and Executrix to the aforesaid Thomas Harte cominge into Court, did owne and acknowlidge that Edward Richmond was her late husbands and her Aturney in the case afore premissed.

On An action of the case for Debt Com[m]enced by **Edward Lay** of Portsmouth Plaintiff against **James Rogers** Generall Serjant Damage therty pownds: The Issue joined is Gen^rl^ Not Guilty.

Jurry on the Case

Mr John Almy fforeman	Anthony Shaw
John Crandall jun^r^	Joseph Parker
Georg Gardner	Nicholas Easton jun^r^
Richard Arnold	Joseph Devell
Richard Dunn	John Sayles
Robert Westcott	Joseph Parker

The Jurrys Verdict: Wee finde for the plaintiff ffive pownds and tenn shillings in currant pay of this Collony and Cost of Court.

An action of Debt upon account Entered by **Joseph Gillam[m]** of Boston plaintiff against **Sam^ll^ Reape** of Pawtuxet in Providence, defend^t^ (damage 200^li^) — a nonsute Entred by the defend^t^ and in Court owned and allowed.

An action Com[m]enced by **John Gerrierdy** plaintiff against Mrs **Sarah Smyton** Exetrix to her late deceased Husband William Smyton, in an action of Debt Dam[m]age 400^li^ st.

This Court upon the Exam[m]ination and inquiry into the action doe see cause to grant a nonsute.

Upon Indictment by the Gran Jurry against **Martha Hicks** of Portsmouth, for Com[m]ittinge the act of ffornication with **Nicholas Browne** of New Jersey.

The said Martha Hicks haveinge Entred her Traverce, and beinge in Court Cald apeered and beinge demanded whither Guilty or Not Guilty she ownes her selfe Guilty.

Lawrance Springard now Husband to the said Martha, doth in the pressence of this Court ingadge him selfe in the behalfe of his wife, to stand to and make good the Courts sentance according to law concerninge his wifes fact: The Court doe sentance her the said Martha to pay the sum[m] of fforty shills. to the Gen^rl^ Treasurer within tenn daies of the dessolution of this Court and pay ffees.

Upon an Indictment by the Gran Jurry against **Nicholas Browne** of New Jerssey for com[m]itting the act of ffornication with **Martha Hicks** of Portsmouth, he being mandamassed and in Court Calld Apeerd, pleads Not Guilty and Referrs him selfe to god and the cuntry for Tryall. The Jurrys Verdict: Not Guilty of ffornication.

Upon an Indictment by the Gen^rl^ Aturney against **Thomas Starr** Resident in Newport for breach of the peace for Resistinge the Cunstable and his ayde —.

The said Starr beinge bound to this Court and in Court Cald appeerd and beinge askt whither Guilty or not Guilty ownes Guilty —.

Mr **John Gould** of Newport doth in Court ingage on the behalfe of Thomas Starr that he shall appeere in Court when Cald for and abide the sentance and Judgment of the Court accordinge to Law for his fact.

The Court doe sentance the said Thomas Starr to pay the su[m]m of fforty shillings to the Gen[rl] Treasurer betweene this and the 25[th] of March next, and alsoe that he Enter into a bond of tenn pownds to be of the good abearinge untill and alsoe to appeere at the next Gen[rl] Court of Tryalls and alsoe to pay pressent ffees. and the Court doe agree to take the said Starrs owne bond in the case.

The said Thomas Starr beinge againe called into Court to Receive his sentance appeered, and M[r] John Gould desireinge to be dismist of his bonds for the said Starr, the Court accordingly dismiss him.

Upon an Indictment by the Grand Jurry against **Grace Lawton** the wife of **Thomas Lawton** formerly the wife of **William Baily** ffor comitting Adulterie with **Thomas Lawton.** The said Grace beinge Mandamassed, Enters Traverce pleads Not Guilty and Referrs her selfe for Tryall to god and the cuntry. The Jurrys Verdict is Not Guilty.

The Court doe declare them selves wholy dissatisfyed with that Verdict and therefore cannot cleere her, The Aturney declareinge there was a failer in the Testimony he depended on or otherwise he had produced other Testimony.

Upon Indictment by the Grand Jurry against **Anthony Emry** of Portsmouth for that he did digg or cause to be diged a well in the Kings high-way wherein a man was drowned. The said Emry beinge Mandamassed and in court called appeerd, and beinge demanded whether Guilty or not Guilty, ownes himselfe guilty of diginge the said well, The Court haveinge had certaine Information that the said Well is fylled up by the said Emry the Court doe thereupon see cause to acquitt him from any further pennalty in the matter he payinge officers ffees.

Upon Indictment by the Gen[rl] Aturney against **Elizabeth Lee** the wife of **Peter Lee** for gran Larceny she beinge in court cald did not appeere: The Court doe order that warrant be Issued forth to M[r] Thomas Ward Cunstable of Newport to bringe the said Elizabeth into Court, accordinge to the said order the said Elizabeth Lee beinge brought into Court and her charge red, beinge demanded of whither Guilty or not Guilty, she pleads Not Guilty and referrs her selfe for Tryall to god and the cuntry: The Jurrys Verdict: Guilty.

[6] The Court doe sentance the said Elizabeth Lee to be whipt with tenn stripes. The Court upon the Humble adress and petition of the said Elizabeth Lee for mercy and pardon and alsoe the peticon of her Husband. This Court doe Referr the Exicution of the Sentance till mundy next beinge the 30th Instant.

M[r] **Lott Strainge** chossen by the Towne of Portsmouth to serve on the Jurry of Tryers in this Court beinge cald and not appeeringe, It was by some pressent said, that he said he could not in conscience serve on a Jurry here because not sworne according as they are in England. But the Court findinge the said Excuse iniffitient doe declare Lott Strainge is fined twenty shillings as the Law detirminith for not serveinge on the Jurry, And doe declare that the previledges of the Charter would be infringed in compellinge any soe to sweare, that differ therefrom in their consciences: Butt if Lott Strainge had appeered in Court and declared his minde as aforesaid he might have been sworne soe as in England.

Mr **Joseph Clarke**, chosen by the Towne of Newport and Mr **Antho. Low** and Mr **Job Almy** chossen by the Towne of Warwicke to attend this Court on the Gran Jurry and they not attendinge that service are fined twenty shillings a peece.

Samuell Stafford beinge chossen by the Towne of Warwicke to attend this Court on the pettitt Jurry and he not appeeringe to attend that service is fined Twenty shillings.

Upon an Indictment by the Grand Jurry against Mr **John Easton** for that the said Easton hath shutt up or caused to be shutt up a high-way in the Towne of Newport.
The Court upon upon veiweinge the Indictment doe judge it invallied.

Upon Indictment by the Gen^{rl} Aturney against Mr **John Porter** for perjury.
The said Mr Porter haveinge been Mandamasd and in court cald did not appeere, and the second time beinge the 27th of October beinge againe cald in court did not appeere: The Court doe sentance him to pay the sum[m] of five pownds unto the Gen^{rl} Treasurer, and pay Court ffees: Alsoe the said John Porter is declared incapable in this Collony to give any Testimony in any case whatsoever in this Collony.

Upon an Indictment by the Grand Jurry against **William Hall** Junr for ffornication — he beinge Mandamassed: and in Court Cald apears .. and pleads the informality of the Bill: and upon the heareinge of the plea, and upon the veiwinge of the Bill of Indictment, the Court doe not Judge the Bill to be fformall.

Upon an Indictment by the Grand Jurry against **John Coggeshall** of the Towne of Portsmouth for ffornication, he being Mandamassed and in Court Cald appeerd, and pleads the informality of the Bill, and upon the heareinge of the plea and veiwinge of the bill of Indictment the Court doe not Judge the Bill formall accordinge to law.

Upon Indictment by the Gen^{rl} Aturney against an Indian Called **Gyles Winnonekin**, for felonious breakinge open the ware house of **Anthony Evernden** of Providence.
The said Indian haveinge been com[m]itted to prison — was in Court Cald for to Answer, The Gen^{rl} Serjant James Rogers made answer that the said Indian had broken prisson and made an Escape.

Upon Indictment by the Gen^{rl} Aturney against **Nicquitticksuck** an Indian, for Gran Larceny the said Indian beinge imprissoned, and in court cald for, The Gen^{rl} Serjant made Answer that the said Indian had broken prisson and made an Escape.

Upon Indictmen^{t} by the Gen^{rl} Aturney against **William Newman** prissoner for conspireinge with the Indians against the English, the said Newman beinge in court cald for. The Gen^{rl} Serjant made Answer he had broken prisson and made an Escape.

Upon Indictment by the Gen^{rl} Aturney against **Mathew Boomer** of Newport for that he the said Boomer did kill severall sheepe that were not his owne and converted them to his owne use which is Gran Larceny: The said Boomer, Beinge in court cald apeerd and Answered. Pleads Not Guilty and Referrs him selfe for Tryall to God and the Cuntry. The Jurrys Verdict: Not Guilty.

The Kings Aturney on the Kings behalfe desireinge a stop of Judgment in the case the court alsoe being unanimously dissatisfyed with the Jurrys Verdict doe see cause to grant the Aturnys Request and doe stop Judgment thereon: Therefore the Court doe see cause and doe continew his former bonds to be of full force untill the next Gen[rl] Court of Tryalls.

John Coggeshall jun[r] (liveinge in the Towne of Portsmouth) the sonn of M[r] **John Coggeshall** of Newport vollentarily cominge into this pressent Court, doth acknowlidge that he is Guilty of the act of ffornication for that before marriage he begott a child upon **Eliza~ Timberleak** his now wife and submitts him selfe to the courts judgment craveing ffavour, The Court doe sentance the said John Coggeshall to pay the sum[m] of fforty shill[s] to the Gen[rl] Treasurer and also pay ffees.

Elizabeth the wife of John Coggeshall Jun[r] liveinge at the Towne of Portsmouth and daughter of **Mary Timberleak** of Newport, vollentaryly cominge into this court did acknowlidge that she is Guilty of the act of ffornication by haveinge a childe by her pressent Husband John Coggeshall before Marraige and submitts her selfe to the courts judgment craveing ffavour. The Court doe sentance her or her to pay fforty shills to the Gen[rl] Treasurer, and alsoe pay ffees. ffor the two afores[d] persons the said John Coggeshall in court ingages to performe the courts sentance.

Upon an Indictment against **Elinor** the wife of **Mathew Boomer** of Newport [7] for aidinge and asistinge **Robin** an Indian (that was prissoner for ffellony) to breake the com[m]on prisson of this Collony. The said Elinor beinge a prissoner and brought forth into Court and the charge beinge Red and she demanded of whither Guilty or Not Guilty pleads Not Guilty and Referrs her selfe for Tryall to god and the cuntry: The Jurrys Verdict, Not Guilty.

Upon an Indictment by the Gen[rl] Aturney against **Elinor** the wife of **Mathew Boomer** of Newp[t] for that she did about the month of Aprill last and before perswade and abett **William Thomas** to Rob and Steale: The said Elinor beinge a prissoner and brought forth into Court, and the charge beinge Red and she demanded off whither Guilty or Not Guilty pleads Not Guilty and Referrs her selfe for Tryall to god and the cuntry: The Jurrys Verdict Not Guilty.

Upon an Indictment by the Gen[rl] Aturney against **Elinor the wife of Mathew Boomer** of Newp[t] for that she did Receive keepe and conceale severall goods stolne by **William Thomas** from M[r] **Kemball** a smith in Boston, The said Elinor beinge a prissoner and brought forth, and her charge Red and beinge demanded of whether Guilty or Not Guilty pleads Not Guilty and Referrs her selfe for Tryall to god and the Cuntry: The Jurrys Verdict. Guilty of consealinge goods accordinge to the Bill of Indictment.

The Court doe declare their sence that it is noe possitive Verdict, and that that matter is in the same state, as at first it was before it came to the Court, and Therefore she is com[m]itted to prisson untill she putt in suffitient Baile of two persons in the sum[m] of fforty pownds for her good and peaceable behaveiour and appeerance at the next Court of Tryalls.

Richard Evernden beinge bound to prosceicute the Indian **Gyles Wonnonequin**, he the said Evernden beinge in court cald, and appeerd is therefore acquitted of his Bonds.

The Court Desolved October the 27th

Att the Gen^rl Court of Tryalls Held in his Maj^ties Name
at Newport the Sixt day of May 1672

Mr Nicholas Easton Governo^r
Captn John Cranston D^t Governo^r
Mr Richard Smith Asistant
M^r ffrancis Brinley Asist-
Mr John Easton Asist-
Captn Arthur ffenner Asist-
Mr Thomas Harris Asist-
Mr Henry Browne Asist-
Mr William Baulston Asist-
Mr Joshua Coggeshall Asist-
Captn John Greene Asist-
Mr Benja. Smith Asist-
John Sanford Recorder
James Rogers Gen^rl Serjant
Mr Peter Easton Ge^l Treas^r
Mr John Easton Ge^l Aturny
Mr Edward Richmond Solicetor

Grand Jurry men
Mr Nathanill Johnson fforeman
Mr Robert Stanton
Mr John Greene
Mr Phillip Smith
Mr Henry Palmer
Mr Thomas Dungin
Mr Thomas Arnold sen^r
Mr Joseph Martin
Mr William Wilbore
Mr Gidion ffreeborne
Mr Natha- Dickins
Mr Thomas Hopkins.

Whereas **John Pearce** of the Towne of Portsmouth Masson being by the last Gen^rl Court of Tryalls bound in the sum[m] of tenn pownds to the peace and good behavio^r and to appeere at this Court, he beinge very lame and ill, and presentinge himselfe to this Court for a Release from his said Bonds, proclamation beinge made in open Court whether any one could charge the said Pearce for breach of his Bond and none appeereinge he is acquitted payinge ffees.

Whereas **Mathew Boomer** of Newport was by the last Court of Tryalls bound to this Court, he beinge in court cald apeard and proclamation beinge made in open Court whither any person had any thinge or cause to Eleadge against the said Boomer, and none comeinge in to Complaine this court doe see cause to acquitt the said Boomer of his Bonds payinge ffees.

This Court upon Many searious Considerations doe see cause to adjourne untill ffryday the Seventeenth day of this instant May at Eight of the clock in the Morning.

May the 17th the Court upon the afore said adjournment Assembled Cald and satt.

Upon an Indictment by the Gen^rl Solicetor against **William Harris** of Providence prissoner, ffor speakinge and writtinge against his Maj^ties Gracious Charter granted to this Collony:

The said Harris beinge brought forth into Court and before him his Indictment Red, and he askt whether Guilty or not Guilty: pleads Not Guilty and Referrs him selfe to the Cuntry for Tryall.

The Jurry of Tryalls owned by William Harris.

Ralph Earll fforeman
Nichol^s Easton jun^r
Thomas Nicolls
Danill Lawton
Samuell Sanford
William Cadman

Vallintine Whitman	Icobod Sheiffeild
Richard Arnold	Hugh Persons
John Bordin	Richard Dunn

The Jurries Verdict Not Guilty of this charge.

[8] Upon an Indictment by the Gen[rl] Solicetor against an Indian by the English Called **William** a prissoner, for Enteringe into the house of **John Odlin** of Newport and there in violent manner did bite and wound the servant of the said Odlin. The said Indian beinge brought into Court and demanded of whether Guilty or Not Guilty Ownes Guilty: The Court doe Sentance the said Indian to pay the sum of Eleven pownds to John Odlin for and in Consideration of his loss charge and Expence, and the sum of Twenty Shillings for Court ffees. And that the said Indian be kept in safe custody untill he pay the said sums or other wise give good securety for it, which if he doe not performe within three months then that the said Indian be sold as a slave by the Treasure to Barbadose or Else where by the first oppertunety to make payment of the said sums.

Upon An Indictment by the Gen[rl] Solicetor **Shadrach Manton** of Providence, for haveing Carnall Copulation with **Mary Pray** the wife of **Richard Pray**. The said Manton beinge bound to this Court and in Court Cald apeerd, and his charge beinge Red and he demanded whither Guilty or not Guilty pleads not Guilty and Referrs himselfe for Tryall to the cuntry. The Jurrys Verdict Not Guilty of the Indictment.

Thomas ffeild of Providence beinge bound to this Court and in Court Cald apeerd, and proclam[ation] in Court beinge made, that if any person or persons had any thinge to Eleadge against him they might come in and be heard, and noe person apeeringe he is acquitted payinge ffees.

Nicholas Power of Providence beinge bound to this Court and in Court Cald apeard and proclamation in court beinge made that if any person or persons had any thinge to Eleadge against him, they might come in and be heard and noe person apeereinge he is acquitted payinge ffees.

Thomas Starr beinge by the last Court bound in a Bond of Tenn pownds to appeere at this Court and in Court Cald appeerd, and owned he had not payd the forty shills ordered by that court to be paid to the Treasurer, and now M[r] **Joshua Coggeshall** haveinge ingaged the payment of the said fforty shillings to the Treasurer, and none appeeringe further to accuse the said Starr he is acquitted of his Bonds payinge ffees.

Upon An Indictment by the Gen[rl] Solicetor against **Mary the wife of Richard Pray** of Providence for haveing had Carnall Copulation with **Shadrach Manton**. The said Mary Pray beinge bound to this Court and in Court Cald apeerd, and her charge beinge Red and she demanded of whether Guilty or not Guilty Ownes Guilty.

The Court doe sentance the said Mary Pray to be twice whipt as the Law hath provided or Else pay the sum of tenn pownds in silver unto the Gen[rl] Treasurer of this Collony: And upon the Consideration of the case the Court doe suspend the Exicution of this Judgment untill the 20th day of August next.

The Court Desolved May the 20th

At the Generall Court of Tryalls Held in his Majties Name at Newport the 23 of October Anno *1672*

Mr Nicholas Easton Governor
Captn John Cranston Dept Governor
Mr Richard Smith Assistant
Mr ffrancis Brinley Assistant
Mr John Easton Asistant
Captn Arthur ffenner Asistant
Mr Henry Browne Asistant
Mr Thomas Harris Asistant
Mr William Baulston Asistant
Mr Joshua Coggeshall Asistant
Captn John Greene Asistant
Mr Benjamin Smith Asistant
John Sanford Recorder
Mr James Rogers Genrl Serjant
Mr Peter Easton Genrl Treasurer
Mr John Easton Genrl Aturney
Mr Edward Richmond Genrl Solicetor

Gran Jurriors
Mr Edward Smith foreman
Mr Robert Stanton
Mr William Case
Mr William Hiscocks Hen. Lilly
Mr Jere. Browne
Lt William Correy
St Jacob Mott
Mr John Brigs
Mr Hugh Persons
Mr John Archer
Mr John Horndell
Mr James Blower

Upon an action of Debt Com[m]enced by Captn **Peleg Sanford** plaintiff against Mr **William Dyre** Defendant

The Jurris Verdict, wee finde for the plaintiff Debt Twenty one pownds Eighteen shillings and two pence, damage five shillings, and Cost of Court. judgment granted and Execution thereon

Upon An Indictment by the Generll Solicetor against **Joan Cowdall** Widdow, for liveinge and Lodginge with **John Deane** and other breaches of the peace; she beinge in Court Cald appeard, Enters Travers, pleads not Guilty and Referrs her Tryall to God and the cuntry: The Jurris Verdict Wee finde Guilty of Lyinge in bed with John Deane, and nott Guilty of breach of peace:

The Courts Centance is that the said Joan Cowdall shall forthwith be brought to the great gunn and there stript to the midle and bound and soe stand for the fourth part of an houres time, and that she alsoe pay ffees.

Upon and Indictment **William Hall junr** of the Towne of Portsmouth, for Com[m]itting ffornication with **Alse** the present wife of the said Hall then **Tripp** before marriage. The Court upon the ple of the case doe see cause to quash the Bill.

[9] Upon An Indictment by the Genrl Solicetor against **Joan Cowdall** for com[m]ittinge Adultery with **John Page** an Irishman: she beinge Mandamassed and in Court Cald, apeard. Enters Traverce, pleads not Guilty, and Referrs her selfe for Tryall to God, and the Cuntry.

The Jurrys Verdict (Not Guilty) whereupon she is cleerd by proclamation in Court payinge ffees.

Upon An Indictment by the Gen^{rl} solicetor against **Susanah Talman** for comittinge ffornication with **Roger Goulding**, she beinge bound to this Court and in Court Calld apeard. Ownes Guilty. The Court doe sentance her to pay the sum of fforty shillings to the Generall Treasurer and pay ffees.

Upon An Indictment by the Gen^{rl} solicetor against **James Browne** for fornication with **Elizabeth Carr**, his now wife, he beinge in Court Calld apeard and ownes Guilty: The Court doe sentance him to pay the sum of fforty shillings to the Generall Treasurer and pay ffees.

Upon An Indictment by the Gen^{rl} Solicetor against **James Parr** for fornication, com[m]itted with a Negro woman, he beinge mandamassed and in Court Calld apeared, and ownes Guilty.

The Court doe sentance the said James Parr to pay the sum of fforty shillings to the Generall Treasurer and pay ffees. Cleerd by proclamation in open Court.

Upon An Indictment by the Generall Solicetor against **John Deane** seaman, for liveinge and Lodginge with **Joan Cowdall** contrary to Law — the said Deane being in Court Calld Did not appeare.

Upon An Indictment by the Generall Solicetor against **Elizabeth Browne** the wife of **James Browne** of Newport formerly **Elizabeth Carr** for ffornication com[m]itted with her said husband before marriage: she beinge in Court Calld apeared, and ownes Guilty.

The Court doe Centance that she pay fforty shillings to the Gen^{rl} Treasurer and pay ffees.

Upon Indictment by the Generall Aturney against **Vallintine Hudleston** for ffornication com[m]itted with **Kathrin** his now wife, before Marriage, he being in Court Calld apeard and ownes Guilty. The Court Centance the said Vallintine, the sum of fforty shillings to the Generall Treasurer and pay ffees.

Upon Indictment by the Generall Aturney against **Kathrin Hudleston** wife of Vallin~ Hudleston for com[m]itteinge fornication with her said husband before marriage, being in court calld apeared and ownes Guilty. The Court Centance the said Kathrin Hudleston to pay forty shillings to the Generall Treasurer and pay ffees.

Upon Indictment by the Generall Solicetor against **Roger Goulding** for com[m]ittinge ffornication with **Susana Talman**: the said Roger beinge in Court Calld apeared Enters Traverce — pleads not Guilty and Referrs him selfe for Tryall to God and the Cuntry. The Jurrys Verdict (Not Guilty) [*in margin*: Juriors on Roger Gouldings Indictm^{t}: Mr Phillip Eads foreman, Weston Clarke, John Greene, Thomas Dungin, John Easton jun^{r}, William Clarke, Nath^{ll} Johnson, Thomas Nicolls, Lawra[nce] Turner, John Holme, John Rathbone, Thomas Gould]

The Court haveinge seariously considered the case by Indictment against Roger Goulding for com[m]itting ffornication with Susanah Talman the daughter of **Peter Talman** of Portsmouth, by whome there is a childe borne and brought into the present Court, and although the Jurry had not cleer Evidence to prove the fact, and thereupon, could not finde the Charge, yett the Court upon Consideration of the motion made in Court by Peter Talman, and the Law, That she haveing upon oath

charged the said Roger Goulding to be ffather of the said Childe: if he by oath would cleere himselfe, there should be noe further charge to the cuntry, and he the said Roger Refusing soe to cleer himselfe the Court doe centance the said Roger Goulding forthwith to give in suffitient Bayle to this Court, to the vallue of ffifty pounds to keep and save harmless and Indemnefied, the Town of Portsmouth from any charge concerninge the Maintaynance of the said Childe.
Roger Goulding haveinge presented his Desire of an Appeal in this Courts Centance unto the Generall Assembly; This Court doe grant his appeal, he haveing in Court Engaged and oblidged him selfe in the sum of one hundred pounds ster^{ll} to prossicute his said appeale in the Generall Adjourned to sitt on Wensday next the sixt of November, and to abide the said Assemblys detirminiation therein —

Whereas **Stephen Sabeere** of Newport was bound to the peace and good behavio^{r} and to appeare at this Court and being in Court Calld apeared, and proclamation beinge made whether any person had any thinge to Eleage against his cleereings, the Generall Solicetor did on his Engagement declare that the said Sabeere had since his beinge bound been drunk and had used uncivill speeches whereupon the Court doe at present suspend the matter.
The said Stephen beinge againe in Court Calld apeared, and owned that he hath done the Gen^{rl} Solicetor wrong and promisses a more Civill deportment for the future, Thereupon the said Stephen Sabeere is in open Court Cleerd by proclamation payinge ffees.

Upon Indictment by the Gen^{rl} Solicetor against **Dennis Lannegan** for fornication com[m]itted with **Mary** the daughter of **Robert Moone** of Newport, he beinge in Court Calld, apeerd, and ownes Guilty — The Court doe centance the said Dennis to pay forty shillings to the Generall Treasurer and pay ffees.

Upon Indictment by the Gen^{rl} Solicetor against **Mary** the daughter of **Robert Moone** for ffornication com[m]itted with **Dennis Lannegan**: she being in Court Calld apeard, the Court upon Veiwinge the Bill doe judge the Bill not formall, as soe she is discharged thereof paying ffees.

Upon an Indictment by the Genr^{ll} Solicetor against Mr **John Paine** for procureing a pattent from the Goverm^{t} of New York for Prudence Island being part of this Collony: The said Mr John Paine being bound to this Court and in Court Calld appeard, the Indictment and Charge to him Read, and he demanded of whether Guilty or not guilty, pleads not Guilty and Referrs himselfe for Tryall to God and the Cuntry. [*in margin:* jurriors on Mr John Paines Indictment: Mr Stephen Arnold foreman, Weston Clarke, John Greene, Thomas Dungin, John Easton jun^{r}, William Clarke, Thom. Nicolls, Lawra. Turner, John Holme, John Rathbone, Latham Clarke, Adam Wooly]
The Jurries Verdict (Guilty) The Court doe pass their Judgment that in this Case the said Mr John Paine hath Trancegressed the law of this Collony and doe centance him accordingly, only doe suspend the Execution untill the Gen^{rl} Court of Tryalls in May next at Newport.

John Smith of Prudence this 29th of October tooke the Engadgement to his Majesty and this Collony.

Thomas Starr, being bound to this Court and to the good behavior, he beinge in Court Calld apeard, and ownes his abusis to the custables and Authorety and saith he was drunk, and is sorry for his Misdemeans therein and humbly craves the Courts favour and pardon promissinge a more Carefull Civill life for the future, and thereupon in open Court he is cleerd by proclamation payinge ffees.

Ephrim Carpenter Carpenter chosen a Jurry-man by Providence and not atendinge is fined twenty shillings.

John Whipple Junr and **Epenetus Olney** chosen Jurry-men by the Towne of Providence, and not atendinge this Court yett haveing sent their Excuse **[10]** that they were [*torn*] to Attend that service the Court doe Remitt their ffines.

Robert Hassard and **George Brownell** chosen Jurry-men by the Towne of Portsmouth and not atending that service are fined twenty shillings a peece.

Benjamin Barton, Thomas Hedge, Benjamin Gorton and **John Carder** chossen Jurry-men by the Towne of Warwick and they not atending that service are fined twenty shillings apeece.

The Court Desolved the 31: October in the Night time

At the Generall Court of Tryalls Held for the Collony
at Newport the: 12th of May *1673*

Mr Nicholas Easton Governor
Mr William Coddington Dep^{t} Gover^{r}
Mr Walter Clarke — Asistant
Mr Daniell Gould — Asistant
Mr John Easton — Asistant
Mr William Harris Asistant
Mr Thomas Harris Asistant
Mr Thomas ffeild Asistant
Mr Joshua Coggeshall Asistant
Mr John Tripp Asistant
Mr Walter Todd — Asistant
Mr Job Almy — Asistant
John Sanford Recorder
James Rogers Genl Serant
Mr Peter Easton Gen^{rl} Treasurer
Mr John Easton Gen^{rl} Aturney

Gran Jurriors Engaged
Lt Joseph Torrey foreman
Mr Robert Stanton
Mr William Case
Mr Thomas Clifton
Mr Thomas Burge
Mr Gidion Freeborne
Mr John Clarke
L^{t} ffrancis Brayton
Mr Phillip Eades
Mr William Hiscox
Mr John Odlin
Mr Henry Lilly

Upon an action of Debt by bill, beareinge date July 31: 1672 Com[m]enced by Mr **Thomas Deane** of Boston Merch^{t}, plaintiff against the Estate of **Nicholas Davis** of Newport late deceased, Defend^{t}. Damage one hundred and twelve pounds, the said case being demurd to this Court, and a Nihill dicett May the 12th Entred by the plaintiff Aturney Mr **Caleb Carr:**

The plaintiff being in Court Calld Mr Caleb Carr appeared and Answered as the plaintiffs Aturney, and presented his power which the Court veiwinge have owned —

Mrs **Sarah Davis** widdow to the deceased Nicholas Davis came into Court and owned Lt **Joseph Torrey** to be her Aturney. The defend^{t} pleads for a Nonsuite.

The Court after a long debate of the matter and heareinge the aligations of Plaintiff and Defend^{t} doe see cause to grant a Nonsuite in the Case.

Upon an action of Debt Due by bond Com[m]enced by Mr **Henry Woolcott** of Winsor in the Collony of Conecticott Lt **Joseph Torrey** Aturney to the plaintiff, against P^{er} **Talman** of Portsmouth Defendant, The Case beinge calld the Defendant apeard in Court, and acknowlidged a judgment for a hundred and sixty pound of sheeps wooll to be paid the plaintiff, between the present Court and the first day of September next which if not then paid Exicution to goe forth:

Upon an action of Trespass upon the case Com[m]enced by Captn **Jonathan Atherton** of Dorchester in the Massachusitts Collony plaintiff against Mr **Timothy Mather** of the said Dorchester defendant, Damage one hundred pounds, beareinge date 3 of Aprill 1673.

May 12 1673 noe Answer beinge in the office the plaintiff Entred a Nihill dicett.

The Court upon hereinge of the case doe finde that there is noe returne of serveinge the writt made to the office, and therefore see cause to declare that the plaintiff is Nonsuited.

Upon an Indictment by the Generall Solicetor against **Emanuall Wooly** of Newport for contempt of Authorety, he beinge mandamassed, and in Court Cald apeared, and the Indictment openly Read and he beinge demanded whether guilty or not guilty, saith he doth not know he is Guilty, yett ownes that in his passion he might use contemptious words beinge over come with drinke: and knows not but that he did soe and Referrs himselfe to the bench.

The said Emanuall Wooly haveinge made his acknowlidgment under his hand for his contemptious expressions and desireinge the Courts favour therein: The Court doe centance the said Emanuall Woolly to pay the sum of five shilings (for beinge drunk) to the Generall Treasurer and alsoe pay court ffees: cleerd in open Court by proclamation.

Upon an Indictment by the Generall Solicetor against **Jobba** a Negro woman servant to Mr **Caleb Carr** for that the said Jobba about the latter end last had Carnall Copulation with **James Gray** — she being mandamassed and in court Cald apeared, pleads Not Guilty and Referrs her selfe for Tryall to the Cuntry: The Jurry sent forth on the case: The Jurrys Verdict Not Guilty. The Verdict accepted by the Court: The Court order she be cleerd by proclamation payinge ffees.

Upon Indictment by the Generall Aturny Mr **John Easton** in the behalfe of our Soverreigne Lord the King against **Thomas Cornell** now prissoner ffor that on the Eveninge of the Eight day of ffebruary last in the 25th yeare of his Maj^{ties} Reigne Ann^{o} 1672 the said Thomas did murther his mother **Rebecca Cornell** or was aydeinge or abettinge thereto. The said Thomas Cornell beinge cald for and brought forth into Court, and his charge Read, and demanded of whether Guilty or Not Guilty — pleads Not Guilty, and Referrs himselfe for Tryall to God and the Cuntry. After all Lawful Liberty granted by the Court as to Exceptions The Jurriors were sollemnly Engaged on the case and sent forth.

Jurriors on the case [*listed in margin*]

Mr Henry Palmer foreman	Daniell Greenell
James Man	William Allin
John Read	John Spencer
Richard Dunn	John Rogers
Serj^{t} Clement Weaver	John Bliss
John Strainge	John Crandell jun^{r}

The Jurry Returne their Verdict publicldy to him declared. Guilty. Thereupon the Court doe pass this followinge centance to the Prissoner.

[11] Whereas you Thomas Cornell have been in this Court Indicted and charged for murthering your mother Mrs Rebecca Cornell Widow. and you beinge by your peers the Jurry found Guilty. Know and to that end prepare your selfe, that you are by this Court Centanced to be Carried from hence to the Com[m]on Goale, and from thence on fryday next which will be the twenty thre day of this instant month May about one of the clock to be carried from the said Goale to the place the Gallowes — and there

to be Hanged by the neck untill you are dead dead.
The Centance beinge pronounced and to him openly declared The said Thomas Cornell is Remitted to the Generall Serjants Custody safely to be kept till the day of Exicution.
A warrant ordered and granted to seize the Estate of Thomas Cornell and make Returne thereof to this Court.
Ordered that a strict Watch be kept in and about the prisson untill the day of the Execution of Thomas Cornell, and that the said Thomas Cornell shall be manacled and surely fastned to the great chaine — And ordered that **James Clarke** and **James Browne** cunstables in Newport are Authorized and desired to Asist the Generall Serjant in settinge and orderinge the watch for secureinge the said prissoner, which watch are to be Eight in the Night time and four in the day time.

Upon an Indictment by the Generall Aturney against an Indian by the English called **John** by the Indians **punneane** for that the said Indian on the Twenty one day of March last past came to the dwellinge house of M[r] **Richard Bulgar** in Portsmouth, and there com[m]itted a Rape on the body of **Lettice** wife of the said Bulgar upon which issued death to the said Lettice.
The said prissoner punneane beinge cald for and brought into Court, and his Indictment publickly Red and Interpreted unto him, and he demanded of whether Guilty or not Guilty, what he had to say for himself: he Answered that he doth not know whether he did the act or not for he was Drunk. The Jurry Impanneld and sent forth on the Case.
Jurrymen: [*listed in margin*]

Georg Lawton foreman	Jeffrey Champlin
Thomas Gould	Thomas Painter
Jerem~ Browne	Willia[m] Rogers
Bened[t] Arnold jun[r]	Ephrim Palmer
James Dexter	Nicholas Easton
Leonard Smith	Barth. Hunt

The Jurrys Verdict Guilty. The Centance of Court Interpreted to the said Indian. Whereas you punneane Indian alias John have been in this Court Indicted and charged for a Rape committed by you on the Body of Lettice the wife of M[r] Richard Bulgar of the Towne of Portsmouth, and you beinge by your peers the Jurry found Guilty of the said fact Know and to that end prepare your selfe for death, And for that end you are to be carried from the present Court unto the Com[m]on Goale there to be safely secured, and from thence to be carried unto the Gallows the place of Exicution on fryday next beinge the 23 day of this Instant May about one of the Clock of the said day and then and there to be hanged by the neck untill you are Dead Dead —

Upon Indictment by the Gen[rl] Solicetor against **George** a Negroe servant (belonging to M[rs] **Sarah Davis**) for com[m]ittinge ffornication with **Maria** Negro servant to M[r] **ffrancis Brinley**, the said Negroe being Mandamassed and in Court Cald apeard: his charge beinge Read and he askt whether Guilty or not Guilty — Ownes: Guilty.
The Court doe centance him to be whipt with fifteene stripes.

Upon Indictment by the Generall Solicetor against **Maria** a Negro woman (servant to M^r^ ffran. Brinley) ffor com[m]itting ffornication with George a Negro servant to Mrs Sarah Davis, the said Negro beinge mandamassed, and in Court Cald apeard, and beinge askt whether Guilty or not Guilty ownes Gulilty. The Court doe centance her to be forthwith whipt with fifteene stripes.

Upon Indictment by the Solicetor against **Hope** a Negro woman (servant to Mr **William Coddington**) for com[m]ittinge the act of ffornication with **James Parr**. The said Negro beinge Mandamassed and in Court Cald apeard, and her charge read, and she askt whether Guilty or not Guilty. Ownes Guilty.
The centance of the Court is That the said Negro be forthwith whipt with fifteene stripes or pay fforty shillings to the Generall Treasury.

Elizabeth Gerrat beinge bound to this Court to answer a Charge of Adultery, layd against her by her husband **Robert Gerrat** and beinge in Court Cald apeard, and none apeareinge to prossicute she is acquitted of her bonds, payinge court ffees, and her bondsman **Samuell Pratt** is acquitted of his bonds.

Robert Gerrat marrine^r^ Charged his wife Elizabeth with the act of Adultry and beinge bound to this Court to prosicute his said Charge, and beinge in Court Cald did not apeare nor any on his behalfe.

William Haukins and **William Vincent** chossen Jurry-men by Providence and they not atendinge are fined twenty shillings a peece.

Samuel Gorton and **Thomas Greene** chosen Jurry men by Warwick and they not atendinge are fined twenty shillings a peece.

Samuel Sanford, Mathew Bordin and **William Hall jun^r^** chossen jurry men by Portsmouth and they not atendinge are fined twenty shillings a peece.

John Warner chossen jurry-man by Warwick Excussed. **Moses Lippitt** fined twenty shillings.

Those following are Testimonys Concerning **Thomas Cornell** Murdering of [**12**] his Mother **Rebeca Cornell**: which was ordered to be Recorded.

Thomas Cornell the son of Rebeca Cornell, being inquired of us the Coroners Inquest, doe declare y^t^ in the eveninge before twas darke, came into the roome and satt downe & discoursed with his Mother Rebeca for ye space of about one houre and a halfe; and then went forth into the next Roome, where he stayd about Threequarters of an houre, then his Wife sent his son **Edward** into the roome to his Grandmoth^r^ to know whether shee would have some milke boyled for her supper; the Child coming in to the roome saw some fire in the roome upon the floore, and the Child came back unto us, and fetcht the candle to see what fire it was, **Henry Straite** went Presently into the roome, my selfe and the rest followed in A Huddle, Henry Straite coming in saw some fire, and stooped, and with his Hands raked fire upon the floore, supposing it to be and Indian that was Drunke, and Burnt, soe he layd hold of the Arme, my selfe Immediately following, by the light perceived it was my Mother, and Cryed out, Oh Lord it is my Mother.

Taken upon oath this Present 9th Day of February 1672/3
Before me William Baulston Assist. & Coroner.

Henry Straite being Examined upon Oath before the Coroner, Testifies, that he knows nothing how Rebeca Cornell came to Her untimely Death, onely sayth that Edward Cornell being sent in unto his Grand mother to Know what shee would have for Her supper, and comeing into the roome, saw fire in the floore, and came out unto us, and tooke the Candle to see what fire twas, he the sayd Henry rann, the Boy with the Candle followed, and Thomas Cornell, he the sayd Henry comeing into the roome, saw fire upon the foore, he stooped down; and with his hand raked fire that was upon the floore, and tooke hold of an Arme, and spake Indian, supposeing it was an Indian, Drunke and Burnt; Thomas Cornell following, and by the Light deserned & called out, and sayd, Oh Lord it is my Mother.

Taken upon oath the yeare and Day above written.

Before me William Baulston Assist. & Corroner.

Wee the Coroners Inquest for his Majestie being Impanelled, and Engaged this Present 9th Day of ffebry 1672/3 by Mr William Baulston Assistt and Coroner for his Matie in the Towne of Portsmouth in Rhod-Island in the Colony of Rhod-Island and Providence Plantations in New-England, have and by these presents doe declare; That being brought to the place where the Dead Body of Rebeca Cornell was Presented, and Inquiry by us made before the Coroner & Mr Joshua Coggeshall one of the Assistants of the sd Towne, and alsoe Coroner. The Body of the sayd Rebeca we found dead upon the floore, her Clothes very much Burnt by fire, and Her Body very much scorched and burnt by fire, And after dilligent Inquirie and Examination of Wittnesses, wee the sayd Coroners Inquest caused the sayd Body of Rebeca Cornell Widdow to Mr Thomas Cornell of Portsmouth to be stripped of the Residue of Clothes upon it (unburnt) turned and Handled, and searched to the best of our Judgments and understandings, doe finde and declare, That upon the Evening after the Eight Day of Febvruary 1672/3 the sayd Rebeca being in or about the age of 73 yeares, was brought to her untimely death by an Unhappie Accident of fire as Shee satt in her Rome, the time afore specified.

That this is our Verdict as the Coroners Inquest, wee give under our hands this Present 9th Day of February 1672/3.

William Dyer fforeman	Edward Lay
John Sanford	Thomas Brook
Georg Lawton	Hugh Parsons
John Albro	Peter Talman
John Anthony senr	ffrancis Brayton
Thomas Wood	William Wilbore

[13] **John Brigs** of the Towne of Portsmouth Aged sixty foure yeares or thereabouts, being According to Law Sworne and In[g]aged befor the Councell, Testifieth That on the Twelfth Day of this Instant month ffebruary in the night as this Depont lay in his Bedd, he being in A Dreame of Mrs Rebeca Cornell Deseased, and being betweene Sleepeing and Wakeing, as he thought he felt something heave up the Bedclothes twice, and thought some body had beene coming to bed to hime, where upon he Awaked, and turned himeselfe about in his Bed, and being Turned, he perceived A Light in the roome, like to the Dawning of ye Day, and plainely saw the shape and

Apearance of A Woman standing by his Bed side where at he was much Afrighted, and Cryed out, in the name of God what art thou, the Aperition Answered, I am your sister Cornell, and Twice sayd, see how I was Burnt with ffire, and shee plainely Apeered unto hime to be very much burnt about the shoulders, fface, and Head.

Taken before the Deputy Govr and Councell mett the 20th day of ffebruary 1672/3 As Atest John Sanford Secretary.

Mr **John Russill** of the Towne of Dartmouth in the Colony of New-Plymouth Aged 65 yeares or thereabouts, being According to Law sworne and Engaged before the Councell, Testifieth, that this Deponant, lately haveing some speech with **Georg Soule** Cunstable of the sayd Towne of Dartmoth. The sayd Soul sayd to this Depon^t^, you being my Anchant ffrind, I have someting to tell you wch I would desire you to be Secret in, and the sayd Soul sayd, he once comeing to Mrs Rebeca Cornells House in Portsmouth, the sayd Mrs Rebeca Cornell sayd to the sayd Soul, that Shee intended in the spring of the yeare, to goe and Dwell with her son Samuell, but shee feared Shee should be made away before that time. And this Relation of the sayd Georg Souls to this Deponant was since the sayd Mrs Rebeca Cornells Decease.

Taken before the Deputy Govr and Councell mett the 20th day of ffebruary 1672/3. As Atest John Sanford Secretary.

We whose names are under subscribed being on the second inquiry after the untimely death, or decease of Mrs Rebeca Cornell of the Towne of Portsmouth, desired to make Dilligent search whether any wound might be found on Her. Doe thus Affirme that wee found A Suspitious wound on her in the upper-most part of the Stomake, Wittness our hands ye 20th day of ffebruary 1672/3.

Henry Greenland Chyr^n^ **Simon Cooper** Chyr^n^

I doe Atest to ye above Written and declare it to be my Judgment, Wittness my hand the Day & yeare above written John Cranston Dept^y^ Govr

The above Premised Henry Greenland & Simon Cooper did both upon their Oaths affirme to the above Premised, Evidence or written, to be truth before John Cranston Dep^ty^ Govr & Practioner in Phisick & Chyrurgery

We whose names are hereunto subscribed being by the Dep^ty^ Govr & major part of the Councell of this his Majesties Colony of Rhod-Island and Providence Plantations, appointed and Empanneled A Coroners Inquest on the Body of Mrs **Rebeca Cornell** (Widdow to ye deceased **Mr Thomas Cornell** of Portsmouth) who came to an untimely, and uncertaine Death, in the night ffollowing the Eight day of this Instant month ffebruary, who this Instant Day, for A Second Inquire, was taken out of Her Grave, upon severall Suspitious reasons Rendered to the Govr, Dep^ty^ Govr, and sayd Councell. And the Corps of the sayd Rebeca, being Dilligently searched by Chyriurgions in our view, and in their search, as under their hands appeares, they findeing A Suspitious wound in the Body of the sayd Rebeca Cornell in the uppermost part of her Stomake. And wee alsoe finding that the Body was much Burnt and Scorched by fire wee doe declare, and returne our Verdict to be, That wee Conceive and Judg, to the best of our understandings, that by the aforesayd Suspitious wound, and fire, shee the sayd Mrs Rebeca Cornell came bye her Death. In witness whereof wee have sett o^r^ hands ye 20th day of ffeb^ry^ 1672/3.

John Sanford foremn	William Wilbore	Phillip Edes
Georg Lawton	James Barker	Caleb Carr
John Albro	Peter Easton	Daniell Gould
Thomas Wood	Joseph Torrey	Henry Bull
Edward Lay	Weston Clarke	Lawrance Turner
Thomas Brooke	Samuell Hubbard	Thomas Nicolls
Hugh Persons	Stephen Mumford	Thomas Dungin
Francis Brayton senr	Edward Greenman	Thomas Burg

[14] **Thomas Cornell** senr of Portsmouth being Examined concerneing the untimely and uncertaine death of his Mother Rebeca Cornell, wch happened on the 8th of ffebruary 1672/3 in the Evening of the same Day: sayth, he coming in to the House from his Occations: a little after sunsett went to visett his Mother, his son Thomas being then with Her, and satt and discoursed with Her in her roome where shee keept, about one houre and halfe, and then Left her and went to Supper, haveing salt-mackrill for Supper, which his Mother cared not for because shee used to say it made her Dry, and haveing supt, his Wife sent his son Edward to his Mother, to know whether shee would have milke boiled for her supper, or what else shee desired, which might be about Three quarters of one houre, from the time he left her, he being the Last that was with Her; the sayd Edward called, Grandmother, Grandmother, and noebody Answering, and perceaving fire in the roome; came out, and sayd lett me have the Candle to see what fire that is in the other roome, whereupon wee all rann in, in hast, and **Henry Straite** ran in ffirst, and Rakeing the fire with his Hands, tooke hold of his Mothers Arme, thinkeing it had been A Drunken Indian, and spake Indian to her; at last sayd here is A Drunken Indian Burnt to Death; But the sayd Thomas Cornell, coming in last, perceaved by Her shoose which he saw by the light of the Candle, that it was his Mother, and sayd, Oh Lord, it is my Mother, and tooke up her head in his Armes to see if any life were in Her; findeing her burnt, lyeing along upon the floore with her head towards the fire, her Cloths burnt of on her below and some above, and the Valins of the Bed burnt, and the upper part of the Curtaines where he Judged Shee stood when Shee was on fire; before Shee fell, her Apron & one of her Petty-coats being Cotton and Wooll, and Judged that her Clothes tooke fire from A Cole that might fall from Her Pipe as shee satt Smoaking in Her Chaire, and haveing seene her in that Condition, as above related, sent out and called in some of the Neighbours liveing neare; which is all that he knows of the Death of his Mother abovementioned; not Judging any one were Instrumentall in any Measure to procure her Death.

Taken before us the 21th
of ffebruary 1672/3

Nich Easton Govr
Jon Cranston Depty Govr
ffrancis Brinley Assistt
John Easton Assistant
Joshua Coggeshall Assistant

April ye 10th 1673

Sarah Cornell the Wife of Thomas Cornell of Portsmouth, being Examined Concerning the Death of her Mother in Law Rebeca Cornell, sayth, yt ye evening her sayd Mothr was found dead in ye House, about one houre or more, or such a quantity of time; before shee was soe found, her Husband Thomas Cornell was with her to see how shee did, hereing that shee was not well, & tooke A Quill of yarne in his hand to winde, after he came out, he winded halfe a Quill of yarne, & then went to Supper, & one of ye Boies was sent to her sayd Moth^{r}, to know what Shee would have for Supper, upon opening of the dore, ye Great Dogg being in her roome, Leaped out over ye Boy, & ye Boy came out in hast, & desired A Candle to see w^{t} fire y^{t} was in ye roome, whereupon most in the House ran in & found her sayd Mother Rebeca Cornell lyeing dead in the floore, being Burnt, but how it came shee knows not, nor can Imagine, but Lookes at it as A wonderfull thing, & the more in regard, part of her Clothes being Cotton and wooll, ye wooll was burnt & ye Cotton Remained whole, which John Gould, John Spencer, & Job Hawkins afterwards saw, comeing to ye House for y^{t} Purpose: ffurther sayth, w^{n} Georg Lawton & John Albro, being sent for, went into the roome, they smelt ye scent of the Burning of the Clothes, & none before, & when Henry Straite went in first he thought it had beene an Indian y^{t} lay there Dead.

Taken before us. Nich~ Easton Govr
ffrancis Brinley Assistant

At a meeting of ye Dep^{t} Govr M^{r} ffrancis Brinley, Mr John Easton & Mr Joshua Coggeshall Assistants, Held at Mr Joshua Coggeshalls House in Portsm^{o} ye 22th of Feby 1672/3.

Henry Straite being brought before ye Dep^{t} Govr & the sd Assist^{ts} & Examined w^{t} he could say and relate concerning the late Deceased Rebeca Cornells death. Answered y^{t} ye night that ye sd Mrs Rebeca Cornell lost her life, he was some part of ye night, at Mr Georg Lawtons & came not to Mr Thomas Cornells (where he Diated & Lodged) untill supper time, & w^{n} he came in, some part of ye supper was upon ye Table, & they were gooing to Supper, & sitting downe to Supper. Mrs Rebeca Cornell, who usialy used to be at Supper with us, not being there, this Examinate saith he inquired where ye sd Mrs Cornell was, & why shee was not at supper wth them, Mr Thos Cornell Answered, we haveing nothing but mackrill to supper, my Moth^{r} will not eate any, for shee saith it makes her dry in the night. The Examinate further saith, y^{t} as soone as they had supped, Tho[m] Cornells wife sd to one of ye boys, by name Edward, goe to yor Grandmother, & ask her whether shee will have any milke for supper; the Ladd going, Emediately returned, and askt for A Candle to see what fire y^{t} was, y^{t} was in his Grandmoth^{rs} roome, whereupon they all ran, & this Examinate came [15] first to the dore, & into ye roome, & espieing fire on ye floore, he clapt his Hands upon it, and raked away ye fire wth his hands, and then thought it had beene an Indian, & tooke hold on ye Arme, and shakt her, speakeing Indian; whereupon Mr Tho[m] Cornell clapt his hands & cryed out, Oh Lord, it is my Mother. And this Examinate also saith, y^{t} there was noe fire in the Curtaines, nor about ye Bedsted when he came in, yett ye Curtins & Valliants at ye foote of the Bedsted was burnt. And alsoe saith y^{t} ye Body lay wth the head towards ye Southmost Dore, & ye feete towards ye other Dore, in wch roome we were & ye Back lay towards ye Bedsteadd ye face towards ye Westmost Window, & lay on ye left side; Also the said Examinate saith y^{t} at other times when they have had Mackrill for Supper, ye sd Mrs Rebeca Cornell used to be called, & did use to come & supp with ye rest in Mr Thomas Cornells roome.

Taken upon Oath.

James Moills, being Examined w^{t} he can relate concerneing ye Death of Mrs Rebeca Cornell. Answered that ye night y^{t} ye said Mrs Cornell lost her Life: The Examinate & Hen~ Straite were at Mr Georg Lawtons, in ye evening & came not to Mr Tho[m] Cornells till about seven A Clocke, when they came in, part of ye Supper was upon ye Table, & after Supper, Tho[m] Cornells Wife bidd one of ye Boys, by name Edward, goe to his Grandmoth^{r}, and ask her w^{t} shee would have for supper; ye ladd goeing in, came Imediately out & askt for A Candle, saying there was fire in his Granmothers roome, upon which every one there Hastened to see what it was. This Examinate, w^{n} he came into ye Entry, was goeing out of dores to see if there were not fire on ye outside of ye House, but before he gott out, hereing Hen~ Straite say here is A Drunken Indian burnt to Death, he returned & went into ye roome, & there he saw, the sd Mrs Rebeca Cornell lyeing on ye floore, wth fire about Her, from Her Lower parts neare to ye Armepits and saith, he knew it to be her by her Shoes, & saith, y^{t} ye Curtins & Valants at ye foote of ye Bedd were burnt, yett ye fire about ye Bedstead was out. And alsoe this Examinate saith, y^{t} he haveing being A Servant, as now he is, to ye sd Mr Tho[m] Cornell, hath observed, y^{t} ye sayd Mrs Rebeca Cornell (except not well) did usually be at Meales wth Her son Thomas &c. and w^{t} the Reason was, y^{t} shee was not y^{t} night at Supper wth them, he knows not. This Examinate also saith, y^{t} at other times in ye Evening it was Usiall, & sildome otherwise, y^{t} one or more of ye Children, were in ye roome wth their gran-mother, but knows not ye Reason they, nor any of them were not wth her then. This Examinate also saith, y^{t} he was in ye roome wth Mrs Cornell y^{t} Morneing before her death, and then shee said shee was not well, & at noone goeing in to see her, shee said shee was something better. This Examinate also saith, y^{t} w^{n} he went into ye roome the night ye sd Mrs Cornell deceased, he saw A peece of her Garment, being Cotton and woollen lyeing upon A Brand on the fire. He alsoe saith shee lay on Her Left side.

Taken upon Oath.

Thomas Cornell (the son of Mr Tho[m] Cornell) Aged 18 yeares or there abouts, being Examined what he can relate Concerneing ye Death of his Gran-Moth^{r} Mrs Rebeca Cornell. Answered and sayth, y^{t} ye Evening his Gran-mother dyed, he was in ye roome wth her, & stayd but A Litle while, but went out againe,and did Leave his ffather in the roome wth her, who stayd wth her about an houre, or an houre & an halfs time, & then in A litle time after his comeing out, went to Supper, & after supper, his Mother sent in his Brother Edward to his Granmother to know w^{t} shee would have for her Supper, who as he s^{d}, called his Gran-Mother, & espieing fire in ye roome, layd his hand on it, & Emediately came runing & askt for A Candle to see w^{t} fire y^{t} was in ye other roome, whereupon we all riseing up, Ran to see w^{t} it was & Henry Strait gott in first, & sayd it was A Drunken Indian, y^{t} had burnt himeselfe to death, but wee Presently espied it to be my Gran-Moth^{r}, whose Clothes were very much burnt, and then on fire. This Examinate alsoe saith, that, y^{t} night his Gran-

Mother was not at Supper wth them, though at other times shee usially used, neither was Shee sent for as at other times, ye Reason was, there being Mackrill to Supper, was A dyet Shee did not like because it used, as Shee sayd, to make her very dry. The Examinate also saith, y^{t} it was formerly usiall for some of them to be in the roome wth their Gran-Mother in the night times, but was not y^{t} night. He alsoe saith, y^{t} w^{n} they went into ye roome, Shee lay on her Left side, wth her Head towards ye fire. And further saith, y^{t} part of ye Curtin & Valants about ye Bedstead was Burnt, but w^{n} they went in, ye fire about the Bedsted was quite out.

Taken upon Oath.

Stephen, Edward, & John Cornell, ye Sons of Mr Tho~ Cornell, being Examined w^{t} they know Concerneing ye Death of their Gran-Mother Mrs Rebeca Cornell. They all being severally Examined, sayd they know not how shee came to Her death, & alsoe said, their ffather was ye Last Person they know of, y^{t} was wth their Gran-Moth^{r}. They further said, that none of them were y^{t} night wth their Gran-Mother, as at other times they use to be.

Taken before John Cranston Dep^{t} Govr John Easton Assist^{t}
ffrancis Brinley Assist^{t} Joshua Coggeshall Assist^{t}

Mary Cornell wife to John Cornell of Plymouth Colony in New-England, Aged 28 yeares or thereabouts, Apeared before mee ye 3^{d} Day March 1672-73 & upon Her sollemn Engagm^{t}, declareth as followeth. That about 3 or 4 yeares past, shee this Depon^{t}, being at her Moth^{r} in Laws House Mrs **Rebeca Cornell** of Portsmth on Rhod-Island, Widdow, & now dead, or Deceast. This Depon^{t} saith that her Mother in Law Mrs Rebeca Cornell, haveing beene in Her Orchard, returneing into ye House, tould this Depon^{t}, y^{t} shee had beene run[n]ing after Piggs, & said shee being weake, & had noe help, & shee being disregarded, shee thought to have stabd A Pen-knife in her Heart, y^{t} shee had in her hand, & then shee should be ridd of Her Trouble. But it came in her minde, Resist ye Devill who will [*illegible*] shee sd shee was well satisfied, & further saith not. Taken upon Oath y^{e} [*illegible*] March 1672/73 before [*illegible*].

[16] **George Soule** Aged 34 yeares or thereabouts being Engaged, saith y^{t} he being at Mr **Tho~ Cornells** House on Rhod-Island ye same day **Mathew Allins** House was Burned in the Winter, last, and this Deponant speaking wth Mrs Rebeca Cornell, shee said shee would goe live wth her son Samuell ye next spring. This Depon^{t} urging her y^{t} shee was better where shee was; shee said y^{t} A differance was arisen between her & her son Thomas, about rent. This depon^{t} sayd shee spoke unadvisedly to say shee would remove. Shee Replyed: w^{t} doth this tend too. Shee said he would have the Hundred Pound bond out of her hand. And this Deponant saith, shee said shee would goe live wth her son in the spring, if shee was not otherwise disposed of, or made away. and further this depon^{t} saith not.

Taken this first day of March 1672/3.

This Depon^{t} further saith he Judged Mrs Rebeca Cornell to Be in a Passion.

Nich Easton Govr
Richd Smith Assistant

Mary ye wife of Mr **John Almy** of ye Towne of Portsmouth Aged Thirty three yeares or thereabouts, being According to Law Engaged & Sworne, Deposeth & Testifieth y^{t} shee hath severall times observed an Undutyfull-ness in **Tho~ Cornell** towards his Mother Mrs **Rebeca Cornell**, & saith y^{t} shee hath severall times spoke of it to others. And further saith, y^{t} ye sayd Mrs Rebeca Cornell told this Depon^{t} y^{t} shee was much neglected, & y^{t} shee was forced in ye Winter season, in ye cold wether to goe to her Bed unmade, & unwarmed, & was therefore forced to procure some woollin Cloth to wrapp her selfe in, before shee went to her could bedd. And alsoe ye sd Mrs Rebeca Cornell, told this depon^{t}, y^{t} if shee could not Eate as all ye foalkes of ye House could, & at their times of Eateing, shee must fast, for there was nothing brought in for Her to Eate; ffurther this Depon^{t} testifieth, y^{t} **Anthony Shaws** wife of Portsmouth (since ye aforesayd Tho Cornell was Imprisened) told this Depon^{t}, y^{t} Tho Cornells Wife coming to ye prison to her Husband, they Desired some time of Privacy, & soe went together into A Private roome, & whilst they were together, ye sd Tho~ Cornell and his Wife had those Expretions each to other, y^{t} if you will keepe my Councell I will keepe yo^{rs}, & soe they spake each together, & then ye Dore of ye roome in which they were was opened.

Taken before ye Dep^{t} Govr & part of ye Gen^{ll} Councell. ye 11th of Aprill. 1673.

John Sanford, Secretary.

Elizabeth ye wife of **Hugh Persons** of ye Towne of Portsmouth, Aged sixty yeares or thereabouts being According to ye Law Engaged, & sworne, Deposeth, & Testifieth y^{t} shee being wth **Goodwife Earle**, desired to lay forth ye Body of the Deceased Mrs Rebeca Cornell, they on ye Sabath Day towards night, Accordingly layd forth the Body of the s^{d} Deceased, & saith y^{t} then there was noe Apeareance of Blood about ye Corps, but comeing thether on ye Munday there had beene in the roome where ye Corps lay, Thomas Cornell wth Wm. Hall to measure ye Corps for ye makeing A Coffin to interr Her in, & some saying ye corps did purge, this depon^{t} went to see whether ye corps did purge or not, & found y^{t} ye corps did not purge, onely saw y^{t} shee had bled fresh Blood at ye Nose; and ffurther saith not.

Taken before ye Dep^{t} Govr & part of ye Gen^{rll} Councell, the 11th day of Aprill 1673.

John Sanford Secretary

Hugh Persons of ye Towne of Portsmouth Aged 60 yeares, or thereabouts, being According to Law Engaged & sworne: Deposeth & Testifieth that y^{t} night Mrs Rebeca Cornell lost Her Life, this Depon^{t} comeing to ye House: went in to ye Roome where shee lay, & Mr **Coggeshall** goeing in before this Depon^{t}, Emediately Mr Coggeshall went to ye outward Doore opening to ye Southward, to see whether it were fast bolted. And this depon^{t} heard Mr Coggeshall say y^{t} Doore was fast Bolted. And further this Depon^{t} saith, y^{t} upon ye hearth there was burnt sinders lay in A traine, & almost covered ye floare in such A manner as if shee had beene drawne thether.

Taken before ye Dep^{t} Govr and part of ye Genll Councell the 11th Day of April 1673.

John Sanford Secretary

Joane Coggeshall ye wife of **Joshua Coggeshall** aged about 38 yeares being Engaged According to Law, affirmeth y^{t} being at the Widdow Cornells House about A yeare & halfe since; as neere as shee can Remember; shee ye sd Cornell Complained to Her, y^{t}

Her son Tho Cornell, carryed himselfe very unkindely to Her, detaineing Her Rent from Her, and would pay Her none, & was soe High & soe Crose, y^t shee durst hardly speake to hime; & y^t shee intended to gett men to speake to hime aboute it, & did nominate **Wm Baulston, John Easton & Walter Clarke**; & further sayd, y^t her son Tho˜ Cornell told her, Her name did stinke about ye Island, or Country, And shee ye sd Widdow Cornell, desired Her y^t shee would not speake of w^t shee told Her, for shee should live A sadd life, wth Her sd son, if he should heare of it.
Taken this 14th of Aprill 1673, before us.

John Cranston Dep^t Govr	Francis Brinley Assist.˜
Richd Smith, Assist	John Easton Assist.˜

Patience Coggeshall ye Wife of **John Coggeshall**, aged about 33 years, being Engaged According to Law, afirmeth, y^t shee and Her Sister **Wait Gould**, & her Sister **Joan Coggeshall**, being with ye Widdow **Rebeca Cornell** about 2 1/2 yeares since, in Her orchard under a Damzen Tree; shee related to y^m y^e sad Condition of Life shee lived wth her son Tho˜ Cornell, wch shee declared wth much weepeing, & sayd, y^t he would not keepe her A mayd, though he was Engaged to it, as to find her Diett, & y^t her son Thomas & his wife, y^t now is, were very cross to her; & this $depon^t$ asked Her how y^e children carryed y^mselves towards her, shee replied; how could they carry it kindly to Her w^n their ffather was soe cross; & y^t shee was afrayd there would be mischiefe don, Her Daughter in Law was of such a Desperate Spirit, for not long since, sayd shee, shee ran after one of ye Children of his ffirst Wife, wth an Axe, into Her House; but shee prevented Her strikeing ye child; & y^t shee did not live wth any of her other children, because shee had made over her Estate to Her Son Thomas; & y^t if shee had thought her son Thomas first Wife would have dyed before Her, shee would not have made it over to hime.

Waite Gould being Engaged According to Law, affirmeth to y^e truth of y^e Premises.
Taken this 14th of Aprill 1673, before us.

John Cranston Dep^t Govr	ffrancis Brinley $Assist^t$.
$Rich^d$ Smith, Assist	John Easton $Assist^t$.

Nicholas Wild of $Newp^t$ aged 73 yeares or there abouts, being According to Law Engaged, & Deposed, Testifieth y^t about a yeare agoe Mrs **Rebeca Cornell** came to this $Depon^{ts}$ House, & there Complained of Her son **Thomas Cornell**; y^t he was [*torn*] Agreemt to pay her yearely (as neere as this $Depon^t$ Remembers Shee sayd) Six pound a yeare, & Diet for A maide Servant, wch shee sayd he refused to pay, & did wth hold it; & further shee sayd, y^t he tould Her, if shee would release hime of y^t Hundred Pound he was Engaged to pay her, y^n he would pay y^e six pound A yeare, & A Maide should have her Diet, as was Promised. ffurther y^e sd Mrs Cornell told this $Depon^t$, y^t her son Told her he must Build, & required y^e Hundred pound toward it, but shee sayd shee could not, unless she should wrong her other Children, for shee thought he had Enough; shee alsoe told this $depon^t$, y^t her son told her shee must pay y^e Rates; Shee alsoe sayd, y^t shee hath been forced to goe out in y^e snow for Wood, & hath falne wth y^e Wood under Her, when they have beene in y^e House & saw it all, wch shee sayd was such A griefe & Trouble to her, y^t shee hath beene afraide of being Provoaked, & hath prayed to ye Lord aga^t it; & ffurther shee sayd y^t Her son Thomas

told Her, y^{t} if shee would forgive ye Hundred pound he would y^{n} pay ye Rent, alow Diet for A Maide for Her, & pay ye rates, & this shee Declared, wth great griefe & Trouble of Spirit, wth weepeing Teares.
Taken before ye Dep^{t} Govr & part of ye Gen^{ll} Councell ye 14th of Aprill 1673.

John Sanford Secretary.

Sarah ye wife of **Nicholas Wilde** Aged 61 yeares or thereabouts, being According to Law Engaged & deposed, testifieth to ye Truth of all y^{t} is above Testified by Her Husband. And further testifieth, y^{t} Mrs Rebeca Cornell told this depon^{t} y^{t} Her Son Thomas, one time being Angry wth her, lookt very firce upon Her, & nasht, or sett his Teeth at her, & sayd shee had beene A Cruell Mother to hime. She told hime shee had not beene cruell, but A [*torn*] & sayd his Carrige & Expressions therein was A great Trouble, or Terror to Her. This depon^{t} askt Mrs Cornell how shee was able to beare such Afflictions. Shee answered y^{t} shee should not be Able to beare it, but y^{t} [17] God did support her, & in Her griefe shee had Scriptures come into Her mind y^{t} did much quiet her.
Taken before ye Dep^{t} Govr & part of the Genll Councell ye 14th of Aprill 1673.

John Sanford Secretary

The Deposition of **Rebeca Woollsey** is y^{t} w^{n} shee was last at Rhod-Island with Her Mother Mrs Rebeca Cornell falling in discourse one with Another, the Depon^{ts} Mother tould her Daughtour Woollsey that shee looked very poorly and the Depon^{t} told her Mother shee had cause soe to doe; her mother did Aske her why; the Depon^{t} told her Mother, y^{t} shee had, had the smal pox, and y^{t} shee was very much Afflicted and Troubled in mind, and y^{t} shee was sometimes Perswaded to Drowne her selfe, and sometimes to stabb her selfe. Soe the Depon^{ts} Mother told her Daughter that shee must pray to God, and he would helpe Her. The Depon^{t} told Her Mother, shee did often call upon God, and he did here her, soe w^{n} the Depon^{t} had done with this Discorce, the Deponants Mother told her Daughter that shee had beene divers yeares possest with an evill spirit, and that shee was divers times Perswaded to make away with Her selfe, and yett the Lord was pleased from time to time to preserve her. The Depon^{t} told her Mother, that shee would tell her Brother Thomas of it, and her Mother charged her not to tell hime, soe shee did not tell hime: And further sayes not.
ffloshin 10 Aprill 1673 — This Testimony taken before me

Robert Coe Justice of Peace

John Pearce of the Towne of Portsmouth Aged 41 yeares or there abouts being According to Law Engaged, Testifieth, that since the Decease of Mrs Rebeca Cornell, this Deponent being at the house of [*torn* - Wm ?] Wood, there was Thomas Cornell, and his Wife, and Thomas Cornell sayd, that his Mother in her life time had A desire to have A good fire, and further sayd, that he thought God had answered her ends, for now shee had it.
Taken the 7th of May 1673 (in the morneing) before me.

Joshua Coggeshall Assistant.

Lift^{t} **Joseph Torrey** of Newport being According to Law Engaged, Testifieth, That on ye Day the Corroners Inquest satt upon the Corps of Mrs Rebeca Cornell deceased (on the second inquiry) comeing to the House of Thomas Cornell, and Inquireing whether the outmost dore were shutt, of the sayd Mrs Cornells Roome that night shee Dyed, Mr Thomas Cornell made Answer, that the dore was not Lockt, neither was there ever any Lock upon the Dore, but sayd he, the Dore was fastned with A Barr upon the Latch, and showed this depon^{t} in what man[n]er it was.

Taken the 16th of May 1673 in Court As Attests John Sanford Record^{r}

Mr. **Phillip Eds** of Newport being According to Law Engaged, Testifieth to the truth of what is above Testified by Lift^{t} Joseph Torrey.

Taken in Court, ye 16th of May 1673. As Attests John Sanford Record^{r}

I Present and Indict **Thomas Cornell** of Portsmouth now Prisoner in his Maj^{ties} Colony of Rhode Island and Providence Plantations Senr. That against the feare of God, the Honour of our Soveraigne Lord the Kinge, and the Law and peace of this Colony, on the Evening of the 8th Day of Feb^{ry} in the 25th yeare of the Reigne of his Maj^{tie} Charles the Second Annoque Domin. 1672. The sayd Thomas Cornell did violently Kill his Mother, Rebeca Cornell, Widdow, or was ayding or Abetting thereto, in the Dwelling House of his sayd Mother in the foresayd towne of Portsmouth, which act of his is Murder, and is against the Hono^{le} Crowne and Dignety of his Majesty the Laws and peace of this Colony.

Dated at A Gen^{ll} Court of Tryalls held ye 12th May 1673

John Easton Gen^{ll} Aturney.

Passed by leave of ye Court to ye Grand Jury As Attests John Sanford Reco^{r}. Grand Jury returne [*blotted*] Bill. Petty Jurys returne. Guilty.

Whereas you **Thomas Cornell** have beene in this Court, Indicted, and Charged for Murdering your Mother Mrs **Rebeca Cornell** Widdow, and you being by your Peers the Jurry found Guilty, Know, and to that end, prepare your selfe, that you are by this Court sentenced to be carryed from hence to the Common Goale, and from thence on ffryday next which will be the 23th Day of this instant month May, about one of the Clocke, to be carryed from the sayd Goale to the place of Execution, the Gallows, and there to be Hanged by ye neck untill you are Dead Dead.—

[18]

At the Gener[ll] Court of Tryalls held in his Maj[ties] Name
at Newport the 22th of October. 1673

M[r] Nicholas Easton, Governo[r]
William Coddington Dep[t] Gov[r]
M[r] Walter Clarke - Asistant
M[r] Daniel Gould - Asistant
M[r] John Easton - Asistant
M[r] William Harris - Asistant
M[r] Thomas Harris - Asistant
M[r] Thomas ffield - Asistant
M[r] Joshua Coggeshall - Asistant
M[r] John Tripp - Asistant
M[r] Walter Todd - Asistant
M[r] Job Almy - Asistant
John Sanford, Recorder
M[r] James Rogers Gen[rl] Serjant
M[r] Peter Easton Gen[rll] Treasurer
M[r] John Easton Gen[rl] Aturney

Gran Jurriors Engaged
M[r] Phillip Eads fore-man
M[r] George Gardner
M[r] John Pepody
M[r] William Devell
M[r] Robert Taylor
M[r] John Stanton
M[r] Willia[m] Correy
M[r] Thomas ffish Sen[r]
M[r] John Potter
M[r] Abiah Carpenter
M[r] Nathanill Johnson
M[r] John Horndall

Upon an action of debt by bill com[m]enced by **Humphrey Hodgis** of Boston plaintiff against **Thomas Starr** Defendant, **Peleg Sanford** the plaintiffs Aturney pleads in Court to a Nihill dicett. The Juries Verdict Wee finde for the plaintiff Eight pounds five shillings Eight pence according to the bill; and six pence damage and charge of court.

Jurry of Tryalls:

Samuell Hubbard foreman
Jerem~ Clarke
John Parker
Samuell Winsor
Dan[ll] Greenell
John Coggeshall
Thomas Eaton
Willia~ Haukins
Clement Weaver
Thomas Brooke
Mathew Boomer
Peter Talman

Upon an action of Debt on account com[m]enced by M[r] **Richard Smith** plaintiff against M[r] **John Porter** Defendant. The defend[t] taken upon a Nihill dicett. The Jurris verdict Wee finde accordinge to these accounts due to the plaintiff Twenty three pounds five shillings; damage two pence; and charge of Court.

Whereas there is an action com[m]enced by **Henry Palmer** of the Towne of Newport plaintiff against **Robert Westcot** of Aquednesett in the Narragansett Cuntry Defend[t] in an action of Debt damage tenn pounds, dated the 13[th] of June 1673 and for want of an answer by the defend[t] to the said action October the 15th 1673 the plaintiff in the office Entred a Nihill dicett, The said case in Court beinge cald plaintiff and defend[t] apeared, and in court the defend[t] acknowlidged him selfe the plaintiffs Debitor and owned the action and confessith Judgment asentinge to an Execution if suddainly the plaintiff be not satisfyed both debt & costs.

Upon an action of Debt Com[m]enced by D[r]. **Henry Greenland** plaintiff against **Clement Weaver** jun[r] bearinge date the 25th of June 1673: The Issue Generall, The Jurrys verdict, wee finde for the defendant Cost of Court, judgm[t] granted, a Reheareinge Entred.

Jurriors:

Samuel Hubard foreman	Thomas Eaton
Jerem~ Clarke	Willia~. Haukins
John Parker	Thom~ Brooke
Sam^ll Winsor	Mathew Boomer
Danill Greenell	Hugh Parsons
John Coggeshall ju^r	Zach~ Dublin

On a Complaint or Declara~. Entred in the office by **Caleb Carr**, the case beinge in court heard and adjetated the court see cause to cast the said action out of Court.

Upon an action of Debt Com[m]enced by **John Sanford** plaintiff against **Jone Cowdall** Widdow defend^t. The defend^t nor any for her appeareinge the plaintiff Enters a Nihell dicett. The jurris Verdict: Wee finde for the plaintiff two pound four shillings, damage two pence and charge of Court.

Upon Indictment by the Gen^rl Atturney against **William Haukins** sen^r of Providence for breach of peace he beinge bound to this Court and in Court cald apeared, pleads Not Guilty and Referrs him selfe for Tryall to God and the cuntry. The Jurries Verdict, Guilty. — The Court upon the consideration of the matter doe see cause to continew the said William Haukins his bonds for his apeareance untill the Court of Tryalls in May next.

Upon an Indictment by the Gen^rl Aturney against **Grace** the wife of **Thomas Lawton** of Portsmouth for com[m]ittinge Adultry with **James Murfie** she Enters Traverce, pleads Not Guilty and referrs for Tryall to God and the Cuntry. The Jurrys Verdict, Not Guilty of Adultry.

Jurriors.

Sam^ll Hubbard foreman	Tho. Eaton
Jer. Clarke	Tho. Brooks
John Parker	Math. Boomer
Sam^ll Winsor	Zach Dublin
Dan^ll Greenell	Joseph Brier
John Coggeshall	Edwd Robinson

The said **Grace Lawton** is by order of Court cleerd by proclamation payinge ffees.

Whereas by examination of **Henry Roberts** of Providence taken before Mr William Harris and Mr Thomas Harris Assistants for that the said Roberts hath against law made sale of Liquors to Indians, and he haveinge by a petition to this Court acknowlidged the charge and craves the courts favour therein pleadinge himselfe a strainger and his Ignorance of the law in that case, The Court doe Referr the Matter to the Generall Assembly for their detirmination therein.

Whereas the Towne of Providence have made choyce of **Lawrance Wilkinson** and **Thomas Roberts** to serve on the Grand and it beinge Eleaged that the said Wilkinson is therein wronged beinge the last Assembly a Deputy, and Thomas Roberts disabled beinge deafe; the Court doe fine the said Towne of Providence fforty shillings for their defect therein. —

According to the Order and Direction of the Gen^rl Assembly to bringe the Indian **Jankesick** to Tryall this court the said Indian beinge accussed for murthering an Indian called **Ossawan** - The Grand Jurry beinge dismist this Court order an other Grand jurry to be Empannalled.

The Grand Jurry [19]

Mr Henry Bull foreman	Tolleratio~ Harris
Willia~. Case	John Bordin
Thom~ Clifton	John Lappum
Thomas Stafford	Willia~ Austin
Adam Mott	Edmund Calverly
Tho. Harris jnr	Richard Morris

The said Grand jurry returned two bills which were by the Court com[m]itted to them - Mr **Peter Talman** haveinge in this Court Misbehaved himselfe, and thereupon com[m]itted to the Cunstables Custody, and he com[m]inge into Court and acknowlidginge his faileinge therein and craveing the Courts favour, the Court doe accept his acknowlidgment with hopes of better deportment —.

Upon Indictment by the Genrl Aturney against the Indian called **Jankesick** ffor Murtheringe the Indian **Ossawan.** — The said Indian Jankesick beinge cald for and brought into Court: his Indictment openly read and distinctly interpreted. he was askt whether Guilty or Not Guilty of the charge to which he could or would give a possetive anser, only sayinge he knew not. soe the case was com[m]ited to the Jurry, whoe were

English:	Indians:
Mr William Dyre foreman	Sawsunkewe
John Parker	Sunkanumskitt
Danill Greenell	Wuttanumpane
John Coggeshall	Weesawwowo
Thomas Eaton	Mamanekanate
Edward Robinson	Acomunat

The Jurrys verdict Guilty.

The Court doe sentence the said Indian **Jan Kesick** to be hangd on the com[m]on Gallows (in the Towne of Newport on Wensday next the 5th instant) by the neck till he be dead dead —.

Samuel Winsor beinge bound to this Court and in Court Cald apeared — : The Court upon the Consideration of the matter see cause to continew his Bonds till the Court of Tryalls in May Next.

Mary Pray of Providence beinge bound to this court, and in court cald did not apeare nor any for her. Therefore the Court doe order that the Majestrates of Providence doe binde the said Mary by suffitient sureties to the peace and good behaviour and to apeare at the Court of Tryalls in May next or Else send her to prison there to be secured.

Benedict Arnold junr and **Jeremiah Browne** chosen by the Towne of Newport to be on the Jurry and they not atendinge that service are fined twenty shillings apeece.

Lott Strainge chosen a jurry-man by the Towne of Portsmouth and not atendinge that service is fined twenty shillings.

Whereas the Towne of Warwick made choyce of **John Gerriardy** to serve on the pettitt jurry and he not apeareinge to serve, the Court Judginge the said John Gerriardy a person not lawfully quallefyed to serve on a jurry in this Collony doe fine the Towne of Warwick twenty shillings.

Jeremiah Wastcot chosen Jurry-man, by Warwick and not atendinge, is fined twenty shillings.

At the Generll Court of Tryalls Held in his Majties Name
at Newport the 11th of May 1674

Mr William Coddington, Governor
Mr John Easton DeptGovernor
Mr Henry Bull Asista~
Mr Walter Clarke Asista~
Mr Daniell Gould Asista~
Mr William Harris Asista~
Captn Arthur ffenner Asista~
Mr Thomas Harris Asista~
Mr Joshua Coggeshall Asista~
Mr John Tripp Asista~
Mr Job Almy Asista~
Mr Samuel Stafford Asista~
John Sanford, Recorder
James Rogers, Genrl Serjt
Mr Peter Easton Genrl Treasur
Mr Peter Easton Genrl Aturney
Mr Robert Williams Solicetor.

Grand Jurriers engaged:
Mr William Dyre foreman
Mr Thomas Dungin
Mr Steph~ Mumford
Mr John Roads
Mr Phillip Eades
Mr Willia~ Hopkins
Mr Thomas Rogers
Mr Thomas Lawton
Mr Hugh Parsons
Mr Thom~ Manchester
Mr Nathnl Dickins
Mr Edward Robinson

Upon the Rehearinge of an action Com[m]enced by Dr **Henry Greenland** plaintiff against **Clement Weaver** defendt

The Jurrys verdict: Wee finde for the plaintiff two pounds in silver and five pounds in cuntry paye and cost of Court and dam[m]age six pence, what of this debt is paid must be deducted out of the debt aforesaid — Judgement Granted. Juriors on the case:

Weston Clarke fore-man
Thom~ Burge
John Rogers
James Clarke
Willia~ Haukins
Henry Brightman
Thom~ Wayte
Icobod Potter
Bartho: Hunt
Thomas Mumford
James Blower
William Rogers

Upon an action Com[m]enced by Dr **Henry Greenland** pla~ against **John Hicks** defendt: the case cald the pla~ and defendt apeard in court, and John Hicks the defendt owned his debt to said Greenland and acknowlidged a judgment for the sum of three pound in silver and Cost of court. The Court thereupon grant judgment — .

Ordered that a warrant be sent forth by the Recorder from this court for twelve men to atend on fryday next the 15th Instant as Jurriors.

Upon Indictment against **George Havens** for com[m]ittinge ffornication with **Ellin Thurston**, pleads not guilty and referrs for Tryall to God and the Cuntry. Upon the Consideration of the pl[*torn*] he pleadinge the womans name is not Ellin the Court see cause to wave the Indictment.

Upon Indictment against **James Murfie** he beinge in court cald did not apeare —

Upon Indictment against **William Haukins** of Providence sen^{r} he beinge in court cald did not appeare.

Upon Indictment by the Aturney Gen^{rl} against **Awassnew** an Indian for murtheringe an Indian he beinge in court cald did not appeare.

Upon Indictment by the Gen^{rl} Aturney against **Henry Dyre** of Newport for [20]
ffornication comitted with **Elizabeth** the daughter of Lt. **ffrancis Brayton** of Portsmouth. The said Henry beinge in court cald apeared. Pleads Not Guilty and Referrs for Tryall to God and the Cuntry. The Jurrys Verdict Guilty.

Jurriors:		
	Weston Clarke, foreman	Willia~ Haukins
	Thom~ Burge	Icobod Potter
	John Rogers	Tho. Mumford
	James Clarke	James Blower
	Hen. Brightman	Willia~ Rogers
	Thomas Wayte	Job Haukins

The Courts Judgment is that the said **Henry Dyre** doe pay the sum[m] of fforty shillings to the Generall Treasury and pay ffees: cleerd by proclamation —

Upon Indictment by the Gen^{rl} Aturney against **John Knight** son of **Richard Knight** of Newport for feloniously takeinge away Bridle of **Zachery Dublins**: — the said John beinge in court cald apeard, Enters Traverse, pleads not Guilty and Referrs for Tryall to God and the Cuntry — : The Jurries Verdict. Guilty — The Courts Judgment is that the said act of John Knight is petty Laceny and therefore accordinge to law to pay twenty shillings or to be whipt and alsoe pay officers fees.

Elizabeth Brayton daughter of **ffrancis Brayton** of Portsmouth beinge by the Kings Aturney for bringinge forth a childe begotten by **Henry Dyre**, she beinge in court cald apeard and ownd her selfe Guilty. The courts Judgment is that the said Elizabeth doe pay the sum[m] of fforty shillings to the Gen^{rl} Treasurer and alsoe pay ffees — : Cleerd by proclamation in open Court.

Upon Indictment by the Kings Aturney against **Harry** an Indian prisoner for actinge abettinge or consentinge to the Death of Mrs **Rebecka Cornell** of Portsmouth

The said Indian, beinge cald for and brought into court, and his Indictment Read and truly interpreted to him, and he askt whether Guilty or Not Guilty: pleads Not Guilty and Referrs for Tryall to God and the Cuntry:

The Jurriors:		
	George Gardner fore-man	Steph~ Sebeere
	Thomas Burge	Thom~ Mumford
	John Rogers	Vall~ Hudleston
	James Clarke	Indians:
	Henry Brightman	Peasaunckquan
	Tho Wayte	Sankeamuaqutt
		Wotiawiceassen

The Juries Verdict: Not Guilty.

The said Indian beinge cleerd of his chaines promissed to apeare at this court at their next sittinge on the 19th instant: the said Indian on the said 19th day beinge in court cald did not apeare.

Upon Indictment: by the Kings Aturney against an Indian, by the Indians called **Quaoganit** by the English called the Old man, for Murtheringe his wife and an other Indian in the month of March last past: — the said Old man beinge Cald for and brought into Court: And his Indictment Read and truly Interpreted to him, and he askt whether Guilty or Not Guilty, ownes Guilty.

Jurry of Tryalls:

George Gardner foreman	Job Haukins
John Rogers	Zach: Dublin
James Clarke	Icobod Potter
Tho. Wayte	Indians:
Stephen Sebeere	Peassaunkckquam
Tho Mumford	Sunkanum[m]aqutt
	Wotiakesete

The Jurrys Verdict, Guilty.

The Court doe centance the said Indian called **old man** to be carried from hence to the com[m]on Goale and there strictly secured, and on the 19th day of this instant month to be carried to the place of Exicution, the Gallows, and there hangd by the neck untill he be dead dead.

Upon Indictment by the Aturny Genrl against **James Hall** for Com[m]itting a rape with his owne childe he beinge in Court Cald apeard Enters Traveres pleads Not Guilty and Referrs him selfe for Tryall to God and the Cuntry

Jurriors:

George Gardner foreman	John Horndall
John Rogers	John Rathbone
Stephen Sebeere	William Rogers
Thom~ Mumford	Henry Brightman
Job Haukins	Thomas Burge
Zach. Dublin	Elkena Johnson

The Jurrys Verdict, Not Guilty.

The Court accept the Verdict and order that the said James Hall be cleerd by proclamation — payinge ffees. Proclamation in open court made —.

Ordered that whereas upon the Complaint of **Daniell Abott** against **William Haukins** senr both of the Towne of Providence the said Haukins was bound to the Genrl Court of Tryalls in October last and there found Guilty, which said court in hopes that a peaceable and loveinge agreement might be had between the said parties before this Court, the said Court in October did continew the said Haukins his bond untill this court and whereas neither the complaint nor defendant though cald have in this court apeared psonaly but the said William Haukins by a letter to the Recorder informinge an agreement, and noe such thing apeareinge to this Court from the said Daniell Abott Therefore, if it doe appeare to the Recorder that what is by the said Haukins Aserted is true then his Bonds to be Voyd, otherwise to continew untill the next Court of Tryalls, and he in the meane time to pay officers ffees for what hath alredy past.

Whereas **Mary Pray** of the Towne of Providence beinge by the securety and obligation of **Joseph Jenks** of the said Towne in a bond of twenty pound sterl[g] to apeare at this court, and she beinge in court cald apeard and Answered. The Court upon considera- of the matter doe order her to be cleerd by proclamation and pay ffees: proclamation made.

Whereas **Anthony Shaw** of the Towne of Portsmouth was bound in a Bond of tenn pounds to the peace and good behaviour and to apeare at this Court, and beinge in court cald did not apeare this Court upon consideration of the matter see cause to continew his Bond to the next Court of Tryalls.

Thomas Arnold Jun[r] chosen a jurry-man by Providence, and he not atendinge is fined twenty shillings — .

Whereas **John Crossman** was chosen by Providence to serve on the jurry and he not apeareinge — Upon searious consideration the Court see cause to suspend his fine till the next Court of Tryalls and if the said Crosman can by law make it apeare he ought to be Exempt his fine shall be remitted.

Whereas the Towne of Warwick have not accordinge to Law made a Returne of their Jurrymen which should have been four to of the Grand and two of the petitt jurry, Therefore the Court doe fine the Towne of Warwick the sum of four pounds.

[*The original sheet containing pages 21 and 22, which must have included records of the beginning of the October 1674 Term, is missing from the book. At some time in the past, the pages were renumbered to page 117, so that each page has the original number at the top center and a second number at the top outside edge.*]

[OCTOBER 1674]

[21/23] . . . for Tryall to God and the cuntry.
Jurry of Tryalls:

M[r] Thomas Ward foreman	Robert Taylor
Nicho. Easton jun[r]	William ffoster
John Allin	Thomas Dorfie
William Peckham	Lawrance Turner
Jerem~ Wayte	John Greene of War[k] jun[r]
John Greene	William Maize

The jurries verdict Guilty of haveinge a childe unlawfully by **Sarah Gregory**. The courts centance is that the said **David Whipple** shall be whipt this instant day beinge the 30th of October, with fifteene stripes or Else pay a fine of forty shillings to the Gen[ll] Treasury and pay officers ffees.

Upon Indictment by the Gen[rl] Aturney against **Sarah Gregory** for ffornication comitted with **David Whipple** of Providence
She beinge in court caled apeard, and beinge askt whether guilty or not guilty — she owned that she hath had a childe by David Whipple, who she saith is her husband, and referrs her selfe to the courts mercy.

The Courts centance: Sarah Gregory Referringe her selfe to the Bench concerninge her Indictm^{t} wee Knowinge that her husband was proved a filthy man before he married her, soe that wee have cause to suspect, that he went away from her unlawfully and that he unlawfully stayeth from her, and never intendith to be a husband to her, but hath broake that bond, but wee doe not permitt that it is lawfull for her to be married, or live as married, or com[m]itt whoredome, with any man, and therefore her centance is for haveinge a childe by an other man, as for fornication to be whiped with fifteene stripes this day or pay fforty shillings to the Treasurer which she will as the law permitith the court to alow her, and if her husband come not sudanily home, that there be intelligence sought after that if it cannot be Knowne in a twelve-months time more, that she may then have liberty to marry as soone as the law will permitt, but if lawfull cause apeare sooner not hereby prevented, to marry sooner: she is alsoe to pay officers ffees.

Upon an Indictment by the Gen^{rl} Aturney against **Peter Lee** for Adultry com[m]itted with the wife of **James Thomas** of Newport: he beinge a prissoner and brought into Court and asked whether guilty or not guilty, owns Guilty and referrs himselfe to the bench — The courts centance, Peter Lee referringe himselfe to the bench concerninge his Indictment although he hath confessed himselfe guilty, it is not soe proveable guilty to us, for then the law provideth the centance Exact which none by Majestracy should alter, but he is proved to Endeavor to be filthely guilty, and soe audatious to afirme that he would have an other mans wife, Therefore in this case is that he the aforesaid Lee, shall be sevearely whipt with Twenty stripes this thirty one instant and pay five pounds to the Generall Treasury and Returne to prison untill he can give suffition securety to be of good behavior to all people and not to come in company with the wife of James Thomas, or to be in prisson untill some Majestrate may see him Tranceportinge out of this Collony, and not to returne without leave, or to be guilty to be punnished as much more and also pay officers ffees: The courts centance of whipinge Executed

Upon indictment by the clerke of the peace against **Robert Moone** of Newport for ffellonius takeinge a horse. He beinge a prissoner and brought into court, and askt whether Guilty or not Guilty, pleads not guilty and Referrs himselfe for Tryall to God and the Cuntry —

The same jurriors above-named only **George Broome** in the roome of Lawrance Turner.

The jurries verdict Guilty of takeinge a horse or Gelding &c without leave — The court upon consideration of the matter doe acquitt him payinge officers ffees—

Upon Indictment by the clerke of the peace against **Charles Wills** for ffelonious takeinge a horse — he beinge in Court Cald apeard, and upon the consideration of his Exceptions the court doe see cause to quash the bill.

At the Gen^{rl} Court of Tryalls Held in his Maj^{ties} Name
at Newport the 10th of May 1675

Mr William Coddington Governo^{r}
Mr John Easton Dept. Governor
Mr Walter Clarke, Assistant
Mr Henry Bull Asista~
Mr Edward Thurston Asista~
Captn Arthur ffenner Asista~
Mr Thomas Harris Asista~
Mr Joshua Coggeshall Asista~
Mr John Tripp Asista~
Mr Benja~ Smith Asista~
Mr Benja~ Barton Asista~
John Sanford, Recorder
James Rogers, Genl Serjant
Mr Peter Easton Gen^{ll} Treasurer
Mr Weston Clarke, Gen^{ll} Aturney
Mr Robert Williams, Solicetor

Grand Jurrymen Engaged:
Mr Edward Greenman, foreman
John Allin
Robert Taylor
Georg Gardner
ffrancis Brayton sen^{r}
Thomas Wood
Anthony Shaw
Stephen Arnold
Walter Newbery
Edward Robinson
Thomas Dungan
James Sweete

Whereas **William Coggeshall** upon the complaint of Mrs **Sarah Smyton** was bound to the peace and to apeare at this Court, and he haveinge petitioned this Court and given Mrs Smyton satisfaction for his abusinge her, he is acquitted in Court by proclamation payinge ffees —:

Zachariah Dublin, beinge bound to this Court and to the peace and good behavior and he apearinge in court and proclamation made and none apeareinge to accuse him he is cleerd payinge ffees —

Upon an action of sclaunder com[m]enced by **William Brownell** of Portsmouth plaintiff against **Thomas Jenings sen^{r}** Defendant, Damage 500^{li} st. ffor want of an answer and the defendant not apeareinge the plaintiffs Nihill dicett is aproved —

[22/24] The Jurry of Tryalls:

Samuell Dyre foreman
Henry Wood
John Stanton
John Vahan
Henry Tew
Eliezar Whipple
John Woodman
Joseph Anthony
Abra~ Anthony
Thomas Eaton
William Rogers
Zache~ Dublin

The Verdict Wee finde for the plaintiff thirty pound dam[m]age and charge of court. Judgment granted and exicution thereon —

Upon an action of Debt by bill Com[m]enced by Captn **Peleg Sanford** plaintiff against Captn **Richard Morris** of Newport Defendant, dated the 19th of Septemb^{r} 1674

The case beinge in court cald the said defend^{t} came into court and acknowlidged the debt and a judgment recorded upon an action Com[m]enced by Captn Richard Morris of Newport plaintiff against **Peter Easton** Treasurer and on the said Towne of Newport defendant, the said action beinge an action of Debt dated the 27th ffebr^{y}: 1674

Upon the debate of the matter the court doe declare that the said action came not leagaly to court —

Upon an action of Debt upon account Com[m]enced by Mrs **Sarah Smyton** plaintiff against **Thomas Jenings** sen^r Defendant: There beinge noe answer in the office nor the defend^t apeareinge the plaint~s Nihill dicett is aproved.
The jurry of Tryalls the same afore Named —
The verdict: Wee finde for the plaintiff debt and dam[m]age seven pounds Eighteene shillings in cuntry pay and cost of court —: Judgment granted and Execution thereon

Upon an action of unjust Detainure Com[m]enced by Mr **Stephen Arnold** of Pawtuxutt plaintiff against Mr **Samuell Reape** defendant, beareinge date the 29th of October 1674 —: The isue joyned by the Aturneyes is Gen^rl Not Guilty of the plaintiffs charge.
The Jurrys Verdict: Wee finde for the plaintiff halfe the mill and five pounds in currant cuntry pay and charge of court — : Judgment granted and Execution thereon —

Upon an action com[m]enced by Mr **Samuell Reape** of Pawtuxet plaintiff against Mr **Benja~ Smith** of the said Pawtuxet defendant, the action beinge an action of Debt beareing date 25th March 1675 The plaintiff in court withdrawes this action —

Upon indictment by the Gen^rl Aturney against **Marke Athy** for selling Liquors to the Indians he beinge Mandamassed and in court cald apeard, ownes Guilty and Referrs himselfe to the Bench. The courts centance [*blank*]

Upon indictment by the Gen^rl Aturney against **Dorothy** the wife of **James Thomas** for Adultery Com[m]itted with Peter Lee — : she beinge in court cald apeard, pleads not Guilty and referrs her Tryall to God and the cuntry—.
Jurry of Tryalls the same aforesaid only Thomas Hopkins Senr in the roome of John Vahan Junr.
The verdict: Guilty: — The courts centance [*blank*]

Upon Indictment by the Kings Aturney against **John ffreeman** for Adultry com[m]itted with **Hannah Larkin alias Bellew** he beinge bound to this court cald and in court cald apeard, pleads not Guilty and referrs him selfe for Tryall to God and the Cuntry —:
The Jurrys verdict, Guilty — : the courts centance [*blank*]

Upon indictment by the Gen^rl Aturney against **Stephen Sebeere** for Contempt of Authority — he beinge bound to this court and in court cald apeard. Ownes Guilty and referrs himselfe to the Bench. The courts centance [*blank*]

Upon Indictment by the Gen^rl Aturney against **Elizabeth** the daughter of **Thomas Hopkins** of Providence for fornication com[m]itted with **Samuell Winsor** — She beinge bound and in court cald apeard, ownes Guilty and referrs her selfe to the Bench.
The courts centance [*blank*]

Upon Indictment by the Gen^rl Aturney against **Samuell Winsor** of Providence for ffornication comitted with **Elizabeth** the daughter of **Thomas Hopkins** — He beinge bound to this Court, and in Court Cald apeard, pleads not Guilty and referrs himselfe for Tryall to God and the Cuntry, — . The Jurrys Verdict. Not Guilty.

Whereas Samuell Winsor was Indicted to have a Childe by Elizabeth Hopkins upon which the Jurry acquitted him the said Winsor, but he being accused by the said

Elizabeth of the act of ffornication, the said Samuell Winsor is bound in tenn pounds Bond to be of good behavior, and to Answer the foresaid charge the next Gen^{rl} Court of Tryalls, otherwise his bond to stand in full force against him the said Samuel:

David Whipple and **Sarah** the Daughter of **Benja~ Hernden** both of [23/25] Providence are centanced to pay four pound to the Gen^{rl} Treasury for not atendinge the Courts order, and if they will marry before this Court they may and it shall be a lawfull Marriage. Married in Court the 15th of May 1675 —.

Upon Indictment by the Gen^{ll} Aturney against **Thomas Jennings**, jun^{r} of Portsmouth for breach of the peace and behavior — : he beinge bound to this Court and in Court Cald apeard. — pleads not Guilty and Referrs for Tryall to God and the Cuntry — . The Jurrys Verdict Guilty —.

Upon indictment by the Grand Jurry against **Peter Talman** for inclosinge a hie-way in the Towne of Portsmouth: The said Talman apeares in Court and Enters Traverse — pleads Not Guilty. Upon the plea and debate of the matter the Court see cause to quash the Bill.

Daniell Williams chosen by the Towne of Providence to be on the grand Jurry this court and not atendinge that service is fined twenty shillings

Abiah Carpenter, Benja~ Gorton and **John Carder** chosen by the Towne of Warwicke to be on the Jurries this Court and they not atendinge that service are fined Each twenty shillings —

At the Gen^{rl} Court of Tryalls held in his Maj^{ties} Name
at Newport the 20th of October 1675

Mr William Coddington Governor
Mr John Easton Dep^{t} Governor
Mr Walter Clarke Assistant
Mr Henry Bull Asista~
Mr Edward Thurston Asista~
Captn Arthur ffenner Asista~
Mr Thomas Harris Asista~
Mr Thomas Bordin Asista~
Mr Joshua Coggeshall Asista~
Mr John Tripp Asista~
Mr Benja~ Smith Asista~
Mr Benja~ Barton Asista~
John Sanford, Recorder
Mr James Rogers, Gen^{ll} Serjant
Mr Peter Easton, Gen^{ll} Treasurer
Mr Weston Clarke Gen^{ll} Aturney
Mr Robert Williams Solicetor

Grand Jurymen engaged:
Mr Caleb Carr fforeman
Samuell Hubbard
Benedict Arnold jun^{r}
John Greene
William Devell
Thomas Painter
Daniell Lawton
Adam Mott
Jacob Mott
Mathew Bordin
John Warner
Samuell Stafford

Upon an action of the case for account comenced by **William Sydney** of Barbados plaintiff against **Sarah Reape**, widow, executrix to the deceased **William Reape** of Newport defendant beareinge date the 12th of Aprill 1675, Dam~ 3000 ^{li}

In the case of William Sydny against Sarah Reap afore-said, she by her aturney apeared and would have gave securety to have been responsible according to law, as the court had ordered an awditt, but not any apeared to give in securety to be responsible accordinge to law as the court had ordered for Cap^{tn} Sydney and soe the case fell

William Cornell stands bound in the sum of one hundred pounds sterll. unto our Sovereigne lord the King, to prosicute a complaint by indictment against **Sarah Cornell** widow.

Ordered that warrant be sent from this court to the cunstables of Portsmouth to aprihend the body of Sarah Cornell widow to the late deceased **Thomas Cornell** of Portsmouth and bringe her before the court.

Upon an action of the case for non performance of covinnant, comenced by **Grace** the wife of **Thomas Lawton** of the Towne of Portsmouth plaintiff against **Daniell Lawton** defendant, beareinge date the 23 of August 1675. Damage 40$^{£}$: sterll.

Upon a long debate of the case the court order that the action shall fall; and it is ordered by this court for the time past and for the future Daniell Lawton shall allow and pay to the said Grace Lawton the sum of four shillings a weeke paid monthly, to be paid to her or her asignes in silver New-England mony in leiw of the use of a horse and fire-wood, the sum of twenty shillings yearly, and this act to be in force untill further care either by her husband or this court to be taken in the premises, and the same to be paid out of his father Thomas Lawtons estate, and ordered that the said Grace Lawton shall give unto the said Daniell Lawton a true inventory of all the partickular estate she hath in her hands, and that the said Daniell Lawton shall forth-with pay the said Grace Lawton the sum of twenty shillings in mony over and above what is afore ordered —.

Upon indictment by the Grand Jury against **John Ward** of Newport for carnall copulation with **Sarah Nicolson** now wife of the said John Ward before they were married, — the said John beinge mandamassed and in court cald, apeard, ownes guilty and referrs himselfe to the bench — : the court doe centance him to pay the sum of forty shillings to the Gen^{ll} Treasurer and alsoe pay ffees and soe is cleerd by proclamation in open court — .

Upon indictment by the Gen^{ll} Aturney against **Hannah Larkin alias Belloo** of adultery comitted with **John ffreeman** in the yeare 1674 — she beinge bound to the court and in court cald and askt whether guilty or not guilty, ownes guilty and refferrs her selfe to the judgm^{t} of the bench.

Hannah Larkin, alias Belloo, the consideration of her case is referred [26/24] this court to the Generall Assemblys consideration and detirmination By act of the Assembly she beinge to pay fforty shillings to the Gen^{ll} Treasury which John Sanford haveinge accepted to discount soe much on the Gen^{rl} account if paid she is cleerd by proclamation payinge ffees —

Upon indictment by **Peter Talman** against **Rebecca Sadler** the wife of **Thomas Sadler** for breach of the peace and thratninge his ffamely — she beinge bound to this court and in court cald, pleads not guilty, and referrs for tryall to the cuntry. The Jurries verdict. Guilty:

The courts centance is that she the said Rebecca Sadler shall pay the sum of tenn shillings to the Generall Treasury and is bound to her good behavior till the next court and pay officers fees —

Upon indictment by **Peter Talman** against **John Hoomery** for breach of the peace by pullinge downe the fence of the said Talman and threatninge his ffamely — He beinge bound to this court and in court cald apeard, pleads not guilty and referrs for tryall to the cuntry.

The Jurries verdict Guilty — The courts centance is that John Hoomery is to pay the sum of tenn shillings to the Gen^{rl} Treasury and is bound to the good behavior till the next court, and shall pay officers ffees.

According to warrant from this court **Sarah Cornell** widow beinge brought to the court she is comitted to the Comon Goale — till cald for by the court.

Upon indictment by the Gen^{rl} Aturney against **Thomas Monsall** of Providence for liveinge and cohabitinge with **Lidia** the daughter of **George Way** of said Providence not beinge lawfully married — He the said Monsall beinge bound to this court and in court cald apeard, and askt whether guilty or not guilty — ownes guilty accordinge to the law of man — The courts centance is that the said Monsall shall finde sureties for his good behavior, and that he shall not company with Lydia the daughter of George Way or be com[m]itted to prison, and pay the sum of forty shillings to the Gen^{rl} Treasury, and if the said Monsall will promise and be bound in a bond of twenty pound to live from the said Lidia in an other towne then his imprisonment to be remitted, and he is to pay officers ffees —

Upon indictment by the Gen^{rl} Aturny against **Joseph Croxford**, prisoner, for begittinge a childe one the body of **Alce Browne** — he beinge cald for by the Court. It was answered he was ffled.

Upon Indictment by the Gen^{rl} Aturney against **Henry Jackmon**, prisoner for cominge into the dwellinge house of **William Weeden** of Newport in the night time, and there broke the civill peace — The said Croxford beinge cald for by the Court It was Answered he was fled.

Upon Indictment by **William Cornell** against **Sarah** widow of **Thomas Cornell** deceast, (of the Towne of Portsmouth, ffor murtheringe of Mrs **Rebecca Cornell**, or beinge abettinge or consentinge thereto, The said Sarah beinge cald for was brought into the Court, —: and beinge askt whether Guilty or not Guilty, pleads not guilty and Referrs her selfe for Tryall to God and the cuntry. The Jurry Empaneld: Their verdict: Not Guilty. Proclamation beinge in open court made and none apeareinge further to prosicute the said Sarah she is cleerd by proclamation payinge ffees.

Whereas **Marke Athy** at the last Gen^{rl} Court of Tryalls was Indicted for breach of the law by sellinge Liquors to the Indians, and there fined five pounds to the Treasury, and bound to this court, he the said Marke beinge in court cald apeard and none apeareinge to accuse him for breach of bonds he is cleerd by proclamation payinge ffees —.

Dorothy the wife of **James Thomas**, and her bondsman **Nicholas Cottrill** and said Thomas, beinge in Court cald did not apeare —: The Court doe therefore declare the forfiture of their bonds, And upon consideration of the matter doe referr it to the Gen^{rl} Assemblys detirmination —.

Stephen Sebeere beinge bound to this Court and to the peace and good behavior and beinge in court cald apeard. Proclamation beinge made and none apeareinge to prosicute him he is cleerd payinge ffees.

Whereas **John ffreeman** was bound to the Assembly, and they haveinge detirmined that freeman shall pay the sum of ffive pounds to the Gen^{rl} Treasury in the charge against him by **Hannah Larkin alias Beloo**, The Gen^{rl} serjant promisinge to accept five pounds on the cuntrys account for the said John ffreeman he is cleerd by proclamation payinge ffees.

Concerninge **Samuell Winsor** and **Elizabeth Hopkins** beinge bound to apeare and answer what should be charged against them in this court but it beinge troublesome times by warr of the Indians, the court did not see cause to prossicute them this court, but continew all bonds concerninge them to the next court —

Isaac Lawton chosen by the Towne of Portsmouth to be on the Jurry of Tryalls this Court and he not atendinge that service is fined twenty shillings.

[25/27]

At a Gen^{rl} Court of Tryalls Held in his Maj^{ties} Name
at Newport the 8th of May 1676

Mr Walter Clarke Govern^{or}
Major John Cranston, Dep^{t} Govern^{or}
Mr John Coggeshall Assistant
Mr James Barker Asist^{a}
Mr John Easton Asit^{a}
Mr William Harris Asit^{a}
Captn Arthur ffenner Asit^{a}
Mr Thomas Bordin Asit^{a}
Mr Joshua Coggeshall Asit^{a}
Mr William Cadman Assit^{a}
Captn Randall Houldon Assit^{a}
Mr Samuel Gorton jun^{r} Assit^{a}

Grand Jurrymen Engaged
Mr George Lawton fforeman
Thomas Dungin
Stephen Mumford
Thomas Burgis
Henry Palmer
John Allin
Samuell Bennitt
Latham Clarke
John Greene
Henry Brightman
William Brinley
James Sweet

Upon an action of the case com[m]enced by **Thomas Burgis** plaintiff against **William Edwards** Defendant bearinge date the 12th of May 1675: The Isue joyned by the Aturneys is a Gen^{rl} Isue Not Guilty. The Court after much plea on the matter, and the Jurries Atendance and Engagement on the Case, plaintiff and defendant did see cause to Referr the matter in difference to Arbitration, whereupon the court doe remitt the said case the Arbitrators by them chosen Viz^{t} Mr William Carpenter, Mr Edward Thurston, Captn John Greene, Mr Jireh Bull and Mr John Wood.

Upon an action of Debt beareinge date the 27th of ffebruary 1675 com[m]enced by **Peter Talman** of Portsmouth plaintiff against Ensigne **Lott Strainge** —

A nonsuite beinge Entred in the office, the case beinge in court cald plaintiff and defendt both apeard in court and the nonsuite pleaded to, and the court did not see cause to owne the nonsuite — whereupon the plaintiff Entred a nihill dicett in Court, and the defendant refussed to put in his answer though with much lenety of the Court advised thereto Therefore the court order the case to proceed to the Jurry :

The Jurry of Tryalls —

Phillip Smith fforeman	John Rise
Thomas ffry	Shuball Painter
Thomas Rogers	John Easton
William Austin	Phillip Long
Adam Mott jun^r^	John ffeild
John Albro jun^r^	William Heiffernan.

The Verdict Wee finde for the plaintiff his demand of five pound cost of court and twelve pence damage. Judgment Granted.

Whereas Ensigne **Lott Strainge** came into this court upon the readinge the verdict, and desired of the court to have a Reheareinge or reveiue of the case, The Plaintiff haveinge as aforesaid taken the Defendant upon a nihill dicett, the Court doe not see cause to graunt the defendants desire therein.

Upon an action of Debt beareinge date the 28th of October 1675 Com[m]enced by Captn **John Cranston** plaintiff against **Edward Robinson** of Newport Defendant — : The case beinge in court cald the plaintiff apeard, but the defend^{t} not apeareinge nor any answser beinge in the office, the Court see just cause to grant the plaint. a nihill dicett and that the case proceed. The Jurrys Verdict, Wee finde for the plaintiff Debt and damage four pounds seven shillings tenn pence in mony and cost of court — Judgment Granted.

Upon an action of Debt beareinge date the 15th of Septem^{r} 1675 Com[m]enced by **William Withington** plaintiff, against **Thomas Starr** defendant: The case beinge in court cald the plaintiff by his Aturny **John Greene** apeard, the defend^{t} not apearinge to answer nor any answer, beinge afore in the office, the court see cause to grant a nihill dicett in the case and, that this case proceed to the Jurry —. The Jurrys verdict Wee finde for the plaintiff his Debt of one pound thirteen shillings four pence Cost of Court and twelve pence damage — Judgment Granted.

Upon an action of Debt Com[m]enced by Mr **William Almy** of Portsmouth plaintiff against **Thomas Harris** of Boston Butcher Defend^{t} beareinge date the 16th of November 1675 — The Jurrys Verdict Wee finde for the defendant Cost of Court and for the plaintiff his just sum.

Emeadiatly upon bringinge in of the Verdict, the defend^{t} paid to the plaint^{f} in the open court his just due which was the sum of thirty three pounds fifteen shillings —

Upon an action of unjust detainure, beareinge the 25th of ffebruary 1675 Com[m]enced by **William, John** and **Samuell Cornell** plaintiffs against **Thomas Cornell** of Portsmouth defendant — The Jurry being Empanneld, were three times sent forth by the Court: their Verdict Wee finde for the Defendant, and Cost of Court.

Upon an action Com[m]enced by **Abiah Carpenter** plaintiff against **Joseph Carpenter** of Musketo Cove on Long Island defend[t] the said action beinge an action of Debt beareinge date the 17[th] of Aprill 1676 — The Case beinge in Court Cald the plaintiff did not apeare, the defendant apeared, and therefore the court see cause to grant a nonsuite in the case —

Whereas Collonell **William Crowne** hath wrote to this Gen[rl] Court of Tryalls sittinge May 1676 and his said beareinge date May 8:76. the said containeinge a desire of a continewance, of an action or atachment upon or against the Estate of Mr **John Paine** deceassed, latly of Prudance, upon which his request and his Reasons shewed of the abscence of his papers proofe of his Debt and his present sicknes, soe wee beinge demanded to give our answer thereto &c, Therefore wee Answer that by the law of England and of this Collony of Rhode-Island the said atatchments seems to us not legall, The law of England not alowinge any atatchment of such nature but either against the Executor or Executrix, Administrator or Administratrix or officiall if he doe not Constitute some one of the said: Secondly by the law of this Collony noe Atatchment can continuew nor come to tryall but must presuppose a person in law to answer, for the law here saith, shall putt in his answer, but in the said writt noe man is put to answer the action Capable by law to answer — therefore the said atatchment not leagall, and therefore not leagall to continew, Thirdly the said atatchment prevents the payment of all other Just debts, by takeinge in or stayinge all the Estate that was the said John Paines there &c — fourthly wee have a presedent of a nonsuite upon the like atatchment, soe Resolves the Judgment of the Court.

Upon an Indictment by the Gen[rl] Aturney against **John Pearce** of Portsmouth Mason, for threatnninge to kill an Indian youth called **Peter** servant to **Peleg Tripp** — the said Pearce beinge in court cald apeard, and referrs the case to the bench, and he in court promissinge that for the future to be of a civill carriage to all persons and Espetially to Peleg Tripp and his famely in the performance thereof the court doe remitt his bonds and is cleered by proclamation payinge fees.

[26/28]

Att a Genrl Court of Tryalls held in his Majesties
name att Newport Octr the 18th 1676

Mr Walter Clarke Govr
Majr John Cranston Depty Govr
John Coggeshall Senr Assita
Mr James Barker Asita
Mr John Easton Asita
Mr William Harris Asita
Capt Arthur ffenner Asita
Mr Thomas Bordin Asita
Mr Joshua Coggeshall Asita
Mr William Cadman Asita
Capt Randall Houlden Asita
Mr Samuell Gorton junr Assita
John Coggeshall Senr Recordr
Mr Peter Easton Genrl Trer
Mr Weston Clarke Genrl Aturny
Henry Lilly Genrl Serjt

Grand Jury-men engaged:
Mr Stephen Arnold ffore-man
Mr Georg Gardiner
Mr Samuel Hubert
Mr Robert Tayler
Mr John Stanton
Mr William Hiscox
Mr John Strange
Mr Daniell Greenall
Mr Daniell Wilcok
Mr Henry Dyre
Mr Thomas ffry
Mr Edmond Calverly

Upon an action of Debt by Bill Com[m]enced by **Stephen Sabeere** of Newport Plant against **William Blanden** of Swansey Defendt beareing date May ye 23th 1676.
Plantiff and Defendt apeareing in Court, the Defendt owned a Judgmt against himselfe acknowledging the Plants debt and cost of Court.
The Courts sentence. Whereas **Stephen Sabeeere** of Newpt com[m]enced A suite against **William Blanden** &c beareing date May the 23th 1676. the sayd suite being for debt, to say seven pounds foureteene shillings and sixpence silver of New-England, as by Bill under his hand & seale beareing date the 17th of Aprill 1676. The Court considering the Defendents poverty haveing not where-with to pay the Debt, and alsoe indebted to other men; And forasmuch as A Law is in the Body of Laws. That poore Persons that have not to pay their Debts shall not lye Languishing in Prison, it being noe way nor meanes to enable them, but in such cases the sd Law Provideth that Officers &c shall apoint & order how such poore Persons shall pay such Debts as they are Able. This Court haveing taken into their serious Consideration the Debters Poverty, and the Crediters due debt, not for Profuce Expences, but diet for himeselfe and wife; doe order and Apoint the sd Debter to pay as followeth; haveing made this Agreemt betweext the sd Credebter and Debter. — That the sd **Stephen Sabeere** shall have the sayd **William Blanden** to worke on Carpentry upon this Island, and the sayd William shall be att the sayd Stephens Com[m]and conserning his worke, and what worke the sayd William shall doe for the sd Stephen shall be vallued by Workemen equally chosen by both parties: And that the sd Stephen shall finde the sayd William foode and Lodging at A Reasonable rate while he workes for hime to pay his debt. And whereas the sayd William hath (as he sayeth) timber supposeing thereby to pay his debt. Therefore this Court doe order, that if the sd William can soe Agree with the sayd Stephen as to take the sayd Timber, or can sell the sayd Timber and pay the sayd Stephen the foresayd debt, (and some costs of Court expressed) then the sayd William

shall be freed from the sayd Stephen and for as much as the sayd William is made as a Prisoner by reason of the foresayd Debt, and the sayd Stephen by Apointm^{t} of this Court to be payd as aforesayd. And Considering that if the sayd William had beene cast into Prison a Second or Third, or more, Arests, or suits could not deafeate the paym^{t} of the ffirst, therefor this Court doe Apoint, that the sayd William shall not be taken out of the hand, or Service of the sayd Stephen by any mans Action whatsoever untill the sayd Stephen is fully payd.

[27/29] Upon an Action of the case for non Performance of Bargains Com[m]enced by **Mary Case** widdow and Executrix to the Late deceased **William Case** of Newport, plantiff against **Lowrance Turner** of the sayd Newport Defend^{t} beareing date July the 8th 1676.

Juro^{rs} on the case betweext Mary Case plant. aga^{t} Lowrance Turner Def^{t}:

Mr Edward Marshall Junr	Thomas Mumford
Wm Coddington Junr	Thomas Hopkins
John Holmes	Benjamin Sherman
John Crandell	Benjamin Mowry
Roger Emson	Thomas Packam
John Lapam	Jerimiah Smith

Generall Isue Joyned, not Guilty. Juryors vardict. We finde for the Plantiff foure Pounds in New-England money Damage, and Cost of Court. —
Judgment granted.

Upon an Action of the case for Detainer Com[m]enced by **Samuell Reape** of Petuxett Plan^{t} against **Benjamine Congden** of Portsmouth Defend^{t} beareing date July the 5th 1676. Plaintiff and Defend^{t} apeareing, both declared they had agreed to leave their Differance to Arbitration, and soe the Action fell.

Upon an Action Slander and Defamation Com[m]enced by **Samuel Reape** of Petuxett Plan^{t} aga^{t} **Benjemin Congden** Defend^{t} beareing date July the 5th 1676. Plantiff and Defend^{t} apearing in Court, did both declare they had Agreed to leave their differance to Arbitration, and soe the Action fell.

Upon an Action of the case for Debt upon Account Com[m]enced by **Mor-decay Bowden** of Newport Plantiff against **Thomas Mill** of sayd Newp^{t} Defend^{t} beareing date Septr 4th 1676. A non-suite entered in the office by the Defend^{t} — upon debate of the matter the Court alow the sayd Nonsuite.

Upon an Indictment by the Gen^{rl} Aturney against **James Dunn** of Newp^{t} for Com[m]itting fornication with **Hanna Moone** of sd Newp^{t}. The sayd James Dunn being called in Court and the Bill redd, was asked whether Guilty or Not Guilty, owned himselfe Guilty.

The sentence of the Court. That the sayd James Dunn shall be Whipped with fiveteene strips, or pay fourety shillings. Richard Dunn of Newp^{t} Promised in The court to pay to the Gen^{rl} Trs^{r} fourty shillings in Currant pay of the Country, for s^{d} fine.

Upon a Bill of Indictment by the Gen^{rl} Aturny against **Hanna Moone** of Newp^{t} for Com[m]itting fornication with **James Dunn**: The sayd Hanna Moone was called in Court, being sick did not Apeare. **Robert & Ebinezer Moone** did in Court Recognize themselves in ten Pounds A Peece, for the sayd Hannas Apearance at the next Gen^{rl} Court of Tryalls.

Benedict Arnold Junr chosen by the Towne of Newp^{t} A Petty Juryman to serve in this Court and he not Attending the service for which he was Chosen, the Court doe fine hime Twenty shillings.

Thomas Manchester Junr chosen by the Towne of Portsmouth A Petty Juryman to serve in this Court, and he not Attending the service for which he was Chosen, the Court doe fine hime Twentye shillings.

ffrancis Brayton Junr chosen by the Towne of Portsmouth, A Petty Juryman to serve in this Court, did Apeare before the Court was Desolved, pleaded his Excuse. The Court fined hime five shillings.

William Hedg being warned by the Gen^{rl} Serj^{t} to Attend this Court to serve on the Jury of Tryalls, did not apeare, but in A slighting way refused, for which the Court doe fine hime Ten shillings.

The Court Desolved, May the 20th

[MARCH 1676/7]

To all Christian People whome these Presents may Concerne. Know yea That his Maj[tie] Charles ye Second, King of England Scotland France and Ireland; haveing out of his Abundant Grace and meere favour, Granted unto this Colony of Rhod-Island and Providence Plantations, A Gratious Charter, with many great liberties, and Previledges therein, which are not to be Parraleled; all which ought the deeper to Engage his subjects here with the greates Aleagiance to soe noble A Prince. And whereas many good and wholesome Laws have frome time to time beene made, in order thereunto, both concerneing the cevill & Millitary power, as upon Record doth Apeare. And I my selfe being very Sick, and neare Death, in Oct[r] Court 1676 doe, since I recovered finde, and it is Published that then & there was A good and wholesome Law Repealed, by the People called Quakers, and their Adherants, Concerneing the Mainetaineing of the Kings Millitery forces here, in their Traineing sixe times A yeare, that soe they might at all times be redy to defend his Majesties Interest, and their owne Lives and their Estates, soe deeply injoyned, & required in our sayd Charter, and finding how all New England hath suffered of late by the Barbaruse Cruelty of the Heathen here, notwithstanding all their uttmost Endevours, and care herein, and how much Christian Blood, hath from time to time beene spilt, and the Warr not being yett over with them, or if it were, yett we know not how soone others of the Kings Enimies may invade us here. I doe therefore for my owne clearing herein, According to my Concerne in this Goverm[t] Declare and Protest against the Repealing of that Law Concerneing traineing, and doe give it under my hand, that it is of Dangerous Consequence unto his Majesties Interest here.

March the 6th 1676/7 James Barker Assistant

A true coppie taken out of ye oreginall, Entered and
Recorded y[e] 9th of March 1676/7 pr John Coggeshall Record[r]

[28/30] At a Gen^{rl} Court of Tryalls held in his Maj^{ties} Name at Newport the 7th of May 1677

Mr Benedict Arnold Governor
Major John Cranston Dep^{t} Gover^{r}
Mr James Barker Asistant
Capt Peleg Sanford Asit^{a}
Mr Joseph Clarke Asit^{a}
Mr John Whipple Junr Asit^{a}
Mr Stephen Arnold Asit^{a}
Captn Sam^{ll} Wilbore Asit^{a}
Captn John Albro Asit^{a}
Captn John Greene Asit^{a}
Mr Samuell Gorton ju^{r} Asit^{a}
John Sanford Recorder
Thomas ffry Gen^{rl} Serjant
Mr Thomas Ward Gen^{rl} Treasur^{er}
Lt Edward Richmond Gen^{rl} Aturny

Grand Jurriors Engaged
Mr Thomas Clifton foreman
Walter Newbery
Christopher Holder
Daniell Gould
John Allin
Walter Roades
Edward Enman jun^{r}
Robert Hassard
William Clarke
Gidion ffreeborne
Edmund Calverly
ffrancis Gisborne.

This Court doe order that each of those in this Court Serveinge on the Grand Jurry shall be allowed and paid by the Gen^{rl} Treasurer as soone as Efects comes into his hands, the sum of twelve pounds a peece in mony or other pay Equivelent for and in leiu of their Dinner by former law and custome of this Collony allowed to the Grand Jurry on the publick charge.

Whereas **James Case** was bound for the appeareance of **Salvadore** a Negro at this Court and the said Case haveinge brought into court the said Negro and desireinge to be Released of his Bonds: The Court doe see cause to Release the said Case, and doe com[m]itt the said Negro Salvadore to the keeper of the Jayle to be secured till cald for by the Court.

Upon an action of the case for Debt com[m]enced by Majo^{r} **John Cranston** of Newport plaintiff against **Daniell Wilcocks** of Portsmouth defend^{t} and beareinge date December 20th 1676. The Issue Joyned is not Guilty of the plaintiffs charge.
Jurriors on the said action:

Myles ffoster fforeman
John Johnson
John Easton ju^{r}
Samuell Bennitt
Vallintin Hudlestone
William Austin
Joseph Anthony
Thomas Dorfie
John Carder
Nathanill Osbourn
John Holme
James Case

Jurrys Verdict: Wee finde for the plaintiff ffive and twenty pounds in mony Debt, and one shillinge Damage and Cost of Court — Judgment Granted by the Court. and alsoe Execution Issued forth.

Upon an action of the case for non performance of covinnant Com[m]enced by **William Clarke** of the Towne of Portsmouth plaintiff, against **John Sanford** and **William Allin** Defendants, Damage 200^{li} sterll. A nihill dicett Enterd by the plaintiff May the 8th the Issue Joyned. Not Guilty of the plaintiffs Charge.

Jurriors on said action:

Myles ffoster foreman	Joseph Anthony
John Johnson	Thomas Dorfie
John Easton ju^r	John Carder
Vallintine Hudlestone	Nathanill Osbourne
Samuell Bennitt	John Holme
William Austin	James Case

Ordered by the court that notwithstandinge the nihill dicitt Entred the defendants shall have Liberty to put in their Answer. The Jurry verdict Wee finde for the defendants cost of court. Judgment Granted by the Court.

Upon Indictment by the Generall Aturney against **Mary Gerrad** aged about ten yeares for cutting **Thomas Goulds** sayles ffrom his boate. The said Mary Garrad beinge cald apeard and pleads not guilty.

The Jurrys verdict not Guilty — cleerd by proclamation in open court.

Upon an Indictment By the Gen^rl Aturny against **Joseph** a Negro, for that the said Negro was suspected to have a hand in burninge the wind-mill, and cutting the sayles from **Thomas Goulds** boate. The said Negro beinge a prisoner and brought into the court and his charge read unto him, and askt whither guilty or not guilty, pleads not Guilty. The Jurrys verdict not Guilty. Cleerd by proclamation in open court payinge ffees.

Upon an Indictment by the Gen^rl Aturny against **Salvadore** a Negro ffor ffelloniously takeinge two bags or sacks, and cuttinge **Thomas Goulds** sayles and Burninge the windmill — The said Negro beinge brought into the Court, and his charges read unto him, and he askt whither Guilty or not Guilty pleads not Guilty: The Jurrys verdict not Guilty — cleerd by proclamation payinge ffees. In this tryall **John Woodman** was on the jurry insteed of **John Easton** Junr

John Sayles of Providence sen^r, **Samuell Sanford** of Portsmouth, **Job Almy** of Warwick, beinge chosen to serve at this Court on the Grand Inquest, and they not atendinge, accordingly are fined each of them twenty shillings.

William Richardson of Newport and **Thomas Havens** of Portsmouth, beinge chosen to atend this court on the Jurry of Tryalls and they not performinge that service, are fined twenty shills a peece.

[29/31]

At a Generall Court of Tryalls held in his Maj^{ties} Name at Newport the 24th of October 1677

Mr Benedict Arnold Governo^r
Majo^r John Cranston Dep^t Govo^r
Mr James Barker, Asist.-
Captn Peleg Sanford Asist.-
Mr Joseph Clarke Asist.-
Mr John Whipple jun^r Asist.-
Mr Stephen Arnold Asist.-
Mr Thomas Olny jun^r Asist.-
Captn Samuell Wilbore Asist.-
Captn John Albro Asist.-
Captn John Green Asist.-
Mr Samuell Gorton ju^r Asist.-
John Sanford Recorder
Thomas ffrye Gen^{rl} Serjan^t
Mr Thomas Ward Gen^{rl} Treasur^r
Lt Edward Richmond Gen^{rl} Atur^y

Grand Jurry-men Engaged:
Mr Thomas Dungin
Richard Dun
Henry Palmer
James Weeden sen^r
Walter Roades
John Lappum
Mathew Borden
Robert Dennis
William Correy
Abyah Carpenter
fforeman Edmund Calverly
William Brinley

Whereas **John Maxon** was chosen by the Towne of Newport to be on the Jurry of Tryalls, and in court called appeared, and Eleaged that his Mother in law and his wife were both sick and ill, and therefore did Request the court, to dismiss him of that service. Thereupon the court see cause to dismiss the said Maxon from the said service and from the fine.

[*in margin:* The Grand-Jurys Engagm^t] Whereas you A. B: are chosen on this Grand Inquest on the behalfe of our sovereigne Lord the King [*written above*: Lady ye Queane]; you doe here promiss and Engage to make a true Returne unto this Court of all such Bills as shall be presented to you, or such breakers of law as shall come to your Knowlidge, and this Engagement you give and make on the perill of the penalty of perjury.

Upon an action of the case for Debt Com[m]enced By **Daniell Wilcock** of Portsmouth pla^t against **William Earll** of said Portsmouth defendant, a Demurr Entred by the defendant: plaintiff and defendant beinge both in court cald there was noe apeareance.

Upon an action of the case for non performance of covenant, com[m]enced by Captn **Peleg Sanford** of the Towne of Newport, Guardian unto **William Brenton**, plaintiff, against **Benjamin Speire** Marriner Defend^t. This case beinge from the last Court of Tryalls Demurrd and nihill dicitt Entred by the plaintiff: The Case beinge in Court cald the Defendant did not apeare.

Jurry-men engaged:

Roger Goulding, foreman
John Rogers
George Brown
Georg Vaughan
Joseph Tripp
Henry Brightman
Jeremiah Browne
Andrew Harris
Jeremia- Smith
Georg Halsall
ffrancis West
Roger Empson

The Jurrys Verdict Wee finde for the plaintiff Eleven pounds ten shillings currant mony Damage and his horse againe and cost of Court. Judgment Granted by the Court.

Upon an Action of Debt Com[m]enced by **Anthony Shaw** of Portsmouth plaintiff against **Edward Marshall** of the Towne of Warwick defend^t^, There being noe answer in the office nor apearance the plaintiff Enters a Nihill dicitt. The Jurrys Verdict: Wee finde for the plaintiff the Contents of the Bill: ffive shillings and cost of Court. Judgment Granted by the Court: Execution given forth.

Upon an action of Detainure beareinge date the 14th of May 1677 Com[m]enced by Captn **Peleg Sanford** of Newport plaintiff against Mr **Myles fforster** of Newport Defendant, Damage 25^li^ sterll. Upon a long debate before this Court, between plantiff and Defendant, The Court doe conclude that they cannot Evade the Tryall, but the case doe proceed to Tryall. And after long debate, the plantiff and defendant not haveinge agreed to Joyne Issue: The Court doe therefore detirmin the Issue to be a Gen^rl^ Issue :

The Jurriors on the said action:

Roger Goulding, foreman	Henry Brightman
John Rogers	Jeremiah Smith
Thomas Mumford	John Woodman
Georg Vaughan	George Halsall
Joseph Tripp	ffrancis West
Andrew Harris	Roger Empson

The Jurry haveinge been three times sent forth by the Court their verdict is Received Vid. wee finde for the plantiff the horse which he sued for, and two pence Damage, and Cost of court. Judgment granted by the Court. The Defendant haveinge paid the Bill of cost, and Given in Bond dated the 14th of Novemb^r^ the said defend^t^ hath procured a Reheareinge of this action at the Court of Tryalls in May next according to law

Upon an action of Sclaunder and Defamation Com[m]enced by **David Lake** plantiff against **John Symmons** defend^t^. The Issue Joyned is Not Guilty of the Charge. The Jurrymen:

Roger Goulding, fore-man	Andrew Harris
John Rogers	Henry Brightman
Thomas Mumford	Jeremiah Smith
George Halsall	John Woodman
Georg Vaughan	ffrancis West
Joseph Tripp	Roger Empson

The Jurrys Verdict. Wee finde for the plantiff twenty shillings damage and cost of Court. Judgment Granted by the Court.

Upon an action of the Case for breach of Covenant Com[m]enced by Mrs **Katherine Dyre,** Widow and Relict to the Deceased **William Dyre** of the Towne of Newport pln^t^ against Mrs **Ann Dyre** Widow and Relict to the deceased **Samuell Dyre** of said Newport Defend^t^ Jurrys aforenamed on this action — Verdict wee finde for the plantiff twenty pounds ten shillings merchant pay and cost of court — Judgment Granted by the Court: Execution given forth.

Upon an action of Sclaunder and defamation, Com[m]enced by Captn [30/32] **Thomas Clowter** of Newport plantiff against **Mordica~ Bouden** of said Newport Defendant: On this case the last afore named jurry: The Verdict Wee finde for the plantiff fforty shillings damage and cost of Court. Judgment Granted by the court. Execution given.

Upon an action of the case for Debt Com[m]enced by **William Clarke** of the Towne of Portsmouth plaintiff, against the Estate of the late deceased Mr **John Paine** of Prudance Island Defendant. The case caled, and there apeard none for the defendant. The plantiff enters a nihill dicitt: The Jurrys verdict Wee finde for the plantiff fforty pound in mony debt and damage, and fifty thre pound Equevelent to mony debt and damage and Cost of Court. Judgment Granted by the Court. Execution given fforth.

Mr **William Browne** merchant of the Towne of Salem plantiff against **William Allin** of Prudance defend^{t}, in an action of Trespass, beareinge date the 10th of September 1677 — : The Isue Joyned, not Guilty of the plantiffs Charge. The Jurrys Verdict Wee finde for the defendant Cost of Court. Judgment Granted by the Court.

Upon an action of Trespass Com[m]enced by Mr **William Browne** of the Towne of Salem merchant plantiff agst **James Sweete** of Prudance Island, Defendant. The Issue a Gen^{rl} Issue. Not Guilty of the plantiffs charge. The Jurrys Verdict Wee finde for the Defendant Cost of Court. Judgment Granted by the Court.

Upon an action Com[m]enced by Mr **Thomas Ward** plantiff in an action of Debt, against the Estate of the late deceased Mr **William Dyre** of Newport Defendant. For want of an answer, or apeareance, the plaintiff Enters a nihill dicitt. The Jurrys Verdict Wee finde for the plantiff Eight pounds, ten shillings debt and damage and Cost of court.

Upon an action of Debt com[m]enced by **Margritt Smith**, Widow and Ex-ecutrix to the deceased **John Smith** of Prudance Island, plantiff against the Estate of the deceased Mr **John Paine** of said Prudance Defendant. A Nihill dicett in open Court. The Jurrys Verdict. Wee finde for the plantiff debt and damage twenty five pound in mony, and thirty seven pounds tenn shillings cuntry pay and cost of Court. Judgment Granted by the Court. Execution given forth.

William Kilbee, beinge bound to the peace, and good behavior, and to appeare at this Court, for Contempt of Authorety — and beinge in Court Cald appeared, and his Bond read. And he acknowlidgeinge himselfe faulty and begs the courts pardon therein, and promissed in court Reformation for the future, and to be obedient to the Kings Authorety, The Court see cause thereupon to acquitt him: payinge ffees — —

Upon an Indictment by the Gen^{rl} Aturny against **Clement Weaver** jun^{r} for declareinge himselfe married to **Rachill Andress** in the presence of the Majestrate Mr **Joseph Clarke** although forewarned by the said Majestrate.

The said **Clement Weaver** Enters Traverce, and beinge in Court Called and his charge read he ownes Guilty. The Court upon Consideration of the Matter, and findeinge the said Case doubtfull in the law, doe referr the case to the Generall Asembly for their advice therein.

Upon an Indictment by the Gen^{rl} Aturney against **Rachell Andress** of Newport for that on the 26^{t} of September last, at the house of Mr **Joseph Clarke** that she tooke **Clement Weaver** to be her husband, &c The said Rachell Enters Traverse, and beinge in Court Cald, and her charge read she ownes Guilty. The Courts Centance is that the said **Clement Weaver** and **Rachell Andress** are bound to the good behavior, and to appeare at the next Gen^{rl} Court of Tryalls, and in the meane time to live asunder, and if it shall be found in that time they doe accompany together without Legall proceeds in the law of Marriage It shall be deemed and accounted in them fornication, as the law hath detirmined.

Hugh Moisser beinge chosen a Juryman by the Towne of Portsmouth, and he haveinge not atended that service is fined Twenty shillings.

Thomas Stafford chosen a jurryman by the Towne of Warwick and he not haveinge atended that service is fined tenn shill^{s}.

Daniell Brownes ffine remitted consideringe his poor condition.

This Court desolved the 6^{t} of November 1677.

At a Gen[rl] Court of Tryalls held in his Majestys Name at Newport the 6th of May 1678.

M[r] Benedict Arnold Governo[r]
Majo[r] John Cranston Dep[t] Gover[r]
M[r] James Barker - Asist.-
Capt[n] Peleg Sanford - Asist.-
M[r] Joseph Clarke - Asist.-
M[r] Stephen Arnold - Asist.-
M[r] Thomas Olney jun[r] Asist.-
M[r] John Whipple jun[r] Asist.-
Capt[n] Samuel Wilbore Asist.-
Capt[n] John Albro - Asist.-
M[r] Samuell Gorton - Asist.-
M[r] Thomas Green Asist.-
John Sanford Recorder
Thomas ffrye Gen[rl] Serja[t]
Capt[n] Peleg Sanford Gen[rl] Treasur[r]
Lt Edward Richmond Aturny Gen[rl]
M[r] Edmund Calverly Solicetor

Grand Jurry men Engaged
M[r] Edward Thurston fforeman
M[r] John Wood
M[r] Thomas Clifton
M[r] Henry Tew
M[r] John Heath
M[r] John Brigs jun[r]
M[r] John Straingе
M[r] John Hulme
M[r] Georg Halsall
M[r] Henry Palmer
Lt Latham Clarke
M[r] Henry Brightman

Upon the Reheareing of an action of Detainure beareing date the 14[th] of [31/33] May 1677 Com[m]enced by Capt[n] **Peleg Sanford** plantiff against **Miles fforster** Defendant Tryed at the last Generall Court of Tryalls held at Newport in October last. Upon a long debate in Court between the plantiff and defendant, the defendant pleading for a Barr in the action. The Court doe not see cause to grant a barr to the action, but that it proceed to Tryall.

Jurry-men Engaged:

Jeremiah Browne foreman
Thomas Rogers
John Stanton
John Maxon
John Clarke
John Steer
John Enman
Anthony Shaw
Samson Shearman
John Albro jun[r]
Walter Roades
John Pocock

Jurrio[rs] Engagement: You. A — B. being of this Jurry of Tryalls You shall well and truly trye the Issue of this Case and all Cases that shall be Com[m]itted unto You, from this Court between the partys plantiff and de-fendant, according to law and Evidence, and this Engagement you make and give upon the perrill of the penalty of perjurry, and to keep together untill you agree of a Verdict in the case or cases Com[m]itted to you and make true Returne of the Verdict or Verdicts unto this Court and to keep your owne and ffellows secretts.

The Court haveing three times sent forth the Jurry, Receive their Verdict which is — : Wee finde for the plantiff the horse sued for damage twelve pence and cost of court.

Whereas there hath been an action, by Reheareing Tryed in this Court wherein Capt[n] **Peleg Sanford** is plantiff against M[r] **Miles fforster** Defendant, and the Jurry haveing found for the plantiff, and the defendant haveing petitioned this Court, that Judgment

Mought be stopt and an Apeale to the Asembly granted: This Court have seariously Considered the defend^ts Motion and carefully Examined the law doe finde that they ought not to stop Judgment in the Case. And therefore doe grant Judgment according to law. Execution Granted.

Upon an action of Debt upon account Com[m]enced by Mrs **Sarah Reape** Wi-dow and Executrix to the late Deceassed **William Reape** of Newport plantiff against Mr **Thomas Wally** of the Towne of Barnstable in the Collony of New Plymoth (or his Estate) now husband to **Sarah** the Executrix to the late deceassed **Nicholas Davis** of the said Newport defend^t the said action beareing date the 5th of Novemb^r 1677.

May the 6^t 1678: for want of an answer the plantiff Enteres a Nihill dicitt. The case being in court Called, and noe defendant appeareing the Nihill dicitt stands

The Jurry afore-named on this case. The Jurrys Verdict: Wee finde for the plantiff Debt and Intrest £55:04s:10d. Damage: three shillings and Cost of Court. Judgment by the Court Granted. Execution given forth.

Upon an Action of Debt upon account beareing date the 9th of November 1677 Com[m]enced by Mr **Stephen Paine** of Rehoboth Plantiff against **Edward Marshall** of Warwick Defendant. The case beinge in Court Called and noe defendant the plantiff Enteres a nihill dicett.

The Jurrys Verdict: Wee finde for the plantiff Debt £40-04s-02d, and damag one shilling; and cost of Court. Judgment by the Court Granted. Execution given forth.

Upon an Action of Debt by Bill Com[m]enced by **Lawrance Turner** of the Towne of Newport Plant^f against **Weston Clarke** of said Newport Defendant. Said action beare-ing date the 18th of January 1677:

May the 6^t 1678 there not being an answer in the office; the plantiff Enteres a Nihill dicett — The said Defendant apeareing in Court, after a long debate, ownes the Bill and the Debt and Referrs himselfe to the Courts Judgment.

Upon an action of the Case, beareing date the 22th of ffebruary 1677 Com[m]enced by Mr **Samuell Appleton** Senio^r of the Towne of Ipswich in the Massachusetts Col-lony; ffor the Mojetie or one halfe of Prudance Island formerly belonging unto the Deceassed Mr **John Paine**: Plantiff against **William Allin** and **James Sweet** joynt Defendants: The Issue Generall Not Guilty.

Jurymen:		
	Jerem- Browne fforeman	John Enman
	Thom Rogers	Antho: Shaw
	John Stanton	Samson Shearman
	John Maxon	Walter Roades
	John Clarke	John Pocock
	John Steere	James Weeden Senr

Jurrys Verdict. Wee finde for the Defendants, the Northermost halfe of Prudence Island for the Children of Mr **John Paine** Deceassed and Cost of Court. Judgment Granted by the Court. Judgment given forth.

Upon an Action of Debt by bill said action beareing date the 23^d of ffebruary 1678 Com[m]enced by Mr **Milles fforster** of Newport plantiff against **Walter Clarke John Coggeshall** Senr **Joshua Coggeshall** and **John Cranston** Dep^t Governo^r all of said Newport Defendants. The case being in Court Called plantiff and defendants appeared. And after a searious debate of the case the Court doe declare that the case cannot proceed.

Upon an Action of the Case for unjust detainure beareing date the 11th of March 1677 Com[m]enced by **Abell Potter** of the Towne of Portsmouth plan-tiff against **Ralph Cowland** of said Portsm^o^ Defend^t^.

Jurriors	Jer: Browne fforeman	John Enman
	Thom Rogers	Antho: Shaw
	John Stanton	Sams: Shearman
	John Maxon	John Albro jun^r^
	John Clarke	Walter Roads
	John Steere	Natha: Coddington

The Issue Generall. Not Guilty.

[32/34]The Jurrys Verdict. Wee finde for the plantiff the three acre Lott that he sueth for, and fifty shillings Damage and Cost of Court; Judgment granted by the Court. Execution given forth.

Upon an Action of the Case beareing date the 18th of March 1677 Com[m]enced by **John Sands** of Block Island Plantiff against **William Edwards** of the Towne of New-port Defendant. The Issue Generall, Not Guilty. The afore-named Jurry on this Case.

The Jurrys Verdict. Wee finde for the plantiff five pounds sterll Damage and cost of court. Judgment Granted by the Court.

Upon an action of Debt by Bill beareing date the 18th of March 1677: Com[m]enced by **William Edwards** of the Towne of Newport plantiff against **John Sands** of New-Shorrum defendant. The Issue Generall Not Guilty. The Jurrys Verdict: Wee ffinde for the plantiff nine pounds in payment according to Bill twelve shillings Damage and cost of court. Judgment Granted by the Court.

Upon an action beareing date the 19th of March 1677 Com[m]enced by **John Warner** and **William Green** Agents for and on the behalfe of the Towne of Warwick plantiffs against **Thomas Gould** of Kings Towne in the Kings province Defendant. The case being called the Defendant did not appeare. Butt **Edward Richmond** appeared saying he is the Defendants Aturney and doth Engage on the behalfe of the defendant to stand to and performe the Judgment of this Court in the case. The Aturneys not agreeing on the Issue; the Issue Joyned by the Court is a Generall Issue.

Jurriors:	Jere~ Browne fore-man	Anth. Shaw
	Tho. Rogers	Sams~ Shearman
	John Stanton	John Albro jun^r^
	John Clarke	Walter Roades
	John Steere	Nath. Coddington
	John Enman	John Pocock

The Jurrys Verdict Wee finde for the Defend^t^ Cost of Court. Judgment Granted by the Court.

Clement Weaver jun^r^ of the Towne of Newport beinge bound by the last Court of Tryalls to appeare at this Court, and in this Court Indicted for ffornication with **Rachill Andress** — he being in court called apeared, and the Indictment Read, and he

askt whether Guilty or Not Guilty of the charge ownes Guilty and leaves himselfe to the mercy of the Bench:
The centance of the Court is that the said **Clement Weaver** shall according to law be whipt with fifteen stripes in the Towne of Newport on the 16th of this instant May, or Else he shall pay a fine of forty shillings to the Generall Treasurer, at or before the last of June next, and is still to stand bound in the Injunctions of his former Bond in October last untill the Court of Tryalls in October next at Newport, and shall alsoe pay all present ffees to Officers.

Rachell Andress of Newport being bound by the last Court of Tryalls to appeare at this Court and in this Court Indicted for fornication with **Clement Weaver** Junr. She being in Court called apeared, and the Indictment Read and she askt whether Guilty or not Guilty of the charge ownes Guilty and Referrs her selfe to the mercy of the Bench:
The centance of the Court is that the said **Rachell Andress** shall according to law be whipt with fifteen stripes in the Towne of Newport on the 16th of this instant May or Else she shall pay a fine of fforty shillings to the Generall Treasurer at or before the last of June next, and is still to stand bound in the Injunctions of her former bond in October last untill the Court of Tryalls in October next at Newport, and shall alsoe pay all present ffees to officers.

Roger Empson of the Towne of Newport being bound to the good behavior and to apeare at this Court, and by the solicetor in this Court Indicted for Misbehavior: he being in Court called apeared, and the Indictment Read, and he askt whether Guilty or not Guilty ownes Guilty — and submitts himselfe to the court mercy. The Court, doe Thereupon see cause; there being noe information of his Misbehavior since his being bound: to acquitt him of his bonds he paying ffees. Cleerd by proclamation.

Thomas Starr, being bound to the Good-behavior and to apeare at this Court and by the Soliceter Indicted for contempt of Authorety — he being in Court called apeared and the Indictment Read and he askt whether Guilty or not Guilty ownes Guilty. and Referrs himselfe to the Courts Mercy. The Court thereupon doe see cause to acquitt the said Starr of his Bonds he paying ffees. Cleered by proclamation.

Upon Indictment by the Genrl Soliceter against **Daniell Dawly** prissoner for diging open and Robin Indian graves; the said Dawly being brought forth into the Court and the Indictment Read and he askt whether Guilty or Not Guilty of the charge ownes Guilty, and Referrs himselfe ot the Mercy of the Bench.
The Court upon the Consideration of the case: doe centance the said **John** [*sic*] **Dawly** to Returne all such things that he had from the Indian graves: unto the house of Mr **Thomas Ward** in Newport, and shall be sevearly whipt with tenn stripes on the 23 day of this instant month May, or Else pay a fine of Twenty shillings in mony to the Genrl Treasury, and shall alsoe pay fees, and shall Remaine a prissoner untill the courts centance be per-formed.

Upon an Indictment by the Genrl Solicetor against **John Cartwright** [33/35] prisoner, for diging open and Robbin Indian Graves, the said Cartwright being

brought forth into the court, and the Indictment to him Read, and he askt whether Guilty or Not Guilty and pleads he had noe hand in it:
Jurriors on the case:

Jeremiah Browne foreman	John Enman
John Rogers	Sams~ Shearman
John Stanton	Anthony Shaw
John Maxon	John Albro jun[r]
John Clarke	Nath. Coddington
John Steere	John Pocock

The Jurrys Verdict (Guilty) The court upon consideration of the case doe centance the said **John Cartwright** to Returne all such things that he had from the Indian graves; unto the house of M[r] **Thomas Ward** in Newport and shall be sevearly whipt with tenn stripes on the 23 day of this instant month May or Else pay a fine of Twenty shillings to the Gen[rl] Treasury in mony and shall alsoe pay ffees, and shall remaine a prisoner untill the courts centance be performed.

Upon an Indictment by the Gen[rl] Soliceter against **Nicholas Utter** prissoner for diging open and Robin Indian graves. The said Utter being brought forth into the Court and the Indictment to him Read, and he askt whether Guilty or not Guilty of the Charge pleads Not Guilty and Referrs himselfe for Tryall to the cuntry.
Jurriors next afore named. The Jurry Verdict (Guilty).
The Court upon consideration of the case doe centance the said **Nicholas Uter** to Returne all such things that he had from the Indian graves, unto the house of M[r] **Thom~ Ward** in Newport, and shall be sevearly whipt, with tenn stripes on the 23 day of this Instant Month May, or Else pay a fine of Twenty shillings in Mony to the Generall Treasury and shall alsoe pay fees, and shall remaine a prisoner untill the courts centance be performed.

Upon an Indictment by the Gen[rl] Soliceter against **John Carr** prisoner for diging open and Robin Indian graves. The said Carr being brought forth into the Court, and the Indictm[t] to him Read, and he askt whether Guilty or not Guilty of the charge pleads Not Guilty and Referrs himselfe for Tryall to the Jurry.
On this case the afore-named Jurriors: The Jurrys verdict (Guilty)
The Court upon consideration of the case doe centance the said **John Carr** to Returne all such things that he had from the Indian graves; unto the house of M[r] **Thomas Ward** in Newport and shall be sevearly whipt with tenn stripes on the 23 day of this Instant Month May or Else pay a fine of Twenty shillings in Mony to the Gen[rl] Treasury and shall alsoe pay ffees and shall remaine a prissoner untill the Courts centance be performed.

Upon an Indictment by the Gen[rl] Soliceter against **John Carr** prisoner; some Resident in the Kings province: for unlawfully and feloniously breaking open his Majestys Goale in Newport in the yeare 1669 or 70: The said Carr being brought forth into the Court, and the Indictment to him Read, and he askt whether Guilty or not Guilty of the Charge, pleads Not Guilty and Referrs himselfe for Tryall to the Jurry.
On this Case the afore-named Jurry — The Jurrys Verdict Guilty.

The Judgment and Centance of the Court is that **John Carr** shall at or before the 30th of June next depart this his Majestys Collony, and if he shall after the said 30th June be found in any part of this Collony: Then it shall be in the power of anyone Justice of the peace to cause him the said Carr to be aprihended and sevearly whipt with 30 lashes in every of the four Townes of this Collony to say Newport, Providence, Portsmouth and Warwick, and then to be Returned unto the Com[m]on Goale, there to Remaine and be kept a close prisoner in Irons untill further order from Authorety. The said Carr is to pay all fees due by law or Else to be levied by Execution on his Estate: And that the Governor or Dept Governor or any two Asistants is to Order and appoint said Carrs Releasment out of prison within the time abovesaid.

Whereas **William Morris** and **Prudance Edwards** stand Indicted in this Court for fornication, he the said Morris haveing been Imprisoned and brought into the Court owned Guilty, upon the Consideration of the matter doe see cause to com[m]itt the said William Morris to prison untill he can procure Sureties for his apeareance at the next Court of Tryalls in October.

Prudance Edwards being in Court Called apeared, and being askt whether she was with childe she answered she was, and said that **William Morris** was the father of it, and William Morris being by owned what was said by Prudance Edwards.

Mr **ffrancis Brinley** doth in Court Engage for the apeareance of the afore said Prudance Edwards at the Next Court of Tryalls in October.

John Peckham of the Towne of Newport, **Abiah Carpenter** and **John Knowels** of the Town of Warwick being chosen by said Townes to serve on the Grand Jury and not attendeinge that service are ffined Each of them twenty shillings.

Georg Brownell of Portsmouth, **William Burton**, and **John Low** of the Towne of Warwick being chosen by said Townes to be on the Jury of Tryalls and not attending that service are fined each of them Twenty Shillings.

This Court Desolved the 15th of May 1678.

Newport August 23 - 1676 [34/36]

At a meeting of the Gen^{rl} Councell of the Collony of Rhode Island and Providence Plantations &c In which were personally present **Majo^{r} John Cranston** Dep^{t} Governo^{r} and Seven Assistants of the said Collony Viz **Mr James Barker, Mr William Harris, Captn Arthur ffenner, Mr Joshua Coggeshall, Mr William Cadman, Captn Randall Houlden and Mr Samuell Gorton.**

Whereas in his Majestys Gracious Charter of Incorporation granted unto this Collony, it is declared to be, that duty of the Governo^{r} and Asistants of the s^{d} Collony for the time being, to aply them selves to take care of the Gen^{rl} Bussines and affaires of the said Collony and the Government of the people thereof, which their duty is afterwards by his Maj^{tie}, more Expresly declared, and their Authorety in the Militia and Millitary affaires granted and confirmed in these words. And wee doe further for us, our heires and successors, give and grant unto the s^{d} Governor and Company and their heires and Successors by these presents, that it shall and may be lawfull for the s^{d} Governo^{r} and in his abscence the Dep^{t}. Govern^{r} and Majo^{r} part of the said Asistants for the time being at any time when the Gen^{rl} Assembly is not sitting, to nominate appoint and constitute such and soe many Com[m]anders Governo^{rs} and Millitary Officers as to them shall seem Requissit for the leading conducting and training up the Inhabitants in the said plantations in Martiall affaires and for the defence and safegard of the people thereof, and that the said officers have power to Exercise the law Martiall in such cases as occassion shall necessarily Require. And upon Just Cause to invade and distroy the Native Indians and other Enemys of the said Collony. And whereas diver Indians are supposed to have been principle actors and contrivers in the late Rebellion and Murthers and other outrages com[m]itted against his Maj^{ties} Authorety, and his good subjects in this Collony, are now in prisson in order to their Tryall, and it being Evident by all the proceedings that have been against the Indians hitherto by the many Com[m]issions that have been granted to the Millitary Officers and by the severall watches that have from time to time been constituted and appointed that this Collony, and all the publick officers thereof have proceeded as in warr for the Mannaging whereof divers Rates have been Levied on the Inhabitants. — : It is Therefore unanimously voted, and declared by the Gen^{rl} Councell and the Authorety thereof according to the power granted to them as is above Expressed That the severall Com[m]ission Officers of the Respective traine bands of this Collony or the major part of them, together with the s^{d} Governo^{r} or Dept. Governo^{r} and any six Asistants or the majo^{r} part of them is and shall be a Court Martiall, and is hereby fully and absolutly Empowred, to hear debate Issue and detirmin to the Tryall and Execution of the said Indians or any of them, or any other that now are or hereafter shall be accussed to be guilty of the said Crimes Relating to the s^{d} warr, and within their Cognizence punishable by them as a Court Martiall, as often as Occassion shall Require, at any time between the date of these presents and the next Gen^{rl} Court of Tryalls to be held in October next. Except the Gen^{rl} Assembly shall see cause to take further order in the meantime. [*councell seal*]

Voted that **Edward Richmond** is constituted and appointed Secretary for the present occassion.

Voted that **Captn Edmund Calverly** is appointed and Constituted Aturny
Voted that **Henry Lilly** is constituted and appointed feild Martiall upon the Occassion and Cryer of the Court.
Voted and ordered that these shall be published and proclamed in Newport, at this Instant by the beat of the Drum. Given under my hand August 24th 1676.

Edward Richmond secretary to ye Councell, by or on ye psent Occassion.

Newport August 24th 1676. The Names of
the Members of the Court Martiall:

Mr. Walter Clarke Governor.
Major John Cranston Dep^t Gover^r
Mr John Coggeshall Asistant
Mr James Barker Asistant
Mr John Easton Asistant
Mr William Harris Asistant
Capt Arthur ffenner Asistant
Mr Thomas Borden Asistant
Mr Joshua Coggeshall Asistant
Mr William Cadman Asistant
Captn Randall Houldon Asistant
Mr Samuel Gorton jun^r

Millitary Officers:
Captn Peleg Sanford
Capt Roger Williams
Captn Samuell Wilbore
Captn John Albro
Captn Edmund Calverly
Captn John ffoanes
Left^t Edward Richmond
Left^t John Green
Left^t William Correy
Left^t Latham Clarke
Left^t ffrancis Gisborn
Left^t Jireh Bull
Ens^n Weston Clarke
Ens^n James Barker
Ens^n Caleb Arnold
Ens^n Hugh Mosher
Ens^n John Potter

Edward Richmond secretary
Captn Edmund Calverlly Aturny Gen^{rl}
Serj^t John Rogers
Henry Lilly Marshall and Cryer

[35/37] I **Edmund Calverly** Aturny Generall in the behalfe of our soveraigne Lord the King Charles the Second of England Scotland ffraunce and Ireland King &c Doe impeach the **Quanpens otherwise Sowagonish** an Indian Sachim Relating to the Narragansett cuntry in the Collony of Rhode-Island and Providence Plantations in New England, for these sundry crimes ffollowing, namly ffor being disloyall to his said Majesty sundry ways: videleset .. ffor that thou hast not faithfully adheared to the Government Established in this said Collony by his said Majesty, but hast rebelliously adheared to Indians of an other Collony called Plymoth namely **Phillip** Cheife sachim of the Indians in that said Collony, whoe with his Indians did within sixteen months past Trayterously Rebelliously Royetously and Routously Arm Weapon and Array them selves, with swords, guns and staves &c, and have killed and Bloodely Murthered many of his said Majestys good subjects whoe lived peaceably under the sundry Governments to which they did belong :
Butt more pertickularly thou hast through thy wicked boody minde and Trayterous Rebellious Roietous and Routous Acts, with swords guns and staves &c, In thy owne

person, within this his Maj[ties] Collony, and many great Companys of Indians with the, some of them yett unknowne Armed and arrayed as afore-said, didst doe great damage to our Soverraigne Lord the King, by killing his subjects, burning their houses, killing and driveing away their cattell, and many more outrages of that nature have been by the and thy confederats done & com[m]itted, all against the peace of our soverraigne Lord the King his Crowne and dignety for all which acts of thine, I doe on the behalfe of his said Majesty impeach the as a Rebell in the face of this Court, And pray Justice against thee the said Quanapen, otherwise Sowagonish &c.

Edmund Calverly Aturny Generall.

Dated at a Court Martiall held in
Newport y[e] 24th of August 1676.

Quanopen owned that he among the Rest was in Armes against the English Nation, and that he was at the swamp fight, and that he had nothing to say against the Indians burninge & distroying Pettacomscutt, and that he was at the Asaulting of M[r] **William Carpenters** Garrisson at Pawtuxet, and that he was in Arms at Nashaway, and did Asist in distroyinge and burninge the Towne, and takeinge and Carrying away the English Captives, to the number of about 20.

Voted. Guilty of the charge, and that he shall be shott to death in this Towne on the 26[th] instant at about one of the Clock in the after-noone.

An Indian with one Eye Quanapens brother saith his Brother **Quanapin** was a Com[m]ander in the warr, but he was not, he being soe defective in his Eye sight that he was incapable.

Voted that at present Judgment is suspended.

August 25[th] **Sunkeecunasuck** upon his Examination owneth that he was at the burning and distroying of Warwick, and that **Wenunaquabin** a Indian that is now in prisson was at the burning and distroying Warwick with him the same time; and that his brother **Quonapin** was the second man in com[m]and in the Narragansett cuntry, that was he was the next to **Nenanantenewtt**. And **Nechett** an Indian owned, that he saw **Sunkeecunasuck** at Warwick and that he was Instrumentall in cheife in saveing his life.

Voted Guilty of the charge and to suffer death the same time and place with his brother.

Ashamattan upon his Examination, owneth, that his brother **Quanapin** had some of the Wampanoags with him, and that his brother Quanapin had many Indians under his com[m]and, but **Nonanantenewtt** was counted the cheifest of the two, and that they had Recrute of powder latly from the Dutch. — : Voted that present Judgment is suspended.

Wenanaquabin of Pawtuxett saith that he was not at the woonding of **John Scott** but was at that time liveing at **Abiah Carpenters**, and he could cleer him; Abiah Carpenters wife being sent for, before his face saith that he went away from their house sometime in May 1675 and did not see him againe nor could heare of him till towards winter, which he saith is true, the s[d] Wenanaquabin further saith that he did not come to Warwick till night after the Towne was burned, and after owned that he saw

Nechett an Indian there. The said **Nechett** to his face afirmed that he saw him at Warwick at the burning the Towne with his gun about noon. The said **Wenaquabin** alsoe confesseth that he was at the fight with **Captn Turner** and there lost his gun and swam over a River to save his life.

Voted Guilty of the charge, and that he shall be putt to death after the same manner, in time and place as Quonapin.

John Wecopeak on his Examination saith he was never out against the English, but one time with other Narragansett Indians, about the month of March last against a Towne upon Conecticutt River called in Indian Pencanasuck, and at that time their company burned a Barne and two dwelling houses, and killed two English-men, and that he was not at the burning of Pettacomscutt, butt was at that time with **Indian John, William heiffernans** man Removinge their wigwams, but shortly after he was sent [36/38] downe by the sachims to fetch off two d[*torn*] Indians from thence, and saith that **Georg Crafts** wife was shott with a slugg, and chopt in some parts of her body with a hatchett, and saith that she did not crye. Hee also saith that he was at the fight with **Captn Turner**, and Run away by reason the shott came as thick as Raine, but said alsoe that he was at a great distance. Butt **John Godfree** and **William Heiffernan** saith that he the said **Weco-peack** told them, that he saw **Captn Turner** and that he was shott in the thigh and that he knew it was him for the said Turner said that was his name. Voted Guilty of the charge and to dye as the others.

Awashawin of Narragansett denyeth that he layd hands on **John Green** of Narragansett, occassioned about the death of a dumb boy, although affirmed by three Witnesses to his face, to witt Mr **Tho. Gould, John Andra** and **Daniell Green.**

The Court adjourned till Thursday next at tenn of the clock in the morning being the 31st of this Instant.

Before the Court Martiall the 31st of August 1676:

Quonachowacont saith he was informed that all the sachims was at the takeing and burning of **Jireh Bulls** Garrison.

Manases Molasses called and Answered to the name, being Examined, concerning **Zow Howland** kild at Pocassett side (being an Englishman) and slaine or murdered by the Indians, and this Molasses being charged or suspected to have a hand in the crime, answers that he did not kill him, but being up in the woods the Indians came and said such a one was kild and offered to sell the coate of the person soe murdered or slaine, and that he the said Mallasses bought the coate of the (said dead man) for ground nutts, and further saith that it was one **Quasquomack** kild the said Howland.

Mr **Almy** declared that at Plymouth being, Examination being then upon the death of Howland it was declared there that this Indian now present, with two others one named **Ohom**[m], the other **Quasquomock** did kill the said Howland.

This Deponant **John Cook** aged about forty five yeares Testefyeth, being at Punckatest in the midle of July or thereabout, did ask of severall Indians named as followeth, **Woodcock, Matowat, & Job**, whome they were that kild **Zow Howland** the fore-sd Indians answer was that there was six of them in company and Manasses was the Indian that fetcht him out of the water ffurther this deponant saith not.

This Deponnant **John Brigs** aged thirty five yeares or thereabouts Testefyeth to the abovewritten Testamony and alsoe that the said **Manasses** shott at **Joseph Russill** as the Indians first above-named relate and further this deponant saith not.

Taken before me this 25th of August 1676 Wm Cadman Asist.

This deponant **William Manchester** aged Twenty and two yeares or thereabout, being at Pocasset asked of **Peter Nonoet** the husband of **Wetomoe**, whoe it was that killed **Zow Howland**, his answer was, that **Manasses** fetcht him out of the water and further saith not.

Augst 25th 1676. Taken before me: Wm Cadman Asist.

Court adjourned while [*sic*] tomorrow Morning Eight of the clock.

Septr 1th 1676 the court called.

Awetamoes sister being Examined what she could say concerning the killing of **Zow Howland** — she saith that she was informed by one of those that was at his killing called **Ohom[m]** that this abovesd **Malasses** was the person that fetcht Zow Howland out of the water at the time when he was kild although the Indians that were with them perswaded him not to persue him, and alsoe further saith that she knoweth him the sd Mallases to be one of the 12 that was of that company that took and kild the said Howland.

Mumuxuack alias Toby, being charged for suspition of killing or Asisting or being in the Company of them that killed **John Archer**, Upon his Examination saith that he was one of four at the killing of John Archer and his sonn, but he was with one more that was about tenn rod distance, and that the other called whether they should shoot or not, but did shoot, but after the said **Mamuxuack** said being over perswaded, and threatned by his brother to carry away **John Archers** head he did doe it, to **Awetamoe** by Reason his brother threatned him, if he Refused to take off his head, and that he carryed the head to Awetamoe, and that his brother gave him a shirt for soe doing for carrying the head.

Jack Havens saith, that he heard the Indians say that John Archer had like to have Escaped by takeing hold of **Mamuxuacks** brother called **Whaweapunet** his hatchett. but that he the sd Mamuxuat came behind the sd Archer and struck him on the head with his hatchitt and soe they kild him.

Wechuncksum, alias Abram, saith, that he well Knoweth the above sd Malasses, and that he heard at the spring of the yeare last, being then at Wachusett, there was then information given what Execution had latly been don against the English, amongst which was affirmed that the abovsd Malasses had latly killed an Englishman at Pocassett:

Suckats squa that lives with **Daniell Wilcocks** saith that she heard the abovsd Malasses say being askt or Examined by the Indians at the spring of the yeare last toward Wachusett whether he had latly killed an Englishman at Pocassett, he answered that he had done it.

Whawinuckshin, Serjt Rogers man, being Examined saith that he was at **Thomas Gould** Garison and the occassion of his coming, was to burry his father or help burry

him, and there found several Indians upon their gard, but stayed not long there but Emeadiatly came away.
Voted that Serj[t] Rogers shall have his Indian man home with him, provided that the said Indian shall be brought forth if Required, which the said Serj[t] Rogers doe in the face of the Court Engage to doe.
The Court adjourned till tomorrow morning at Eight of the clock.

S[r] The Letter sent by the Governor of Plymoth to your selfe, and by your selfe to us bearing date August 28th last past purperating the Massachusetts [37/39] and New Plymoths demand of Indians on this Island &c, an answer to which concerns in a speciall manner yo[r] selfe and need of all Expedition for divers reasons, besides safety and charge, Wee therfore pray yo[r] pressence at the ussiall place of Meeting this day to consider what Answer or to Require a full apearance of the Councell, or otherwise as you please; with speed doe what seems best to you; wee are Redy to doe our service to the publick peace and safety.
These are to certefy all whome it may concern that Capt[n] **Benjamin Church** is Authorized, and fully Empowered by the Authorety of this Collony of New Plymoth, in the name of the said Collony and for their use and benefitt, to demand and Receive of the Governo[r] and Authorety of Rhode Island, all such of our Indian Enemys whether men women or children, as whilst our fforces were abroad Ranging the adjacent parts of our Collony in pursute of the said Enemys, were Received by and are Entertained, upon the s[d] Island. And haveing Received them he is ordered to guard and conduct them to Plymoth aforesd and alsoe Impowered to sell and dispose of such of them and soe many as he shall see cause for there: to the Inhabitants or others, for tearm of life or for shorter time as there may be Reasons. And his actings herein shall at all times be owned and Justefyed by the said Collony.
August 28th 76 Pr Josiah Winslow Go[v]

Voted that **Malosses** and **Mamxuat** and **Quanachuagat** are ordered to be delivered out of the prison to Capt[n] **Benjamin Church**, and seven more to be delivered to Capt[n] **Anthony Low**, whoe have Engaged to Tranceport them out of the Collony and that they shall not Returne here againe, and one more to be at the dispose of **Henry Lilly** which he Receives in full satisfaction for his Atendance at this Court, and to be tranceported as the other to Capt[n] Low, and that at or before the delivery of these the Marshall shall take all their names, and give Returne thereof to the clerk of this present Court.
Whereas It is Reported that divers Indians are now brought to Newport, and severall other upon the maine land neer shoers of Rhode Island. Wee doe therefore declare and in his Majesty name Requier that noe Indian Either great or small be landed on any part of Rhode Island aforesd or any Island in the Narraganett Bay upon the penalty as formerly, Impossed upon such ofenders, and they shall be taken as being Contemners of the Authorety of this Collony, Always provided that if any bee or may bee upon Just cause detected, he or they at all times, shall be lyable to be brought forth

to Answer the same by warrant from the Govern^{r} or Dep^{t} Governo^{r} or any two Asistants.

Dated at a Court Martiall held in Newport
on Rhode Island August 24th 1676. Pr Edwd Richmond Sec^{ty} to the Court.

Voted that the Dept. Governo^{r} shall have Copys of the Tranceactions of this court between this and the next sitting.

Voted that the Court is adjourned till the 25th this Instant, except the Dep^{t} Governor shall see cause to call the s^{d} Court in the intrim between this and the 25th of this instant as aforesd and upon any such Occassion the Dep^{t} Govern^{r} have full power to call a Court Martiall as aforesaid.

[38/40]

At a Gener[rl] Court held in his Maj[ties] Name
at Newport the 23 of October 1678

M[r] William Coddington Governo[r]
Majo[r] John Cranston Dept Gov[r]
M[r] James Barker Asista-
Captn Peleg Sanford Asista-
M[r] Joseph Clarke Asista-
M[r] Stephen Arnold Asista-
M[r] Thomas Olney Jun[r] Asista-
M[r] John Whipple jun[r] Asista-
Capt[n] Samuell Wilbore Asista-
Capt[n] John Albro Asista-
Capt[n] Samuell Gorton Asista-
M[r] Thomas Green Asista-
John Sanford Recorder
Thomas ffry Gen[rl] Serja[t]
Capt[n] Peleg Sanford Gen[rl] Treasurer
L[t] Edward Richmond Gen[rl] Aturny
M[r] Edmund Calverly Soliceter

Grand Jurrymen engaged:
M[r] Phillip Smith foreman
M[r] Henry Tew
M[r] Richard dunn
M[r] Robert Taylor
M[r] John Vaughan
M[r] Walter Roades
M[r] Gidion ffreeborne
M[r] Mathew Borden
M[r] Richard Knight
M[r] John Rice
M[r] William Edwards
M[r] Weston Clarke

Upon an action com[m]enced by M[rs] **Kathrin Dyre** plaintiff against **Thomas ffry** Gen[rl] Serjn[t] Defend[t] It being an action of the case. Damage two hundred pounds sterling beareing date the 21[th] day of June 1678. The Issue: Generall not Guilty.
Jurriors:

William Coddington foreman
John Bliss
Henry Wood
Georg Way
John Steer
John Borden
Benja[n] Shearman
John Houldon
John Heath
John Smith
John Odlin
David Lake

Verdict: Wee finde for the plantiff cost of court and forty shillings damage (Equivelent to mony) and the debt according to the former Judgment to be paid her forthwith. Judgment granted. Execution given forth.

Upon an action of Detainure bearinge date the 27[th] of January 1678 damage: two hundred pounds sterling. Com[m]enced by **David Lake** Husband to **Sarah**, Relict of the deceased **Thomas Cornell** of the Towne of Portsmouth plantiff against **Thomas Cornell** of said Portsmouth defend[t]. The Issue Joined. Not Guilty of the charge.
Jurriors:

W[m] Coddington foreman
John Bliss
Georg Way
John Steer
Benja[n] Shearman
John Holdon
John Heath
John Odlin
John Smith
Nathaniell Coddington
Thomas Mumford
William Brinley

Verdict: Wee finde the plantiffs wife her dowry in the proper Estate of her deceased Husband Thomas Cornell that he was lawfully possessed of when he dyed. With Cost of Court. Judgment granted. Execution given forth.

Upon an action of Debt upon account debt and Damage tenn pounds sterll. Com[m]enced by **Andrew Thorne** plantiff against **Caleb Carr** sonn of **Robert Carr** of Newport defend^{t}.
Issue: Gen^{rl} not Guilty of the Charge: on this case Enoch Place in Rome of Nath^{ll} Coddington.
Verdict: Wee finde for the plantiff his Debt and five shillings Damage and Cost of court. Judgment Granted. Execution given forth.

Upon an action of Debt by bill beareing date 29th of August 1678. Damage 20^{li} sterll Com[m]enced by **John Carder** of Warwick pla~. against **John Pococke** of Newport defend^{t}. Issue Gen^{rl} not Guilty. Verdict: Wee finde for the plantiff his debt due and Cost of Court. Judgement Granted. Execution given forth.

Upon an action of Debt upon account Damage tenn pounds sterling beareing date the 31th Augt 1678. Com[m]enced by Mrs **Dameris Arnold** Widow and Executrix to the late deceased Mr **Benedict Arnold** of Newport plantiff against **Benjamin Congdon** of Portsmouth defend^{t}. ffor want of an answer the defend^{t} is taken upon a nihill dicett.
Verdict Wee finde for the plantiff her debt & Damage three pound and Cost of Court. Judgment granted. Execution given forth.

Upon an action of Debt by bill debt & damage five pounds sterling bearing date 13th August 1678 com[m]enced by **Stephen Sebeere** of Newport plantiff against **John Green** jun^{r} of Warwick Defend^{t}. Upon the plea of the case the Court see just cause to grant a non suite.
Judgment granted. Execution given forth for the defend^{ts} costs.

Upon an action of the case damage twenty five pounds sterling, beareing date 28th August 1678 com[m]enced by **Robert Malins** plantiff, against **Robert Taylor** ropemaker defend^{t}. A Nihill dicett Entered. The defendant apearinge in court acknowlidged a Judgment. Judgment granted by the court.

Benjamin Shearman one of the Jurry being sick **Weston Clarke** is putt on the Jurry in his Roome and **Hugh Persons** in the Roome of **Enoch Place.**

John Heath being bound for the Apeareance of **Thomas Case** at this Court and presenting the said Case unto the Court desireing to be Released of his bonds, the Court doe Release the said John Heath and doe com[m]itt Thomas Case to the keeper of the Goale to be safely kept till called for by the Court.

Emanuall Wooly of the Towne of Newport being Indicted at the last Gen^{rl} [39/41] Court and Mandamassed to appeare at this Court to answer said Indictment, and being in Court Called did not appeare.

Upon Indictment by the Gen^{rl} Solicetor against Mr **Christopher Almy** of Portsmouth, for breach of peace, against **John Pocock** and his wife. Enters Traverce. The said Christopher Almy being in Court Called apeared. Being Demanded whether Guilty or not Guilty. Answers Not Guilty and Referrs him selfe for Tryall to God and the Cuntry.
Jurriors:

Willia~ Coddington foreman	John Heath
John Bliss	John Smith

John Steer	Thomas Mumford
Georg Way	William Brinley
John Houldon	Hugh Parsons
John Odlin	John Clarke

The Jurrys Verdict Not Guilty. Cleerd by proclamation in open Court paying ffees.

Whereas the Gen[rl] Aturny hath been in the Court Called and sent for and not appeareing, and the Gen[rl] Solicetor being detained from Atending by the death of his wife:

Therefore that the Court may not be deterred in goeing on with such matters as doe concerne this Court. The Court doe appoint John Sanford Recorder to Officiate in the Aturnys Office dureing the time of this Courts sitting.

Upon Indictment by the Gen[rl] Solicetor against **Thomas Case** of Long Island, for misbehavior. The said Case being Called for and brought into Court, and demand whether Guilty or not Guilty pleads not Guilty. and Refferrs himselfe for Tryall to God & the Cuntry.

Jurriors:

John Bliss fforeman	Hugh Parsons
John Steer	John Clarke
Georg Way	ffrancis West
John Odlin	Barthol. Hunt jun[r]
John Smith	Georg Lawton jun[r]
Thomas Mumford	Alexander ffenix

The Jurrys Verdict not Guilty according to the Indictment.

Cleerd by proclamation in open Court paying ffees.

Upon indictment by the Grand Jurry against L[t] **Edward Richmond** for keeping unlawfull Gaming in his house. Enters Traverce. Pleads not Guilty and Referrs himselfe for Tryall to God and the Cuntry.

[*in margin: list of jurors*]

Will Coddington foreman	Wm Brinley
John Bliss	Hugh Parsons
John Heath	John Clarke
John Steer	John Smith
John Odlin	Barthol. Hunt jun[r]
Thomas Mumford	Georg Lawton jun[r]

The Jurrys Verdict Not Guilty.

Upon Indictment by the Gen[rl] solicetor against **Jabesh Cotterill** of Newport for ffelonious takeing away a sheep out of the custody of **John Easton jun[r]**. he being bound to this Court Called appeared, and being askt whether guilty or not guilty, ownes Guilty and prays the favour of the Court.

M[r] **Peter Talman** Recognized in open Court to stand to and performe the Bonds given in for the said Jabesh Cotterill.

The Courts centance is That the said Jabesh Cotterill shall be seveerly whipt with 15 stripes in the Towne of Newport tomorrow beinge the 9th of this instant Novemb[r] about one of the clock afternoone, or Else shall pay unto the Gen[rl] Treasury before that time the sum of forty shillings in silver for his said offence. and shall alsoe Repay to M[r] John Easton jun[r] two good sheep or the vallue to the satisfaction of the said Eston, and shall pay officers ffees. The Gen[rl] Treasurer paid in mony.

Upon Indictment by the Gen[rl] Solicetor against **James Thornton** of Newport for felonious takeinge away a sheep out of the custody of **John Easton** jun[r]. The said Thornton being in Court Called apeared: And beinge asked whether Guilty or not guilty: pleads not guilty and Referrs him selfe for tryall to God and the cuntry. The Jurrys verdict (Not Guilty): Cleered by proclamation in open Court paying ffees.

Upon Indictment by the Gen[rl] Solicetor against **Thomas Starr** for misbehaviour towards said solicetor **Edmund Calverly**: the said Starr Enters Traverce. Being brought into Court and askt whether Guilty or not Guilty: pleads not Guilty and Referrs him selfe for Tryall to the Cuntry. The Jurrys Verdict Guilty.

Upon Indictment by the Gen[rl] Solicetor against **Thomas Starr** for Misbehaviour against the cunstables. The said Starr being brought into Court and askt whether Guilty or not Guilty pleads not guilty. The Jurrys Verdict Guilty.

Whereas Thomas Starr was afterward called for in Court and being vissitted with sickness and cannot come into the Court: This Court doe sentance the said Thomas Starr to remaine in the Charge of the keeper of the Goale untill he putt in to the Authorety suretye according as the law in that case provides and pay officers their present ffees.

Upon Indictment by the Gen[rl] Solicetor against **Samuell Cumstock** of Providence for breach of the peace &c: beinge in Court Called Enteres Traverce pleads not Guilty and Referrs for Tryall to the Cuntry.

The Jurrys verdict, Guilty. The Courts sentance is that Samuel Cumstock shall forthwith pay to the Gen[rl] Treasurer of this Collony in mony the sum of fforty shillings for his aforesaid offence and pay officers ffees, and his former bonds to continue till the performance of this sentance.

Upon Indictment by the Gen[rl] solicetor against **Elizabeth** the wife of **Benja- Hernden** of the Towne of Providence ffor breach of the peace: being in Court Called apeared: pleads not Guilty and Referrs her selfe for Tryall to the Jurry. The Jurrys Verdict, Guilty: The Courts sentance is that the said Elizabeth Hernden shall in the Towne of Newport be severly whipt with tenn stripes on the 6th instant and kept in durance till that time, or Else forthwith pay in mony unto the Gen[rl] Treasurer of this Collony the sum of the sum [*sic*] thirty shillinge, or Else give in to this Court suffitient securety for the payment thereof on or before the 5th of this Instant November: **Benjamin Hernden** of the Towne of Providence doth in this Court Recognize and firmly Engage and binde over unto our Soverreigne Lord the King of England &c, a percell of Land in the said Towne of Providence containninge Twenty four Acres more or less lyinge & scittuate at a place called Robins Brooke, The Condition whereof is that if the said Benjamin Hernden doe pay or cause to be paid unto the Gen[rl] Treasurer of this his Maj[ties] Collony the sum of thirty shillings the sentance of this Court against his wife Elizabeth Hernden, upon an Indictment found against her in this Court, and truly pay the said sum on or before the first day of Aprill next, that then the said land to be cleer of this Bond, otherwise to be levied and Executed on for the use and bennefitt of this

Collony, And this the said Benjamin acknowlidgeth in open Court the 5th of No^{r}: 1678.

Upon an Indictment by the Gen^{rl} Solicetor against **Joseph Woodward** of Providence for breach of the peace: he being in Court Called apeared, Ownes Guilty. The Courts sentance is that Joseph doe forthwith pay unto the Gen^{rl} Treasury the sum of tenn shillings in mony, and alsoe give in to this Court suffitient Bond with sureties for his good behaviour untill, and appeareance at the next Gen^{rl} Court of Tryalls in May, and pay officers ffees and the former bonds to continue till the performance of this sentance. **William Haukins** Inhabiting in Newport doth in this Court on the behalfe of Joseph Woodard Recognize unto our soverreigne Lord the King, That the said Joseph Woodard shall pay or cause to be paid unto the Gen^{rl} Treasurer the sum of tenn shillings in mony. It beinge for the payment of soe much this Court hath sentanced the said Joseph to pay, and the said sum to be paid on or before the 5th day of December next. Owned in Court. Joseph Woodard of the Towne of Providence, doth Recognize himselfe and his house and Land in said Providence unto his Maj^{tie} of England in the sum of tenn pounds sterling to apeare at the next Gen^{ll} Court of Tryalls to be held at Newport in May next, and in the meane time to be of good and peaceable behaviour, unto all his Maj^{ties} Leige subjects in this Collony, and to answer to such things as shall be Eleaged against him. Read and owned in Court, and from his fformer bonds cleerd by proclamation.

Upon Indictment by the Gen^{rl} Solicetor against **Roger Empson**, for ffalonious taking sheep, which were the proper Estate of Mr **Caleb Carr** Senr and Captn **John ffoanes** of Quononoqutt Island. The said Empson beinge brought into Court and askt whether Guilty or not Guilty ownes Guilty. The Courts sentance is that Roger Empson shall be severly whipt with twenty stripes in the Towne of Newport tomorrow the 9th of November about one of the clock after noon, or Else before that time shall pay to the Gen^{rl} Treasury the sum of forty shillings in silver for his ofence, and shall alsoe repay unto Mr Caleb Carr and Captn John ffoanes or Either of them five good sheep or the vallue to the satisfaction of the said Carr and ffoanes, and shall pay officers ffees.

Upon Indictment by the Gen^{rl} Solicetor against **Charles Hill** for ffalonious takeinge sheep which were the proper Estate of Mr **Caleb Carr sen^{r}** and Captn **John ffoanes.** The said Hill beinge brought into Court and askt whether Guilty or not Guilty, ownes Guilty. The Courts sentance is that Charles Hill shall be severly whipt with twenty stripes in the Towne of Newport tomorrow the 9th of November about one of the Clock after noon or Else before that time shall pay to the Gen^{rl} Treasury the sum of fforty shillings in silver for his offence, and shall alsoe repay unto Mr Caleb Carr and Captn John ffoanes or either of them five good sheep or the vallue to the satisfaction of the said Carr and ffoanes, and shall pay officers ffees.

Upon indictment by the Gen^{rl} solicetor against **Richard Cowley** prissoner for ffaloniously stealing and takeing away sheep which were the proper Estate of Mr **Caleb Carr sen^{r}** and Captn **John ffoanes** on the Island Quononoqutt. He being brought into Court and asked whither Guilty or not Guilty; pleads not Guilty and referrs him selfe for Tryall to God and the Cuntry. The Jurrys verdict: Not Guilty. The Court com[m]itt him unto the keeper till called for. The said Cowley being called for, the keeper made answer that he had broken prisson and made his Escape: The Court doe Empower the officers to seise on any Estate they can finde of the said Cowleys to pay their Just ffees. [41/43]

Peter Lee comeing into this Court and misbehaveing himselfe by saying to a prissoner at the barr to have a care of what he said, whereupon he was Com[m]itted to prison, And he haveing petitioned this Court to be released, acknowlidging his fault therein, and promissinge a better behaviour for the future, The Court doe Release him, payinge officers ffees.

Upon Indictment by the Gen^{rl} Solicetor pl against **Mathew Taylor** for ffalonious takeing away boards and Timber from **Josiah Lendall.** He beinge brought into Court and askt whether Guilty or not Guilty: pleads Not Guilty. And Referrs himselfe for Tryall to God and the Cuntry.

The Jurry:

John Bliss foreman	Hugh Parsons
John Steer	John Clarke
John Heath	Bartho: Hunt
John Smith	Georg Lawton jun^{r}
Thom~ Mumford	James Huling
William Brinley	John Green junr

Verdict Guilty. The Courts sentance is that the said Mathew Taylor shall be severly whipt with twenty stripes in the Towne of Newport, tomorrow the 9th of November or Else within that time shall pay to the Gen^{rl} Treasury the sum of forty shillings in silver, and shall pay unto Josiah Lendall the sum of Twenty shillings and pay officers ffees.

Upon Indictment by the Gen^{rl} Solicetor against **Samuell Winsor** of Providence for an Asault and Battery. He being called in Court, apeared and being Askt whether Guilty or not Guilty pleads not Guilty, and Referrs him selfe for Tryall to God and the cuntry.

The afore named Jurry: Verdict. Not Guilty. Cleerd by proclamation in Court payinge officers ffees.

Upon Indictment by the Gen^{rl} Solicetor against **Samuell Winsor** of Providence for Contempt of Authorety &c He beinge in Court Called appeared. Plead not Guilty and Referrs him selfe for Tryall to God and the Cuntry:

The Jurrys verdict: Guilty. The Courts sentance is That the said Samuell Winsor doth Recognize himselfe unto our soverraigne Lord the King in the sum of tenn pounds sterling to be Levied on his goods and Chattells To make his personall appearance at the Gen^{rl} Court of Tryalls in May next at Newport, and shall in the meanetime be of good and peaceable behaviour unto all his Maj^{ties} leig subjects in this Collony and alsoe pay officers ffees. Acknowlidged in Court.

Upon Indictment by the Gen^{rl} Solicetor against **Samuell Winsor** of Providence for maliciously useing words of Contempt against Mr **Thomas Olney** and Mr **John Whipple** Asista^{ts} in the Execution of their office. He being in Court Called appeared: pleads not Guilty and Refers for Tryall to God and the Cuntry:

Juriors on this case:

John Bliss foreman	John Odlin
Henry Wood	Hugh Persons
John Heath	John Clarke
John Smith	Bartho. Hunt jun[r]
Tho Mumford	Georg Lawton jun[r]
Will. Brinley	James Huling

Jurrys verdict Not Guilty: Cleerd by proclamation in open court paying officers ffees.

Upon Indictment by the Gen[rl] Solicetor against **John Andrew** of Narragansett for Contempt he beinge in Court caled, pleads not Guilty, and referrs for Tryall to God and the cuntry.

Jurrys verdict Guilty. The Courts sentance is that the said John Andrew doth Recognize himselfe unto our soverraigne lord the King in the sum of tenn pounds to be levied on his Lands Goods or Chattells, and shall appeare at the Gen[rl] Court of Tryalls, in May next at Newport, and shall in the meane time be of peaceable and good behaviour unto all his Maj[ties] leige subjects in this Collony and pay officers fees: Acknowlidged in Court.

Upon Indictment by the Gen[rl] solicetor against **Emanuell Wooly**, at the last Court of Tryalls for com[m]on tipling and Neglecting his ffamely.

He being Mandamassed and in court three times called did not appeare, and sent for by the serja[t] **Lilly** — the serja[t] made returne that he would not come and said would you were hanged for your Newes: yett afterward cominge to the Court The Court see cause to binde him to the peace and good behaviour. Therefore Emanuell Woolly doth in Court Recognize unto our soverraigne Lord the King in the sum of tenn pounds sterling, to be of good and peaceable behaviour unto all his Maj[ties] leige people, and to make his appeareance at the Gen[rl] Court of Tryalls in May next, and pay officers ffees. Acknowlidged in Court.

Richard Pray of Providence beinge bound in the sum of tenn pounds for his appearance at this Court, and he haveing at the severall times Called in Court, and he not appearing nor any to answer for him, the Court doe declare he hath forfitted his Bond the same to be distrained on and pay officers fees.

John Angell of Providence, beinge bound to this Court, and in Court called did not appear yett the Court Considering the Bill of Indictment formed [42/44] against him for the charge he was bound, the Grand Jurry found Ignoramus, therefore the Court doe remitt the forfiture of his Bond and he is cleer paying ffees.

Whereas Capt[n] **John Roades**, upon Complaint against him for makeing his Escape from the Authorety in New Yorke was apprihended and Com[m]itted to prison, and the Authorety here haveing Indeavored, by severall vessalls bound to Yorke to send him thither but could not: The Court haveing sent for the said Roades into Court, and seariously considered the matter; doe see cause to discharge his imprisonment, and permitt him liberty upon parowle, he haveinge promissed to Attend the Authorety when Called for.

Whereas **William Morris** was the last Court of Tryalls Indicted for fornication Com[m]itted with **Prudance Edwards**, and he then owninge Guilty, the Court then suspended sentance and Com[m]itted the said Morris to prison, untill he putt in sureties for his appearance at this Court: This Court doe sentance the said William Morris for his said ffact to be severly whipt with fifteen stripes in the Towne of Newport, or else shall pay unto the Genl Treasurer the sum of forty shillings in mony or as mony; And the time of his punishment is Referred unto the Judgment of the Governo^{r} or any two Asistants — and shall alsoe pay officers ffees.

Whereas **Prudance Edwards** was the last Court Indicted for ffornication Com[m]itted with William Morris and she then owneinge Guilty: The Court then did see cause to suspend sentance, And M^{r} **ffrancis Brinley** then Engaged for her appeareance at this Court, and she being in Court Called said Mr Brinley came into the Court and declared that she was sick and Could not come. This Court doe sentance the said Prudance Edwards to be severly whipt with fifteen stripes in the Towne of Newport, or Else shall pay unto the Gen^{rl} Treasurer the sum of fforty shillings in or as mony, and shall alsoe pay officers ffees: And the time of her punishment is Referred to the Judgment of the Governo^{r} or anny two Assistants —

Whereas **Abraham Butterworth** was Com[m]itted to prison for Misbehavior in and towards his famely: he beinge brought into Court and acknowlidging his fault and faillinge therein: The Court upon his promiss of liveing more peaceably with his famely for the future, doe see cause to cleere him he paying fees: Only if the said Butterworth shall breake his promiss made to this Court, and Misbehave himselfe, Then it shall be in the power of any Assistant upon lawfull Complaint made to Com[m]itt the said **Abraham Butterworth** to prison as the Authorety shall see cause —

Thomas ffeild of Providence, **Joseph Card** of Newport, **Amos Westcott** and **John Knowles** of Warwick, and **John Bordin** of Portsmouth, being chosen and not attendinge the Jurry are fined twenty shillings apeece —

This Court desolved the 21^{t} of November 1678

Att A Gener^{ll} Court of Tryalls Held in his Majesties Name
at Newport the 12th of May 1679

Majo^{r} John Cranston Governour
Mr Walter Clarke Dep^{t} Governo^{r}
Mr Caleb Carr — Asista~
Mr Thomas Ward Asista~
Mr Joseph Clarke Asista~
Mr Stephen Arnold Asista~
Captn Arthur ffenner Asista~
Mr John Whipple jun^{r} Asista~
Captn John Albro Asista~
John Sanford Asista~
Captn Samuell Gorton Asista~
Mr Thomas Green Asista~
John Sanford Recorder
Mr Edmund Calverly Gen^{rl} Serja^{t}
Majo^{r} Peleg Sanford Treasur^{r}
Capt Edward Richmond Atturny
Mr Edm^{d} Calverly Soliceter

Grand Jurrymen Engaged —
Mr William Hiscox foreman
Mr Bartholomew Hunt
Mr Thomas ffish
Mr Adam Mott
Mr Daniell Lawton
Mr Thomas Dungin
Mr John Stanton
Captn John Sands
Mr John Rathbone
Mr John Coddington
Mr William Allin
Mr Henry Tippitts

Whereas Mr **John Saffin**, in a Bond of 2000^{li} sterling, was bound for his appeareance at this Court, and Mr **Richard Smith** and M^{r} **ffrancis Brinley** his sureties — the said Mr Saffin coming into Court and declareing him selfe he was here redy to answer, and that his and his sureties Bonds were Voyd: Therefore the Court doe com[m]itt the said Mr Saffin unto the safe custody and keeping of the serjant untill the Court see cause to Call for him.

[43/45] Whereas **William Haukins** with his surety **John Stanton** appeared in Court desireing to be releassed of their Bonds: The Court doe therefore com[m]itt the said Haukins to the safe keeping and Custody of the Serjan^{t} till called for by the Court.

Upon an action of the case for Debt, debt and Damage 20^{li} sterling beareing date the 9th of November 1678: Com[m]enced by **Peter Talman** plantiff against **Nicholas Cotterill** defend^{t}. A nihill dicett —

Jurrio^{rs} Mr James Green foreman
James Barker jun^{r}
Willia~ Heiffernan
Nathan^{ll} Tomkins
Thomas Gould
Joseph Jencks
Joseph Williams
Benja~ Hall
Peter Green
Willia~ Wilbore jun^{r}
William Maize
William Hedge

Verdict Wee finde for the plantiff Debt five pounds, one peny damage and cost of Court. Judgment Granted, and alsoe Execution given forth.

Upon an action of the case for Trespass Damage tenn pounds sterling Com[m]enced by **William Earll** plantiff against **Daniell Wilcocks** Defend^{t}. The Issue Joyned a Generall Issue.

Jurrys Verdict: Wee finde for the defend^{t} Cost of Court — Judgment Granted —.

Upon an Action of Debt by Bill. Debt and Damage ten pounds sterling bearing date the 12th of ffebruary 1678 Com[m]enced by **Samuell Robinson** of Salem plantiff

against **William Chadwick** of Newport defend[t]: — May 9th 1679: there not being an answer in the office, the plantiff by his Aturny **John Smith** Entred a nihill dicett.
The Defend[t] being in Court Called, and noe appeareance to answer, the Court approve the nihill dicett, and that the case pass to the Jurry —
Verdict wee finde for the plantiff his Bill of five pounds, and Damage Eighteen pence and Cost of Court: The Court accepts the Verdict and allow the Bill of Cost one pound Eleven shillings Eight pence: And grant Judgment.

Israell Arnold plantiff against Lt. **Edward Richmond** Defenda[t] in an action of Debt, debt and damage tenn pounds sterlinge: beareinge date the 18th of ffebruary 1678.
Verdict wee finde for the plantiff his debt for malt two pounds ninteen shill[s] & six pence silver mony, damage two pence and Cost of Court: Judgment granted.

Miles ffoster plantiff against **John Wright** defend[t] in an action of the case damage forty pounds sterling: May 13th there being noe answer in the office the plantiff enters a nihill dicett: none appeareing in Court to answer the Court aprove the nihill dicett.
Verdict Wee finde for the plantiff upon Bills and accounts debt forty four pounds one shilling tenn pence, and damage four pounds and Cost of Court, Judgment granted.

Upon an Action of Debt by Bill debt and Damage tenn pounds sterling beareing date the 27th of ffebruary 1678/9 Com[m]enced by **Marke Athy** plantiff against **William Downing** defenda[t]. The Issue Not Guilty; and are not Indebted to the plantiff.
Verdict Wee finde for the plantiff due by bill two pounds fifteen shillings: Damage, one shilling and Cost of Court: Judgment granted.

Upon an action of Debt damage 60[li] sterling beareing date the 24th of March 1678/9 Com[m]enced by **Christopher Almy** and **Job Almy** joint plan-tiffs against **John Pocock** defenda[t]

Upon an action of the case for Trespas Damage 50[li] sterling beareing date the 30th of January 1678: Com[m]enced by **William Earll** against **Daniell Wilcocks** defenda[t]: Issue Joyned Not Guilty of the charges. Verdict wee finde for the defend[t] Cost of Court.

Samuell Winsor of Providence being bound to this Court and to the peace and good behavior in Court Called appeared, and proclama~ made, none appeareing to the contrary he is in Open Court cleard paying ffees.

Joseph Woodard of Providence being bound by the Court in October last to appeare at this Court and to the peace and good behavior: in Court Called, did not apeare, yett upon his petition this Court see Cause to continew his bonds untill the Gen[rl] Court of Tryalls in October next.

Emanuell Wooly of Newport being by the last Court of Tryalls bound to appeare at this Court & to the peace and good behavior: in Court Called appeared: proclamation in Open Court made he is cleard paying ffees.

Upon Indictment by the Gen[rl] solicitor against **Kathrine Dyre** of Newport for Misbehavior she being in Court Called appeard: pleads Not Guilty and Referrs for Tryall to God & the Cuntry — The Court upon searious consideration of the matter se cause to quash the bill.

Upon Indictment by the Grand Jurry against **William Hiefernan** of Newport for keeping unlawfull gaming &c: being mandamassed and in Court Called appeared: pleads not Guilty and Referrs for Tryall to God and the cuntry: Verdict not proved Guilty: he being in Court Called did not [44/46] appeare: This Court doe therefore desire and Authorise the Governo^{r}, Dept. Go^{r} or any one of the Asistants in Newport, forthwith to take a five pound bond of the said **William Hieffernan** for his good behavior, and appeareance at the next sittinge of this Court in October next.

Upon Indictment by the Gen^{rl} Solicetor against **John Remington** jun^{r} of Quononoqutt Island for ffornication Com[m]itted with **Abigall Richmond, alias Remington** &c: being mandamassed and in Court Called appeared: pleads not Guilty, and Referrs for Tryall to God and the Cuntry.

Verdict Not guilty by Evidence: cleard by proclamation paying ffees.

Upon Indictment by the Gen^{rl} Solicetor against **John Albro** jun^{r} for ffornication Com[m]itted; by begetting a childe on the Body of **Margrett Hall**, being bound and in court called appeared pleads not Guilty to God and the Cuntry: The Jurry being three times sent forth in the case. Their Verdict Guilty. This Court upon Consideration doe referr this case to the Gen^{rl} Assembly. Jurry men on John Albros case:

Weston Clarke foreman	Benja~ Hall
Daniell Gould jun^{r}	Peter Green
William Brenton	Willia~ Wilbore ju^{r}
Joshua Coggeshall jun^{r}	Will Maize
Nathan^{ll} Tomkins	Willia~ Hedg
Thomas Gould	John Remington

Mr **Joseph Jenks** chosen by the Towne of Providence on the Jurry and he Aledging to this Court the debillety of his body to Atend that service, the court thereupon see cause to dismiss him.

Upon Indictment by the Grand Jurry against **John Saffin** of the Town of Boston for Indeavoring the subverting of great part of this Collony, and draw away the Inhabitants of this Collony from the Obediance of his Majesties Authorety in this Jurisdiction. The said John Saffin being in Court Called appeared: and demanded whether Guilty or not Guilty pleads not Guilty and Referrs for Tryall to God and the Cuntry.

The Jurry Impanneled on the case:

Weston Clarke foreman	Peter Green
James Barker jun^{r}	William Wilbore ju^{r}
William Hieffernan	William Maize
Nathaniell Tomkins	William Hedg
Thomas Gould, jun^{r}	Jeremiah Browne
John Hulme	James Browne

The Jurrys verdict Guilty: the Court after three times sending the Jurry forth accept the verdict. The said Mr John Saffin is com[m]itted to the serja^{ts} custody till called for by this Court:

Whereas you **John Saffin** have been Indicted for breach of law and contempt of his Majestys Authorety in this Jurisdiction, the bill being found against you; and the Jurry of Tryalls yor Tryers haveing found you Guilty: Therefore if you have any thing lawfully to say, why the sentance of this Court shall not be Read and pronounced against you; You may speake otherwise the sentance shall be given against you. The sentance of this Court is against You John Saffin that all your Estate both Reall and personall that you are lawfully possessed of in this Collony is fforfitted unto his Majestys Authorety in this Jurisdiction. And for your Contemptious behavior and Intrutions, the Court doe fine you thirty pound in silver which you are forthwith to pay or cause to be paid in to the Gen^rl Treasurer of this Collony, or to Remaine in Dureance till it is paid as afore-said: and alsoe pay ffees of Court: This court doe order the Recorder according to law to grant forth Execution on the lands and Estate of the said Saffin within Collony. This Court upon the Request of Mr John Saffin doe see cause to grant him the favour — that if Mr John Saffin doe procure two suffitient sureties to be bound for him in the sum of sixty pounds sterling that he the said John Saffin shall not depart out of the liberties of this Towne of Newport, untill he have paid and performed this Courts sentance which if he does not observe and performe then the Bonds to be forfitted.

Upon an action of the case damage 100^£ sterling bearing date the 14th of ffebruary 1678 Com[m]enced by **John Sanford** plantiff against **Elias Williams** defend^t. The said Williams defend^t being called in court and none appearing to answer the plantiff withdrawes this action in Open Court.

Thomas Starr beinge by the last Court of Tryalls Com[m]itted to the Custody of the serja^t till suffitient bond putt in according to law for his good behavior and appearance at this Court being called for was brought into the court, and is com[m]itted to the serja^ts custody till cald for by ye court. Upon the petition of Thomas Starr craveing of this court pardon for his former offences and promissing for the future a better behavior; the Court see cause to acquitt him of his bonds paying ffees: Cleerd by proclamation in Open Court.

Upon Indictment by the Gen^rl solicetor against **William Haukins**, for that the said Haukins did before the Corroner falsly sweare if not perjure him selfe: he enters Traverce: This court upon the searious Consideration of the matter see cause to suspend the case and continew the said William Haukins in the Bond of twenty pounds sterling for his appearance at the Gen^rl Court of Tryalls in October next, and in the meane time to be of peaceable and good behavior to all his Maj^ties leige subjects in this Collony.

Upon Indictment by the Gen^rl Solicetor against **Margrett Hall** for ffornication com[m]itted by her with **John Albro** jun^r: she being bound to this Court and in Court Called; appeared and being demanded of whether Guilty or not Guilty ownes Guilty: Upon consideration of the case of Margrett Hall, the court finding that the [45/47] case of John Albro jun^r is Referred to the Gen^rl Assembly doe alsoe Referr the said Margrett Halls case to the said Assembly for their Detirmenation therein.

Mary Ridgly being by warrant brought into this Court she standing Indicted for Adultery with **John Andrews** of Narragansett, In Court being Examined said Andrews being present, she declared and affirmed that the child then in her armes was begotten by the said John Andrews at the said Andrews house in Narragansett, about the beginning of the month of June last and saith that severall times he the said Andrews had the use of her body even at his pleasure and that she was induced therto by the over perswassion of the said Andrews; and that since that time in June last never had to doe with any other man in that nature but with said Andrews.

Mr **Thomas Gould** and **John Andrews** both of Narragansett doe Recognize unto our soverraigne Lord the King in the sum of Twenty pounds sterling that the said Andrews shall appeare at the Gen^{rl} Court of Tryalls to be held in October next.

John Andrews doth recognize in the sum of twenty pounds sterling to be levied on his lands goods cattell or chattells for his apeareance at the Gen^{rl} Court of Tryalls to be held at Newport in October next, and in the meane time to be of good and peaceable behavior unto all his Maj^{ties} leige subjects in this Collony.

Upon Indictment by the Gen^{rl} Solicetor against **Shuball Painter** of Newport for contempt of Authorety, he being in Court Called appeared. Ownes Guilty and Referrs himselfe to the Mercy of the bench.

The Courts Judgment and sentance is that the said Shuball Painter shall forthwith pay unto the Gen^{rl} Treasury of this Collony the sum of thirty shillings in or as mony, and stand bound in the sum of tenn pounds to be of the peace and good behavior, and to appeare at the Gen^{rl} Court of Tryalls to be held in October next at Newport and pay present ffees.

Mr **Henry Bull** chosen by the Towne of Newport one of the Grand Jurry and he appearing, and Aledging that he is cleer by law: This Courts Judgment is that if the said Mr Henry Bull can make it appeare by law that he is cleared from such service, Then the Towne of Newport is fined twenty shillings, otherwise the said Bull is fined Twenty shillings.

Mr **Nathaniell Coddington** and Mr **Jeremiah Clarke** chosen by the Towne of Newport on the Grand Jurry and **John Ward** on the Jurry of Tryalls they not attending that service are fined each of them twenty shillings.

Daniell Williams and **Samuell Tieft** chosen Jurrymen by the Towne of Providence, and they not atending that service are fined each of them twenty shillings.

Jonathan Knight, William Hopkins, and **Joseph Stafford** chosen Jurrymen by the Towne of Warwick and they not attending that service are fined each of them twenty shillings.

This Court is Adjourned untill the next Tuseday before the last Wensday save one in October next then to Assemble againe at Newport.

At a Gener[ll] Court of Tryalls Held in his Majesties Name at Newport the 22th of October <u>1679</u>:

Majo[r] John Cranston, Governour
Mr Walter Clarke Dep[ty] Governo[r]
Mr Caleb Carr, Assista[t]
Mr Thomas Ward Asista-
Mr Joseph Clarke Asista-
Mr Stephen Arnold Asista-
Capt Arthur ffenner Asista-
Mr John Whipple jun[r] Asista-
Capt[n] John Albro Asista-
John Sanford Asista-
Capt[n] Samuell Gorton Asista-
Mr Thomas Green Asista-
John Sanford, Recorder
Edmund Calverly Gen[rl] serja[t]
Majo[r] Peleg Sanford Gen[rl] Treasurer
Capt[n] Edward Richmond Gen[rl] Aturny
Mr Edmund Calverly, Solicetor

Grand Jurrymen engaged:
Mr Peter Easton fforeman
Mr James Weeden
Mr John Wood
Mr Samuell Hubbard
Mr Thomas Cliften
Mr Robert Hodgson
Mr Mathew Borden
Mr Hugh Persons
Mr John Green jun[r]
Mr Thomas ffry
Mr Joseph Bennitt
Mr William Allin

[46/48] Upon an action of Debt debt and damage tenn pounds sterling bearinge date ye 14th of aprill 1679 Com[m]enced by **Clement Weaver** plantiff against **Benja- Congden** defend[t]: This case with the consent of plantiff and defend[t] is suspended.

Upon an Action of Debt debt and Damage sixty pounds sterling bearinge date the 15[th] of May 1679 Com[m]enced by **Christopher** and **Job Almy** joynt Executors to the Estate of the late deceassed Mr **William Almy** of Portsmouth plantiffs against **John Pococke** and **Mary** his wife Executrix to the late deceassed John Almy of said Portsmouth defendants. There being a nihill dicett taken in the Recorders office, and the matter debated the Court doe see cause to grant the defendants liberty to put in their answer.

There being the mistake of a word in the Declaration writting Septem[r] for Decemb[r] the plantiff hath liberty granted to mend that Expresssion. The Issue Joyned by the Court: is not Guilty of the charge.

Jurrymen:

Joshua Coggeshall fforeman
James Man
John Rogers
Thomas Burgis
John Crandall
Joseph Tripp
Mallica Roades
Charles Mecarta
Georg Halsall
Samuell Stapleton
John Rise
Henry Wood

The Jurry haveing been three times sent forth. The verdict Wee finde for the plantiffs debt and damage seventeen pounds Equivalent to mony and Cost of Court.

Whereas **John Sweet** of Narragansett was bound to this Court, and to the peace and good behavior, being in court called appeared: proclamation made and none coming in to accuse him for breach of his Bond, he is acquitted by proclamation paying fees.

An action of the case for Trespas damage 40£ sterling bearing date the 15th of May 1679 Com[m]enced by **Christopher Almy** plantiff against **John Pococke** defendant. The Issue joyned A Gen[rl] Issue:

Jurymen:

Joshua Coggeshall foreman	Mallecai Roades
James Man	Charles Mecarta
John Rogers	Georg Halsall
Tho Burgis	Samuell Stapleton
John Crandall	John Maxon
Joseph Tripp	John Rise

Verdict wee finde for the defendant cost of court: Judgment Granted: cost paid.

An action of unjust mollestation damage one hundred pounds sterling bearing date the 15th of May 1679 Com[m]enced by **Christopher Almy** plantiff against **John Pococke** defendant. The issue joyned A Gen[rl] Issue. Verdict Wee finde for the plantiff damage three pounds and Cost of Court.

An action of Debt debt and damage five hundred pounds sterling bearing date the 9[th] day of August 1679 Com[m]enced by **Phillip Smith** the surviveinge Executor of **John Clarke** late of Newport phiscitian deceassed plantiff against Majo[r] **Peleg Sanford** Gen[rl] Treasurer of the Governo[r] and Company of the English Collony of Rhode Island and Providence Plantations, defendant on the said Collonys behalfe. Issue Joyned Generall Not Guilty: Judgment Granted.

Jurrymen:

Josh. Coggeshall fo-ma.	Georg Halsall
James Man	Sam[ll] Stapleton
John Rogers	Charles Mecarta
John Crandall	John Rise
Joseph Tripp	Edward Lay
Malica Roads	John Manchester

The Jurry haveing been three times sent forth the Court accepts the verdict: Verdict wee finde for the defendant Cost of Court.

An action of the case for unjust Mollestation damage 60£ sterling beareing date the 16[th] of August 1679 com[m]enced by **Christopher Almy** plantiff against **John Pococke** defenda[t], The defenda[t] pleading a nonsuite in this case, It being a matter that had its beginning in the Collony of Plymoth upon the plea of Lands: The Court upon the consideration of the matter doe see cause to grant a nonsuite in the case.

An action of Debt Damage tenn pounds sterling Com[m]enced by **William Downing** plantiff against **Marke Athy** defenda[t]. The Issue Joyned by the Aturnys a Gen[rl] Issue Not Guilty. The Jurry haveing been three times sent forth the Court accepts the verdict.

Verdict wee finde for the plantiff Debt and Damage five pounds Equivelent to mony and Cost of Court; Judgment granted.

An action of Debt debt and Damage 8£ sterling beareing date the 12[th] of July 1679 Com[m]enced by **William Allin** plantiff against **Samuell Reape** defendant The Issue joyned by the Aturnys a Gen[rl] Issue not Guilty. Verdict wee finde for the plantiff Debt and Damage three pounds seven-teen shillings and tenn pence and Cost of Court: Judgment Granted.

An action of sclaunder and Defamation Damage four hundred pounds [47/49] sterling beareing date the 12[th] of July 1679. Com[m]enced by **William Allin** plantiff against **Samuell Reape** Defendant. Upon the Reading and peruseing the Declaration and answer, and much adjetation thereon, finding that there was a mistake in the plantiffs declaration. Incertinge towards the latter part thereof five hundred pounds in stead of four, the Court doe Judge it to be only mistake or misprission in the scribe, and therfore see cause that it shall be noe barr in law, but that the case proceed to Tryall and the Declaration mended.

Jurrys verdict Wee finde for the plantiff, twelve pence Damage and Cost of Court. Judgment granted.

An action of the case Damage one hundred pounds sterling beareing date the 21[th] of July 1679 Com[m]enced by **John Sanford** of the Towne of Portsmouth plantiff against **Elias Williams** late Inhabitinge in the said Towne defendant. The partys plantiff and defendant in the action last above Entred have severally oblidged them selves each to other in Open Court in the sum of one hundred pounds sterling to abide and stand unto the award and detirmination of M[r] **Walter Clarke** and Major **Peleg Sanford** of the Towne of Newport, and **William Wodell** of the Towne of Portsmouth or any to of them in or concerning the matter of difference Relating to the said action: And it is further agreed between the said plantiff and defendant, that the said partys have power to meet at the house of Capt[n] **William Correy** on the Twentith day of November next insueing, and soe from time to time untill the 20th day of December next to detirmin the said differance: The plantiff and defendant have in confirmation of the above-written severally to each other Interchainged the sum of one shilling of mony in Court.

An action of the case for unjust Mollestation damage seventy pounds sterling bearing date the 26 of July 1679 Com[m]enced by **John Pococke** plantiff against **Christopher Almy** and **Job Almy** defendants. The Issue Joyned is Gen[rl]. Not Guilty.

Jurrymen:

Josh. Coggeshall foreman	John Manchester
James Man	Charles Mecarta
John Rogers	Georg Halsall
Tho Burges	Samu[ll] Stapleton
John Crandall	John Rise
Jos. Tripp	Mallica Roades

The Jurry haveing been three times sent forth the Court accepts the verdict. Verdict Wee finde for the defendants Cost of Court.

An action of Debt due by bill debt and Damage forty pounds sterling bearing date the 26[th] of July 1679 Com[m]enced by **John Pococke** plantiff against **Christopher Almy** defendant. The defendant in his Answer Craveing a Nonsuite in the case, for that the declaration is not agreeable to the Origonall writt, upon a long debate of the matter the Court see cause to give leave to the plantiff to mend his declaration. Upon the consent of plantif and defendant this case is Referred for Tryall to the Gen[rl] Court of Tryalls to be held in May next.

An action of Debt upon account damage tenn pounds sterling, bearing date the 12[th] of Septemb[r] 1679 Com[m]enced by **Anthony Shaw** plantiff against **John Pococke** defend[t]. The Jurry haveing been three times sent forth the Court accepts the verdict. Jurrys Verdict Wee finde for the plantiff debt one shilling & fivepence, two pence damage and Cost of Court — Judgment granted.

An action of unjust Mollestation Com[m]enced by **Kathrine Dyre** widow plantiff against **Ann Dyre** widow defendant. The Court haveing heard much debate on the case: with consent this case is Referred to the Gen[rl] Assembly, for them to appoint and Authorize persons to give their detirmination for the Issuinge the said Widows differences.

An action of Debt by bill debt and damage tenn pounds sterlinge, beareing date the 6[th] of Septemb[r] 1679 Com[m]enced by **Seath Pope** plantiff against **Georg Halsall** Defendant. Issue Not Guilty.

Jurry:

Josh. Coggshall foreman	John Manchester
James Man	Charles Mecarta
John Rogers	Mallica Roades
Thomas Burgis	Edward Stapleton jun[r]
John Crandall	John Rise
Joseph Tripp	Nicholas Carr

Verdict wee finde for the plantiff the contents of the Bill and twelve pence damage and Cost of Court. Judgment granted.

On an Indictment by the Gen[rl] Solicetor against **Henry Timberlake** for ffornication com[m]itted with **Sarah Comby** alias **Megron**: he being **[48/50]** Mandamassed and in Court Called appeared: And demanded whether Guilty or not Guilty ownes Guilty. The court doe sentance him according to law to be whipt with fifteen stripes or to pay the sum of fforty shillings in or as mony to the Gen[rl] Treasury and pay fees.

On Indictment by the Gen[rl] Solicetor against **Sarah Comby** alias **Megram** for fornication Com[m]itted with **Henry Timberlake**, she being Mandamassed, and in Court called apeared by Henry Timberlake, who on her behalfe owned Guilty. The Court doe sentance her according to law to be whipt with fifteen stripes or to pay the sum of forty shillings in or as mony to the Gen[rl] Treasury and pay ffees. Henry Timberlake in Court Engageth the payment of forty shillings in or as mony for him selfe and forty shillings for Sarah Comby, to be truly paid to the Gen[rl] Treasurer, and pay officers ffees.

Upon Indictment by the Gen[rl] Solicetor against **John Mackandrew** alias **Andrews** for com[m]itting Adultery with **Mary Ridgly**: Hee being by the last Court bound to the court, and in Court called appeared. being askt whether Guilty or not Guilty, pleads not Guilty and Referrs for Tryall to God and the Cuntry.

Jurry:

Josh Coggeshall	John Manchester
James Mann	Charles Mecarta
John Rogers	Mallica Roades

Tho Burgis
John Crandall
Joseph Tripp
Edward Thurston jun^r
William Earll
John Remington

The Jurrys verdict. Guilty.

The court doe sentance the said John Andrews according to law to be sevearly whipt at two Townes and alsoe pay a fine of tenn pounds in or as mony unto the Gen^rl Treasury of this Collony.

Upon Indictment by the Gen^rl Solicetor against **Rowland Robinson** for ffornication Com[m]itted with **Mary Allin**. Being Mandamassed and in Court Called appeared being askt whether Guilty or not Guilty pleads not Guilty and Referrs himselfe to the Cuntry for Tryall.

Jurrymen:

Josh Coggeshall
James Man
John Rogers
John Crandall
Joseph Tripp
John Manchester
Mallica Roades
Charles Mecarta
Edwd Thurston ju^r
William Earll
John Remington
Lt James Barker

Verdict Not Guilty. The Court accepts the Verdict; And he is cleerd by proclamation paying ffees.

Upon Indictment by the Gen^rl Solicetor against **Mary Allin** for fornication Com[m]itted with **Rowland Robinson**, being Mandamassed, and in Court Called did not appeare.

Shuball Painter being by the last Court of Tryalls bound to the peace and good behaviour and his appearance at this Court, he being in Court Called appeared and proclamation made none appearing to accuse him, he is cleered paying ffees.

Upon an Indictment by the Gen^rl Solicetor against **John Ward** of Newport for misbehaveing himselfe and speaking in his own house contemptious words against the Authorety of this Collony: he being bound over and in Court Called appeared And being askt whether Guilty or not Guilty, pleads not Guilty, and Referrs himselfe for Tryall to God and the Cuntry:

Jurrymen:

Mr Phill: Smith foreman
John Rogers
John Crandall
Charles Mecarta
Ed: Thurston jun^r
Jer: Browne
John Paine
Hen. Tew
Phil. Doderidg
John Vaghan
John Bennitt
Tho: Brookes

Verdict not Guilty: The Court see cause to cleer him paying ffees.

Upon Indictment by the Grand Jurry against **Richard Smith** of Narragansett Merchant, for Indeavouringe to subject a part of this Collony to another Jurisdiction, he being bound to this Court and in Court Called, appeared, and being Askt whether Guilty or not Guilty: pleads that before he give his Answer the Court will consider his Exceptions to the Bill of Indictment. The said Mr Richard Smiths Exceptions haveing been in Court Read and seariously considered, and findinge the said Exceptions to be against two bills of Indictment not distinguishing Each, The Court order that the said Mr Richard Smith draw his Exceptions to each Bill pertickularly. The said Mr Richard Smith haveing presented his Exceptions to the aforesaid Bill and signed them under his hand, The Court on Serious Consideration thereof accept his Exceptions and see cause thereon to quash the Bill of Indictment.

Upon an Indictment by the Grand Jurry against **Richard Smith** of Narragansett ffor uttering many Contemptious words and speeches against the Authorety of this Collony, The said Mr Richard Smith haveing putt in his Exceptions against this second bill of Indictment, The Court Inquired of said Mr Smith, whither he owned himselfe to be one of the Inhabittants at Kings Towne in the Narragansett in the Kings province. He owned himselfe soe to be, Thereupon (that being omitted in the Indictment). The Court accept the Exceptions and quash the Bill.

The Court order that the said Mr Richard Smith be cleerd from both the Indictments against him, by open proclamation, he paying fees.

[49/51] Upon Indictment by the Gen^rl Solicetor, against **Peter Pylatt** a Negro, servant to **Christopher Holder** of Newport for Asaulting Battering and Ravishing **Elizabeth** the daughter of said Holder: The said Petter being called for and brought into the Court: his Indictment to him Read and he demanded off whither Guilty or not Guilty pleads not Guilty and Referrs himselfe for Tryall to God and the Cuntry.

Jurrymen:

Phillip Smith fo:man	Jerem~ Browne
James Man	John Paine
John Rogers	Henry Tew
John Crandall	Christopher Almy
Charles Macarta	John Cooke
Edwd Thurston ju^r	John Bennitt

Verdict: Guilty: The Court accept the Verdict.

The Courts sentance. That according to law he the said Peter Pylatt Negro shall suffer Death And that he shall from hence be carried to the Goall and there safely secured untill munday next which will be the tenth day of this instant month Novemb^r, and from the Goale on the said 10th day about two or three of the Clock after noone to be carried to the place of Execution the Gallos, and there to be hangd by the neck untill he be dead Dead.

Upon Indictments by the Gen^rl Solicetor against **Mary Ridgly**, for Adultery com[m]itted with **John Mackandrew alias Andrews**, and she in the last Court of Tryalls owning Guilty: This court doe sentance her to be punished and to pay a fine accordinge to the law of this Collony: And that the Governo^r or any two Asistants doe order and see the due Execution. And the Governo^r is desired to send to the Governo^r or Governm^t of Plymoth for her Returne to Authorety here.

Marke Athy and **Mercy** his wife being bound to the peace and good behavior and appearance at this Court being called appeared: and none accusing them for breach of bonds they are cleerd by proclamation paying ffees.

Joseph Woodward being bound by the last Court to the peace and good behavior: none appearing to accuse him, he is cleerd by proclamation paying ffees.

William Hieffernan being bound to this Court, and in Court Called did not appeare: The Court considering the great ilnes and weaknes he is under doe Excuse his non apearance, proclamation beinge made and none accussing him he is cleered paying ffees.

William Haukins being bound in the sum of twenty pound to the peace and good behavior, and his appearance at this Court, and hee haveinge been two severall times Called in this Court did not appeare nor any for him.

Aderman an Indian being bound to this Court and to the peace and good behavior, he being in court called, appeared, and proclamation made for his delivery Mr **Peter Talman** in court said that he the said **Alderman** [*sic*] had Indeavored to destroy the said Talmans ffamely: The Court see cause to cleer him: cleerd by proclamation paying ffees.

This Court upon the searious consideration of two actions the one an action of debt Com[m]enced by **Christopher Almy** and **Job Almy** plantiffs, against **John Pococke** defendant, the other an action of unjust Mollestation com[m]enced by **Christopher Almy** against **John Pococke** defend^t^ This Court upon the Consideration of the Exceptions put in by the defend^t^ doe see cause to Suspend Judgment at present in both actions, and doe Referr the consideration of the said action of unjust Mollestation unto the Gen^rl^ Assembly: And doe Referr the other case to the next sitting of this Court of Tryalls which on weighty consideration Is Adjourned untill the first Tuseday in January next then to sitt at this Towne of Newport.

Samuell Winsor, John Tillinghast and **Daniel Williams**, Chosen by the Towne of Providence to be on the Jurry, they not attending that service, are fined, each of them twenty shillings, and **John Dexter** chosen by said Towne is fined tenn shillings.

Abiah Carpenter chosen juryman by the Towne of Warwick, he not atending is fined twenty shillings.

January the 6th being Tuseday according to the aforesaid Adjournment the Court Called and satt.

In the action of Debt Com[m]enced by **Christopher** and **Job Almy** Executors to the Estate of the deceased **William Almy** joynt plantiffs, against **John Pococke** and **Mary** his wife Executrix to the deceased **John Almy** Defendants, wherein the Jurry found for the plantiffs as Exprest in their verdict: The Court then saw cause to suspend Judgment Referring it to this sitting: and upon debate of the matter the court see cause and doe grant Judgment in the case.

The Dep^t^ Governo^r^ Mr Walter Clarke doth enter his desen to this act of the Court.

Upon the action of unjust Mollestation Com[m]enced by **Christopher Almy** plantiff against **John Pococke** defend^t^ by this court Referred to the Gen^rl^ Asembly, who haveing againe Returned the matter to this Court, with their Advice, that they suppose Judgment in this case and all others of that Nature ought to be barred. This Court upon the searious consideration of the matter, doe see cause to Barr Judgment in the said case:

January the 6th this Court Desolved:

[50/52]

At a Generall Court of Tryalls held in his Majesties
Name at Newport the 10th of May *1680*

Major Peleg Sanford Governor
Mr Walter Clarke Dept Governor
Mr Thomas Ward Asistant
Mr Caleb Carr Asista-
Mr William Coddington Asista-
Mr Stephen Arnold Asista-
Captn Arthur ffenner Asista-
Mr Joseph Jenkes Asista-
Captn John Albro Asista-
Mr Georg Lawton Asista-
Captn Samuel Gorton Asista-
Captn John Green
John Sanford Recorder
Mr Edmund Calverly Genrl Serjant
Major Peleg Sanford Genrl Treasr
Mr Weston Clarke Genrl Aturney
Mr Robert Williams Solicetor

Grand Jurrymen Engaged
Mr Joshua Coggeshall foreman
Mr John Hulme
Mr John Pebody
Mr Richard Dunn
Mr Bartho- Hunt
Mr John Vaughan
Mr Robert Dennis
Mr Daniell Lawton
Mr Mallica Roades
Mr Thomas ffry
Mr Edward Thurston junr
Mr John Sisson

Proclamation in his Majties Name Openly made

Mr **John Carder** chosen by the Towne of Warwick to be on the Grand Jurry, and this court being informed that upon extraordnary occassion he is detained, and Mr **Malica Roades** by desire of said Carder presenting himselfe to serve in his stead the court doe accept the said Mallica Roades to be one of the Grand Jurry in the roome or stead of said John Carder.

On the Rehearing of an Action of Debt Com[m]enced by Mr **Christopher Almy** and Mr **Job Almy** Joint Executors to the Estate of Mr **William Almy** deceased, plantiffs against **John Pococke** and **Mary** his wife Executrix to the Estate of the deceassed **John Almy** defendants:

Jurrymen

Mr Jeremiah Browne foreman
John Vaughan junr
Thomas Peckham
William Edwards
Gyles Slocum junr
Thomas Cornell
Henry Brightman
Clement Weavour
James Browne
Samuell Hagbourne
Zachery Gant
William Hedge

Verdict: Wee find the Estate of John Almy to be Indebted to the plantiffs the Debt sued for with two pence damage and Cost of Court. The Court accept the Verdict and signe the Bill of Cost one pound nine shillings eight pence. Judgment Granted and alsoe Exicution thereon.

On the Rehearinge of an Action of debt Com[m]enced by **William Downing** plantiff against **Marke Athy** defendant Verdict. Wee find for the plantiff the debt sued for with three pence damage and Cost of Court. The Court accept the verdict and allow the Bill of Cost two pounds Eight shilling one penny. Judgment Granted. Appealed to the next Generall Asembly.

On the Rehearing of an Action of Debt Com[m]enced by **William Allin** plantiff against **Samuel Reape** defendant. The action being in court called plantiff and defendant appeared, and in Open Court mutualy agreed to withdraw the action: And Referred their differences, not only in and concerning the aforesaid action, but alsoe all other differences between the said plantiff William Allin and said defend^t Samuell Reape, untill the day of the date hereof unto Arbitration, of the Arbitrators hereafter named and doe Engage themselves each to other in the sum of one hundred pounds sterling, to stand to abide and performe the Award Arbitterment and detirmination of the Hono^rd Governo^r Peleg Sanford, and John Sanford Recorder, to be given and, singed [*sic*] under their hands, and the said Arbitrators to appoint the first time of their meeting, and the place where, and soe from time to time untill the matter be finished alwaies provided that the said agreement and award be drawne up in writeing on or before the last day of June next: This is owned and acknowlidged in Open Court the 12th May 1689.

On an Action of Debt due by bill Com[m]enced by **John Pococke** plantiff against **Christopher Almy** Defendant, and Referred by the Court in October unto this Court. The case called and after a long debate thereon between [51/53] plantiff and defendant The court finding the Declaration to be in the name of **John Pococke** and **Mary** his wife (who since is deceased) doe see cause that in the station the action is now in, the action cease.

On the Rehearing of an action of debt on account Com[m]enced by **Anthony Shaw** plantiff against **John Pococke** defend^t: The case being Called the defenda^t apeared, the plantiff did not apeare nor any for him.
The Court Grant Judgme^t to the defend^t and allow his bill of Cost, 2^li 07^s 02^d.

On an action of the case for unjust detainure Damage one hundred pounds sterll. beareing date the 12th of March 1679: Com[m]enced by **Jeremiah Mallice** and **John Roades**, plantiffs against **David Sheppe**, Resident at Pawtuxett in Warwicke, Defendant: The case in Court Called, and the defend^t not appeareing to answer nor any for him the plantiff Enters a Nihill dicett.
After the plantiffs plea the case Com[m]itted to the aforenamed Jurry:
Verdict, Wee finde for the plantiffs, and three pounds damage in mony or pay Equivelent with Cost of Court: The Court accepts the Verdict. Judgment Granted: A Rehearing Entered.

On an Action of debt damage Twenty pounds bearing date the 18th of March 1679 Com[m]enced by Mr **Paul Dudly** of Boston Merch^t plantiff against **Mordice Bowden** Resident at East Greenwich defend^t. The Case Called the defendant not appeareing The plantiff Enters a Nihill dicett: The Case Com[m]itted to the Jurry:
Verdict, Wee find for the plantiff the debt sued for, with five shillings damage and Cost of Court: The Court accepts the Verdict, and allow the Bill of Cost one pound sixteen shillings Eight pence: Judgment Granted.

On an Action of Debt said debt being due by Covennant damage thirty pounds ster-

ling: Com[m]enced by M[r] **John Pococke** in Right of his wife **Mary** formerly the widow and Relict of the deceased **John Almy** of Portsmouth plantiff against **Christopher Almy** of said Portsmouth defend[t] s[d] action bearing date the 18[th] March 1679/80. The Issue is Generall, not Guilty of the charge:
Verdict Wee find for the plantiff the debt sued for with six pence damage and Cost of Court: The Court accepts the Verdict, and allow the Bill of Cost, two pounds four shillings nine pence. Judgment Granted: A Rehearing Entered.

On an Action of unjust detainure damage tenn pounds sterll. bearing date the 27[th] day of March 1680 Com[m]enced by **Arthur Cooke** of Portsmouth plantiff against **Benjamin Congden** of said Portsmouth defendant: The Issue Joyned Gen[rl]: Verdict Wee find for the plantiff the mare sued for, and thre pence damage with Cost of Court: The Court accepts the Verdict: and allow the Bill of Cost, two pounds five shilings & one peny.
Judgment Granted — and Execution thereon.

On an Action of the Case for nonperformance of Covennant Damage thirty pound sterling: bearing date the 30[th] of March 1680 Com[m]enced by M[r] **William Browne** of Salem Merchant plantiff against **Thomas Brigs** of Prudance defend[t]. The action Cald: The defend[t] by his Aturny **John Pococke** acknowlidgeth a judgment owning he hath broaken Covennant, and promisseth payment of the Damages: The plantiff by his Aturny Majo[r] **Peleg Sanford** promisseth that if the said acknowlidgment and promiss be by the defend[t] truly performed, Execution shall not proceed and doth consent to allow one months time from the Desolution of this Court for the performance thereof: Judgment Granted, and the Bill of Cost allowed — nine shillings and Eleven pence.

On an action of debt Com[m]enced by **John Williams** of New-Shorrum plantiff against **Joshua Lamb** of Roxbury defend[t] the plantiff haveing not put in his Declaration the defendant Enters a Nonsute, The Court Grant Judgment and allow the Bill of Cost Eleven shillings and one peny.

On the Nonsute of an action of the case Com[m]enced by **James Barton** of Boston plantiff against **John Pococke** of Newport defend[t]: The Court Grant Judgment and signe the Bill of Cost Eight shillings four pence.

On the Nonsute of an action of the Case for Non-performance of Covennant, Com[m]enced by **Samuell Reape** plantiff against **Thomas Eldred** defendant: The Court Grant Judgment [and] allow the bill of Cost fifteen shillings and seven pence.

An Indictment by the Aturny Gen[rl] against **Shuball Painter** of Newport for Indeavoring Contrary to law to publish marriage in two publick meetings, about the month of March last in the Yeare 1679:80 unto **Hannah** the wife of **Thomas Martin**, and for keeping company with said Hannah, after being forbiden and forwarned by Authorety: he being bound to this Court and in Court Called, appeared. Pleads not Guilty, and Refers himselfe for Tryall to God and the Cuntry.
[52/54] The Jurry

Jeremiah Browne foreman	Clement Weaver
John Vaughan	James Browne
Thomas Packham	Zachery Gant

Gyles Slocum	William Hedge
Thom- Cornell	William Edwards
Hen. Brightman	James Renolds jun^{r}

Verdict Guilty: By the Court com[m]itted to the Gen^{rl} Serja^{ts} Custody till called for.

The Sentance of the Court is That **Shuball Painter** either be sett in the stockes for six howers time or pay twenty shillings to the Gen^{rl} Treasury, in mony betwixt this & next Thursday twelve of the clock — and that his bonds be continued while next Court and alsoe pay officers ffees.

An Indictment by the Gen^{rl} Aturny against **Georg Halsall** of Newport for breach of peace by abussing the Gen^{rl} serja^{t} in the Execution of his office being bound to this Court, and in Court Called appeared, Pleads not Guilty and Refers himselfe for Tryall to God and the Cuntry

The Sentance of the Court is that Georg Halsall pay a fine of twenty shillings in mony to the Treasury, and in the mean time to stand Com[m]itted till the said sum be paid and alsoe pay officers ffees.

An Indictment by the Gen^{rl} Aturny against **Samuell Reape** for breach of prisson &c — he being bound to this Court and in Court Called appeared: pleads not Guilty and Refers him selfe for Tryall to God and the Cuntry.

Jurry:

Jerem- Browne	Clement Weavor
John Vaughan	James Browne
Thomas Peckham	Zachery Gant
Gyles Slocum	William Hedge
Tho. Cornell	James Renolds
Hen. Brightman	Ebeneasar Slocum

Verdict Guilty; Com[m]itted to the Gen^{rl} Serj^{ts} Custody till called for.

The sentance of the Court is That Samuell Reape shall pay a fine of forty shillings mony to the Treasury and in the mean time to stand Com[m]itted till the said sum be paid and alsoe pay officers ffees.

An Indictment by the Gen^{rl} Aturny against **Thomas Starr** for breach of peace for speaking Abusive and Contemptious words against Authorety: he being in Court Called for appeared: Pleads Guilty: The court Com[m]itt him.

The sentance of the Cour[t] is That Thomas Starr doe give tenn pound bond for his good behaviour and appeareance at the Next Court and pay Officers ffees

An Indictment by the Gen^{rl} Aturney against **Thomas Starr** for breach of the Goale &c he being brought into Court, pleads Not Guilty, and Refers for Tryall to God and the Cuntry

The Verdict Guilty: The Court Com[m]itt hm to the Gen^{rl} Serjants Custody till called for

The sentance of the Court is That the said Thomas Starr shall pay a fine of forty shiling to the Treasurer, or else be whipt with fifteen stripes on the naked back, the 15th Instant and alsoe pay officers ffees.

An Indictment by the Gen^{rl} Aturney against **Arthur Dudly** now prissoner, for abuseing and [*illegible*]ing officers, and threatning the burning and ruening of houses: he being Called for and brought into Court: Ownes Guilty: The Court Com[m]itt him to the Gen^{rl} Serjants Custody till called for. The sentance of the Court is that Arthur Dudly shall either pay a fine of forty shillings mony to the Treasury, or be whipt with fifteen stripes on the naked back in the Towne of Newport on the twenty fifth of this instant May, and alsoe pay officers ffees.

Mr **John Coggeshall** being bound to this Court and in Court Called appeared. The Court see Cause to Continue the said Mr John Coggeshalls Bonds untill the next Court of Tryalls And Mr John Coggeshall in open Court did owne the said continuation of his Bonds.

Whereas this Court finding on Record of the Gen^{rl} Court of Tryalls held in October last That **William Haukins** was bound in a Bond of Twenty pounds for his appeareance at that Court, and twice in that Court Called, and he at the said Court not appearing nor any for him: This Court doe declare his Bonds of Twenty pounds fforfited to the Collony.

Epenetus Olny of Providence, **Moses Lippitt** of Warwick, and **Henry Hall** of Westerly chosen to be on the Grand Jurry and they not accordingly attending this Court are fined each of them twenty shillings

Jahleel Brenton of Newport, **Samuell Whipple** and **Zachery ffield** of Providence, **Benjamin Gorton**, and **John Low** of Warwick; and **John Randall** of Westerly Chosen to be on the Jurry of Tryalls. And they not accordingly attending this Court are fined each of them twenty shillings.

May 17th This Court desolved.

[53/55] At the Gen^{rl} Court of Tryalls held in his Majestys Name at Newport the 7th of September 1680

Present

Majo^{r} Peleg Sanford Governo^{r}
Mr Walter Clarke Dep^{t} Governo^{r}
Mr Thomas Ward Asista-
Mr Caleb Carr Asista-
Mr William Coddington Asista-
Majo^{r} John Albro Asista-
Mr George Lawton Asista-
Capt John Green Asista-
John Sanford Recorder
Edmund Calverly Gen^{rl} Serjant
Majo^{r} Peleg Sanford Gen^{rl} Treasu^{r}
Mr Weston Clarke Gen^{rl} Aturney

Grand Jurrymen Engaged
Mr Daniell Gould foreman
Mr Phillip Smith
Serja^{t}Clement Weaver
M^{r}Thomas Clifton
Mr Samuell Tieft
Mr Gidion ffreeborne
Mr William Wilbore
Mr Daniell Vaughaun
Mr Bartholomew Hunt Senr
Mr Peter Easton Senr
Mr Nathaniell Tomkins
Mr Thomas ffry

Proclamation openly made

Thomas Case being brought into this Court for Contempt of Authorety and he promissing to appeare, **Joseph Tripp** Engageth the said Thomas Case shall appeare at this Court when Called for by the Court

ffrancis Brayton jun^{r} in the sum of five pound Engageth to atend this Court on Thursday the 9th instant

Susanah Townsend Engageth to appeare tomorrow the 8th instant —

On the Rehearing of an action of debt due by Covenant Com[m]enced by **John Pococke** plantiff against **Christopher Almy** defend^{t} Tryed at the Gen^{rl} Court of Tryall held in September last:

Jurrymen

Mr John Stanton foreman	Edwd Thurston jn^{r}
Thomas Burge	John Paine
Richard Barnes	Willia~ Griffith
Thomas Rogers	Tho ffish jun^{r}
William Vincent	Tho Gould jun^{r}
John Albro jun^{r}	Hen. Timberlake

Verdict Wee finde for the defend^{t} Cost of Court: The Court accepts the Verdict and allow the Bill of Cost, two pounds four shillings. Judgment Granted.

On an action of Debt by Bill Damage twelve pounds sterll. Com[m]enced by **Thomas Eldred** plantiff against **Samuel Reape** defend^{t}, The said action bearing date the 13th of Aprill 1680: and now at this Court the defend^{t} taken on a Nihill dicet. The case Comitted to the Jurry

The Verdict: Wee finde for the plantiff five pounds thirteen shilling debt mony 12^{d} damage and cost of Court. The Court accepts the Verdict and allow the Bill of Cost one pound sixteen shillings and Eight pence

On an action Com[m]enced by Mrs **Kathrin Dyre** plantiff against **Robert Lavis** defend^{t}. The defend^{ts} Aturny **Henry Lilly** in open Court acknowlidged Judgment in the Case, The Court grant Judgment and allow the Bill of Cost tenn shillings six pence:

On an action Com[m]enced by **Robert Lavis** against Mrs **Kathrin Dyre** defend^{t} said action being in Court Calld plantiff and defend^{t} appeareing: with the advice of the Court doe Referr this case to the detirmination of Mr **Henry Bull** and Mr **John Williams**, and doe Engage them selves in the sum of five pounds each to other to stand to the award and Detirmination of said Arbitrators.

On an action Com[m]enced by **Samuell Batte** plantiff against **Benjam~ Congden** defend^{t} by **Weston Clarke** the plantiffs Aturny in Open Court withdrawne

An action Com[m]enced by **James House** plant^{f} against **Elias Williams** Defend^{t} in Court Called, and noe appeareance

On an action Com[m]enced by **Stephen Sebeer** plant^{f} against Sam^{ll}Reape defend^{t} in Court Called and noe appearance

On an action com[m]enced by **John Albro** jun^{r} plant^{f} against **Willia~ Champlin** Defend^{t} — the Courts Result and Judgment

Whereas there hath been an action Com[m]enced in this Court by **John Albro** jun^{r}

against **William Champlin** concerning the Title of a Certaine percell of land lying and being in the Narragansett or Niantick Cuntry in the Kings province in this his Maj^{ties} Collony of Rhode Island &c; and this Court haveing seariously Considered the premisses, and haveing on the debate of the matter Read his Maj^{ties} letter to us, dated ffebruary 12th 1678/9 wherein his Maj^{tie} hath Required all persons that lay any claime to the propriety of the soyle of the said lands, to make their claime thereunto before his Maj^{tie}, and that all things Relating thereunto, should Remaine in the same Condition as now they are or latly have been in, untill his Maj^{ties} pleasure be further Knowne whereupon the Resolve of this Court is at present to suspend the Tryall of the said Case [54/56]

On an action Com[m]enced by **Richard Bulgar** plantiff against **Thomas Dorfie** defend^{t}

In the Case last above mentioned the Court Resolves that the writt shall abate — because the Trespass was Com[m]itted in Plymouth Collony —

On an action Com[m]enced by **Kathrin Dyre** plant^{f} against **Ann Dyre** defend^{t} after a long debate the court see cause to sease the action.

On a Nonsute Entred in the office in an action Com[m]enced by **Christopher Almy** plantiff against **John Pococke** defend^{t}. The Court approve the Nonsute and allow the defend^{ts} Bill of Cost ffive shillings two pence.

On Indictment by the Grand Jurry against **William Maize** of Newport for selling strong drink by Retaile without a lycence: he being Mandamassed and in Court Called appeard, pleads Not Guilty and Referrs himselfe for Tryall to God and the Cuntry.

Jurriors	John Stanton foreman	Edwd Thurston
	Thomas Burge	John Paine
	Richard Barnes	Willia~ Griffith
	Thomas Rogers	Hen. Timberlake
	Willia~ Vinsent	Thomas Gould jun^{r}
	Gyles Perce	William Weeden

Verdict Guilty. William Maize is sentanced by this Court to pay the sum of fforty shillings in or as mony to the Gen^{rl} Treasury and alsoe pay officers ffees

On Indictment by the Grand Jurry against **Robert Litle** of Newport for selling strong Drinke by Retaile: he being Mandamassed and in court Called apeared — pleads not Guilty, Referrs himselfe for Tryall to God and the Cuntry. Verdict Guilty. Rober Litle sentanced by this Court for his offence to pay the sum of fforty shillings in or as mony to the Gen^{rl} Treasury and alsoe pay Officers ffees —

On Indictment by the Gen^{rl} Aturney against **Marke Athy** of Newport for sellinge strong drink by Retaile, he being Mandamassed and in Court Calld appeared pleads Not Guilty and Referrs for Tryall to God and the Cuntry. Verdict Guilty. Marke Athy sentanced by this Court to pay the sum of forty shillings in or as mony to the Gen^{rl} Treasury and alsoe pay officers ffees.

On Indictment by the Grand Jurry against **James Blower** of Newport for selling strong drink by Retaile to Negros and Indians, he being in Court Called, appeared. Pleads

Not Guilty and Referrs for Tryall to God and the Cuntry — Verdict Guilty. James Blower sentanced by this Court to pay for his offence the sum of forty shillings in or as mony to the Gen^{rl} Treasurer and alsoe pay officers ffees.

On Indictment by the Grand Jurry against **Elizabeth Holdersbee** [*sic*] of Portsmouth for selling strong drink by Retaile not haveing a lycence, she being in Court Called appeared. Pleads Guilty and Referrs to the mercy of the Bench. The Court sentance the said Elizabeth Holderbee [*sic*] for her offence to pay the sum of forty shillings in or as mony to the Gen^{rl} Treasury and alsoe pay officers fees

On Indictment by the Gen^{rl} Aturney against **Stephen Richardson** Liveing on the west side of pawcatuck River for Exercissing Authorety contrary to law — he being bound to this Court and in Court Called appeared and Referrs himselfe to the Bench. The Court on the searious Consideration of the Case and being desireous to prevent future troubles doe agree and detirmin that the said Stephen Richardson be Releassed of his bonds, he Engageing for the future, not to attempt the Mollestation of any of the Kings Subjects in this his Maj^{ties} Collony of Rhode Island and Providence Plantations and Kings Province, by any Authorety derived from any other Collony.

On Indictment by the Gen^{rl} Aturny against **Richard Rowland** for breach of the peace he being bound to this Court appeared, Ownes Guilty and Craves the favour of the Court. The Court sentance him to pay the sum of five shillings unto the Gen^{rl} Treasury and alsoe pay officers ffees.

On Indictment by the Gen^{rl} Aturney against **John Marshall** for breach of the peace being bound to this Court and in Court Called appeard; Ownes Guilty and Craves the Courts favour. The Court sentance him to pay the sum of five shillings unto the Gen^{rl} Treasurer and alsoe pay officers fees.

On Indictment by the Grand jurry against **Edward Lay** of Portsmouth for selling strong drink by Retaile without a Lycence: The Court on the Consideration of his Exceptions doe Referr the Case to the next Court.

On Indictmen[t] by the Gen^{rl} Aturney against **Thomas Case** for Contempt of Authorety and Breach of peace, he being bound and in Court Called appeared. Pleads not Guilty.

Jurriors

John Stanton f-man	Henry Timberlake
Thomas Rogers	Robert Brownell
William Vincent	John Crandall
Gyles Pearce	John Sisson
John Paine	William Weeden
Willia~ Griffith	William Haukins

Verdict Guilty: The sentance of the Court Concerning Thomas Case is that he stand bound in a Bond of tenn pounds mony, for three months time to be of good behaviour, towards all his Majesties leige people in this Collony but Espetially to them in Authorety and alsoe pay present ffees, and shall Remaine in durance untill bond as afore said be given. [55/57]

On Indictment by the Gen^{rl} Aturney against **ffrancis Brayton** jun^{r} of Portsmouth for Contempt of Authorety and breach of peace: Being bound and in Court Called, pleads not Guilty.

Jurriors

John Stanton ff.m	John Paine
Richard Barnes	Willia~ Griffith
Thomas Rogers	Hen~ Timberlake
Willia~ Vincent	Thom~ ffish jun^{r}
Gyles Pearce	John Sisson
Edwd Thurston	Robe^{t} Brownell

Verdict Guilty. The sentance of the Court concerning ffrancis Brayton ju^{r} is that he stand bound for three month time in a bond of tenn pound mony to be of good behavior towards all his Maje^{ties} liege people but espetially to those in Authorety and pay present fees, and to remaine in dureance untill he give in bond as afore-said.

Lt. **ffrancis Brayton** of the Towne of Portsmouth ffather unto ffrancis Brayton ju^{r} doth before the Governo^{r}, and Mr Thomas Ward, Mr William Coddington and Majo^{r} John Albro Asistants Recognize in the sum of tenn pounds in or as mony unto our soverraigne Lord the King, for the peaceable and good behavio^{r} of his aforesaid sonn ffrancis Brayton according to the sentance of this Court Concerning him — and alsoe promissed to pay officers ffees.

On Indictment by the Gen^{rl} Aturney against **Hannah Spooner** for haveing begotten and brought forth a childe of her Body not being lawfully Married. She being bound to this Court and in Court Called appeared, with the childe Ownes Guilty and affirmed in Open Court that Mr **John Coggeshall** Senr was the father of the said childe, acknowlidging her former Examinations and Relations to be truth.

The Courts Sentance is that the said Hannah Spooner doe truly pay unto the Gen^{rl} Treasurer of this Collony the sum of one pound six shill^{s} eight pence in or as mony — On or before the 30th day of this instant month September — or else to be severly whipt with 15 stripes on the naked back in the Towne of Newport by the Order of the Governo^{r}, Dep^{t} Governo^{r} or any two Asistants and alsoe pay officers ffees.

On Indictment by the Gen^{rl} Aturney against **John Coggeshall** of Newport being the Reputted ffather of a childe begotten begotten [*sic*] of **Hannah Spooner** and by her lately brought forth — he being bound to this Court and in Court Called appeared; and owned that according to the law of England, by the womans accusation, guilty of being the Reputed ffather, and Referrs himselfe to the Judgment of the Bench.

The Courts Sentance is that the said John Coggeshall shall well and truly pay or cause to be paid unto the said Hannah Spooner, the sum of three pounds fourteen shillings, for and toward, the Maintanence of and for the charges of the birth of the male child borne of the Body of said Hannah Spooner on the ninteenth of May last whereof the said John Coggshall is by law the Reputed father; on or before the fifteenth day of this instant in Manner following that is to say the one halfe of the said sum being thirty seven shillings currant mony the other halfe of the said sum being thirty seven shillings to be paid in good provissions fitt for famely uses at mony price, and alsoe that from and after the said fifteenth of this Instant the said John Coggshall shall pay or cause to be paid unto the said Hannah Spooner the sum of three shillings in pay as above-said every week weekly untill there shall be further Order taken in the matter by two or more of the Majestrates liveing in the Towne of Newport, for the future Maintanence of the said child according to Law; and alsoe pay officers ffees:

Shuball Painter beinge bound by the last Court, and his appeareance at this Court in Court Called appeared; And This Court on the Consideration of the case doe see cause and doe continue his Bonds untill the next Court of Tryalls —

Thomas Starr being bound by the last Court and his appeareance at this Court and in Court Called did not appeare. The Court doe therefore sentance him the forfiture of his Bond unto the Gen^{rl} Treasurer and alsoe payment of officers ffees.

Jonathan Knight of Warwick and **John Badcock** of Westerly chosen to serve on the Grand Jurry and not attending that service are fined.

Thomas Rogers of Newport, **Isaac Lawton** & **Thomas Wayte** of Portsmouth **Thomas Hopkins** of Warwick and **Nicolas Cotterill** of Westerly chosen to serve on the Jurry of Tryalls and not attending that service are fined

New Shorrum fined for noe Returne of Jurrymen

Kings Towne fined for noe Returne of Jurrymen

James Towne fined for noe Returne of Jurrymen

The Court desolved the 14th of September

[56/58]

At the Gen[rl] Court of Tryalls held in his Majestys Name
At Newport the 29th of March *1681*:

Present

Majo[r] Peleg Sanford Governo[r]
M[r] Walter Clarke Dep[t] Governo[r]
M[r] Thomas Ward Asista~
M[r] Caleb Carr Assista~
M[r] William Coddington Assista~
M[r] Joseph Jencks Asista~
Majo[r] John Albro Asista~
M[r] George Lawton Asista~

Grand Jurrymen Engaged
M[r] Edward Greenman foreman
M[r] Benedict Arnold
M[r] Henry Wood
M[r] Stephen Mumford
M[r] Joseph Nicolson
M[r] Hugh Parsons
M[r] Josiah Arnold
M[r] Henry Timberlake
M[r] Clement Weaver
M[r] George Halsall
M[r] James Man
M[r] Thomas ffry
M[r] Henry Palmer

Elias Williams plantiff. **James House** Defendant: In Court Called noe appeareance.

Major **Peleg Sanford** plantiff against **Richard Tarr** defend[t] in an action of Debt (by Bill) bearing date the 14[th] of September 1680. Debt and damage Seven pounds sterling: The Case being Cald the defendant not appearing the plantiff Enters a Nihill dicett

The case com[m]itted to the Jurry whoe were

James Barker jun[r] foreman
Thomas Coddington
John Ward
James Weeden
Samson Shearman
Richard Pearce
John Maccoone
Stephen Mumford
Caleb Carr jun[r]
Samuell Cranston
William Brenton
Charles Crosthwait

Verdict Wee finde for the plantiff ffour pounds four shillings as is due by Bill, Damage twelve shillings and Cost of Court: The Court accepts the Verdict and allow the Bill of Cost one pound Eight shillings: Judgment Granted: Execution given forth.

Samuell Bennett plantiff. **Thomas Gould** Defendant:
In Court Called. Noe appearance.

Kathrin Dyre plantiff. **Thomas ffry** Defendant:
In Court Called. Noe appearance.

Walter Todd Plantiff. **Eleazer Collins** Defendant.
In Court Called. Noe appearance.

James Dennis Plantiff **John Veale** Defendant.
Withdrawne in Court by M[r] John Williams

James Dennis Plantiff: **Symon Pullen** Defend
Withdrawne in Open Court by M[r] Caleb Carr

Zacheriah Curtice Plantiff: **Clement Wever** Defendant In Court Called the plantiff not appearing the defendant Enters a Nonsute —

Edward Lay of the Towne of Portsmouth, being Indicted for sellinge strong drink by Retaile without a Lycence, and the case being Referred by the last Court unto this Court, and he being in this Court Called did not appeare: This Court doe sentance him the said Lay to pay the sum of fforty shillings unto the Generall Treasury — and pay officers ffees.

Upon Indictment by the Gen[rl] Aturney against **Rebeckah Sanford** for ffornication, She being Mandamassed, and in Court Called did not appeare: The Court doe sentance the said Rebeckah to pay to the Gen[rl] Treasury the sume of forty shillings in cuntry pay or one pound six shillings eight pence mony.

Emanuall Wooley of the Towne of Newport being bound in the sum of tenn pound to the peace and good behaviour, and his appeareance at this Court. And he being in Court Called did not appeare: The Court doe therefore sentance him the said Wooley the fforfiture of his said bonds to be paid to the Gen[rl] Treasury and alsoe pay officers ffees.

Upon Indictment by the Gen[rl] Aturney against **Thomas Joanes** of Newport for being an abetter or Reciever of a firkin of Butter ffelloniously taken by a Negro Called **Rutter** Servant to M[rs] **Layouge**: said Joanes being a prissoner, and brought into Court, his charge to him Read and he askt whether Guilty or not Guilty. Ownes Guilty: The Court doe sentance the said Thomas Joanes to pay the sum of Twenty shillings in mony to the Gen[rl] Treasury or soe much in his Service as the Authorety of this Collony shall see cause to Order: and alsoe pay Officers ffees:

Edward Bayly of the Towne of Newport being by the Gen[rl] Aturney Indicted for breach of peace, and he beinge bound to this Court, and in Court Called appeared, and ownes Guilty. The Court doe sentance the said Edward Bayly to pay three shillings four pence in mony to the Gen[rl] Treasury, and alsoe pay Officers ffees.

Upon Indictment by the Gen[rl] Aturney against **Christopher Almy** of the Towne of Portsmouth for Breach of peace and Misbehavior, for which [57/59] Charge being Bound unto this Court: And in Court Called, and askt whether Guilty or not Guilty — desired of the Court some time to Consider, before he gave his possetive answer which being Granted he after presented the Court with his Exceptions

The Court upon the seriouse Consideration of the Case and the Exceptions of the said Christopher Almy: doe see cause to quash the Bill.

Shuball Painter of Newport being bound by the last Court of Tryalls for his appeareance at this Court and in Court Called Appeared:

This Court upon the seariouse Consideration of the Case doe continue his Bonds unto the next Court of Tryalls —

Job Almy of the Towne of Portsmouth being bound to the peace and good Behaviour and his appeareance at this Court: In Court Called appeared, and his accuser Christopher Almy in Court Owninge what was said by him was in passion

Proclamation being made and none appearing to accuse him the said Job Almy he is cleerd by proclamation payinge officers ffees —

Amos Wastcott of Warwick chosen to serve on the Grand Jurry and not attending that service is fined twenty shillings —

John Peckham of Newport, **Edward Enman** and **John Angell** of Providence, **John Coggeshall** of Portsmouth, and **Henry Tew** for James Towne, chosen to serve on the Jurry of Tryalls, and not attending that service, are fined Each of them Twenty Shillings —

This Court desolved the 31st of March.

At the Gen^{rl} Court of Tryalls Held in his Maj^{ties} Name
at Newport the 6th of September *1681*

Majo^{r} Peleg Sanford Governo^{r}	Grand Jurrymen Engaged
Mr Walter Clarke Dep^{t} Governo^{r}	Mr William Hiscox foreman
Mr John Easton Assista-	Serj^{t} Clement Weaver
Mr Caleb Carr Assista-	Serj^{t} John Stanton
Mr William Coddington Assista-	Serj^{t} John Pebody
Capt Arthur ffenner Asista-	Captn William Correy
Mr Joseph Jencks Asista-	Lt ffrancis Brayton
Mr Richard Arnold Asista-	Mr John Odlin
Majo^{r} John Albro Assista-	Mr Benedict Arnold
Mr George Lawton Assista-	Mr Mordica Bowden
John Sanford Recorder	Mr Edward Inman
Thomas ffry Gen^{rl} Serja^{t}	Mr Samuell Hagbourne
Mr Weston Clarke Treasurer	Mr Walter Roades
Mr Edmund Calverly Gen^{rl} Aturney	
Mr Edmund Calverly Solicetor	

On the 4th day of October added by the Court to the Grand Jurry (in the roomes Edward Inman, Sam^{ll} Hagbourne and Walter Roads) Mr John Williams, Joseph Morie, Mr John Easton jun^{r}: And the 5th day of October Mr Lawrance Turner Mr Walter Roades Mr Barthol. Hunt sen^{r}, Mr Henry Timberlake Mr James Blower

David Lake plantiff against **Joseph Cowell** of Boston defenda^{t} in an action of [*sic*] bearing date the 31st of March 1681: damage 20$^{£}$ sterling —
a Nihill dicett: The case Com[m]itted to the Jurry:
Jurrio^{rs}:

James Weeden foreman	Joseph Smith
John Vaughan jun^{r}	Thom. Eaton
Thomas Peckham	John Manchester
William James	Tho. Manchester
John Crandall	Dan^{ll} Vaughan
Henry Austance	George Havens

Verdict wee finde for the Plantiff Debt and damage Eight pounds & one shilling in New England silver mony & cost of Court. The Court accept the Verdict and allow the bill of Cost one pound sixteen shillings & eight pence

Robert Brooks plantiff against **Samuel Banks** defendant in an Action of Assault and battery bearinge date the 4th of July 1681 damage. a Nihill Dicett, the defend^{t} Refuseing to answer the case according to law — The Case Com[m]itted to the jurry: John Crandall Excepted against in his roome added to the Jurry Edward Thurston jun^{r}
Verdict wee finde for the plantiff fifty shillings in silver and Cost of Court. The Court accept the Verdict and allow the Bill of Cost, 2$^{£}$ 1^{s} 1^{d}.

Sep^{tr} the 8th in the Roome of Ser^{t} Clement Weaver Bened^{t} Arnold & Mordica Bowden were added Dan^{ll} Stanton, Thomas Brooks & Caleb Carr jun^{r}:

[58/60] **Robert Brookes** of Newport plaintiff against **Gersham Lockwood** Defenda^{t} in an action of Asault and Battery beareing date the [?]th of July 1681 Damage. a Nihill

Dicett the defend[t] Refuseing to answer according to law. The Case Com[m]itted to the Jurry. Verdict Wee finde for the plaintiff fifty shillings in silver and Cost of Court. The Court accept the Verdict, and allow the Bill of Cost — 2£. 1s. 1d.

Benedict Arnold of Newport plaintiff against Serjt **Clement Wever** defendant in an action of Trespass, bearing date the 6th of July 1681: damage 100£ sterling in the case in the roome of **Thomas Peckham** One the Jurry **Edw[d]** Thurston jun[r]. The Case Com[m]itted to the Jurry : Verdict wee finde for the plantiff tenn shillings in mony damage and Cost of Court — The Court accept the Verdict and allow the Bill of Cost 2£. 6s. 10d.

On an Indictment in March last by the Gen[rl] Aturny against **Christopher Almy** of the Towne of Portsmouth for Misbehaviour: being mandamassed and in Court Called appeared Haveing been three times (after his charge openly read in Court) asked whether Guilty or not Guilty would not give a possetive answer, on which the Court granted him liberty to Consider the matter till next morninge:

September the 10th the Court againe Called him and his Indictment againe Read, and he three times asked whether Guilty or not Guilty and still he would not give a possetive answer Therefore the Court doe Com[m]itt him to the Cunstables Custod[y] till Cald for.

Whereas M[r] Christopher Almy of the Towne of Portsmouth was at his Maj[ties] Gen[l] Court of Tryalls held in Newport in March 1680 Indicted by the Gen[l] Aturny for his Misbehaviour as by the Indictment found by the Grand jurry will appeare And being in this present Court Called and asked whether he was Guilty or not guilty would not give answer according unto law, Butt in most Contemptious upbraiding manner abussed the Kings Authorety and Offices saying that he was as good a man as the best of them, their places only Excepted, that the Recorder and Gen[rl] Aturny were Knaves petifull begerly fellows, with many other Revileing abussive and unbeseeming expressions nevertheless the Court in their Moderation, gave time unto the said M[r] Almy untill the next day to make answer: and on that day the said Almy being againe Called to make answer unto the Bill of Indictment which he Refuseing the Court see cause for the preservation of the Kings peace, and the prevention of such like Misbehaviours for the future if it may bee, To sentance the said M[r] Almy as followeth —

The Court haveing taken into their searious Consideration the severall abusses and Reflections cast upon his Maj[ties] Authorety in this Collony and the officers thereof, by M[r] Christopher Almy of Portsmouth, Doe therefore Adjudge and sentance the said Christopher Almy to make and Humble acknowlidgment satisfactory to the Govern[r] & Assistants on the Island for his Misbehaviour and abussis as aforesaid. And the same to be done in writeing under his hand, and delivered unto the Governo[r] Dep[t] Governo[r], or any one Assistant on this Island that it may be presented and veiwed by the Governo[r] and Assistants on the Island at or before the 16th Instant September; and pay officers fees. Otherwise the sentance and Judgment of this Court is That the said Christopher Almy shall pay a fine of five pounds in mony or pay Equivolent to mony unto the Gen[rl] Treasurer of this Collony at or before the 20th of this Instant September: And in case the said Christopher Almy within the time aforesaid doe not make the aforesaid acknowlidgment or pay the said sum, then the said sum of five pounds shall be taken by distraint by a warrant under the hand of the Governo^{r}, and Dep^{t} Governo^{r}, or any two Asistants directed to the Gen^{rl} Serja^{t} who shall Execute and performe the same. Ordered: that the officers fees shall be paid out of the afore-said five pounds if said Christopher Almy pay the same or it be distrained.

On an Indictment of the Grand Jurry in March last against **John Baily** of Portsmouth for fornication with widow **Sutten Browne**, he being [in Court, *crossed out*] Mandamassed and in Court Called appeared, The Court upon the Consideration of his Exceptions doe see cause to quash the Bill.

On Indictment of the Grand Jurry in March last against the widow **Sutten Browne** now wife of **John Baily** for fornication, she being mandamassed and in Court Called did not appeare, yett the Court see Cause to quash the Bill.

On Indictment by the Gen^{rl} Aturny against **John Peckham** jun^{r} of the Towne of Newport for Contempt of Authorety — being bound to this Court and in Court Called appeared his Indictment Read and he askt whether Guilty or not Guilty plead, Not Guilty:

On this Case in the Roome of Thom~ Peckham and John Crandall, were [59/61] on the Jurry: Thomas Rogers, John Albro jun^{r}: The Case Com[m]itted to the Jurry: — Verdict Guilty. The Sentance of the Court is that the said John Peckham doe on or before the 20th of this instant month September make his Humble acknowlidgment in writeing under his hand for his said misbehaviour, to the satisfaction of the Governo^{r} and Councell on the Island and pay officers fees otherwise shall on or before the said 20th of Septem^{r} pay unto the Gen^{rl} Treasurer of this Collony the sum of forty shillings in mony or pay Equivelent to mony, which if he doe not performe Then the said sum of forty shillings shall be taken by distraint by the Gen^{rl} Serja^{t} by vertue of a warrant under the hands of the Governo^{r} and Dep^{t} Governo^{r}, or any two Asistants: And the officers fees to be paid out of the fine.

On Indictment by the Gen^{rl} Aturny against **Thomas Deway** for breach of law &c beinge a prissoner and Called for was brought into Court his Indictment Read and he asked whether Guilty or not Guilty and Referrs his Tryall to ye jurry. Verdict Not Guilty. The Court accept the Verdict and order the said Deway to be cleerd by proclama~ paying officers ffees. The ffees being Engaged for by the Asistants of Providence, cleerd by proclamation.

On Indictment by the Gen^{rl} Aturny against Mr **Benedict Arnold** of Newport for breach of Law &c: Enters Traverce: pleads Not Guilty. Verdict Not Guilty: The Court accept the Verdict and Order his cleering by proclamation paying ffees.

On Indictment by the Gen^{rl} Aturny against **James Exeny** for ffornication with **Elizabeth** the daughter of **John Parker**: Confessed Guilty. The Court sentance the said James Exeny to pay the sum of one pound six shillings eight pence in or as mony to the Gen^{rl} Treasurer and pay ffees, John Parker aforenamed hath Engaged the payment of the fine &c.

On Indictment of the Gen^{rl} Aturny against **Elizabeth Exeny** the daughter of **John Parker** for fornication: by her said father confesseth Guilty. The Court doe sentance her to pay the sum of one pound six shillings eight pence in or as mony to the Gen^{rl} Treasury and pay ffees:

Shubell Painters fformer Bonds are Continued untill the next Court. This Court on searious Consideration of some matters of Consequence yett depending and cannot now be finished, Doe Adjourne untill the first Tuseday in October next, then to meet and sitt at the house of **William Maize** in Newport.

October the 4th 1681: The Court Called and Satt.

On Indictment of the Gen^{rl} Solicetor against Captn **Jacob Steers** now prissoner for being a Sea Rober, and that hee and his Confederates did Rob some of his Maj^{ties} subjects &c — : Said Captn Steers being brought into Court, and his Indictment to him Read and he being askt whether Guilty or not Guilty pleads Not Guilty, and Referrs for Tryall to God and the Cuntry:

Jurry:

James Weeden foreman	Daniel Vaughan
Thomas Peckham	Joseph Carder
William James	John Cooke Junr
John Crandall	Alex^{r} Coleman
John Manchester	John Ireson
Tho. Manchester Junr	William Griffith

The case Com[m]itted to the jurry: Verdict Not Guilty: The Court Recieve the Verdict. The Court on the Searious Consideration of the matter, their sentance is that all and every part of the Estate Seized from Captn **Jacob Steers**, that lys now under Seizure in this Collony shall soe continue for the full time of one whole yeare and one day from the time of the first Seizure thereof; Except any person in the intrim doe appeare and lay claime thereto or any part thereof, and in a due progress thereof Recover the same: Only Excepted the present discharge of all Necessary Expences, and the Charges and Expences of others of his Company that have been here apprihended and Tryed:

On Indictment of the Gen^{rl} Solicetor against **William Adams** now prissoner for being a Sea Rober &c: he being brought into Court and his Indictment to him Read, and he askt whether Guilty or not Guilty — Pleads Not Guilty and Referrs himselfe for Tryall to God and the cuntry — objects against **William James** in whose Roome on the Jurry was **Gilbert Magick**. Verdict Not Guilty: The Sentance of the Court against him is the same as afore Exprest against Captn Jacob Steers.

On Indictment of the Gen^{rl} Solicetor against **John Osbourne** now prissoner for being a Rober &c, hee being brought into Court and his Indictment to him Read, and he askt whether Guilty or Not Guilty — pleads Not Guilty. The Case Committed to the Jurry: Verdict Not Guilty: **[60/62]**

The Sentance of the Court is that John Osbourne shall depart this Collony within three days after this 7th of October, and shall not continue here longer Except by leave of the Governo^{r}. And if he bee found in this Collony Contrary to this sentance, then by warrant under the hand of the Governo^{r}; Dep^{t} Governo^{r}, or any Assistant or more to be apprihended, and sent to prisson for his Contempt there to Remaine till by Authorety Released.

On Indictment by the Gen[rl] Solicetor against **John Johns** now prissoner, for Robery &c: he being brought into Court, and his Indictment to him Read, and askd whether Guilty or not Guilty: — pleads Not Guilty, and Referrs for Tryall to God and the Cuntry. The Case Com[m]itted to the Jurry: Verdict Not Guilty: The Sentance of the Court against him is the same as is afore Exprest against John Osbourne:

On Indictment of the Gen[rl] Solicetor against **Archebell fforest** now prissoner for Contempt of Authorety — he being brought into Court and his Indictment to him Read and he Askt whether Guilty or not Guilty ownes Guilty: The Courts Sentance is That Archebell fforest within tenn days after his cleering himselfe of the prisson by paying ffees shall depart this Collony, and shall not returne againe to Inhabitt within any parts thereof without leave of two Assistants of this Collony under their hands signed; And if Contrary to this Sentance he shall at any time hereafter be found It shall be in the power of any Asistant Warden or Conservator of the peace in this Collony to Cause the said fforest to bee apprihended, and sent to the Goale in Newport, and in the said Towne to be severly whipt with twenty five stripes on the naked back, and the same to be done by the appointment of any one Majestrate or more in Newport, and then againe to depart out of this Collony: And soe often as found Transgressing this Sentance to Recive the like punnishment.

On Indictment of the Gen[rl] Solicetor against **Richard Knigh** [*sic*] Inhabiting in Ports[mouth] for breach of law by Contempt: he beinge a prissoner and brought into Court and askt whether Guilty or not Guilty, pleads Not Guilty. The Jurrys Verdict Guilty: The Sentance of the Court is That **Richard Knight** for his Transegresion shall soe long as he Remaines in this Collony be that person that shall be the whipper of **Archebell fforest** at all times when the said fforest by his Transegressing the Sentance of this Court shall be brought to punnishment, and if the said Knight upon the Com[m]and of any one or more Assistants in this Collony from time to time shall refuse soe to doe, then shall he forfitt the sum of forty shillings to be forthwith paid to the Gen[rl] Treasury or Else the said sum shall from time to time be taken by distraint by warrant under the hands of any one or more Assistants & pay fees.

Westerly fined for noe Returne of Jurrymen
Shorrum fined for noe Returne of Jurrymen
Kings Towne fined for noe Returne of Jurrymen

[61/63]

Att the Gen^rl Court of Tryalls held in his Maj^ties Name at Newport the 28th day of March *1682*

Majo^r Peleg Sanford Governour
Mr Walter Clarke Dep^t Governo^r
Mr John Easton - Assistant
Mr Caleb Carr - Asista~
Mr William Coddington - Asista~
Mr Joseph Jencks - Asista~
Mr Richard Arnold - Asista~
Majo^r John Albro - Asista~
Mr George Lawton - Asista~
Captn John Green - Asista~
John Sanford - Recorder
Thomas ffry Gen^rl Serja^t
Mr Weston Clarke Gen^rl Treasu^r
Mr Edmund Calverly Atturney
Mr Edmund Calverly Soliceto^r

Grand Jurrymen Engaged
Mr Daniell Gould fforeman
Mr John Vaughan
Mr John Allin
Mr Benjamin Carpenter
Mr Gidion ffreeborne
Mr Israell Arnold
Mr John Maxon
Mr John Sisson
Mr Benjamin Devell
Mr Henry Lilly
Mr Henry Palmer
Mr John Rathbone

On the Rehearing of an Action of Trespass Comenced by Mr **Benedict Arnold** Plantiff against Serja^t **Clemant Weaver** Defendant: after a long plea the case com[m]itted to the Jurry:

Jurriors: Henry Tew foreman
Mr John Rogers
Edward Thurston jun^r
Lt John Holmes
Bartho. Hunt jun^r
John Wilkinson
Benj^a Shearman
John Albro jun^r
John Cooke jun^r
Jeremiah Browne
Caleb Carr jun^r
Henry Timberlake

Verdict Wee find for the plantiff fifteen shillings in mony damage Cost of Court. The Court accepts the Verdict: and allow the bill of Cost two pounds seventeen shillings five pence:

An action Com[m]enced by Lt **John Green** plantiff against **Marke Athy** defendant, in Court Cald noe appeareance.

An Action by **Robert Litle** against **George Smith** defend^t. Cald noe appeareance

On an Action of the Case Com[m]enced by **William Maize** of Newport plantiff against **Joseph Cowell** of Boston Defend^t Dammag 20^£ sterll. bearing date the 8th of September 1681: in this action **Henry Lilly** on the Jurry in the Roome of **John Albro**: Verdict Wee find for the defendant Cost of Court. The Court accept the Verdict and allow the Bill of Cost

On an Action Com[m]enced by Capt **Josiah Hubbart** Aturny unto Mr **Thomas Partridge** of fflushing on Long Island plantiff, it being an Action of the Case for detayning a parcell of land Damage 150^£ sterlinge against **John Williams** of Newport defendant — and bearing date the 15th of October 1681: The Case being Called the Plantiff and Defendant appeared. The defendant putt in his Exceptions for a Barr to the Action; And the Court haveinge seariously Viewed and Considered the Plantiffs declarations and finding that in the declaration there is not such certainty and verety as law Requires doe therfore detirmin the abatement of the said action.

On an action Com[m]enced by **John Abraham** against **John Simons** in Court Cald noe appearance

On an action Com[m]enced by M^{r} **ffrancis Brinley** against **Daniell Crum**[m] in Court Called noe apperance

On an Indictment by the Genl Solicetor against Serja^{t} **Clement Weaver** for breach of law by fenceing in a hie-way — Entred Traverce: in Court Called appeared: Serjant Clement Weaver being Indicted in Court for takeing in the Com[m]ons and hie-way of the Towne of Newport, and makeing his alligation, that any of the Towne of Newport might not be Judge or Jurry in said Case: which alligations though the Court Could not altogether allow of — yett notwithstanding the said Clement Weaver makeing a Rationall motion in Court that himselfe and Mr **Benedict Arnold** might choose either of them one man, and the Court be pleased to add three unto them, and so the Major of the five to fully detirmin the difference concerning the hieway and Com[m]on betwixt the Towne of Newport, Mr **Benedict Arnold** and said **Clement** Weaver, as alsoe the hie way and Com[m]on, betwixt the said Weavers land and Mr **John Goulds**: soe as to putt a final Issue thereunto: said lands being in Newport neer said Weavers.

The Court assent thereunto: The men chossen are by Serja^{t} Clement Weaver, Capt John Green by Mr Benedict Arnold, Mr Richard Arnold, of [62/64] Providence, by the Court Majo^{r} John Albro Mr George Lawton & Mr John Sanford Recorder: And it is agreed that all differences about either the hieways or Com[m]ons as aforesaid are Referred to the full Judgment and Detirmination of the Major part of the Arbitrators afore-named, giveing their award under their hands: allways provided they doe detirmin the same betwixt this and the last of June next insuing the date hereof, and that Execution shall goe forth from the Recorder to the Gen^{rl} Serjant according to their award or detirmination in Case either party Refuse or Neglect to performe the same, and that the Charges shall be paid according as the said Arbitrators or the Major part shall detirmin.

And the said Arbitrators doe in Court agree to have their first meeting on the first day of May next.

On an Indictment by the Grand Jurry against **Howlong Harris** of Providence for Carnall Copulation with **Thomas Deway**. She being Mandamassed and in Court Called appeared, the Indictment to her read leaves the matter to the Judgment of the bench, alleadging that the man being cleerd, she could not be guilty.

The Court haveing seariously Considered the Case doe detirmin that although she cannot be lawfully Convict according to the Indictment yett never-the-less by her Confession it appearing that she was soe surprissed by drink that brought her into such inconveniency: doe therefore order that she be cleared of the Indictment paying five shillings to the Treasury and Costs of Court.

On Indictment by the Gen^{rl} Solicetor against **Ruth Bayly** of New Shorrum for haveing had sundry Bastards: she beinge in Court Called appeared, and putts in her Exceptions against the Bill:
The Court on searious Examination of the Case see cause the Case proceed to Tryall. She being askt whether guilty or not guilty: pleads not guilty as to the whole bill. The sentance of the Court: That Ruth Bayly shall forthwith pay unto the Gen^{rl} Treasury of this Collony the sum of one pound, six shillings Eight pence in or as mony, and upon default thereof then with two months after her being delivered of the childe she now goes withall she shall be severly whipt, with fifteen stripes on the naked back, and this punnishment to be done at New Shorrum and the Warden or Wardens there are to see the performance of the said punnishment and she shall alsoe pay officers ffees.

On Indictment by the Gen^{rl} Solicetor against **Ruth Burdick** for fornication com[m]itted with **John Phillips** she being mandamassed and in court Called did not appeare. The Gen^{rl} Serjant haveing in Court affirmed she was Mandamassed, The Court detirmin her nonappearance a Contempt.

On Indictment by the Gen^{rl} Solicetor against **John Phillips** for fornication with **Ruth Burdick**, Mandamasse sent forth he being in Court Called noe appeareance.

On Indictment by the Gen^{rl} Solicetor against **Andrew Edmands** of the Towne of Providence for breach of law &c, he being bound in a Bond of twenty pounds for his appeareance at this Court Called did not appeare, Mr **Joseph Jencks** in Court declareing that the Reason of his nonappearance was not in Contempt but the ilnes of his ffamely as he said: Therefore the Court doe Continue his Bond, untill the next Generall Court of Tryalls.

On Indictment by the Gen^{rl} Solicetor against **John Joanes** of KingsTowne for ffornication with **Maria** a Negro woman servant to Mr **Richard Smith**, he being bound in a Bond of forty pounds for his appearance at this Court, and in Court Called noe appearance. The Court declare his Bonds fforfitt.

On Indictment by the Gen^{rl} Solicetor against **Nathaniell Osband** of Newport for perjury — he being bound and in Court Called appeard: his Indictment Read, he Enters Traverce, pleads not Guilty and Refers himse[lf] for Tryall to God and the Cuntry — The Case Com[m]itted to the Jurry. Verdict Verdict Guilty: The Court accept the Verdict, and Com[m]itt the person. The Sentance of the Court that Nathaniell Osband shall on or before the last day of September next pay the sum of three pounds six shillings Eight pence in or as mony unto the Gen^{rl} Treasury of this Collony, and shall not for the future beare any office either in the Civill or Millitary affaires nor his Testamony to be taken in any Case Authentick, and shall alsoe pay officers ffees.

On Indictment by the Gen^{rl} Solicetor against **Benjamin Whipple** of Providence for breach of law and Misbehavior, he being Mandamassed and in Court Called appeared: And haveing put in his Exceptions to the Bill: The Court haveing seriously considered the Matter doe quash the bill.

Shuball Painter being by the last Court bound to this Court and in Court Called noe appearance — The Court see cause to Continue his Bond, untill the next Court of Tryalls.

Thomas Ustance chosen by the Towne of Providence on the Jurry of Tryalls and not attending is fined

John Roades chosen by the Towne of Warwick on the Jurry of Tryalls and not attending is fined.

Shorrum ffined for noe Returne of Jurry men

Kings Towne fined for noe Returne of Jurry men

James Towne fined for noe Returne of Jurry men.

[63/65]

At the Genl Court of Tryalls held in his Maj^ties Name
at Newport the 5th day of September 1682

Present

Major Peleg Sanford Governour
Mr John Easton - Assistant
Mr Caleb Carr - Asista~
Mr Joseph Jencks - Asista~
Mr William Cadman Asista~
Mr George Lawton Asista~
Captn John Green Asista~
John Sanford Recorder
Edmund Calverly Genl Serja^t
Mr Weston Clarke Genl Treasurer
Mr John Pococke Genl Atorney

Grand Jurrymen Engaged -
Mr Phillip Smith foreman
Mr James Weeden Senr
Mr John Maxon
Mr Robert Taylor
Mr John Morrey
Mr Mathew Borden
Mr Adam Mott
Mr James Carder
Mr John Rathbone
Mr Stephen Mumford
Mr Thomas ffry
Mr Joseph Bryer

The Grand Jurry allowed to part untill Called for by the Governo^r.

On an action Com[m]enced by Mr **Richard Smith** Administrator to the Estate of **Edmund Oliver** Deceased Plantiff against **Jarad Talbott** of Tanton defendant beareing date the 7th of March 1681/2 Said action beinge an action of the Case for detaininge goods delivered him by **Edmund Oliver** deceased Damage tenn pounds sterlinge. The Case in Court Called the plantiff appeared, the defendant did not appeare.

The Jurry:

Mr Jeremiah Browne foreman
Nathaniell Coddington
John Easton jun^r
Henry Dyre
Samuell Wilkinson
Robert Brownell
John Cooke jun^r
John Warner
Thomas Nicolls jun^r
John Williams
Joseph Remington
Anthony Wood

The Case Com[m]itted to the Jurry: The Verdict Wee find for the Plantiff thre pounds five shillings in mony and Cost of Court. The Court accepts the Verdict and allow the bill of Cost one pound twelve shillings Eight pence. The defendant according to law Entered a Rehearing.

On an action of the Case for breach of Bond debt and damage 1000£ Sterlinge bearing date the 29th of March 1682 Com[m]enced by **John Williams** plantiff against **Joshua Lamb** defendant. The Court on a searious Debate and Consideration of the Case doe see cause to abate the action for as much as the plantiff in his Declaration, doth not pertickularly declare in what Collony the lands he suith for is and lyeth: and allow the bill of Cost, thirteen shillings.

On an Action of Trespass upon the Case Damage thirty pounds sterling, bearing date the 24th of June 1682 Com[m]enced by Mrs **Kathrine Dyre** Widow plantiff against **Charles Dyre** Defendant. The Case Comitted to the Jurry.

Jurrymen:

Jeremiah Browne, foreman	John Williams
John Easton junr	Thomas Nicoll, junr
Samuell Wilkinson	Joseph Remington
Robert Brownell	John Borden
John Cooke junr	William Allin
John Warner	John Paine

Verdict Wee find for the defendant Cost of Court. The Court accepts the Verdict and allow the bill of Cost one pound and five pence.

On an Action of Debt Damage Eight pounds sterling beareinge date the 1st of July 1682 Com[m]enced by Mr **Stephen Arnold** plantiff against Mr **Joseph Jencks** defendt. The case called plantiff and defendant appeared. On the plea the plantiff [*written over* Defendant] quieried whether the Governor ought to sitt Judge of the Court in this Case, for as much as the Governor had in the Genl Assembly held in May 1681 Entred his decent [dissent] to the act of the said Asembly concerning the Collonys Asesment for the payment of the 60£ Rate Asessed in July 1679. The Major part of the Court viz Mr Caleb Carr, Mr William Cadman, Mr George Lawton, & Captn John Green Assistants doe Conclude that the Governors said decent is suffitient grounds for his not sitting Judge in said action and all other actions of that Nature: The Dept Governor not being present there could not be a further proceed.

On an Action of the Case for Trespass Damage twenty pounds Sterling bearinge date the 1st day of July 1682 Com[m]enced by **Elizabeth Holderbee** plantiff against **Daniell Wilcocke** defendant. The Court on Searious debate of the case doe see cause to abate the action — and allow the bill of cost twelve shillings eight pence.

On an Action of the Case for detaininge a percell of Land containinge Eight acres more or less lying and beinge in the Towne of Newport, and is between the land formerly belonginge to Capt **Robert Harding**, and the land formerly belonging unto **Marmaduke Ward**, Damage 150£ as pr writt beareing date the 4th day of July 1682: Com[m]enced by **Josiah Hubbert** of East Hampton on Long Island Attorney unto **Thomas Partridge** of the Towne of fflushing on sd Long Island, son of the late deceased Capt **Allexander Partridge** of Newport on Rhode Island plantiff against **John Williams** of said Newport defendt. Mr Caleb Carr appeared the plantiffs Attorney.

The Court on the searious veiwing of the Letter of Attorney and Consideration of the Case doe see cause to abate the Action fforasmuch as the said origonall plantiff in the probation of the letter of Attorney is only said the Reputed son of Capt[n] Allexander Partridge — and allow the bill of Cost twelve shillings Eight pence.

On an action of account Damage 20£ sterling beareing date the 12th of July 1682 Com[m]enced by **John Pococke** plantiff against **Edmund Calverly** Gen[rl] Serja[t] Defendant. The Court see cause to Referr the case to the next Gen[rl] Asembly.

On an Action of the case for Dower Damage 100£ sterling beareing date the 10th of July 1682 com[m]enced by **Modecay Bowden** and **Rebecka** his **[64/66]** wife, said Rebecka beinge formerly the widow and Relict of **Thomas Tooly** of Newport deceased plantiff against **Thomas Burge** of s[d] Newport Defendant on the Consideration of the Case the Court see cause to abate the Action — and allow the Bill of Cost twelve shillings eight pence.

On Indictment against **Andrew Edmunds** for breach of his Maj[ties] peace, he being bound to the last Court of Tryalls, and by said Court Referred to this Court, and now beinge in Court Called noe appearance. This Court see cause to refer the Case to the Next Court of Tryalls.

On Indictment against **Trustram Dodge** sen[r] of Block Island alias New Shorrum for being strongly suspected to be sheep-stealler, he beinge bound to this Court and in Court Called appeared: pleads not Guilty, and Refers himselfe for Tryall to God and the Cuntry.

Verdict Guilty of Suspition. The Court on the searious Consideration of the Case finding nothing against the said Dodge but suspition, doe see cause to acquitt him of his bonds paying ffees.

On Indictment against **Nathaniell Brigs** of New Shorrum for being a sheep stealler — Mandamass being sent forth, and he in Court Called noe appeareance.

On Indictment against **Richard Barnes** of Newport for ffellony, he being bound to this Court and in Court Called appeared, ownes Guilty: The Court doe sentance the said Richard Barnes for his transgretion to deliver unto **Edward Thurston** sen[r] of the Towne of Newport two good sheep each equal to the sheep by him stolne, on or before Thursday next the 14th of this Instant September, and shall forthwith pay to the Gen[rl] Treasurer, the sum of forty shillings in or as mony and pay fees: And if he doe not pay the said forty shillings to the Treasurer, then he shall be sevearly whipt with twenty stripes on the naked back in the Towne of Newport on the 14th Instant.

On Indictment against **John Pearce** Mason for fornication Comitted with **Mirriam Tyler** — he beinge bound and in Court Called pleads Not Guilty — and Referrs for Tryall to God & the Cuntry. Verdict Guilty: The sentance of the Court, That John Pearce shall well and truly pay or cause to be paid unto Mirriam Tyler the sum of twenty shillings in or as mony towards the charge of her lying in at the birth of the Male Childe whereof the said John Pearce by law is the Reputed father, and alsoe for the future and untill further order from this Authorety the said John Pearce shall pay or cause to be paid unto the said Mirriam Tyler in or as mony every week for the maintanence of the said Childe the sum of two shillings six pence, and pay officers ffees.

On Indictment against **Mirriam Tyler** for fornication Com[m]itted with **John Pearce** Mason, she being in Court Called, appeared, ownes Guilty. The Court sentance Mirriam Tyler for her Trancegretion to pay forthwith the sum of twenty six shillings Eight pence in or as mony to the Gen^{rl} Treasurer, or else shall be sevearly whipt on the naked back with fifteen stripes in the Towne of Portsmouth on the 14th day of this instant month, an shall pay officers ffees.

Richard Sutton beinge bound to the good behaviour, and his appeareance at this Court: he being in Court Called appeared: proclamation beinge made and none appeareinge against him he is cleerd paying ffees.

Shuball Painters bonds being Continued from the last Court to this Court, and in Court Called noe appeareance, The Court on Consideration of the Matter doe Continue his bonds untill the next Court of Tryalls.

This Court is Adjourned untill the last Thursday save one in March next then to sitt at Newport only if there doe appeare Necessary Occassion unto the Governo^{r} or in his abscence the Dep^{t} Governo^{r} it shall be in the power of either of them to Conveane the Court sooner.

At the Gen^{rl} Court of Tryalls held in his Majesties Name
at Newport the 27th day of March *1683*

Present

Majo^{r} Peleg Sanford Governo^{r}
M^{r}Walter Clarke Dep^{t} Governo^{r}
Mr Caleb Carr — Assistant
Mr Joseph Jencks — Assista-
Mr Richard Arnold — Assista-
Mr William Cadman — Assista-
Mr George Lawton — Assista-
Captn John Green — Assista-
John Sanford Recorder
Mr Edmund Calverly Genl Serja^{t}
Mr Weston Clarke Genl Treasur^{r}
Mr John Pococke Genl Attorney

Grand Jury from the severall Townes Returned
Grand Jurrymen Engaged
M^{r}Nathaniell Coddington foreman
Serja^{t} John Stanton
Serja^{t} John Pebody
Mr Richard Dunn
Lt ffrancis Brayton
Mr William Wilbore
Mr Job Green
Mr John Maxon
Mr John Odlin
Mr Joseph Morrie
Mr Caleb Carr
Mr John Sisson

Serja^{t} **John Stanton** being bound in the sum of forty pounds for the ap-peareance of **Shuball Painter** at this Court to answer the Complaint of Mr **John Williams** in a Charge for takeing sheep ffeloniously &c. The said John Stanton bringinge the said Shuball into the Court, and presentinge his person to be Released of his Bonds: The Court doe acquitt the said Serjant John Stanton from his said Bonds. And the said Shuball Painter is by the Court Com[m]itted to the Genl Serjants Custody. **[65/67]**

On An action of the Case for unjust Detainure Damage 200$^{£}$ sterling, beareing date the 20th of July 1682 Com[m]enced by **William Clarke** plantiff against **William Ales-**

worth, Jane Saxby widow and **Rebeckah Saxby** defend^ts^. The Case Called, the plantiff appeared, and the defendants by their Attorney.

Jurrymen:

Cap^tn^ James Barker fforeman	John Coggeshall
Thomas Peckham	Jacob Mott
Jireth Bull jun^r^	John Rice
John Vaughan jun^r^	John Bennett
John Ward	Edward Thurston jun^r^
Thomas Pattey	John Sheldon

The case Com[m]itted to the Jurry. The Court three times sent for the Jurry. The Jurrys Verdict: Wee find for the plantiff Cost of Court and five pounds damage in mony or Equivalent to mony:

The Court on the searious Consideration of the Case doe see cause to suspend Judgment and Referr the Case to the further Consideration of the next Gen^rl^ Court of Tryalls.

On an Action of Debt by bill debt and damage 7^£^ sterll. beareing date the 5th of Septemb^r^ 1682 Com[m]enced by **Peter Lee** plantiff against **Richard Sutton** defend^t^, plantiff and defendant appeared in Court, the Issue joyned Not Guilty of the charge, The Case Committed to the Jurry. The Jurrys Verdict. Wee find for the plantiff the debt due by bill which is three pounds five shillings: two pence damage, and Cost of Court: The Court accept the Verdict and allow the bill of Cost: one pound twelve shillings and one peny. Judgment granted.

On an Action of Debt: debt and Damage Eight pounds beareinge date the 8th of Septr 1682: Com[m]enced by Mr **Stephen Arnold** plantiff against Mr **John Williams** Defendant. The Case Called, the plantiff appeared, the defend^t^ did not appeare; only his Answer in the ofice — On the said Action the Governo^r^ withdrew himselfe Aleadginge that the Court of Tryalls in September last on an Action Com[m]enced by Mr Joseph Jencks have declared that there was suffitient grounds for his not sittinge as Judge in that Case and all other Actions of that Nature — And the Dep^t^ Governo^r^ by lawfull Exceptions beinge off the Bench, Therefore, the Court in this Case Consisted of these Judges Viz: Mr Joseph Jencks, Mr Richard Arnold, Mr William Cadman Mr George Lawton and Captn John Green Assistants. The Case Com[m]itted to the Jurry: The Jurrys Verdict Wee find for the plantiff ffour pounds in New England silver mony Damage five shillings and Cost of Court. The Court Accept the Verdict, and allow the Bill of Cost One pounds twelve shillings and one peny: Judgment granted.

The Governo^r^ and Dep^t^ Governo^r^ tooke their Places.

On an Action of Debt by bill damage 40^£^ sterlinge beareing date the 2nd of January 1682/3 Com[m]enced by **Anna Cole** and **Hugh Cole** plantiff against **John Pococke** defendant. Plantiff and defendant appeared in Court. And on Request in hopes of Agreement the Court doe Referr this Action to be the last of Actionall Cases in this Court.

On an Action of Sclaunder and Defamation Damage 40^£^ sterling beareing date the 30th of January 1682/3 Com[m]enced by **Shuball Painter** plantiff against Mr **John Williams** defendant. The plantiff appeared. Noe appearence of the defendant only his

Answer in the Office: The Court haveinge heard and Considered the plantiffs declaration, and the defendants Answer, and findinge that the plantiff stands Indicted for that declared the grounds of the Action, Doe see cause to Demurr the Action to the Next Court of Tryalls.

On an Action of Debt debt and damage 17£ sterl. beareinge date the 5th of ffebruary 1682/3 Com[m]enced by Mr ffrancis Brinley plantiff against Mr **William Brenton** defendant. In Court Called noe appeareance of the plantiff: The Governor on behalfe of the defendant Answered.

On an Action of Debt by Bill, debt and damage tenn pounds sterl. bearing date 8th ffebruary 1682/3 — Com[m]enced by Lt **ffrancis Brayton** plantiff against **Thomas Manchester** Senr defendt. In Court Called, the plantiff appeared; noe appeareance by the defendant. The Case Com[m]itted to the Jurry: The Jurrys Verdict, Wee find for the plantiff three pounds in mony or Equivolent to mony. three pence damage and Cost of Court. The Court Accept the Verdict and allow the Bill of Cost one pounds sixteen shillings and tenn pence.

Whereas **Samuell Gardner** and **John Booth** Negro, as privateers have been some time past, by the Authorety of this Collony secured, and there not appeareing any persons to accuse the said parties, This Court Court [*sic*] doe Confine them on their perrill not to depart this Collony dureing the full time of one yeare from the time of their first Imprissonment.

On Indictment by the Genrl Attorney against **Shuball Painter** for liveing with **Hannah** the wife of **Thom~ Martin** contrary to law &c: Being brought into Court pleads Not Guilty, And Referrs for Tryall to God and the Cuntry. The Case Com[m]itted to the Jurry: The Jurrys Verdict, Guilty. The Court accept the Verdict. The Court Sentance him the forfiture of his Bond which is 20£ and pay ffees.

On Indictment Against **Andrew Edmunds**, he being bound to the last Court, and by that Court Referred to this. In Court two severall days Called Noe appeareance. The Court doe Sentance him the said Edmunds the forfiture of his Bond twenty pounds.

On Indictment by the Genl Attorney (on the Complaint of Mr **John Williams**) Against **Shuball Painter** for ffellonious takeing up sheep &c: Called appeared, pleads Not Guilty, and Referrs himselfe for Tryall to God and the Cuntry: The Case Com[m]itted to the Jurry: The Jurrys Verdict, Not Guilty: The Court accept the Verdict, and cleer him paying ffees.

On Indictment by the Genl Attorney against **Mary Garrett** for felloniously stealing and purloyninge severall goods from **Sarah Mills** allias **Williams**. — In Court Called noe appeareance. [66/68]

Gabrill Jenings beinge Bound in a Bond of tenn pounds for the ap- peareance of **Mary Garrett**. And in Court twice Called Noe appeareance: Therefore the Court Sentance said Jenings the forfiture of his Bond.

James Man beinge bound in a Bond of tenn pounds for the appeareance of his wife at this Court: — beinge Cald he bringinge his wife into Court, and none appeareing to accuse her, his Bonds are Remitted.

Benjamin Devell beinge bound in a Bond of tenn pounds for his appeareance at this Court, And Court Called did not appeare, Therefore the Court Sentance the forfiture of the said Bond.

m^{r} **Benedict Arnold**, m^{r} **John Thornton** jun^{r}, and m^{r} **Peleg Shearman** Chosen Jurry men and not attendinge are fined.

The Towne of New Shorrum and Kings Towne fined for not makeing Legall Returns of Jurrymen.

At the Genl Court of Tryalls Held in his Maj^{ties} Name
at Newport the 4th day of September *1683*:

Present

Mr William Coddington Governo^{r}
Mr Walter Clarke Dep^{t} Governo^{r}
Mr John Easton Assistant
Mr Caleb Carr Assistant
Majo^{r} John Coggeshall Assistant
Majo^{r} John Albro Assistant
Edmund Calverly Gen^{rl} Serja^{t}
Weston Clarke Gen^{rl} Treassu^{r} & Genl Attorney
John Sanford Recorder beinge sick: Ordered that Thomas Ward supply the Recorders Place

Grand Jurrio^{rs} that appeared and Engaged

Mr Edward Greenman foreman
Serja^{t} Clement Wever
Mr John Vaughan Senr
Mr John Sailes
Mr Hugh Parsons
Mr Job Green
Mr William Clarke
Mr John Heath
Mr John Timberlake
Mr John Tillinghast
Mr Bartho: Hunt
Mr Edward Thurston jun^{r}

Whereas Mr **Edward Pellam**, was bound for the appeareance of **Shuball Painter** at this Court and he have presented the said Painter to the Court he Desireing to be Releassed of his bonds this Court Doe discharge the said Mr Pellam of his said Bond: And the said Shuball Painter is Committed to the Gen^{rl} Serja^{t} till Called for by the Court.

Rebecka Hobson, being brought into the Court: Mr **Samuell Hagbourne** Doth Recognize in the sum of tenn Pounds to bring the said Rebecka in this Court, when by the Court Called for.

On An Action of Debt by bill Damage tenn Pounds Sterling bearinge date the 27th of June 1683 Com[m]enced by **Thomas Burge** of the Towne of Newport Plantiff against **Henry Head** of Saconett in the Collony of New Plymouth Defendant: The Case in Court Called the Plantiff appeared, yett noe appeareance of nor for the defendants. Therefore the Plantiff Enters a Nihill dicett against the defendant.

Jurrio^{rs}:

Joshua Coggeshall foreman
John Rodman
Andrew Willitt
Charles Crossthwaite
Sylas Carpenter
Willia~ Wilbore jun^{r}
George Havens
Phillip Long
John Pebody
Henry Timberlake
Samuell Cranston
Emanuall Wooly

The Case pleaded and Com[m]itted to the Jurry: Verdict, the Jurry find for the Plantiff five and forty shillings mony Debt, Damage five shillings and Cost of Court: The Court Accept the Verdict, and allow the Bill of Cost, two pounds four shillings Eight Pence: Judgment Granted.

On An Action of Sclaunder and Defamation Damage 40£ sterlinge bearing date 30th January 1682/3 — Com[m]enced by **Shuball Painter** of Newport Plantiff against **John Williams** of said Newport defendant said Action being by the last Court of Tryalls Demurrd. The Plantiff and Defendant in Court three times Called noe appearance: Yett soon afterwards the Plantiff appeareing in Court, the Court allow it the last Action Tryable in this Court.

On an Action of Batterie, Damage seven hundred Pounds sterling bearing date the 23 of July 1683 Com[m]enced by **Henry Tibbitts** of Kings Towne Plantiff against **Thomas Gould** of said Kings Towne Defendant, Septr 6: 1683: there being noe answer putt in, the Plantiff Enteres a Nihill dicett, The Case Called the Plantiff and defendant appeared And after a long debate of the matter, and time by the Court allowed the partys for their Consideration, Plantiff and defendant came into the Court and freely themselves fully agreed in the difference depending between them.

On the above mentioned Action depending between **Shuball Painter** and **John Williams** — The Case againe Called, the Plantiff appeared, noe appearance of or for the Defendant only an Answer in the Office, The Case Com[m]itted to the Jurry:

Jurriors:

Joshua Coggeshall foreman	Phillip Long
John Rodman	Hen. Timberlake
Andrew Willitt	Samuell Cranston
Charles Crossthwaite	Emanull Woolly
Sylas Carpenter	Tho: Gould junr
Willia~ Wilbore junr	Mathew Greenell

Verdict Wee find for the Plantiff three Pounds Damage and Cost of Court: The Court accept the verdict, and allow the bill of Cost one pounds Eleven shillings four Pence: Judgment Granted. [67/69]

On Indictment by the Genrl Attorney Against **Uriah Clemence** a youth, now Prissoner, for ffelloniously stealing a Watch from **Joseph ffoard** of Bristoll, he being brought in to the Court and askt whether Guilty or not guilty, ownes Guilty, and alsoe ownes that he stole a silver hook from said ffoard. The Court Doe Sentantance Uriah Clemence, for his Severall Transgressions by him owned in this Court to pay the sum of Twelve Pounds in or as mony unto the Genrl Treasurer and alsoe to be severly Whipt on the Naked back with fifteen stripes in the Towne of Newport: And this Court doe Order, That if the aforesaid Uriah Clemence Doe not forthwith pay downe to the Treasurer the afore-said sum of Twelve pounds, then it shall be in the power of the Genrl Treasurer to make sale of the said Uriah for a Servant the full tearme of seven yeares from this Court: Out of which twelve pounds officers Fees to be paid which is one fourth part being three pound, the Remainer to Returne to the aforesaid Joseph ffoard of New Bristoll.

On Indictment against **Rebeckah Hobson**, for ffornication, She being in Court Called appeared: the Charge to her Read and she askt whither Guilty or not Ownes Guilty: The Court doe sentance the said Rebeckah, for her Transgression, Shall forthwith pay unto the Gen^{rl} Treasurer the sum of One Pound Six shillings Eight pence in or as mony, or Else be sevearly whipt, with fifteen stripes on the Naked back in the Towne of Newport, and shall alsoe pay officers ffees.

On Indictment by the Gen^{rl} Attorney against **Shuball Painter** for ffellonious takeing up a Sheep belonging to **Daniell Gould** jun^{r} Out of the ffarme of **John Easton**, he the said Painter being in Court Called appeared, and the Charge to him Read and askt whither Guilty or not Guilty: Ownes that he did take up a sheep out of John Eastons farme, for **Abraham Burge** a Jew, which he doth now Really think was the said **Daniell Goulds** Sheep — And Referrs himselfe to the Judgment of the Bench. The Court doe Sentance the said Shuball Painter forthwith to pay unto Daniell Gould two good Sheep in leiue of that Sheep by him taken, and shall forthwith pay unto the Gen^{rl} Treasurer the sum of tenn shillings in or as mony, or Else for his not payment of the said tenn shillings he shall be sevearly whipt with tenn Stripes of the Naked back in the Towne of Newport and pay fees.

On Indictment by the Gen^{rl} Attorney against **Sarah Dye** daughter of **William Dye** belonging to the Collony of New Plymouth, for ffornication, She beinge being brought into Court, her charge Read, and She askt whither Guilty or Not Ownes Guilty. The Court doe sentance Sarah Dye for her Transgression forthwith to pay unto the Generall Treasurer the sum of One Pound six shillings Eight pence in or as mony or Else be sevearly whipt with fifteen stripes on the Naked back in the Towne of Newport and pay ffees.

On Indictment by the Gen^{rl} Attorney against **Hannah Archer** for ffornication: in Court Called appeared, her charge Read, and She askt whither Guilty or not — Ownes Guilty — and saith **Job Manchester** is the father of her child. The Court doe sentance the said Hannah Archer forthwith to pay unto the Gen^{rl} Treasurer the sum of one pound six shillings Eight pence, in or as mony or Else shall be sevearly whipt with fifteen stripes on the Naked back in the Towne of Newport and pay ffees.

On Indictment by the Gen^{rl} Attorney against **Deborah Allen**, Daughter of **Mathew Allen** of the Towne of Dartmouth in the Collony of New Plymouth for ffornication, and for Indeavouringe the distruction of the Child in her womb: being brought into the Court, her Charge Read and askt whither Guilty or not Ownes Guilty: The Court doe Sentance Deborah Allen for her Transgression forthwith to be severly whipt in the Towne of Newport with fifteen stripes on the Naked back and pay officers ffees.

Job Manchester being bound to this Court & Called appeared. **John Manchester** doth Recognize in the sum of thirty pounds to bringe into this Court the said Job Manchester when Called for.

Whereas **John Warner** of the Towne of Warwick was bound to this Court and being Called appeared — The Court Declareing the said Bonds to be voyd Butt **Ann Warner** wife of the said John Warner appearing in Court and declared in said Court that still she went in fear of her life by her said husband and did desire to have his bonds renued againe, The premisses Considered this Court doe see Cause to binde the said John Warner in a Bond of fifty pound sterling to his Maj^{tie} Payable upon all demands to be levied on his lands, goods cattell or chattells, the Conditions are that he be of the good behaviou^{r} to all his Maj^{ties} Liege subjects but more Espetially to his said wife untill the next Court of Tryalls to be held for the Collony in Newport being the last Tuseday in March 1684 or untill the Governo^{r} Dept Governo^{r} or two Assistants doe otherwise order.

Whereas **Job Manchester** of the Towne of Portsmouth hath been on the Complaint of **Hannah Archer** charged to be the father of a Childe by her borne in the month of Aprill last, and he the said Job & Hannah being in this Court face to face, and the Child alsoe, said Hannah affirming, and said Job denying, yett according to law the said Job being the Reputed father: This Court doe order and Detirmine That the said Job Manchester shall forthwith pay or cause to be paid unto the said Hannah Archer, on and towards the charge of the Nurssing and Maintanence of that Child the sum of two Shillings in or as mony for every week since the birth of the said Child And shall alsoe for the future from this 7th of Septemb^{r} weekly **[68/70]** and every week untill the Authorety in this Collony see Cause other wise to Order, allow and truly pay unto the said Hannah Archer, and to the maintanence of the said Child the full sum of two shillings in or as mony. And the said Job Manchester shall alsoe give in good and suffitient securety unto the Governo^{r} Dept. Governo^{r} or any two Assistants for the true and absolute performance of this Courts Judgment aforesaid, or Else be kept in prisson untill such securety given.

Peter Easton of Newport, **Robert Hodgson** of Portsmouth, and **Robert Burdick** of Westerly beinge chosen to serve on the Grand Jurry and not attending are fined.

m^{r} **Edward Pellam** of Newport and **Jonathan Holme** of s^{d} Newport and **Abraham Man** of Providence being chosen to serve on the Jurry of Tryalls and not attendinge are fined.

New Shorrum and Kings Towne fined for not making Returnes.

This Court Desolved.

At the Gen^{rl} Court of Tryalls Held in his Maj^{ties} Name
at Newport the 25th of March *1684*

Present
Mr William Coddington Governo^{r}
Mr Walter Clarke Dep^{t} Governo^{r}
Mr John Easton Assistant
Mr Caleb Carr Assista-
Majo^{r} John Coggeshall Assista-
Mr Joseph Jencks Assista-
Mr Richard Arnold Assista-
Majo^{r} John Albro Assista-
Mr George Lawton Assista-
Majo^{r} John Green Assista-
John Sanford Recorder
Edmund Calverly Gen^{rl} Serja^{t}
Mr Weston Clarke Gen^{rl} Treasurer
& Attorny

Grand Jurriors that appeared and Engaged
Mr William Hiscox foreman
Mr Henry Tew
Mr Jeremiah Brown
Mr William Wilbore
Mr James Carder
Mr John Odlin
Serj^{t} John Pebody
Mr Stephen West
Serj^{t} John Pearce
Mr Thomas Burge
Mr John Parker
Mr Robert Tayler
Mr Thomas Manchester jun^{r}
Mr Zachery Gant

John Pearce of Prudance being bound for the appearance of **Ellin Hitt** the wife of **James Hitt** at this Court and he bringing the said Ellin into the court desireing to be dismist of his bonds not being willing to be bound any longer, The court doe discharge him of his said Bonds And the said Ellin Hitt is Com[m]itted to the serjants Custody.

On the Rehearing of an Action of Sclaunder and defamation damage 40$^{£}$ sterling Com[m]enced by **Shuball Painter** Plaintiff against **John Williams** Defendant Tryed at the last Court of Tryalls. The Court on the searious debate of the matter see cause to Referr this Case to the Gen^{rl} Asembly in May next and order the Recorder to give the partys notice thereof.

On an Action of Debt debt and damage 20$^{£}$ sterling bearing date the 10th of October 1683 Com[m]enced by **Thomas Terrey** of Tanton Plantiff against **Hudson Leverett** of Boston defendant. The case being Called the plantiff appeard but noe appearance of the defendant nor any for him. A Nihill dicett Entred. The case pleaded and Com[m]itted to the Jurry.

Jurrymen:
Serja^{t} John Holmes foreman
John Ward
Thomas Rogers
John Clarke
John Easton jun^{r}
Samson Shearman
Abiell Tripp
Anthony Shaw
Peter Green
Daniell Vaughan
Thomas ffry
John Davis

Verdict, Wee find for the plantiff Debt and damage twelve pounds fifteen shillings silver mony of New England and Cost of Court. The Court accept the verdict and allow the bill of Cost one Pound fifteen shillings. Judgment granted. Execution Issued forth on the Estate of the defendants Bondsman Mr Samuell Hagbourne of Newport.

On an Action of the Case for Trespass damage 20$^{£}$ sterling bearing date the 22th October 1683 Com[m]enced by **John Parker** Plantiff against **Edward Robinson** defendant. Verdict Wee find for the Plantiff thirty shillings silver mony Damage and Cost of Court. The Court accept the Verdict and allow the bill of Cost two pound one shilling seven pence: Judgment granted also Executed.

On an action of the Case damage 20$^{£}$ sterling bearing date the 23 October 1683. Com[m]enced by **Thomas Dorfee** plantiff against **Richard Bulgar** Defendant. Verdict Wee find for the Plantiff Cost of Court and twelve pence damage. The Court accept the verdict and allow the bill of Cost One Pound Ninteen shillings Six pence. Judgment granted. Execution given forth.

On an action of Debt debt and damage 20$^{£}$ sterling bearing date the 2nd of January 1683/4 Com[m]enced by **Stephen Sebeer** Plantiff against **Joseph Timberlake** defend^{t}. March 18: noe answer in the office the plantiff Enters a Nihill Dicett. The Case Called the plantiff appeared. Noe appearance of or for the defendant. Verdict Wee find for the Plantiff debt and Damage Eleven Pounds of silver mony and Cost of Court. The Court accept the verdict and allow the bill of Cost one pound fifteen and six pence. Judgment granted & Executed.

On an action of the Case for Detainure of Lands & Damage forty pounds sterll. bearing date the 10th day of January 1683/4 Com[m]enced by **Richard Waterman** plantiff against **Samuell Winsor** and **Mercy** his wife. The Defen^{t} Samuell Winsor in Court ownes his appearance on behalfe of his wife as well as himselfe. **[69/71]**

Verdict: Wee finde for the Plantiff Cost of Court and twelve pence damage. The Court accept the verdict and allow the bill of Cost two pounds fifteen shillings five pence. Judgm^{t} granted. Plantiff and defendant in open Court declared themselves that as to the devission ofahe widows thirds from the heires Right they leave it fully to Captn **Arthur ffenner** to devide between this and the last of Aprill at furthest: Execution Issued forth for the Costs.

On an Action of the Case for cloathing maintenance with Education Expended bearing date the 11th of February 1683/4 Com[m]enced by **Samuell Winsor** Plantiff aginst **Richard Waterman** Defend^{t}. The Plantiff did not proceed but lett fall his action, The Court allow the defendants bill of Cost thirteen shillings four pence.

On an action of the Case for detaininge **John Waterman**, &c damage forty pound bearing date the 11th of February 1683/4 Com[m]enced by **Samuell Winsor** Plantiff against **Joseph Williams** defendant. Mr **Thomas Olney** appeared Attorney for the defendant. Verdict: Wee find for the defendant Cost of Court. The Court accepts the verdict and allow the bill of Cost One Pound fifteen shill. & seven pence. Judgment granted to the defendant.

On an Action of Debt due by Bond debt and damage 24$^{£}$ sterll. bearing date the 12th of January 1683/4 Com[m]enced by **Edward Thurston** Plantiff against **William Maize** defendant.

Jurriors:

Serj^{t} John Holmes	Anthony Shaw
John Ward	Peter Green
John Clarke	Daniell Vaughan

John Easton jun^r^ | Thomas ffry
Sam^ll^ Shearman | John Davis
Abiell Tripp | John Parker

Verdict Wee find for the Plantiff the bond sued for and Cost of Court. The Court accept the verdict and allow the bill of Cost one pound fifteen shill[s] four pence. Judgment granted.

On an action of Detainure Com[m]enced by Widow **Ann Jenings** Plantiff against **Isaac Lawton** defend[t]: the case Called Pla~ & defend[t] appeared. The Court on the Debate of the matter finding the writt to be served by the Town Serja[t] and the Gen[rl] Serja[t] afirminge he had not made him his deputy to serve said writt Doe see cause that the Action abate.

On an Action of the Case for dower Damage one hundred and forty pounds sterling bearing date the 29[th] of January 1683/4 Com[m]enced by **Mordecay Bowden** and **Rebeckah** his wife Plantiff against **Thomas Burge** defendant. There being a Nonsute entred in the office The Court after a long debate on the Case do judge the Nonsute to be Leagall. The Court allow the defendants bill of Cost nine shillings two pence.

On an Action of Debt upon accompt Debt and damage 16[£] sterll. bearing date the 5[th] day of January 1683/4 Com[m]enced by **John Williams** Plantiff against **Josiah Arnold** defendant. On the debate of the matter the Court allow a Nonsute And allow the Defendants bill of Cost tenn shillings two pence. Execution given forth.

On an action of Debt by Bill of Exchaing Damage 75[£] sterling, bearing date the 28[th] January 1683/4 Com[m]enced by Majo[r] **Peleg Sanford** Attorney to **John Winslow** and Capt[n] **Elisha Hutchinson** Administra[r] to the Estate of **Joseph Winslow** of Boston Marriner deceased Plantiff, against **Mordeacah Bowden** Defendant.

On the Jurry in this Case **John Rathbon** in the room of **Daniell Vaughan.**

The Issue Joyned by the parties, a Gen[rl] Issue: The Jurrys Verdict Wee find for the Plantiff Debt and Damage Thirty five Pounds two pence silver mony and Cost of Court. The Court accept the Verdict and allow the bill of Cost One Pound sixteen shillings and Eleven pence Judgment granted and Execution thereon.

On Indictment by the Gen[rl] Attorney against **John Williams** of Newport for feloniously takeing and was abetting to the takeing a Pigg which was the proper Estate of **George Halsall.** he being Mandamassed and in Court Called appeared and askt whither Guilty or not Guilty pleads that without an accusser he will not answer to the bill. The Court see Cause to quash the bill.

On Indictment by **Henry Tibbitt** against **Thomas Gould** of Kings Town for that he the said Gould did Mallitiously Asault and batter the said Tibbitts by Cutting his hand with an axe. Thomas Gould being bound and in Court Called appeared. The Indictment Read and he askt whither Guilty or Not Guilty. Owns Guilty of Cutting Henry Tibbotts hand.

On Indictment by the Gen[rl] Attorney against **Thomas Gould** of Kings Town for Misbehaviour. Said Gould in Court Called appeared. being demanded whither Guilty or not guilty, Refussed to give a Possetive Answer. Therefore the Court Refer the Tryall of the Case to the Jurry.

Jurriors:

Serj^{t} John Holme foreman	Abiell Tripp
John Ward	Anthony Shaw
Thomas Rogers	Peter Green
John Clarke	Daniell Vaughan
John Easton jun^{r}	Thomas ffry
Samuell Shearman	John Davis

Verdict: Guilty: The Court accept the verdict.

On Indictment by the Generall Attorney against **Thomas Gould** of Kings Town for battering the Cunstable **James Hasselton** in the Execution of his office. Said Gould Called, appeared, the Indictment Read and he askt whether Guilty or not Guilty — pleads Not Guilty and Refers himself to the Tryall of his pears.

Edward Thurston and **Charles Dyre** in the Room of **Sam^{ll} Shearman** and **Daniell Vaughan.**

The Case Committed to the Jurry: And the Jurry haveing been by the Court three times sent forth their verditt: Not Guilty. [70/72]

On Indictment by the Gen^{rl} Attorney against **Thomas Gould** of Kings Town for threatning the life of **Henry Tibbitts** and stricking at him: said Gould in Court Called appeard: the Charge Read and he askt whither Guilty or not Guilty pleads not Guilty and Refers himselfe for Tryall to the cuntry his peers. The Case Com[m]itted to the Jurry: Their Verdict. Guilty.

On Indictment by the Clerke of the peace against **Thomas Gould** of Kings Town, on suspition of being Instrumentall to the burning of a Barne belonging to Captn **John ffoane** at said Kings Town &c. Said Gould in Court Called appeard. The Charge Read and he askt whether Guilty or not guilty pleads not Guilty and Refers himselfe for Tryalls to his Pears. The Case Com[m]itted to the Jurry who were

John Holme foreman	Anthony Shaw
John Ward	Peter Green
Thomas Rogers	Thomas ffry
John Clarke	John David
John Easton jun^{r}	Charles Dyre
Abiell Tripp	Gilbert Magick.

Jurrys Verdict: Not Guilty.

Thomas Gould whereas you are found Guilty by Confession and Verdicts of Jurry concerning three bills of Indictment, Viz. by **Henry Tibbitts** for cutting his hand, for misbehavio^{r} to Capt **John ffoanes** in the Execution of his Office, for Threatning the life and stricking at **Henry Tibbits.** The Court Do Sentance that said Thomas Gould do forthwith pay to the Generall Treasurer five pounds in silver mony, and all the Charges of the Cunstables and aide, and all Officers ffees. And the said Thomas Gould is so Confined that he shall be Restrained from going to any part of the main land within this Jurisdiction of Rhode Island and Providence Plantations or Kings Province without further order from his Majesties Gen^{rl} Court in this Collony. And in case he presume to go Contrary hereunto; then it shall be lawfull for any Generall Officer of this Collony or Conservator of the peace in the Kings Province to Cause the said Thomas Gould to be aprihended and sent to his Maj^{ties} Goale in Newport without bail or mainprize. And that the said Thomas Gould shall give one hundred pound bond with two suffitient sureties to be of a peaceable and good behaviour to all his Maj^ties^ Leige people and in espetiall manner towards Captn John ffoanes Henry Tibbitts and their famelies. And further that his breaking of said Confinement shall be a brea[c]h of his bond.

On Indictment by the Gen^rl^ Attorney against **Precilla Knight** for fornication. She being in Court Called appeard, and askt whether Guilty or not guilty - Owns Guilty and saith that **William ffoster** Junr is the father of her child. The Court doe sentance the said Precilla Knight for her Transgression, forthwith to pay unto the Generall Treasurer the sum of Twenty six shillings Eight pence in Mony or else to be sevearly whipt with fifteen stripes on the Naked back in the Town of Newport and pay officers ffees.

William ffoster jun^r^ being brought into the Court, and **Precilla Knight** unto him before the Court affirming that he was the person by whome she was begotten with childe, and the only father of that childe by her born into the world ... and the said child being dead. The Court doe see just cause and doe adjudge the said William ffoster the Reputed father, forthwith to pay unto the said Precilla Knight towards the Charge of her lying in and the burriall of the child the sum of thirteen shillings four pence in mony, & be com[m]itted till the mony be paid.

On Indictment by the Clerke of the Peace against **Rebeckah Saxbey** for fornication. She being in Court Called appeard, and askt whether Guilty or not guilty Owns Guilty: and saith that **James Kinion** is the father of her child. The Court doe sentance the said Rebeckah Saxbey for her Trancegression, forthwith to pay unto the Gen^rl^ Treasurer the sum of twenty six shillings eight pence in mony or else be sevearly whipt with fifteen stripes on the Naked back in the Town of Newport and pay officers fees.

James Kinion being brought into the Court and **Rebeckah Saxbey** unto him in open Court affirming that he was the Person by whome she was begotten with child and the only father of that child by her born into the world: The Court adjudge according to law the said James Kinion the Reputed father of the said child shall forthwith pay unto the said Rebeckah Saxbey the sum of two shillings pr week in or as mony towards the charge of the birth and bringing up of said child for every weak from the time of the birth thereof the this present fourth of Aprill, And shall also for the future untill Authorety sees cause otherwise to Order, pay to said Rebeckah Saxbey every week and weekly towards the maintenance of the said Childe the sum of two shillings in or as mony.

Forasmuch as **Mallato Tom** servant to **Thomas Gould** hath been charged and it appears that he layd voyolent hands on **James Hasleton** Cunstable, This Court doe sentance him forthwith to be sett in the Stocks, in the Town of Newport and there to Remain dureing the Courts Pleasure.

Captn **John ffoans** Conservator of the peace in Kings Town, doth Recognize unto his Maj^tie^ in the sum of twenty pounds to Prossicute a charge against **James Green** at the next Gen^rl^ Court of Tryalls for suspition of being Instrumentall of fyreing the sayd ffoanes his barne at Kings Town, the 26th of December last.

James Green and **Henry Tibbitts** of Kings Town and Lt **John Green** of Newport said James Green at the next Court of Tryalls to answer the aforesaid charge by Suspition against him by Cap[t] ffoanes.

Whereas **John Peckham jun[r]** was bound for the lawfull appeareance of **Mordicah Bowden** at the sute of Majo[r] **Peleg Sanford** Attorney to the Administrators of the deceassed **Joseph Winslow**, And haveing brought the said Mordicah Bowden into this Court and desired a Release of his said Bonds the Court doe see just Cause according to Law to Release the said Peckham of his said bonds.

Samuell Whipple of Providence & **Daniell Crum**[m] of Westerly chosen to be on the grand jurry for not attending that service are fined. **Eliezer Whipple** & **Joseph Woodard** of Providence, chosen to be on the jurry of Tryalls for not attending that service are fined.

New Shorrum, Kings Town and James Town fined for not makeing Returne of Jurrymen.

[71/73]

Att the Gen[rl] Court of Tryalls held in his Majesties Name
at Newport the 2nd of September *1684*:

Present
M[r] William Coddington Governo[r]
M[r] Walter Clarke Dep[t] Governo[r]
M[r] John Easton Assistant
M[r] Caleb Carr Assista-
Majo[r] John Coggeshall Assistant
M[r] Joseph Jencks Assistant
M[r] Richard Arnold Assistant
Majo[r] John Albro Assistant
M[r] George Lawton Assistant
Majo[r] John Green Assistant
John Sanford Recorder
M[r] Edmund Calverly Gen[rl] Serja[t]
M[r] John Pococke Gen[rl] Att[y] & Soliceto[r]

Grand Jurrymen and Engaged
Retained by the severall Towns
M[r] Peter Easton foreman
M[r] Clement Weaver sen[r]
M[r] John Allin
M[r] Thomas Burge
M[r] Nathaniell Mawrey
M[r] Peleg Shearman
M[r] John Borden
M[r] Moses Lippitt
M[r] Stephen Mumford
M[r] William Edwards
M[r] John Coggeshall jun[r]
M[r] John Sisson
after John Rathbon in the roome of John Borden
Mathew Greenall in the roome of Peleg Shearman.

On an Action of Debt upon Account Damage ffifty pounds sterling bearing date the 4[th] of July 1684 — Com[m]enced by **John Williams** Attorney to **John Baker** of Boston Braissier, Plantiff against **Josiah Arnold** as Administrator to the Estate of the deceassed **Robert Williams** of Newport Defendant: after the Calling of the Case the defendant Pleading that the Originall Plantiff was a strainger and had noe Visible Estate in this Collony and desired Securety from the Plantiff before the case proceed, Thereupon M[r] John Williams in open Court doth oblidge himselfe and Estate, on the behalfe of the Origonall Plantiff Lawfully to stand to performe and abide the Judgment of this Court in said Case:

Jurriors:

L[t] John Green foreman	Clement Weaver jun[r]
Henry Brightman	John Pain
James Weeden	Samuell Gardner
William Peckham	John Timberlake
Samuell Cranston	Gilbert Magick
Isaac Lawton	Ens. John Crandall

The Case pleaded and Com[m]itted to the Jurry.

Verdict: Wee find for the Plantiff Twenty Eight pound Eleven Shillings and nine pence currant mony of New England three pence damage and Cost of Court. The Court accept the Verdict and allow the bill of Cost one pound ninteen shillings eight pence. Judgment granted.

On an Action of unjust mollestation by false Imprisonment damage five hundred Pound sterling bearing date the 27[th] of Aprill 1684. Com[m]enced by **ffreelove Morris** Plantiff against Capt[n] **Richard Smith** of Kings Town Defendant. Issue Joyned not Guilty of the Charge.

Jurio[rs]:

Lt John Green foreman	Robert Carr
Edward Thurston jun[r]	John Pain
James Weeden	Samuell Gardner
William Peckham	John Timberlake
Samuell Cranston	Gilbert Magick
John Easton jun[r]	Ens. John Crandall.

The Case Pleaded and Com[m]itted to the Jurry. Verdict: Wee find for the Plantiff. Damage Twenty Pounds Currant mony of New England. The Court accept the Verdict and allow the bill of Cost One Pound seventeen shillings three pence. Judgment Granted: and 17[th] Septemb[r] 1684 Execution.

Edward Robinson of Newport being charged for haveing a Child or children by **Margrett Hall** the wife of **James Hall**, and appearing in Court with a child in his Armes Owned that he had had to doe with that sd woman, and Owned the Child to be his and Referred himselfe to the Judgment of the Bench. Margrett Hall also appearing in Court with a child in her armes owned the same. This Court takeing the premisses into Searious Consideration and for weighty matters presented before the Court doe see cause to leave the whole matter to the next General Asembly to be held the last Wensday in October next Ensuing at Warwick.

M[r] **James Green** of Potowomett being bound to this Court, in Court appeared and is cleerd of his Bond.

John Andrew of Kings Town being bound to this Court and Called appeared and none appearing to prossicute him he is cleerd by proclamation in Open Court.

M[r] **James Renolds** sen[r] of Kings Town being bound to this Court and Called appeared and no one appearing to prossicute him he is cleerd by Proclamation in Open Court.

Whereas the Majestrate **John Green** com[m]itted **John Andrew** Cunstable and **James Renolds** both of Kings Town to lye in Prison without baile or mainprize, but in the Mittimas Expressed that it was for what the Majestrate proffered to take their own bond and that therefore he so com[m]itted them. But those Com[m]itted afterward tendered to the Governo^{r} suffitient baile, and therefore the Governo^{r} upon suffitient bond given to answer to all Complaints that should according to law be brought against them they were not kept in Prison but appeared at Court according to Law, but the Majestrate Complained that the Governo^{r} had not such power to take bond although the Governo^{r} had the Councell of the Deputy and other Majestrates soe to take bond. But that Majestrate said his brother whome he had bound to inform against those he gave baile was freed from being soe bound, but the Majestrate would have had the Gen^{rl} Attorney to have made a bill for them to be indicted for a Riot. The Attorney informed the Court that the Cunstable and his aide being by a warrant or at least he pretended in the Execution of his office, and therefore could not make a [72/74] Riott of it, and the Court allowed of the Attorneys information, and informed the Majestrate and his brother, that if they would Charge the Cunstable in any other way then for a Riot, for any other Crime the law was open.

Captn **John ffoanes** being the last Court of Tryalls bound to this Court, and Called appeared.

James Green of Kings Town being at the last Court of Tryalls bound to this Court, and Called appeared.

On the searious Consideration of the decease of Mr **John Spencer** of East Greenwich, in the Kings Province Conservator of the peace there, and for the maintaninge and upholding his Majesties Authorety and the peace of his Subjects in this Collony. The Honord Governo^{r} and Dep^{t} Governo^{r} and Rest of this Court being the Major part of the Generall Councell doe see good Cause and Doe Authorize and Empower Mr **John Heath** of said Greenwich in the place office and Authorety of a Conservator of the peace in and throughout said Town of East Greenwich untill the Authorety of this Collony see Cause otherwise to Order.

Johnathan Sprauge and **Zachery ffield** of Providence chosen to be on the Jurry of Tryalls & not appearinge are fined, **John Keese** of Portsmouth chosen to be on the Jurry of Tryalls and not appearing is fined.

Shorrum, Westerly and James Town for not makeing Returns of Jurriors are fined.

At the Generrl Court of Tryalls Held in his Majesties Name
at Newport the 31 of March *1685*

Present
Mr William Coddington Governor
Mr Walter Clarke Depr Governorr
Mr John Easton - Assistant
Mr Caleb Carr Assista-
Major John Coggeshall Assista-
Major John Albro Assista-
Mr George Lawton Assista-
Major John Green Assista-
John Sanford Recorder
Edmund Calverly Genrl Serjat
Mr Weston Clarke Genrl Treasurer
Mr John Pococke Genrl Attorney & solic.
by Reason of William Wilbores sickness
Mr Henry Palmer Engaged on the grand Jurry

Grand Jurriors Engaged
Mr Phillip Smith foreman
Mr Jonathan Holmes
Mr Robert Tayler
Mr Lawrence Turner
Mr Gyles Slocum
Mr Wiliam Wilbore
Mr Joseph Morie
Mr Thomas Burge
Mr John Parker
Mr Barth. Hunt senr
Mr John Sisson
Mr Walter Roades

In Answer to the Petition of Captn **Richard Smith** concerning his being Imprissoned by Execution, sd Petion bearing date March 31 1685. What is Cognizable to this Court they are Redy and willing to do without Respect to persons in Judgment.
The proceeds of the preceeding Court of Tryalls, wee are not to question, Judgment haveing past, and Execution thereupon, which is the end of that Court: and he that neglects his libertie in law (a Rehearing) implicitly Owns the Judgment, and can have noe lawfull appeall, because a due Progress hath been neglected by himselfe.
On an Action, of unjust Mollestation by falce Imprissonment Damage fifty pounds sterling Com[m]enced by **John Borden** of Portsmouth Plantiff against Captn **Richard Smith** of Kings Town Defendant. A nihill dicett entred in the Office.
After much debate on the Case the defendant puts in a paper said in barr of the action. The Court after much debate and on Searious Consideration thereon Detirmin the action to Tryall. The Court after many adjutations demanded of the defendant to joyn Issue, his Attornys Viz. **Mr Wharton** and **Captn Thomas** answered they could not joyn Issue in the Case.
Jurriors:

John Rodman foreman
Henry Timberlake
Thomas Gould junr
Benja- Hernden
John Pearce mason
Ens John Pearce
John Correy
John Weeden
Benja- Smith junr
George Halsall
Alexandr Colman
Josiah Lindon

The Case Com[m]itted to the Jurry: Their Verdict: Wee find for the Plantiff damage Thirty Pounds Currant mony of New England and Cost of Court. The Court accept the Verdict and allow the bill of Cost, one Pound Eighteen shills four pence. Judgment granted and Execution thereon.

On an Action of Debt debt and Damage five Pounds sterling Com[m]enced by **Samuell Hagbourn** Plantiff against **Shuball Painter** Defendant: bearing date the 21st August 1684. The Case Pleaded and Com[m]itted to the Jurry. Verdict Samuell Hagbourn Plantiff, Shuball Painter Defendant, Wee find for the Plantiff forty three shillings and that the Defendant pay Cost of Court with damage two pence. The Court accept the Verdict and allow the bill of Cost one Pound three shillings six pence.

On an Action of account Damage tenn Pounds Sterling bearing date the 21st of August 1684: Com[m]enced by **Shuball Painter** Plantiff against **Samuel Hagbourn** Defend^{t} Verdict Shuball Painter Plantiff, Sam^{ll} Hagbourn defendant, Wee find for the defendant two pence and that the Plantiff pay Cost of Court.The Court accept the Verdict, and allow the bill of Cost: [73/75] seventeen shillings eight pence. Judgmen[t] Granted.

On an Action Com[m]enced by **Benjamin Newbery** Plantiff against **George Halsall** defendant. In Court Called noe appearance.

On an Action Com[m]enced by **John Williams** Plantiff against **Nathaniel Niles** defendant. In Court Called noe appearance.

On an Action Com[m]enced by **John Thornton** jun^{r} against **Edward Enman** defendant. In Court Called noe appearance.

On an Action or Complaint of Majo^{r} **William Dyre** as Survayer Gen^{rl} against **Mordica Campanell, Saul Brown, Abraham Burgis, Rachell** the widow and Relict of **Symon Mendes** dec^{d} and others Jews fforeigne borne. ffor want of a declaration in the office according to Law, the defendants enter a Nonsuit. The Case in Court Called. the afore-named Majo^{r} Dyre the Complainant did not appear only Edward Uster his Attorney appeard. The defendants appeared.

Whereas upon the Information of Majo^{r} William Dyre to Our Honord Governo^{r} against **Mordica Campanell, David, Daniell & Abraham Campanell, Saul Brown, Abraham Burges, Rachell the Widow and Relict of Symon Mendes** deces^{d} and **Aron Verse** Jews. Our said Governo^{r} granted a warrant to the Generall Serja^{t} to sease the said Jews goods or Estates to answer the said informer his charge against them as Aliens at this Court. And whereas he hath not brought the matter in such forme as our law Requires; Yett for weighty Reasons moveing, This Court doe see Cause with the defendants Consent, that the action shall Come to a Tryall forthwith.

The Case Pleaded, and Com[m]itted to the Jurry.

Verdict Wee find for the defendants and that the Plantiff pay Cost of Court. The Court accept the Verdict and allow the bill of Cost fifteen shillings Eight pence.

Whereas Majo^{r} William Dyre Esqr survayer Gen^{rl} as informer hath Caused the Estates of severall Jews Viz. Mordecai, David, Daniell & Abraham Campanell, Saul Brown and Abraham Burgis, Rachell the Widow and Relict of Symon Mendes dec^{d} and Aron Verse to be seized to bring them to a Tryall as Aliens &c and the Jurry haveing found for the defend^{ts} and the Informer disappearing in Person, and a nonsute granted, as also haveing given noe bond. The Court therefore unanimously order that the distraint upon the defendants goods be taken off and their Estates so seized be Restored by the Generall serja^{t}.

On a Bill of Indictmen by the Gen^{rl} Attorney against **John Williams** — being Mandamassed in Court Called appeared. On Consideration of the matter the Court doe quash the bill.

On Indictment by the Grand Jurry against Captn **Richard Smith**, for breach of Law by Causing Inhabitants of this Collony to be arrested and imprissoned in Plymouth Colony &c: he being mandamassed and in Court Called appeared. On the debate of the matter, and seariouss Considerations of the Reasons Rendered by the said Captn Smith, The Court see just Cause to quash the bill.

On Indictment by the Gen^{rl} Attorney against **Edward Ewster** for Publishing scandelus Lybills. In Court Calld appeared. The Indictment Read and he askt whether Guilty or not Guilty: answerd that he owned the truth to the Honord Governo^{r} &c and Referrs himselfe to the judgment of the bench. The Court upon his acknowlidgement, and Promiss for the future better behaviour doe see cause to pass by his offence therein.

Richard Speare affirming himselfe Batchelor of Arte, said to be a person that assumeth the Authorety and hath married Persons in Kings Town, in Court owned he had so done, and that for the future he will do soe noe more without Legall Lycence, and desires the favour of the Court.

Walter Newbery, Josiah Arnold, & Bartholomew Hunt Junr chosen to be on the jurry of Tryalls by the Town of Newport, and not attendinge are fined.

The Towns of Warwick, Westerly, New Shorrum, Kings Town, East Greenwich, & James Town fined for not makeing Returns of Jurry-men.

[*Pages 74/76 through 78/80 are blank, and this ends the double numbering of pages. No further entries were made in the book until June 1687.*]

[81]

Att the Generall Quarter Sessions and Inferior Court of Common Pleas holden in his Maj^{ties} name at Newport for Rhode Island Narrogansett or Kings Province and Providence Plantations the 14th day of June *1687*

Justices Present
ffrancis Brinley Chairman & Judge
Leiu[t]: Collonell Peleg Sanford
Maj[r] Richard Smith
Capt[n] John ffones
M[r] John Coggeshall
M[r] Caleb Carr Seni[r]
M[r] Symon Ray
Capt[n] Arther ffenner
Capt[n] James Pendleton

Grand Jury Sworne
Thomas Olney foreman
James Greene
Andrew Willet
Jeremiah Browne
John Whiple
Peleg Shereman
John Knowles
Joseph Mory
Rouse Helmes
Thomas ffry
Nathanell Niles
Thomas Burge
John Rise

Constables Sworne in Court
Henry Briteman)
George Sisson)
Thomas Durfee) for Portsmouth
Jacob Mott)
Robert Westgate)
Jireh Bull)
John Easton Jun[r]) for Newport
John Headley)
William Hancock - for New Shorum
Joseph Mory - for James Towne

Petty Jury Sworne
Leiu[t] John Stanton foreman
Benedict Arnold
Thomas ffeild
Nathaniell Waterman
John Peirce
Isaack Lawton
William Knowles
John Thomas
Robert Burdick
Capt[n] Clement Weaver
Ensig. John Hulme
Joshuah Coggeshall Jun[r]

The Court Adjorned till 7 A clock tomorrow morning

June 15th Court Called and Sate —

Ordered that the Clarke write Orders and Deliver to the Constables that appeared at Sessions to warne the persons appointed for constables to Serve the year Ensueing to appear in Sessions or before one of the Justices of the peace to give their Oath to said office.

Upon the Pettition of **Sarah Potter** of Warwick it is Ordered that the Consideration thereof be Referred to the Justices of the peace of Providence, Warwick and Rochester to Inquire Into and Take Care concerning the Promisses therein Contained.

James Herbert Prisoner in his Maj[ties] Goale in Newport being Indicted was called in Court and his Indictment being read to him and he demaunded Guilty or not his Answer was, that he would not say any thing and soe was remaunded to Goale.

Robert Brownell being bound to the Good behaviour and his appearance at this Court, he being in Court Called appeared, Proclamation being made and none Appearing against him: he is cleered paying officers fees. [82]

Thomas Gould & Clement Weaver being bound to the Good behaviour and Appearance at A court at Rochester and by Order of Law to this Court they being in Court called, Appeared Proclamation being made and noe man Appearing Against them they and either of them are Cleered paying officers fees.

Samuell Meads being bound to the peace and Appearance at A Court At Rochester and by Order of Law to this Court he being in Court called appeard Proclamation being made and noe person Appearing aganst him hee is Cleerd paying officers fees.

John North being bound to the peace and his Appearance at this Court he being in Court Called Appeared Proclamation being made and none Appearing Against him he is cleard paying officers fees.

John Wood, John Knight, Thomas Nichols, being bound to the peace and good behaviour and Appearance at a court at Rochester and by order of Law to this Court they being in Court Called Appeared Proclamation being made and none Appearing Against them they and Either of them are cleard paying officers fees.

Henry Underwood of James Towne being bound by Recognizance to this Sessions being Called Appeared and **Nicholas Carr** of the Same place being his Surety and sd Nicholas Carr Desiring to be Discharged from his bond the Court doe Discharge the said Nicholas Carr and Order the Said Henry Underwood to Stand Bound in the Sum of twenty pound to Appear personally at the next Generall Quarter Sessions to be holden for this Province.

The Court Adjourned till to morrow 7 A clock

the Inferior Court of Common Pleas Calld and Sate

The Wittnesses to the Will of **Richard Barnes** of Newport on Rhode Island Dated 8th of Aprill 1687 Appeared in Court did Testifie to the Same

John Hulme } Sworne
William James } did Solemnly
James Clarke } Testifie
Samuell Stapleton }

The Inventory of the estate of the Said Richard Barnes was presented in Court Amounting to 148£ 9s 0d and the [*blotted*] appeard in Court and did testifie thereunto
Robert Little Sworne

James Clarke did Solemnly Testifie

The will of **John Pebody** of Newport on Rhode Island Dated ye 22d day of March 1686/7 Presented in Court, ye Wittnesses alsoe Apeared in Court and did Testifie to the Same

Jonathan Hulme }
Peter Tailer } Sworne

The Inventory of the Estate of the said John Pebody Dated Aprill 18th 1687 Presented in Court, Amounting unto 103£ 04s 00d.

The Apprisers appeared in Court and did Testifie thereunto
Henry Tew }
John Ward } Sworne

[83] June 16th the Court of Sessions called and Sate

James Herbert Prisoner being Indicted, called in court and his Indictment being Read to him and Demaunded Guilty or not — Answered he would not Answer — and Soe was remanded to goale

John Maxson } appointed to be
John ffairfeild } Overseers of the poor
James Reinalls } for feversham

Samuell Albro } appointed to be
Captn Clement Weaver } Overseers of the
John Heath } Poor for Dedford

Nathaniell Waterman } appointed to be
Parden Tillinghast } Overseers of the Poor
Shadrach Manton } for Providence

Samuell Stafford } appointed to be
Moses Lippitt } Overseers of the Poor for Warwick

Nicholas Carr } appointed to be Overseers
Oliver Arnold } of the Poor for James Towne

Gedion ffreeborne } appointed to be Overseers
John Borden } of the Poor for Portsmouth

Mathew Borden } appointed
John Woodman } to be
Benedict Arnold } Overseers
Lawrence Turner } of the Poor
Peter Easton } for Newport

Robert Guthridge } appointed to be Overseers of
Nathaniell Niles } the Poor for Newshoram

Whereas Severall Persons being bound by their Recognizance of Good behaviour and to Appear at a court at Rochester in the Kings Province and the said Court being not held at the time Appointed and all the Persons did there at the time and Place appear, which said Recognizances the Justices weer by commission to hear and Determin all things Relateing there unto at this court and the said Persons being called not appearing this Sessions doe order that the said persons shall be Summoned to Appear at the next Generall Quarter Sessions to Answer —

Persons Admitted to have Licences
William Mayes }
Charles Beere }
John Davis } of Newport
George Halsall }
Robert Little }

James Herbert now Prisoner in his Maj^{ties} Goale being Twise caled in Court and his Indictment Read to him he was Demaunded Guilty or not Guilty he said hee would not Answer. The Sentance of the Court is that the said James Herbert pay five pounds in money and Give his Owne Bond of twenty pounds to be of Good behaviour and Appearance at the next Quarter Sessions and to remaine in Prison till hee performe the Sentance

Ordered that **Edmund Calverly** Late Generall Serjeant and Goaler bee Allowed 20 Shillings for his Service.

[84] Ordered that the Clerke write Prohibitions to Prohibbet the Selling of all Sorts of Strong Drinkes in the Kings Province Without Licence on the Penalty by Law Appointed

The Sessions Adjourned till 3 aclock in the after noone

The Inferiour Court of Common Pleas Called and Sate —

The Will of **Bartholomew Hunt** of Newport on Rhode Island Dated the 11th day of february 1686 Being Presented in Court — and the Wittness alsoe appearing in Court did Testifie to the Same

John Vaughan — Testified thereto —

The Inventory of the Estate of the Said Bartholomew Hunt Dated the 5th day of the first moneth 1686/7 Presented in Court amounting unto - 106$^{£}$ 17^{s} 0^{d} — The Apprisers alsoe apearing in Court and testified thereunto.

Joshuah Coggeshall }
Dan^{ll} Gould } Solemnly Testifie

The Will of **Roger Basterd** of Newport on Rhode Island Dated the 22^{d} day of Aprill being Presented in Court and the Witnesses also Appearing in Court Did testifie to the Same

John Woodman }
Samuel Minott } Sworne

The Inventory of the Estate of the said Roger Basterd Dated Aprill the 27th 1687 Presented in Court amounting unto 16$^{£}$ 17^{s} 3^{d} the Appisers also appearing in Court Did Testifie to the Same

John Woodman }
Thomas Ward } Sworne

The Gen^{rll} Quarter Sessions called and Sate ———

—— the Courts Desolved ——

[85]

Att a General Quarter Sessions and Inferior Court of Common pleas holden in his Maj^{ties} Name at Rochester for Rhode Island
Narroganset or Kings Province and Providence Plantations the 14th day of Septemb^{r}: *1687*

Justices Present
ffrancis Brinley Chairman & Judge
Leiu^{t} Colon^{ll} Peleg Sanford
Maj^{r} Richard Smith
Capt John ffones
Randall Holden
Captn James Pendleton
Captn Arther ffenner

The Grand Jury sworne
Phillip Smith foreman
John Wood
John Greene
Samuell Gorton
Nicholas Carr
Ephraim Moss
Daniell Lawton
Benjamin Shearman
George Whitman
Thomas Mumford
Rouse Helmes
John Maxson
Samuell Winsor
William Cory

On an action of Debt, Debt and Damage ten pound Sterling comenced by **William Edwards** Plaintiff against **William Wood** Defendant bearing Date the Eight Day of July 1687
The Case called the Plaintiff and Defendant appeared, the Issue Joined not Guilty of the Charge.
The case pleaded and Committed to the Jury.
Juriors
John Cole foreman
Capt John Bliss
John Ward
John Heath
Joshuah Coggeshall ju^{r}
Samuell Shereman
Thomas Hasard
Samuell Eldridge S^{r}
Caleb Carr juni^{r}
Moses Lippitt
Epenetus Olney
Benjamin Carpenter

Verdict Wee finde for the Plaintiff two pounds Eighteene Shilings and Seven pence Sterling money of New England twelve pence Damage and Cost of Court. The Court accept the Verdict and allow the Bill of Cost one pound Nineteene Shillings and Eight pence. Judgment Granted.

On an action of Defamation Damage ten pounds Sterling commenced by **Samuell Meads** Plaintiff against **Aaron Jakewise** Defendant bearing date the 25th day of July 1687. The Case Called and noe appearance.

On an action of Trespass Damage five pound Sterling commenced by **Daniell Greene** Plaintiff against **Zerubbabell Wescot** Defendant bearing Date the Eighteene day of July 1687. The Case Called and noe appearance.

On an action of Defamation Damage ten pound Sterling commenced by **Rouse Helmes** Plaintiff against **Samuel Tift** Defendant bearing Date the 29th of August 1687. The Case Called and noe appearance.

The Court Adjourned for one howers Time
The Court being Sate

ffrancis Renalds being bound to the peace and appearance at a Court at Rochester and by Order of Sessions Summoned to appear at this Court hee being in Court Called appeared. Proclamation being made and noe person appearing against him he is cleered of his Bond paying officers fees. [86]

Arther Aylworth, James Renolds Senr, Henry Matteson, John Brigs Senr: Phillip Long, Charles Hazelton Junr, Giles Peirce, John Nichols, Benjamin Bennet, William Bennet, James Renolds Junr. John Spencer, John Greene, Henry Tippet Junr, Daniell Greene, Henry Tippets S^r^, Samuell Bennet, each of them being bound to the peace and appearance at A Court to have beene Holden at Rochester and by Order of Gen^rll^ Quarter Sessions Summoned to appear at this Court they being Severally Called in Court Appeared and Proclamation being made and noe person appearing against them they and Either of them are Cleered from his bond paying officers fees.

The Court Cald and Sate

James Herbert his Bond Continued untill the next Quarter Sessions.

The Bills found by the Grand Jury the Last Generall Quarter Sessions against the Townes of Portsmouth and Newport for not haveing in them a pound are refered to a further Consideration in Gen^rll^ Quarter Sessions.

Upon the Request of the Overseers of the poor of Newport what way they Should Raise maintinance for the poor.

It is Ordered that the Overseers of the poor of each Towne Within this Province or County Shall have power to make and assess A Rate or Levy on all and Every the Estates of the Inhabitants and Others Within their Towneships according to the Custome of England for the Releife of the poor of each of their Respective Townes.

John Whipple and **William Turpin** both of Providence are forbidden Selling of any Sort of Strong Drink by Retaile by his Maj^ties^ Justices of the Peace Sitting in Generall Quarter Sessions at Rochester September 14th 1687 — Except they or Either of them Shall appear before two of his Maj^ties^ Justices and give Bond according to Law.

Henry Underwoods Bond is Continued Untill the next Gen^rll^ Quarter Sessions.

Edward Greene, George Vaughan and **John Andrew** each of them being bound to the peace and appearance at A Court to have been holden at Rochester and by Order of Generall Quarter Sessions Summoned to appear at this Court they being Severally in Court Called appeared and Proclamation being made and noe person appearing against them they and Either of them are Cleered from his bond Paying officers fees.

Henry Renals being bound to the peace and appearance at A Court to have been holden at Rochester and by Order of Generall Quarter Sessions Summoned to appear at this Court he being Called appeared Proclamation being Made and noe person appearing against him he is Cleered from his bond Paying Officers fees.

Whereas **George Havens** was Summoned to appear at this Quarter Sessions and there Called appeared and withDrew himself not being Discharged for which offence of his the Court Doe Order the Said George Havens to pay A fine of five shillings in money and give bond before his Maj^ties^ Justices to be of peaceable behaviour and his appearance at the next Quarter Sessions and then and there to Answer to Such matters of misdemeanour as he Shall be charged with by his Maj^ties^ Authority according to former Bond.

Whereas **Mary** An Indian Squaw having been formerly committed to Goale upon Suspition of fellony and not being brought to this Sessions this Court doe Order the Said Squaw to be brought forth to the next assises or General Goale Delivery to be holden in Newport the Second Tuesday in Octob^r^.

Joseph Nicholson being bound by Recognizance to appear at this Court to [87] Prosecute **John Coggeshall** Juni^r^ of Newport and **Daniell Coggeshall** of Portsmouth for Assault and Battery made on the said Nicholson and he being Caled appeared and the Grand Jury haveing found a True Bill against the s^d^ John and Daniell Coggeshall they being in Court Called appeared & **Joshuah Coggeshall** their ffather and bondsman Requested of the Court that they might have Leave to answer at the next Court which Request the Court accordingly Granted.

The Quarter Sessions Desolved

Att A Petty Sessions held in Newport on Rhode Island Octob^r^ 25th *1687*

There being present

ffrancis Brinley Esqr Judge of the Inferior Court of common Please
Lieu^t^: Colo^ll^: Peleg Sanford } Esq^rs^ his Maj^ties^ Justices
and Caleb Carr ———— } of the peace

Anna Williams Relict and Executrix of **John Williams** Late of Newport on Rhode Island Deceased appeared and presented the Will of the Said John William Dated the 18th day of Aprill 1687 and the Wittnesses to the Said Will also appearing at the Same time Did Testifie to the Trueth of the Said Will.

William Hiscox } Sworne
Christopher Hargall } Did Testyfie

The Inventory of the Estate of the Said John Williams dated May 6th 1687 was also presented in Sessions amounting to 393^£^-0^s^-6^d^ the apprisers also being present.

John Woodman
William Hiscox

—— The Sessions Ended ——

Att a Gener[ll] Quarter Sessions and Inferior Court of common Pleas holden in his Maj[ties] Name at Newport for Rhode Island Kings Province &c the 13th day of December *1687*

Justices Present
ffrancis Brinley - chairman & Judge
Left: Colo: Peleg Sanford }
Capt John ffones } Esqrs
Caleb Carr Sr }
John Coggeshall }

The Grand Jury Sworne
Capt Benjamin Gorton foreman
Capt James Barker
Henry Bull junir
Henry Tibbits Senr
Henry Hall —
James Badcock Senr
James Blackmer
Abiah Carpenter
Thomas Brooke
Charles Tillinghast
Robert Carr
George Cooke
Stephen Braiton

William Allen, Thomas Cornell, John Albro Junir, Jonathan Sprage, John Hawkins all being returned by the Sheriff to Serve on the Grand Jury and they Refuseing to Take the Oath in Court when Called there unto they and Every of them are for their Said offences Sentanced to pay A fine of Six Shillings Eight pence in or as mony each Person.

[**88**]The Petty Jury Sworne

Capt Robert Lawton
John Paine
Charles Beere
Henry Reinalls
Thomas Greene Junr
Silas Carpenter
John Low
Peter Greene
John Cory
Thomas Coddington
John Carr
John Haris

In An action of the Case comenced by **John Blount** Plaintiff against **Shuball Painter** and **Isaac Naphtaly** Defendts there being a nonsuite Entred by the Defendt: the Court allowed the nonsuite and allow the Defendts Bill of cost in the Case fourteen Shillings Eight pence.

In an action of Unjust Detainer commenced by **Isaac Naphtaly** Plaintiff against **John Blount** Defendt: there being in the Case a nonsuite Entred and the Case withdrawne in Court: The Court Allow the Defendts Bill of Costs Seven Shillings ten pence.

John Coggeshall of Newport &c Junir Husbandman being Presented by the Grand Jury in the Quarter Sessions held at Rochester the 14th Sept Last for an assalt and battery made on **Joseph Nicholson** being Called in Court and his Indictment Read to him and Demaunded Guilty or not Answered not Guilty, and Referd for Tryall to God and the Country. The Jurys Verdict (Guilty). The Court Acepts the Verdict and Sentance the Said John Coggeshall for his offence to pay A fine of three Shillings four pence in money and pay officers fees.

Daniell Coggeshall of Portsmouth &c Husbandman being Presented by ye Grand Jury in the Quarter Sessions held at Rochester the 14 Sep^{t} Last for an assault and Battery made on **Joseph Nicholson** being Called in Court and his Indictment Read unto him and Demanded Guilty or not Answered Not Guilty, and Referd for Tryall to God and the Country. The Jury^{s} Verdict (Guilty). The Court Accepts the Verdict and Sentance the Said Daniell Coggeshall for his offence to pay a fine of three shillings four pence in money and pay officers fees.

Ordered that all cord Wood Put to Sale in the Towne of Newport on Rhode Island shall be corded Except the parties concerned Shall Otherwise agree and that the Justices of the peace Liveing in the s^{d} Towne of Newport or the major part of them Shall have power from time to time to appoint a fitt person to be A Corder of Wood In the Said Towne and the person by them appoynted Shall be Sworne to the true performance of his office when called thereunto, and to be allowed for his Se[r]vis four pence A cord.

For Prevention of Damage by ffire

It is Ordered that if any Chimney in any Street or other parts of the Towne of Newport on Rhode Island, betweene the Places commonly Called and Knowne by the name of the pound and the Lands Late the Lands of Thomas Clifton Deceased, Shall be foule and take fire and burne above the Tunnell that the Person useing the said Chimney Shall forfeit for each time two Shillings Six pence in or as money — And also it is further Ordered that Every Owner of A house or houses in the said Parts of the said Towne Shall provide for every dwelling house A Ladder to Stand against Each the said Houses that Shall reach up to or near the Ridge of the said Houses within nine monethes after the End of this Sessions or pay a fine of five Shillings for his or her Default.

[89] **Edward Wilcockes** and **Nicholas Cotterell** being both Returned by the Sheriff to Serve on the Jury of Tryalls being Called in Court did not appear, for which offence of theirs, Each of them are Sentanced to pay a fine of thirteene Shillings four pence in or as money.

Upon the Request of the Overseers of the poor of the Towne of Newport It is Ordered that Leu^{t}: Colon^{ll} Peleg Sanford and Thomas Ward are Added unto them to help them in makeing A Rate on the Estates of the Inhabitants and Others Within the said Towneship for the Releife of the poor of the said Towne of Newport.

The Court Adjorned Untill tomorrow Eight of the Clock
or Ring of the Bell

The Court Called and Sate

Mary ffish Reliect and Executrix of **Thomas ffish** Late of Portsmouth on Rhode Island Deceased, appeared in Court and Presented the Will of the said Thomas ffish Dated the 9th day of february 1686/7 and the Wittnesses to the said Will also appearing at the Same time did upon Oath Testifie to the Truth of the said Will

Caleb Arnold }
Juriell Hall } Sworne

The Inventory of the Estate of the said Thomas ffish Dated Octob^{r} 12th 1687 was also presented in Court Amounting unto 49$^{£}$-10^{s}-0^{d} — the apprisers alsoe being present.

John Albro
ffrancis Brayton

Thomas Wells of ffeversham and **John Wells** his Sonn being bound by Recognizance for Appearance at this Court, and being Called in Court appeared and noe person appearing against them they and Either of them are acquited paying officers fees.

Hanah Clarke of James Towne Widdow appearing in Court and being Sworne Did Testifie that **Henry Underwood** was the father of the Child then in her armes and that it was borne the 28th of August Last and that the Child was named **Henry**. Hanah Clarke of James Towne Widdow haveing in Court Confesed that the male Child in her armes was A Bastard Child borne of her Body on the 28th of August Last — for which fact of hers the Court doe Sentance the said Hanah to be well whipt with ten strips on her Naked Back in the Open Street in the Towne of Newport — or pay a fine of twenty Shillings in or as money.

Henry Underwood of James Towne alias Cononicut Island being bound by Recognizance of twenty pounds for his appearance at the Quarter Sessions held at Newport the 14th day of June Last and by Order of Sessions then Continued to the Quarter Sessions held at Rochester the 14th of September Last, and by Order of Sessions then Continued to This Quarter Sessions — hee being Charged by **Hanah Clarke** Widdow for being the father of the Child then in her armes and begotten of her body, and he being Called in Court did not appear the Courts Sentance is that the said Underwoods Re- cognizance is forfeited.

[90] **Mary** An Indian Squaw being formerly committed to goale on Suspicion of felony and brought to this Court, It is Ordered that the said Squaw Remane in the Custody of the Sheriff to be brought to the next Quarter Sessions to be holden at Rochester.

This Court being Informed that **William Palmer** and **Daniell Mackinees** both of Rochester victuallers have misbehaved themselves and Otherwise not being fitly Quallifed for that Imployment, This Court doe Order that the said William Palmer and Daniell Mackinees be Suspended from Keeping Victualling houses or Seling Ale Bear Sider or any Other Strong Drink by Retaile on Penalty by Law Prescribed.

Samuell Stapleton and **Christopher Hargall** Both of Newport being Sent for appeared in Court and Demanded the Rason Why they Kept not their Shops Shutt on the first day of this Instant Decemb^{r} it being A day Sett apart by his Exelency the Governor and Councill for Thanckes Giveing and praise to god. Samuel Stapleton^{s} answer was that he was above the observation of Dayes & times. Christopher Hargalls answer was that his boy Opened his Shop and what worke his Sonn did was on his Owne account and that he was Lame or else he did not Know but that himselfe might have then wrought.

Ordered that the Constable, or Constables, or major part of them in each the Respective Townes in this Province or County being assisted with one or more Justices of the Peace Shall have power to appoint Such and Soe many meet Persons to be Surveyors of the Highways as by them Shall be Judged convenient to take Care for the Repaireing the wayes in their Respective Towneships which said Surveyors are to be appointed in each Towne on or before the Last Tuesday in february next, which said Surveyors are to Attend their said Service on Penalty by Law appointed.

The Court Adjourned till tomorrow morneing 8 of the Clock

The Court Called and Sate

Ordered That all Arrests to the Inferior Court of Common Pleas Shall be made tenn Dayes compleat before the day of the Court besides the day of Arrest

And that Every Plaintiff Shall put in his Declaration in the office Six Dayes compleat before the Sitting of the Court besides the day of putting in the Declaration Otherwise the Defendant is allowed the Advantage of A nonsuite at any time after untill the Plaintiff put his Declaration in ye office.

Ordered that Every Defendant Shall put in his answer four Dayes compleat before the day of the Courts Sitting, Otherwise the Plaintiff is allowed to take the Advantage of A nihildicet at any time after before the Defendant put in his Answer.

[91] **William Turpin** of Providence victualler not appearing in Sessions ac- cording to his Excelencies Order for the Takeing of a lycence It is Ordered that the said William Turpin be Suspended from Keeping A victualing house or Selling Ale, Beer, Syder or Other Strong Drinke by Retaile on penalty by Law Provided.

Ordered that the Clerke write to the Constables of Providence to acquaint the said William Turpin of the affore written Order, and if he Submitt not to make Presentment in the Case according to Law.

Ordered that Maj^{r} **Roger Golding, Weston Clarke** and **Robert Aires** Shall have Power to Apprise all and Every part of the Estate of **James Herberts** in whose hands or custody Soever It is and an Inventory thereof returne to the Clerke of the Court.

This Court is Adjourned for one hour

Cald & Sate

Ordered that if any Person or persons Shall Entertaine **James Herbert** in their Dwelling House or Other place Day or night Except the Persons whoe have him in Keeping Or Sell or give any Sort of Strong Drinke ale bere or sider to the said James Herbert Shall for Every his or her soe doeing pay A fine of five Shillings in or as money.

Mary Gardiner of Newport Single Woman being Delivered of A child and Declareth that **Peter Easton** (the Sonn of **John Easton** of Newport) is the father of the said Child, and the said Peter Easton brought into Court before his Maj^{ties} Justices and the said Woman not being in a capassity to be brought before the Court to be Examined the Court Order that the said Peter be bound with Sureties to appear before his Maj^{ties} Justices when Called for to Answer to the said Charge, John Easton of Newport Juni^{r} and the said Peter Easton Doe obleige themselves Jointly and Severally in the sum of Twenty pounds to Our Lord the King that the said Peter Easton shall appear before one or more of his Maj^{ties} Justices of the peace of this Province when there unto Required to Answer the said Charge.

Ordered that there be A Rate of one hundred and Sixty pounds Levied and Raised on the Severall Townes and places in this Province or County for and toward the Building of A Court House in Each of the Townes of Newport and Rochester and Repairing the Prison in Newport and paying of Debts Lately Contracted Within this Province or County and to be paid unto the Treasurer of this Province or County on or before the first day of July next Ensueing in the Specias hereinafter named that is to Say in money or Sheeps Wooll at Seven pence halfe penny a pound Butter made in the Spring at four pence half Penny a pound, Indian Corne at twenty pence the bushell Rye at Two Shillings Six pence a bushell Porke at fourty two Shillings A Barrill all the said Specias to be Good and merchantable.

The Proportion that Each Towne is Levied and assessed to pay is as followeth

Newport -	38£
Portsmouth	31
Providence	27
Warwick	12
Dedford*	03
Rochester*	18
ffeversham*	10
Newshorum	11
James Towne	10
	160

Ordered that the Constables of Each the Respective Townes within this Province or County of Rhode Island Kings Province & Providence Plantations Shall Warne the Inhabitants of their Towne to meet Togerther on or before the first Wensday in Aprill next to choos three or five men of the In-habitants of their Towne to Assess and Levy the Rate assessed and Levied on their Towne (by his Majties Justices sitting in Generall Quarter Sessions [92] held in Newport the 13th day of December 1687) on each the Estates of the Inhabitants and Others within the Precincts of their Towneship which said Rate is to be Made and the List thereof Perfected under the hands of the said Rate Makers or the major part of them on Or before the third Wensday in the said moneth of Aprill and forthwith to be delivered to the Constables of each Towne Whoe are heerby Required to gather and Collect the Same and the said Rate by them Soe Gathered and Collected the said Constables Shall Send unto the Treasurer of this Province or County of Rhode Island &c on or before the first day of July next and the better to Inable the Constables to gather and Collect the said Rate the said Constables are Impowred if any Person or Persons Refuse to pay the Rate Soe Assessed on them to Distraine of the Estate of the Person or Persons neglecting or Refuseing to pay the Same.

It is alsoe Ordered that Mr **ffrancis Brinley** Leiut Colonell **Peleg Sanford** and Capt **John ffones** or the Major part of them are hereby Impowred and Requested to Bargaine and Agree to and with Such and Soe many Workemen Artists and Others for the

* During the administration of Gov. Edmund Andros, East Greenwich was known as Dedford or Deptford, Kingstown as Rochester, and Westerly as Feversham or Haversham (the spelling in Book A is clearly ffeversham).

the said Two Court houses as in their Discretion Shall Seeme meet and That an Order under the hands of Them or the major part of them to The Treasurer of this Province or County to pay to any person or Persons Either for Materialls to be Used or Worke Done about the Building the said Houses Shall be A Sufficient Warrant for the said Treasurer to pay the Same.

John Woodman nominated to be Treasurer and Sworne

Ordered that the Clerke Write A Letter to be Sent to his Exelency ye Governer to acquaint him that this Court have In Persuance to the Advice of ye Judges to them given, Considered the necessity and Charge of two Court Houses one to be built in the Towne of Newport and the Other in Rochester and to give his Exelency an account what they have at Present Computed the Charge may be.

Ordered that if any person or Persons Shall Sitt Tippling or Drinking in any Victualling house Within this Province or County on the first day of the Weeke or be found Playing or Sporting on the first day of the Weeke Shall for every of the said offences be Prosecuted and punished as by Law is apointed and all masters of famalies are Strictly required to take Care of their Servants and children for whome they are to be accountable and the Constables in each Towne are Strictly Required to take care that this Order be duly Observed.

[93] Ordered that the Clerke Coppy and Send forth the Orders concerning the Rate to the Constables of the Severall Townes and all Such Other Orders alsoe as are to be Published according to the Use they are Intended.

The Quarter Sessions Ended

Att A Sessions held in Newport on Rhode Island &c the
4th day of January *1687*

There being Present

ffrancis Brinley Esq[r] Judge of the Inferior Court of Common Pleas
Leu[t]: Colo: Peleg Sanford } Esq[rs] his Maj[ties]
Caleb Carr Sen[r] } Justices of the Peace

Sarah Timberlake Widdow and Relict of **Henry Timberlake** Late of Newport on Rhode Island aforesaid Deceased, appearing and Requesting Administration on the Estate of the said Henry Timberlake It was accordingly Granted Shee giveing Bond With Security Well and Duly according to Law to Administer the said Estate.

The Inventory Presented Amounted Unto 31£-6s-10d

And Shee haveing Given Bond according to Order, Letter of Administration was given to the said Sarah Timberlake.

The Sessions Desolved

Att A Generall Quarter Sessions and Inferior Court of common
Pleas holden in his Maj[ties] name at Rochester for Rhode Island Kings
Province and Providence Plantations &c the 6th day of March *1687*

Present
ffrancis Brinley - Chairman & Judge
L[t] Peleg Sanford }
Ma: Richard Smith } Esqrs.
Ca[n] John ffones }
James Pendleton }
Arther ffenner }
Randall Holden }

The Grand Jury Sworne
Nathaniell Waterman foreman
Job Greene
Lodawick Updike
Henry Gardiner
William Knowles
Clelment Weaver
Enoch Plaise
Ephraim Moss
John Clarke
John Maxson
Samuell Bennet
Thomas Mumford
Henry Bull

Mary the Indian Squaw formerly committed to Prison on Suspicion of felony being called in Court and Proclamation being Made and noe person appearing against her the said Mary is Discharged from her said Imprisonment. [94]

John Peirce of Prudence Island being comitted to Prison for mis-demeaneour by him committed on the 20th day of february Last Appeared in Court and confesed his fault, where upon the Court Discharge the said John Peirce from his said Imprisonment.

Mary Gardiner of Newport being Summoned to Court for that the said Mary being A Single Woman had a feamale Child Borne of her Body in the moneth of June Last past, the Courts Sentance is that the said Mary Gardiner for her said offence to pay a fine of 20s in money or be whipt in Rochester with ten Stripes.

Elizabeth Palmer the Wife of **William Palmer** of Rochester Late Victualler Being Presented in this Sessions by the Grand Jury for an assault and Battery on the Body of **Rose Mackinees** being Called in Court and her Indictment Read to her and Shee Demaunded Guilty of the Charge or not, Answered not Guilty and Refered to Tryall, the Jurys Verdict not Guilty, the court accepts the verdict.

The Jury Sworne Were

Joseph Davell foreman	John Mancester
Roger Burlingham	John Baily
James Carder	Thomas Rogers
Benjamin Carpenter	Thomas Rimington
Stephen Northup	fregift Coggeshall
George Vaughan	Gilbert Magick

Daniell Mackinees of Rochester being Presented in this Court by the Grand Jury for an assault and Battery by him made on the Body of **William Palmer** of the Same Place and Other Misdemeanours being Called in Court and his Presentment Read unto him and he demanded Guilty or not — Ansered not Guilty and Refered to Tryall. The Juryes Verdict, Guilty, the Court accepts the Verdict and Sentance the said Daniell Mackinees for his offence to pay a fine of Six Shillings Eight pence in or as money.

Rose Mackinees the Wife of **Daniell Mackinees** of Rochester being Presented by the Grand Enquest in this Court for an asault and Battery by her made on the Body of **Elizabeth Palmer** the Wife of **William Palmer** of Rochester being Called in Court and her presentment Read to her and Shee Demanded Guilty or not ansered not Guilty, and Referd to Tryall. The Juryes Verdict (Guilty) the Court accept the Verdict and Sentance the said Rose Mackinees for her offence to pay a fine of three shilling four pence in or as money.

George Brownell being Returned by the Sheriff to Serve on the Grand Enquest being called in Court appeard not for which offence of his the Court Sentance the said George Brownell to pay a fine of thirteen Shillings four pence in or as money.

Giddion Freeborne being Returned by the Sheriff to Serve on the Grand Enquest and he refuseing to take the Oath in Court when Required for which offence of his the Court Sentance the said Giddion Freeborne to pay A fine of Six Shillings Eight pence in or as money.

[95] For the Encouragement of fishing

if any Person or Persons Inhabitting at or neer Pettaquamscut Shall make A ware this Spring to Take fish in Pettaquamscut River for their Encoragement therein it is Ordered that noe Person or Persons Shall disturb them in their fishing in their said Ware When made nor fish with them therein Except Such Persons as shall help them to make the said Ware or allow to them that make it and it is alsoe further Ordered that noe person or Persons shall Presume ot make any new Ware above the said Ware thereby hindering the fishing in the said Ware, Notwithstanding this order It is not Intended to hinder any of the neighboure Inhabitants of fishing in the said River above or below the said Ware.

William Palmer of Rochester being Presented in this Court by the Grand Enquest for Selling of Rum by Retaile and Suffering the Same to be Dranke in his said house being Cald in Court and his Presentment Read to him and he Demanded Guilty or not answered (Not Guilty) and Refered to Tryall. The Juryes Verdict (Guilty) the Court accept the verdict and Sentance the said William Palmer for his said offence ot pay a fine of five Pounds.

Ordered that if any Person or Persons Shall Kill any Woolfe or Woolves Within this Province or County, and Shall Demand pay for the Same according to Law Shall bring or Cause to be brought the said Woolfes or Woolves by him or them Soe Killed Within twenty four houres after to a Justice of the Peace who is to Keep Record thereof and Certifie the Same to the Treasurer.

Ordered that there shall be A Rate Levied and assessed on the Severall Townes and Places in this County or Province of fifty three pounds Six Shillings and Eightpence for and toward the Paying for the Killing of Woolves in this Province and to be assessed and Proportioned on each the Townes proportionably At the Rate of one hundred and Sixty pounds is and to be Levied collected and paid at the Same time and in the same manner and forme as in & by the said Order is Directed and Prescribed, The Proportion that each towne is Levied and Assessed to pay is as followeth

Newport	12-13-4
Portsmouth	10-06-8
Providence	09-00-0
Warwick	04-00-0
Deptford	01-00-0
Rochester	06-00-0
feversham	03-06-0
New Shorum	03-13-4
James Towne	03-06-8
	£ 53-06-8

Samuell Eldred being the Informer against **William Palmer** for Selling Rum by Retaile, in Court forgave his part of the fine being the halfe thereof to the sd Palmer

[96]

Upon the Applycation of William Palmer to this Court that hee might have Liberty to Keep An Ordinary, Alehouse or Common Victualing house the Court doe Admitt him to Keep an Ordinary, Ale house or Common Victualling house Untill one year be fully compleat and Ended from and after the day of the Date of his former Lycence.

Upon Complaint to this court made by **Robert Spinke** and others of the Towne of Rochester that Severall Highwayes in the said Towne are Stoped up, to the Great Damage of the Inhabitants of said Towne. It is Ordered that Mr **Daniell Vernon** and Mr **Henry Tibbits** are Impowered to Take Care that the highway which Leads from **George Whitemans** to the Country Road and comes Out to ye said Road between the Land of Mr **James Reinalds** and **John Briggs** be forthwith Layd Open for the Use and Benefit of the Inhabitants.

In an action of Debt Commenced by **William Palmer** Plaintiff against **Henry Mattison** Defend^t^ and there being noe Answer in the office — The Plaintiff Enters a nihildicet. The Debt being under fourty Shillings the Court Declare it not Tryable in this Court.

In an action of Assault and Battery commenced by **William Palmer** of Rochester Plaintiff against **Daniell Mackinees** of the Same place Defendt Pleading, Variance, betweene the writt and Declaration the Court allowed the Plea and Grant a nonsuite in the Case.

Ordered that **John Trip** of Portsmouth on Rhode Island Exucutor and Testament of **John Trip** Late of Portsmouth aforesaid Deceased be Summoned With all convenient Speed to make his appearance before ffrancis Brinley Esqr Judge of the Inferior Court of Pleas and other his Majties Justices to Give his Answer Whether he accept of his Trust as Executor to the said Will of the said John Trip Deceased.

The Sessions and Inferior Court Ended

Att A Meeting in Newport on Rhode Island the
22d day of March *1687*

Justices Present

ffrancis Brinley - Judge of the Inferior Court of common Pleas
Peleg Sanford }
Caleb Carr Senir } Esqrs

John Trip of Portsmouth on Rhode Island who was by the Last will and Testament of his father **John Trip** of said Portsmouth Deceased to be An Executor to his Will being Summoned to give his answer whether hee would accept of the place and Trust of An Executor and he appearing being Demanded Whether he would accept thereof Answered, that hee would not Accept, And **Peleg Trip** of said Portsmouth Sonn of the said John Trip Deceased being also Subpenaed to give his answer Whether hee woold Administer on the Estate of the said John Trip Deceased, being called answered that hee would not accept of Administration on the said Estate.

[97] Upon the Desire and request of **Benjamin Ingell** of Portsmouth on Rhode Island Concerning certaine Goods that weer in his Possession and weer Seized by **Henry Lilly** Dept Sheriffe upon the Complaint of **Christopher Almy** as Attorney to the Children of **John Trip** It is Ordered that the said Goods Shall be apprised by Indifferent Persons and that if the said Benjamin Ingell Shall give bond of the Sum of fifty pounds With Security not to Imbezell nor Wast the said Goods, and that the said Goods according to the Inventory thereof Returned by the said Dept Sheriff Dated the 22d day of february 1687 or 8 Shall be Well Secured and Kept Safe Untill the Same Shall have had Legall Judgment passed on them Whether the said Goods are parcell of the Estate of the said John Trip Deceased or not and that if the said Goods shall be proved to be part of the said Estate of the said John Trip Deceased to well and Truly Surrender and Deliver them to whome according to Law the Same Ought to be Delivered and Surrendred That then the said Benjamin Shall have the Same Delivered to him by the Sheriff Into his Possession hee Receiveing them where they now are.

This Sessions Adjorned untill Thursday come three weekes
being the 12th day of Aprill next

Att A Meeting in Newport on Rhode Island &c
the 10th day of Aprill *1688*

There Being Present

ffrancis Brinley Esqr Judge of the Inferior Court of common Pleas
Peleg Sanford — }Esqrs his Majties
John Coggeshall } Justices of the Peace

Caleb Carr of Newport aforesaid Apearing and being Willing to have Administration on the Estate of **Moses Pacheco** Late of Newport aforesaid Deceased it was Granted Granted that he Should have the Administration of the said Estate he giveing Bond Well and Duly according to Law to Administer on the said Estate. And he haveing Given Bond according to Order Letter of Administration was Given to the said Caleb Carr

The Inventory of the said Estate Being 11£-8s-4d —

The meeting Desolved

[98]

Att a Meeting in Newport Aprill 12th *1688*

Present

ffrancis Brinley Esqr Judge of the Inferior Court of common Pleas
Peleg Sanford }
Caleb Carr Senior } Esqrs Justices of the Peace

Zuriell Hall of Portsmouth on Rhode Island in the Province of Rhode Island Kings Province and Providence Plantations and **Elizabeth** his Wife being Willing to Have Administration on the Estate of **John Tripp** Late of said Portsmouth Deceased it was Granted that they should have Administration on the said Estate Giveing Bond according to Law to Administer on the said Estate.

And he haveing Given Bond according to Order Letter of Administration was Granted to the said Zuriell Hall and Elizabeth his Wife.

The Meeting Ended

Att a Meeting of his Maj[ties] Justices in Newport on Rhode Island the 4th day of Aprill 1688 there were Proved the Wills hereafter mentioned, and al-lowed of By Francis Brinley Esq[r] Judge of the Inferior Court of com[m]on Pleas

Present

Peleg Sanford }
Richard Smith }
John ffones } Esq[rs] Justices of the Peace
Caleb Carr Sen[r] }
James Pendleton }

Joseph Smith the Son & Executor of **John Smith** of the Towne of Providence Deceased Appeared and Presented the Will of the said John Smith Dated the 26th day of March 1686 or 87 and the Wittnesses also to the said Will appearing at the same time did upon oth Testifie to the Truth of the said Will.

John Arnold }
James Browne } Sworne

The Inventory of the Estate of the said John Smith Dated August y[e] 10th 1687 was also Presented which amounted to 19£-13[s]-6 ½

The aprisers being also Present

Thomas Arnold
John Whipple

[99] **Elizabeth Hearnton** Relict and Executrix of **Benjamin Hearnton** Late of the Towne of Providence in New England Deceased appeared and Presented the Will of the said Benjamin Hearnton dated the 1st day of february 1686 - 1686/7 and the Wittnesses to the said Will also appearing at the same Time did upon Oath Testifie to the Trueth of the said Will

John Dexter }
Thomas Arnold } Sworne

The Inventory of the Estate of the said Benjamin Hearnton dated May 27th 1687 was also Presented being which amounted to being brought together 42£-7[s]-4[d] ½ the Aprisers being part Present.

Att a Meeting in Newport on Rhode Island in the Province or County of Rhode Island Kings Province &c May 16th 1688

Present

ffrancis Brinley Esq[r] Judge of the Inferior Court of common Pleas
Peleg Sanford }
Caleb Carr Senior } Esqrs his Majties Justices of the Peace

Richard Clemens of Providence in the Province &c aforesaid the Son of **Thomas Clemens** of said Providence Decesed requesting Administration of the Estate of the said Thomas Clemens, and It was Granted that hee should have Administration on the said Estate he giveing Bond to Administer according to Law on the said Estate, **Elizabeth Clemens** the Relict of the s[d] Thomas Clemens Signifieing her desire that her Son Richard Clemens Should be Admitted Administrator and he haveing Given Bond

according to Order Letter of Administration was Given to the said Richard Clemens. The Inventory of the Estate of the said Thomas Clemens Dated March 9th 1688 was presented which amounted to 38£-04s-0d
The apprisers Being

Epenetus Olney
John Dexter

The Meeting Ended [100]

Att a Generall Quarter Sessions holden in his Majties Name at Newport for Rhode Island Narroganset or Kings Province and Providence Plantations the 12th day of June 1688

Justices Present	The Grand Jury Sworne
ffrancis Brinley Chairman	Edward Greenman foreman
Peleg Sanford	francis Braiton Senior
Richard Smith	Sampson Sheerman
John ffones	John Lewis
John Coggeshall Esqrs	William Gardiner
Caleb Carr Senr	John Shelden
James Pendleton	Peleg Mumford
Symon Ray	John Heath
Arthur ffenner	William Burton
	John Sailes
	Isaac Lawton
	Joshua Raymond
	Robert Guthridge
	Oliver Arnold

John Wells of Feversham Being Presented In the Assises or Generall Goale Delivery holden in [*blank*] Last for Killing Slaying Sundry Swine of **George Denison** of the Same Place and Bearing them away Being Called in Court and his Indictment being Read to him and he Demanded Guilty of the Charge or not Answered not Guilty and Refered to Tryall.
The Jury Sworne wear

Henry Hall foreman	Randall Holden
William Burlington	Stutly Stafford
Samuell Tift	Eleazer Whiple
Joseph Case	Eleazer Arnold
Samuell Browne	John Smith
John Wood	John Coggeshall Junr

The Juries Verdict not Guilty the Court accepts the verdict. The said John Wells Cleared by Proclamaton.

Samuell Whipple }
Giddion Crawford } Sworne
Ephraim Peirce }

The Court Adjourne for an hours Time
the Court Called and Sate

Allexander Gordon of Newport Admitted to have a Lycence

Constables for Feversham:

Nicholas Cotterell }
Joseph Stanton } Sworne

Constables for Warwicke:

James Carder }
John Roads } Sworne

Constables for Portsmouth:

Jeremiah Smith }
Thomas Durfee } Sworne
John Keas }

Edward Wilcox of Feversham being returned by The Sheriff to Serve on the Jury of Tryalls at the Quarter Sessions held in Newport ye 13th day of December 1687 and for not appearing was fined, Applycation being made and Information Given in Court that he had not warning to appear the Court Remitt the fine.

Benjamin Sherman appointed to serve in the office of Constable Sworne

[**101**] Constables for Rochester:

William Gardiner — Sworne

The Court Adjournd till to morrow morning - 8 -
of the Clocke The Court Caled and Sate

Constables for Newport:

Nathanell Coddington
Shuball Painter - being Presented by Ralph Chapman was accepted and after suspended
John Bailey
Charles Dyre
Ezechiell Hunt
John Bennet Appointed by the Court to Serve in the office of Constable Sworn

John Wood and **Symon Parret** both being Chosen by the Inhabitants of ye Towne of Newport in May Last to the office of Constable and in Court Called Refused to Take the Usuall Othe of a Constable

Daniell Vaughan being Chosen by the Inhabitants of Newport in May Last to serve in the office of Constable being Called in Court aledged the Insufficiency of Body was Discharged

Constables for James Towne:

Robert Allen being Chosen to serve in the office of Constable for James Towne and haveing not beene two months an Inhabitant thereof at the Time the Court Discharge him

George Cooke Appointed by the Court to serve in ye office of Constable for James Towne

William Rathbone Appointed by the Court to serve in ye office of Constable for New Shorum

Thomas Star of Newport haveing misbehaved him selfe in Court & Submit himselfe to the Court, the Court sentance is that the said Thomas Starr pay a fine of three shilling four pence.

Whereas the Late Constables of the Towne of Providence have neglected to Call the Inhabitants of the said Towne together to Choose Rate makers to assess and Levy the County Rates Assessed on their Towne for and toward the Erecting and building Court houses &c and for payment for Killing of Woulves this Court order that the said Constables Takeing to their assisstance two or three of their Sufficient Neighbours Shall assess and Levy the said Rates assessed and Levied on their Towne according as by the former orders is Appointed and Directed on or before the first Monday in July next Ensueing and if none of their said neighbours will assist them in makeing the said Rates assessed on their Towne according to the said Orders the said Constables shall Levy the said rates themselves and are hereby also Impowred to gather the said Rates so assessed by Warrant from one Justice are Impowred to Distraine for neglect or refusall of payment of the same and shall forthwith Returne the said Rate by them Soe gathered to the Province or County Treasurer.

Ordered that the Treasurer shall forthwith pay to Mr West Deputy [**102**] Secretary the sum of four pounds one shilling and three Pence in money

Ordered that Every Towne in this Province or County in the next Rate to be Levied shall be Rated the Sum of ten Shillings for and toward their repaying Into the Treasury the said money paid to the D Secretary.

It is Ordered that the Constables of the Townes of Newshorum, feversham, Rochester, Deptford, Warwick, and Providence shall be allowed Resonable Charge for the Transportation by Water of the Rates of Their Towns To the Treasurer or Soe much thereof as shall be sent to him to Newport to be paid in the said Species.

Upon the Request of **Richard Dengley** It is Ordered that he Shall be Discharged from his rate of two Shillings Six pence assessed on him by the Rate makers of the Towne of Newport.

John Tillinghast appointed Gauger Packer and Measurer of salt for the Towne of Newport — and Sworne.

Whereas **John Eldred** of Rochester his Lycence being not fully Expired and he Requesting that it may be continued untill the next Quarter Sessions, It is Ordered that the Lycence of the said John Eldred Shall Continue in force untill the next Quart Sessions and also the Lycence of **Samuel Eldred** of said Rochester is Continued to the next Quarter Sessions.

It is Ordered that the Selectmen Townesmen and Overseers of the Towne of Newport or any one of them Shall Veiw all Cattle Transported from Out of the said Towne by Water and shall have for their Service therein the former and usuall allowed fees

The Court Adjourned untill to morrow morning 8
of the Clock — The Court Called and Sate

Whereas the Late Ratemakers Chosen by the Inhabitants of the Towne of Newport to assess and Levy the Rates assessed on theirTowne by the Justices Sitting in Generall

Quarter Sessions in Newport Decemb^r 13th 1687 and Rochester March 6th 1687 have neglected to Rate some Persons haveing Estates in the Precincts of their Towne that according to Order Ought to have beene Rated It is Ordered that the said Ratemakers doe and shall meet together on Or before the one and Twentieth Day of this Instant June to perfect and finish the list of the said rates and to make Returne thereof forthwith to the Constables of the said Towne

[**103**] The account of **Thomas Ward** Clerke of the Peace Presented in Court being two pounds seven shillings for sending forth of Orders of Sessions is allowed.

ffrancis Brinley & **Peleg Sanford** Esq^rs and **Thomas Ward** are Appointed and Audit to Audit the Sheriffs account.

Henry Lilly Deputy Sheriff is allowed the sum of one pound four shillings for his attendance on the Courts to this Time.

The Sessions Desolved

Att an Inferior Court of Comon Pleas holden in Newport
for Rhode Island Kings Province and Providence Plantations
June 14th 1688

Present
ffrancis Brinley - Esqr Judge
Peleg Sanford }
Richard Smith }
John ffones }
John Coggeshall } Esq^rs
Caleb Carr Senr }
John Pendleton }
Symon Ray }
Arther ffenner }

Daniell Coggeshall of Portsmouth on Rhode Island Executor of **Joshua Coggeshall** of Portsmouth afore said Deceased Appeared in Court and Presented the Will of the said Joshua Coggeshall dated the thirteenth Day of July one Thousand Six hundred Eighty and Seven and the Wittnesses to the said Will also appearing at the same time did Upon Oath Testifie to the Trueth of the said Will

Thomas Townsend }
John Coggeshall } Sworne

The Inventory of the Estate of the said Joshua Coggeshall Dated the 4th day of May 1688 was also Presented in Court amounting unto 185^£-13^s-8^d Present The Apprisers
Thomas Nichols
Robert Lawton

The Court Desolved

[104]

Att a Generall Quarter Sessions holden at Rochester for
Rhode Island Narroganset or Kings Province and Providence
Plantations the 1st Tuesday in Septembr: 1688

Justices Present
ffrancis Brinley }
Capt John ffones } Esqrs
John Coggeshall }
Caleb Carr Senir }
Randall Holden }

Grand Jury Sworne
Edward Pelham foreman
Henry Brightman
Robert Lawton
James Coggeshall
Robert Little
John Rathborne
James Reinalls Senr
Thomas Gould
John Watson
Capt William Hopkins
John Low
Charles Hasleton
John Thomas
Henry Tibitts

Persons Lycenced
William Mayes } of Warwick
George Halsall }
John Davis } of Newport
Stephen Sabeer }
Charles Beer }
John Cooke — of Portsmouth
Samuel Albro — of Rochester
Abraham Campanall
Mary Sanford } of
Joseph Timberlake } Portsmouth
Benjamin Gorton
John Eldred }
Benjamin Mory } of Rochester
Samuel Eldred }

Retailers not Less then a Pottle
Gidian Crawford - 163
Andrew Willet — of Rochester
Margarit Huling — of Newport

The Court Adjourned for an howers Time the Court Called & Sate

Marey Cory of Portsmouth Single Woman Being Called in Court to Answer to An Indictment by the Grand Jury found against her for haveing a child Borne of her Body, June Last past appeared and being Demaunded who was the father of the said Chilld She Answered **John Wickham**.

The Court sentance the said Marey Cory for her offence to pay a fine of twenty shillings in money and also that shee secure the Towne of Portsmouth from all Charges Concerning maintaineing and bringing up the said Child.

Martha Cooke (alias Cory) of Portsmouth on Rhode Island Single Woman being Summoned to Appear at this Court to Answer to a Presentment for haveing a child borne of her Body found by the Grand Jury in June Last past being Called did not ans-

answer by the Court is Ordered that an attachment goe forth against her to appear at the next Quarter Sessions.

[105] **Mary Blower** of Newport on Rhode Island Single Woman being Summoned to Appear at this Court to Answer for haveing Lately had a child borne of her body and being called in Court Did not Answer by the Court it is Ordered that an Attachment goe forth to attach her Body to appear at the next Quarter Sessions.

ffrancis Braiton of Portsmouth on Rhode Island being Summoned to apear at this Court to Answer to a Presentment for seling Drinke to Indians on the first day of the weeke Being Called in Court appeared and Demanded Quilty or not Confessed the fact and Refered himself to the Judgment of the Court. The Courts Sentance is that the said francis Braiton pay a fine of ten shillings in money for his offence.

Robert Lawton of Portsmouth on Rhode Island Sworne Sealer of the said Towne.

The Court Adjourned untill to morrow moring.

The Court Caled and Sate

The Sessions Ended

Att an Inferior Court of Common Pleas holden at Rochester for Rhode Island Kings Province and Providence Plantations Septemb[r] 5th 1688

Justices Present
ffrancis Brinley Judge
Cap[t] John ffones
John Coggeshall
Caleb Carr Seni[r]
Randall Holden

The Jury
John Davis
Latham Clarke
Zuriell Hall
Thomas Manchester
James Danielson
Thomas Arnold
John Knowles
Samuell Eldred Juni[r]
Giles Peirce
Stephen Wilcockes
Thomas ffry Juni[r]
Elisha Berry
John Greene

Actions Entred for Triall

Mungo Crawford Plaintiff **John Cooke** Defend[t] in an action of Debt
Debt and Damage 20£ Sterling Dated 21st August 1688
John Cooke the Defend[t]: in Court Called appeared and Pleads hee owes nothing. The Plaintiff haveing Sattisfied the Court that one of his Wittnesses being Weak of Body and not Capable to appear in Court, the Court grant an Imparleance in the said action untill the next Inferior Court of Pleas to be holden in Newport the Second Tuesday in December next.

Joshua Brodbent Plaintiff, **Charles Beer** Defend[t]: in an action of Debt Debt and Damage 20£ Sterling Dated 30th July 1688. Charles Beer Defend[t] in Court Called appeared and Pleads hee Owes nothing. The Plaintiff haveing sattisfied the Court that his Wittness being Incapable of Body to appear in Court the Court Grant an Imparlance in the said action untill the next Inferior Court of Pleas to be holden in Newport the Second Twesday in December next.

William Baker of Portsmouth being Suppenaid in 20£ to Give Evidence in a case Depending in Court betweene Mungo Crawford and John Cooke being called appeared not and Othe being made in Court that he was Sup-pinaid [*rest of line heavily crossed out*]

Stephen Wilcockes being Returned by the Sheriff to Serve on the Jury of [**106**] Tryalls being Called in Court Answered not for which offence the Court Sentance the said Stephen Wilcockes to pay a fine of thirteene shillings and four pence in money.

The Court Desolved

Att a Generall Quarter Sessions held at Newport for
Rhode Island Kings Province and Providence Plantations the
11th day of December 1688

Justices Present

ffrancis Brinley }
Peleg Sanford }
Richard Smith }
Capt John Fones } Esqrs
John Coggeshall }
Caleb Carr Senior }
Arther ffenner }

Grand Jury Sworne

Lawrence Turner foreman
Thomas Paine
Daniell Stanton
Thomas Brookes
George Sisson
Stephen Cornell
Enoch Plaise
Lodawick Updicke
William Palmer
John Warner
Joseph Woodward
George Vaughan
Stephen Rimmington

Persons Lycenced

Samuel Wilson of Rochester
Job Card of Newshorum
James Sweet of Prudence

John Mory being Returned by the Sheriff to Serve on the Grand Jury being Called in Court Answered, and being Required to Take the Oath Refused for which the Court Sentance the said John Mory to pay a fine of [*blank*]

Whereas there was an Order made in the Quarter Sessions held in Newport the 12th day of December 1687 for the Prevention of Damage by fire in the Towne of Newport that if any Chimney in the said Towne shall be foule and take fire and burne above the Tunnell thereof that the Person useing the said Chimney shall pay Two shillings six pence and by the said Order there was noe means Provided for the Collecting and Receiveing the same, It is Ordered that if any Person or Persons shall give notice of any Chimney Takeing fire and Burning above the Tunnill to the next Justice of the Peace shall have Sixpence for the same Out of the said fine and it is further Ordered that one of the Constables of the said Towne shall demand and receive the

Same and if the Person offending Refuse on demand to pay the Same that then by Warrant from one Justice of the Peace to a Constable he shall Levy the same by Distress on the Goods of the offender together with the Charge thereof and the said fine (Except the Sixpence [107] aforesaid to deliver to the Selectmen and Overseers of the Pore of the said Towne of Newport for the use of the Poor, And also at the Time aforesaid it was Ordered that the Owner of Every Dwelling house in the Parts of the said Towne between the Places called the Pound and the Lands of **Thomas Clifton** Deceased should Provid a Ladder to Stand against the said houses that would conveniently Reach to or neer the Ridge of the said houses within nine moneths on the forfeiture of five shillings and the said Order haveing beene heitherto generally Neglected, It is Ordered that all and Every Person or Persons Owners of Houses as aforesaid shall within three moneths after the End of this Sessions Provide a Ladder or Ladders according as is Directed by the said Order (Except such Persons as have already Provided Ladders accordingly) or shall forfeit the sum of five shillings to be to the use of the Poor of the said Towne of Newport, and it is further Ordered that the Constables of Newport shall take Care to see this Order be Performed and if any shall neglect their Duty herein to Receive and Collect the said fine and if any Person or Persons offending shall Refuse to pay the same on demand the said Constables or any of them by Warrant from one Justice of the Peace shall Levy the same by Distress together with the Charge for Levying the same.

The Court Adjourd for an howres Time

— Called and Sate —

William Baker of Portsmouth being Attached to Appear at this Courte to Answer for his Contempt in not appearing at the Inferior Court of Pleas held at Rochester in September Last, being Called in Court Appeared and submitted himselfe to the Judgement of the Court in the Case the Courts Sentance is that the said William Baker for his said offence to pay a fine of twenty shillings in money.

Whereas the Treasurer of this Province or County hath made Report to this Sessions that severall of the Constables have neglected to Collect and Gather the Severall Rates Levyed on the Estates within their Respective Townes, It is Ordered that the Constables and Each of them that have Neglected to gather and Collect Any the said Assessments shall forthwith Collect and Gather the Same or else for the Neglect of their said Duty they and Every of them shall be Lyable to pay the Sum or Sums by them Neglected to be Collected and Gathered as by the said Orders are Provided and Directed, and that if all or any of the Constables shall neglect to pay the said Assssments and finish their accounts with the said Treasurer it shall and may be Lawfull for any two Justices of the Peace of This Province &c to grant forth a Warrant to the Sheriff or Other Person as to them shall seem meet to Distraine the same of the Goods and Chattles of all and every the Constables that shall neglect their Duty herein.

Marth Cory of Portsmouth being called in Court to Answer for her misdemeanour in not appearing according to Summons at the Sessions held at Rochester the first Tuesday in September Last, appeared appeared Submitted to the Judgment of the Court In the Case, the Courts Sentance is that the said Martha for her offence to pay a fine of ten shillings in money. [**108**] Whereas by the Order of Sessions held at Rochester the sixt day of March 1687 It was Ordered that if any Person or Persons shall Kill any Woolfe or Woulves Within this Province or County and shall Demand pay for the Same according to Law shall within twenty four howres bering the Bodys of the said Woolves to A Justice of the Peace, which Order is found Difficult to Performe, It is therefore Ordered that if the head and skin of Any Woolfe by any Person Soe Killed shall be Brought to A Justice of the Peace in the said Time it shall be Sufficient for the Justice of the Peace to make Record of the Killing the said Woolfes and to certifie the same to the Treasurer.

Mary Blower of Newport Singlewoman being Attached to Appear at this Sessions to Answer for her Contempt in not appearing at the Sessions held at Rochester in September Last to Answer for haveing a Child borne of her Body and being in Court Called Appeared and it being affirmed that shee was then unable to appear the Courts Judgment was that shee should save the Towne of Newport harmless from Charge in bringing up the said Child and her father **James Blower** Engageing to save the said Towne harmless the Court Dismist the said Mary.

It is Ordered that the Seller of Cordwood in the Towne of Newport shall pay the four pence A Cord for Cording ye s^d^ wood

The Court Adjourned till tomorrow Morning

the Court Called and Sate

James Greene Sworne Sealer of the Towne of Rochester

the Seale of the said towne is - **R** -

Jeremiah Browne being appointed sealer of the Towne of Newport and not being Capable to come to Court **Caleb Carr** Senr Esqr was by the Court Ordered to give him his Oath — and he Returne that hee was sworne to his s^d^ office.

Ordered that there shall be A Rate of one hundred and Twenty pounds Levyed and Raised on the Severall Townes in this Province or County for the Defraying of the Publick charge thereof and to be Paid unto the Treasurer of this Province or County on or Before the first day of July next Ensueing in the Specias herein after named and at the Prisses hereafter That is to say Sheeps Wooll at Eight Pence the pound Butter at four pence a pound Indian Corne at fourteene Pence the Bushell, and if any Person or Persons shall pay money hee or they shall be Abated the one Six part, all which Specias to be Good and Merchantable.

The Proportion that Each Towne is Levyed and Assessed to pay is as ffolloweth [**109**]

	£ s
Newport	28-10
Portsmouth	23-05
Providence	20-05
Warwick	09-00
Deptford	02-05
Rochester	13-10
feversham	7-00

Newshorum	8-15
James Towne	7-10
	120-00

Ordered that the Select men in Each the Respective Townes Within this Province or County shall meet together on or before the first Wednesday in Aprill next to assess and Levy the Rate assessed and Levyed on their Towne by his Maj^ties Justices Sitting in Generall Quarter Sessions held in Newport the Eleventh day of December 1688 on Each the Estates of the Inhabitants and Others Within the Precincts of their Towne-ships which said Rate made and the List thereof Perfected under the hands of the said Selectmen or the Major Part of them on or before the third Wensday in the said moneth of Aprill and forthwith to be delivered to the Constables of each Towne who are hereby Required to gather and Collect the same and the said Rate by them So Gathered and Collected the Said Constables shall send unto the Treasurer of this Province or County of Rhode Island &c on or before the first day of July next and the Better to Enable the Constables to gather and Collect the said Rate the said Constables are Impowred if any Person or Persons shall Neglect or Refuse to pay the Rate so assessed on them to Distraine of the Estate of the Person or Persons neglicting or Refuseing to pay their Rate

It is Ordered that Leiu^ts Colonell **Peleg Sanford** and **Thomas Ward** shall Examin all the accounts concerneing the Publick Charge of this Province or County and the accounts which shall be by them approved and allowed shall be paid by the Treasurer of this Province or County.

This Sessions Adjourned till to morrow

The Clerk shall Transcrib the Orders of this Sessions in Order for the makeing the Same Knowne to all Persons Concerned that they may conforme accordingly.

The Sessions Ended

Att The Inferior Court of Pleas held in Newport on Rhode Island &c
the 12th day of Decemb^r 1688

In an action of Debt commenced by **Mungo Craford** Plaintiff against **John Cooke** Defend^t: Debt and Damage 20^£ Dated August 21st 1688 and the action Entred for Tryall at the Inferior Court of Pleas held at Rochester the 5th of Septemb^r Last past, the Defend^t being called Appearing Pleaded he owes Nothing. And upon the Plea of the Plaintiff that his Wittness was sick and Incable to come to Court the Case was Emparled to this Court.

[**110**] The Plaintiff Called appeared, the Defendant Called Apeared. The Case Pleaded and Committed to the Jury.

The Jury Sworne

Peleg Shearman foreman	Samuell Eldridge
Bartholomew Hunt	Rouse Helmes
Thomas Weaver	Moses Lippit
John Odlin Jun^ir	Thomas Nichols Junr

Isaac Lawton	Lot Strainge
Richard Peirce	John Bliss

The Jury^s Verdict, Wee find for the Defendant

In an Action of Debt Commenced by **Joshua Brodbent** Plaintiff against **Charles Beere** Defendant, Debt and Damage 20£ Dated July 30th 1688 and the action Entred for Tryall at the Inferior Court of Pleas held at Rochester September 5th Last past, the Defendant being Called Appeared & Pleaded he owes nothing. And upon the Plea of the Plaintiff that his Wittness was Incapable of Body to Appeare in Court, the Case was Emparled to this Court. The Plaintiff Called Appeared, The Defendant Called Appeared. The Case Pleaded and Comitted to the Jury.

The Jury Sworne

Peleg Shearman foreman	Samuell Eldridge
Bartholomew Hunt	Rouse Hulmes
Thomas Weaver	Moses Lipit
John Odlin Junir	Thomas Nichols Junr
Isaac Lawton	Lot Strainge
Richard Peirce	John Bliss

The Jury^s Verdict, Wee finde for the Defendant. Entred for Tryall

Joshua Brodbent and **Mungo Craford** Plaintiff **ffrancis Braiton** Defendant in an action of Debt Dated September the 4th 1688

The Plaintiff Called Appeard, the Defendant Called Appeared. The Plaintiff Demured to the Plea and Answer of the Defendant for the Insufficiency thereof, Where Upon the Justices, take time till the Inferior Court of Pleas to be held at Rochester the first Twesday in March next to Advise on the Premises.

Proclamation being made for **Samuell Moone**, to appeare in Court to give in Evidence in a case Depending between **Joshua Brodbent** Plaintiff and **Charles Beere** Defendant in an action of Debt, Debt and Damage 20£ Dated July 30th 1688 appeared not.

John West of Swansey in the County of Bristol misbehaveing himselfe in Court, the Court Sentance the said John West for his offence to pay a fine of 3s-4d in money.

The Court Adjourned till to morrow morning

Called and Sate

Anthony Shaw haveing misbehaved himselfe and Broken the Peace the Court Sentance the said Anthony Shaw to pay a fine of 3s-4d in money and to give Bond to be of Good behaviour. [111]

Joshua Brodbent and **Mungo Craford** Plaintiff, **Thomas Cooke** Defendant in an action of Debt, Debt and Damage 20£ Sterling Dated October 16th 1688. The Plaintiff Called Appeared, the Defendt Called **John West** Attorney Appeared. The Case Refered to the next Court, and afterwards Agreed.

Thomas Cooke Plaintiff, **Mungo Craford** Defendt in an action of Debt, Debt and Damage 50£ Sterling Dated November 17th for want of a Declaration the Defendant Entred a nonsuite.

Thomas Cooke Plaintiff **Mungo Craford** Defendant in an action of Slaunder Damage 200£ Dated November 17th 1688 there being noe Declaration in the office the Defendant Enters a nonsuite.

Nathaniell Mory being Returned to serve on the Jury of Tryalls being Called in Court Answered, and being Required to Take the Oath Refused for which offence the Court Sentance the said Nathaniell Mory to pay a fine of 5s.

The Court Adjourned for an howers Time

Caled and Sate

—— The Court Desolved ——

Att a meeting of his Majties Justices in Newport on Rhode Island in the Province or County of Rhode Island Kings Province and Providence Plantations January 2d 1688

Present

ffrancis Brinley Esqr Judge of the Inferior Court of Pleas
Peleg Sanford }
Caleb Carr Senior } Esqrs Justices of the Peace

Nicholas Carr of James Towne in the Province or County aforesaid appearing and Requesting to have the Administration of the estate of **William Hadley** of James Towne aforesaid Deceased it was Granted the hee should have the Administration of the said Estate hee giveing Bond well and Duly to Administer the same according to Law

The Inventory of the Estate Presented amounted unto - 4£-13s-6d and he haveing Given Bond according to Order Letters of Administration was Given to the said Nicholas Carr.

[112]

Att a Generall Quarter Sessions held at Rochester for
Rhode Island Kings Province and Providence Plantations
the first Twensday in March 1688

Justices Present
Richard Smith }
John ffones } Esq^rs
Arther ffenner }
ffrancis Brinley Esqr

Grand Jury Sworne
foreman William Champlin
Thomas Hassard
John Peirce
William Turpin
James Angell
John Sweet
John Potter
Henry Rennalls
Thomas Mumford
Jeffery Champlin
George Whiteman
Henry Knowles
John Whipple
Arthur Kerke
ffreegift Coggeshall

The Court Adjourned till to morrow morning

The Court Called and Sate

Persons Lycenced

Paull Collin, Jaco Rattier, Peter Ayrault of Rochester.
Providence: John Whipple, William Turpin.
Newport: Thomas Case.
ffeversham: Joseph Pemberton.
Deptford: Clement Weaver.

Anthony Shaw of Portsmouth being bound by Recognizance to the Good behaviour and appearance at this Court being Called appeared, and Proclamation made and no Person appearing against him he is Discharged paying fees.

James Wilson of Rochester in this Province &c being bound by Recognizance to this Court and to the Good behaviour being Called appeared, the Court Order the said Wilson to Give bond with Surety for his appearance at the next Sessions and to be of good behaviour.

Job Greene Returned by the Sheriff to Serve on the Grand Jury being Called Appeared and then Required to Take the Usuall Oath Possitively Refused for which offence the Court sentance the said Job Greene to pay a fine of thirteen shillings four pence in money.

Robert Allen Returned by the Sheriffe to Serve on the Grand Jury being Called Appeared and then Required to take the Usuall Oath Did Scroople & Refuse to take the Oath for which offence ye Court sentance the said Robert Allen to pay a fine of six shillings Eight pence in money.

The Court Adjourned for an howres time Called and Sate

William Palmer of the Towne of Rochester Presented by the Grand Jury for Planting a Peach Tree on the first day of the Weeke being the third day of this Instant March was Called in Court and his Presentment Read to him and Demanded whether hee would Travers the Case this Court, Answered Yes.

The Court Adjourned Untill to morrow morning

The Court Called and Sate

William Palmer Called in Court appeared and Confessed the fact and submitted to the Judgment of the Court in the matter, the Court sentance ye s^d^ William Palmer to pay a fine of three shillings four pence in money.

Mongo Crawford being Presented by ye Grand Jury for that the said Mongoe vexatiously molested and Trobled his Maj^ties^ Subjects with Vexatious Suits being Called in Court and his Presentment Read to him and he Demanded whether he would Travers the Case this Court or not Answered he Would not.

The Sessions Ended

[113]

Att An Inferior Court of Common Pleas holden at Rochester for Rhode Island Kings Province and Providence Plantations the 20th day of March 1688

Present

ffrancis Brinley Esqr Judge
Richard Smith }
John ffones } Esq^rs^
Arther ffenner }

Joshua Brodbent & **Mungo Craford** Pla^nt^: **ffrancis Braiton** Defend^t^: in an action of Debt Dated September 4th 1688 the Plaintiff Called appeared the Defend^t^ Called Appeared, the Plaintiff Demurred to the Plea & answer of the Defend^t^: where upon the Justices take time untill the Inferior Court of Pleas to be held at Rochester in this Instant March to Advise on the Premisses, the Plaintiffe and Defend^t^ being Called appeared the Court Over Rule the Demur and Order the Defend^t^: to pay to the Plaintiff nine shillings and there upon Grant Leave to the Defend^t^ to Amend his Answer.

Entrys for Tryall

Savill Sampson of Boston Shoomaker Pla^t^: **Henry Rawlins** of Prudence Island in the Township of Portsmouth marriner Defend^t^: in an action of Debt, Debt and Damage 300^£^ Dated January 11th 1688 The Plan^t^ Called Appeared the Defend^t^ Called appeared The Plant[iffs] Wittnesses not being Within this Province and at this time Cannot appeare in Court and there upon he Requested An Emparleance in the Case Untill the Inferior Court of Pleas to be holden in Newport on Rhode Island the Second Twesday in June next, which was Granted.

Joshua Brodbent and **Mungo Craford** Pla^ts^: **Thomas Hickey** Defend^t^: in an action Debt and Damage 60^£^ Sterling Dated Decemb^r^ 14th 1688 The Plan^ts^ Called Appeared, the Defend^t^ Called Appeared. The Plan^ts^ Informed the Court that his

Wittnisses Weer not in a Capassity to appear in Court where Upon the Plaintiffs Requested An Imparleance in the Case to the Inferior Court of Pleas to be holden at Newport the second Twesday in June next which was accordingly Granted

Abigall Remington Widdow and Relict of **John Remmington** Late of Rochester Deceased Presented in Court an Inventory of the Estate of her said Deceased Husband and Requested Administration on the said Estate which was accordingly Granted.
The Inventory of the Estate of the said John Remmington Dated the 18th day of february 1688 Amounting unto - 46£-17s-09d.

The apprissers Henry Gardiner
Henry Bull Junir

Benjamin Hall returned by the Sheriffe to serve on the Jury of Tryalls being Called Appeared not for which offence the Court Sentance the said Benjamin Hall to pay a fine of thirteene shillings four pence.

The Court Ended

Att a Meeting of his Majties Justices in Newport on Rhode Island in the Province or County of Rhode Island Kings Province and Providence Plantations March 18th 1688

Present

ffrancis Brinley Esqr Judge of the Inferior Court of Pleas
Peleg Sanford }
Caleb Carr Ser } Esqrs Justices of the Peace

Benjamin Newberry of Newport aforesaid appeared and Requested Administration on the Estate of his Brother in law **Robert Twin** Late of London Deceased which was accordingly Granted he giveing bond according to Law Well and Truly to Administer the said Estate.
The Inventory of the Estate of the said Robert Twin was also Presented which amounted unto - 8£-0s-0d.

Apprisers Weston Clarke
John Scot

The Meeting Ended

[*There is a gap in the records, to September 1693. Three pages were evidently left blank and the following two documents entered much later, out of chronological order*]

[115]

Know all men by these presents that I **Martain Anderson** of ye Island Neyeve [?] in ye Province of New Yorke marr^r^ have Nominated & Constituted Ordained & by these presents doe Nominate Ordaine Constitute Appointe & in my stid & place putt my Trusty and well Beloved friend **Abraham Rideout** of ye town of Newport in ye Colony of Rhoad Island as my true & lawfull attorney to aske demande levey recover and receive for mee &, in my name and to my use of **William Squire** of ye town of New Bristall in ye province of ye Masachusett in New England marr^r^ & now or late Commandr of ye vessell called ye Newport belonging to ye sd town of Bristall ye sume of twenty foure pounds & five shillings, Cur^t^ silver mony of ye Collony of Rhoad Island, which ye sd William Squire oweth unto mee ye remaining part of my wages Now dew unto mee for servis done by mee on borde ye sd vessell as by a certaine writing und^r^ ye hand of ye said William Squire written in ye s^d^ town of Bristoll & directed unto my s^d^ Attorny & delivered unto him in ye town of Newport baring date with these p^r^sents, bouth for day & year being ready to be produced, doth & may more at Large Appear Giving & by these presents Granting to my sd Attorney my whole & full power and Authorety in ye premises to sue arest Imprison Implead & Condem ye said William Squire his Executors or Adm^rs^ or any othr pson or psons which shall or may becom liable to pay sd debt for mee & in my name & to my use in Any Court before Any Judg or Justis & them or Either of them out of prison Againe to deliver and upon ye receipt of ye sd sume of twenty foure pounds & five shillings or Any part thare of: One or more Lawfull Acquittance or Acquittances Discharge or Discharges for mee & in my name to make signe seall and deliver And also one or more Attorny or Attornies under him to substitute and appoint & at his pleasure againe to revoake & further to doe touching or Conserning ye premices as throughly & holy as I the sd Martaine Anderson in my owne pson might or could doe in ye same Rettifing confirming & Allowing whatsoever my sd Attorney shall Lawfully doe or Cause to be done in ye premises by these presents. In Witness whareof I the sd Martain Andresson have heare unto sett my hand & seal the seventh day of July ye 7th year of ye Reigne of o^ur^ Soveraigne Lady Ann Regina over England & Annq Domij 1708

Signed sealled & delivered in ye presence of us Robt Carr Nath^ll^ Sulvester

The marke of ye sd Marten *W* Andresson

Compared with ye Originnall & Entred upon Record ye 25th of Augt pr Wes^t^ Clarke Recd^r^

July ye 17th 1708 Appered ye within named Martain Andreson and Acknowledged ye with in written power to be his Act & Deed before mee James Brown Justis

[116] Know all men by these presents y^{t} I **Elisha Cole** of Kings town in ye Collony of Rhoad Island & Providence Plants &c In New England youman am holden & Stand firmely bound & Obledged unto **Thomas Coop**^{er} of Boston in ye County of Suffolk in New-England aforesd march^{t} In ye full & Just Sume of five hundred And Sixty pounds Currant Mony of New-England to be payd unto ye s^{d} Thomas Coop^{r} his Attorney Ex^{rs} Adm^{trs} or Assignes To which Payment well and truly to be made I bind my Selfe my heires Executo^{rs} And Adm^{rs} formerly by these p^{r}sents Sealed with my seal Dated ye twenty third day of Desemb^{r} Anno Domi 1704 Annoq R R Anne Anglies &c Tertio
The Condition of this Obligation is Such that whareas **John Cole** of Kings town Aforesd youman father of ye Above Bounden **Elisha Cole** and **Susanah** his wife in And by their Certaine Letters of Attorney or provisation and or their hands & Sealls duly Executred Baring date of ye Seventeenth Day of Desemb^{r} Anno Domi 1703 did Impower ye s^{d} Tho Coop^{r} to receive of And from **Edmond Soames** of London in ye Relme of England, Draper ye full And Just Sume of two hundred pounds Sterling mony of England vallue received of s^{d} Coop^{r} viz, two hundred & Eighty pounds Currant mony of New England Tharefore ye s^{d} Sume of two hundred pounds sterling shall or hath bene well & truly paid unto ye s^{d} Thomas Coop^{r} his Attorney Ex^{r} Adm^{r} or Assignes by ye s^{d} Edmond Soames his heires Ex^{rs} or Adm^{rs} According to ye purport of ye s^{d} Letters of Attorney Either before ye Date of these presents or at Any time within six months next Insuing ye Date heare of or in Defalt thareof If ye Above bounden Elisha Cole his heires Ex^{rs} or Adm^{rs} shall & doe well And truly pay or Cause to be payd unto ye s^{d} Thomas Coop^{r} his Attorney Ex^{rs} Adm^{rs} or Assignes in Boston Afore s^{d} ye full & Just Sume of two hundred & Eighty pounds Currant Silver mony of New England with Lawfull Intrest for ye same unto ye day of Payment (viz) ye time of Six months Above [——] After ye rate of Six pounds p^{r} Cent p^{r} Anum with out fraud or delay then This Obligation to be void or Else in full force
Sealled & delivered in y^{e}
Presence of us Elisha Cole (seal)
John Vincent testes
Thos Danford The Above Written is A true Coppy of y^{e} Originall Bond
as Attest West^{n} Clarke Recd^{r}
Suffolk SS
Boston July y^{e} 5th = 1706
Thomas Danford of full Age parsonally Appered & mad Oath y^{t} hee was p^{r}sent & saw y^{e} within named Elisha Cole Signe Seall And as his Act & Deed Deliver the within written Obligation to y^{e} use within mentioned & y^{t} hee y^{e} deponant together with John Vincent sett to their hands as Wittnesses of ye Execution thareof At ye same time
Jurat Corom Is Addington JP:

[*page 117 is blank*]

[118] At A Gen^{rll} Court of tryall held for his Maj^{ttys} Collony of Rhoad Island & providence plantations the 5th of Sep^{t} 1693 being Called at the Gov^{rs} hous by reason of Sickness of the Govr & Deputy Govr that they Could not Attende the Court in Order to Discharge ye Collonies Consernes &c

These are to publish & declare that this present Court of tryall is Adjorned to the Last Tusday of this Instant & that all psons that have Any Actions Depending in Sd Court by bond Recognizence or other wise by bill or obligation are to be Continued in as full forse And power as they ware at this present Court & all Such psons are Required then to Attend as had Either Action Som[m]ons or bound Over or in Custody of ye Shriffe shall neglect of their Apperance at ye time the Court is adjorned to Shall have Judgment Entred Against them upon none Apperance as Aforesd & all Jury men Chosen by ye severall towns Are Requird to Attend as Aforesd & upon ye penalty as the Law derects

Septemb^{r} 26th 1693 The Court being called at the Gov^{r}s hous Aforesd
& by Reason the sickness still Continuing on ye Govr & Deputy Govr
The Court is Adjourned to the Second Tusday in Novemb^{r} next Insuing
And all persons are Required to Attend as Aforesd.

Novemb^{r} 14th 1693 the Court Againe Called According to Adjornment

John Easton Govr
Maj^{r} John Green Dep^{ty} Govr
Mr Caleb Carr As^{t}
Mr Edward Thurston As^{t}
Mr Benj Arnold As^{t}
Mr Jeames Barker As^{t}
Mr Steven Arnold As^{t}
Mr Joseph Ginks As^{t}
Mr Giles Slocom As^{t}
Mr Henry Brightman As^{t}
Mr Benjn Smith As^{t}
West^{t} Clarke Recd
Epharim Turner Attorny
Charles Tillinghast G Sarg^{t}
John Hulms G^{rl} Tresuar

Grand Jury
William Jeames ffDoreman
Andrew Langworthy
William Peckham
John Clarke
John Pepody
John Holm
Richard Ebing
John Scott
Daniell Parce
Joseph Palmer
Nath^{ll} Shiffield
John Roades

The Jury of tryalls
Charles Crosewhaitt foreman
Robert Tailor
Thomas Case
Thomas Dawson
Johnathan Mash
John Paine
Thomas Gould
ffreegift Coggeshall
Alixand^{r} Gordon
John Greenman
Edward Boss
Pall Stevens

The Case Commenced by **Charles Dyre** pl^{f} Against **ffrancis Brinley** Def^{t} called in Court the Jury of tryalls Impannalled & Sworne in An Action of Deten[ure] The Court see Cause that the Action Abate.

John Greenman pl^{f} Against **Samuell Dyre** Def^{t}, in An Action of Debt by bond the Case pleaded in Court & Committed to ye Jury: The verditt of the Jury is wee find for

John Greenman pl^f^ husband to **Elizabeth** Second Daughter **William Dyre** Deceased fourty pounds Currant Mony with Cost of Suitt. The Court Exsept ye verditt & Causes Judgment to be Entred

William Potter pl^t^: **John Hicks** Def^t^: After much Debate ye Court see Cause to Abate ye Action

Thomas Rodman pl^t^ Against **John Stanton** Def^t^ in An Action of Debt debt & Damage twenty pounds the Case being Called the pl^t^ Appered but no Appearance of ye Def^t^ ye pl^t^ Enters A Nihil decett The Case Committed to ye Jury, the Verditt of the Jury is wee find for ye pl^f^ the debt According to Account 17^£^ 15^s^ & Cost of Court five Shilling Damage ye Verditt Axsepted & Judgment given.

Martha Hews being Indicted for Selling of Lickors by retaile & hir Indictment Read she pleads not Guilty & putt hir Selfe upon tryall by god & ye Cuntry ye Returne of the Jury is Not Guilty & Shee Cleared by procklamation paying hir fees.

Jeames Phillips being Indicted for burning **Nath^ll^ Moris** hay Spoiling his barn killing his Cattle & Severall threatts pleads Not Guilty & Refers him Selfe to ye Jury. The Returne of ye Jury is Not Guilty & Ordred to be cleared by procklamation paying his fees but thare being A Stope in ye procklamation ye Court for Severall Reasons see Cause to bind ye sd Jeames Phillips in a bond of twenty pounds with two Surties for his good behaviour till ye next Court of tryalls.

Abraham Anthony being bound by recognizance for Contempt of Authority to Appr at Court And being Called in Court did not Appeare the Determanation is that his bonds are forfited.

John Albro being bound over & not Appering the Sence of ye Court that his bond is forfited.

Benjamin Star being Indicted for helping his father **Thomas Star** out of [119] prison & braking ye prison & by the Jury found guilty the sentance of the Court is that ye said Benj^a^ Starr for his offence pay tenn shillings mony to ye Genrll tresuar & officers fees or to be whipt on his naked backe ten Stripes forth with.

Joseph Stanton being presented in Court for Contempt of Authority & hee Owning him selfe guilty & Refers him selfe to ye hon^r^ bench And upon serious Consideration of the Court hee the sd Joseph Stanton is for his Contempt of Authority fined six pounds ten Shillings to be payd forth with to ye Gen^r^ll Tresuar & Offices ffees & to remaine in Durance till ye Sentence is fullfiled; The Court Desolved:

At A Court of Tryalls held for ye Collony of Rhoad Island And Providence Plant^{s}. at ye Collony hous in Newport The 27th day of March 1694

John Easton Govr
Mr John Green Dep^{ty} Govr
Caleb Carr As^{t}
Benj Arnold As^{t}
Edward Thurston As^{t}
Jeames Barker As^{t}
Stephen Arnold As^{t}
Joseph Ginks As^{t}
Giles Slocom As^{t}
Henry Brightman As^{t}
Benj Smith As^{t}
Wes^{t} Clarke Recd^{r}
Charles Tillinghast G Sarg^{t}
Epharim Turner G Atty
John Hulmes G Tre^{a}su^{r}
Joseph Card foreman
John Clarke
Richard Dunn
Phillip Tillinghast
William Arnold
John Sanford

Grand Jury
Capt Edward Pelham foreman
Thomas Rogers
Thomas Burge
Sam^{ll} Stapelton
Mathew Grenall
John Carr
John Smith
Jireh Bull
Charles Beere
George Bradly
Phillip Harwood
Sam^{ll} Cranston

Jury of tryalls
John Hedley
Sam^{ll} Minott
Thomas Casse
John Rogers
Sam^{ll} Davis
Obadiah Coates

Charles Dyre p^{lt} Against **ffrances Brinley** Def^{t} by A writt of Ejectment the sd Brinly not Appearing Either by him selfe or Attorney the Case is Committed to ye Jury for Judgment According to Law the verditt of the Jury is wee finde for ye p^{lt} title of Land sued for Coste of Court & twelve pence Damage the verditt Accepted & Judgment Given

Robart Davis being by bond bound to this Court & Appering is Cleared of his bonds paying officers fees

John Green being by bond bound to this Court & Appering is Cleared of his bonds paying Officers ffees

John Carr of Kingstown is Cleared by proclamation from his bonds paying officers ffees

Henry Gardner being bound Over to this Court for being Charged by **Abigall Rimington** for gitting on hir body two bastard Children And he being the Reputitife father in the Law he is Sentanced by this Court to Keepe ye town of Kings town Indemnifide from Any Charge that may Arise for ye Maintenance of ye sd Children & that ye Children Shall be Maintained by the sd Henry Gardner.

Abigall Rimington being bound to Appear at Court to Answer for the Act of fornication Committed with **Henry Gardner** & being taken sick Could not Appear the sd Gardner payd hir fine in Court being twenty six shillings & Eight pence & officers fees:

The Court Desolved

[120]

At A Gen^{rll} Court of Tryalls held for ye Collony of Rhoad Island & Providence Plant^{s} the 4th day of Sepr 1694

John Easton Govr
Mj^{r} John Green Dep^{ty} Govr
Caleb Carr As^{t}
Edward Thurston As^{t}
Benj Arnold As^{t}
Jeames Barker As^{t}
Joseph Jenkes As^{t}
Stephen Arnold As^{t}
Joseph Williams As^{t}
Giles Slocom As^{t}
Henry Brightman As^{t}
Benj Smith As^{t}
Wes^{t} Clarke Recd
John Hulmes Tresuar
Charles Tillinghast G Sarg^{t}
John Easton Junr G. Attorny

Grand Jury
Jeremiah Clarke
Sam^{ll} Stapelton
Thomas Peckham
Walter Roads
Thomas Paty
John Ward
William Waddall
Andrew Langworthy
Thomas Gould
John Rathbon
John Godfrey
Gilbart Majgack

Jury of tryalls
Sam^{ll} Winsor foreman
Nath^{ll} Bowdish
Will Peckham
Dan^{ll} Vaughan
Robart Fish
Benj Shearman
Nath^{ll} Sheffild
Charles Dyre
Obadiah Coates
William Allin
Thomas Casce
Nath^{ll} Dyre

Ordred by the Gen^{rll} Court of Tryalls that Mr **Epharim Turner** is Appointed their Maj^{ttis} Attorny in the rome of **John Easton** Gen^{rl} Attorney Chosen by the Collony hee being Gon to Phillidelph & the sd Turner hath taken his Engagment thareonto for this Court or untill the next Election

Majo^{r} **Roger Goulding** pla^{t} Against **William Wanton** Def^{t} in An Action of trespas the Case being Called & pleaded & Committed to the Jury the verditt is wee find for ye Def^{t} ye verditt Accepted

Capt **Jeffery Champlin** p^{lt}: Against **Joseph Pemberton** Def^{t} in An Action of Detinue & keeping from ye plantif A hors Damage six pound The Action being Called pleaded & Committed to the Jury the Juris verditt wee find for the pla^{t} three pounds damage & Corst of Corrt The verditt Accepted & Judgment given

Nathaniell Blagrave plan^{t} Against **John Rhoads** Def^{t} for breach of Covenant Damage foure pounds the Case being pleaded in Court & Committed to ye Jury the verditt we find for the pla^{t} twenty shillings Damage & Coust of Court the verditt Accepted

John Harding being Chosen by the town of Newport for A grand Jury man & would not serve is fined ten Shillings

Jeames Clarke being Chosen A grand Jury man & Refusing to serve is fined 20*s* & hath payd it in Court

ffrancis Waste of kings town being bound over to Courte for breach of pesce & by the grand Jury found Ignoramos was Cleared by proclamation paying fees

Epharim Higing Chosen A grand Jury man & not Appearing is find ten Shillings

John Vaughan Chosen A grand Jury man for the town of Portsmouth & not Appearing is by the Court fined 13^s^: 4^d^

John Carder Chosen A grand Jury man for the town of Warwicke & **Stutly Wascott** A petty Jury man they not Appering in Court are Sentananced to pay Each A fine of 13^s^: 4^d^

Robert Davis being under bonds for his good behavor & Called in Court & no Apperance Left **John Low** & **John Warner** being bound in twenty pound bond for his Apperance the Court doe Deame the bonds to be forfited yett never the Less for ye Respect the Court hath to ye Surties that if they bring the sd Davis to the next Genrll Court of tryalls & hee thare stand & Abide the Sentance of the Court their forfiture shall be Remitted:

[121] **Thomas Starr** being presented by the Attorny Genrll for breach of his Maj^tty^ Gole & Contempt of Authority & found Guilty by the Jury the Sentance of the Court is that ye sd Thomas Starr pay A fine of twenty shilling to ye tresury & officers fees

The Court Desolved

At A Court of Tryalls held at Newport in his Maj[tt] Name
The 26th of March 1695

John Easton Gov[r]	Grand Jury Ingaged
M[r] John Green Dep[ty] Gov[r]	Cap[t] Henry Tew
Caleb Carr As[t]	Thomas Burge
Edward Thurston As[t]	ffreegift Coggeshall
Benj Arnold As[t]	Robart Ayres
Jeames Barker As[t]	Dan[ll] Lawton
Joseph Jenkes As[t]	Joseph Cook
Stephen Arnold As[t]	David Shippe
Joseph Williams As[t]	Nath[ll] Dyre
Henry Brightman As[t]	Nath[ll] Sheffild
Giles Slocom As[t]	Joseph Gardner
Benj Smith As[t]	John Rathbon
West[t] Clarke Recd	John Bayly
Charles Tillinghast G Sarg[t]	
Epharim Turner G. Attorny	
John Hulmes G Tresuar	

Jury of tryalls Engaged

Nicholas Carr foreman	Jeremiah Clarke
John Coggeshall	John Pepody
Nich Easton	John Davis
Thomas Manchester	Robart Carr
John Corey	Richard Dunn
Andrew Langworthy	John Spencer

Robart Davis of providence tailo[r] being Indicted as An Accessary or Confederett of feloniously takeing A hors & pleads not Guilty & Refers himselfe to god & y[e] Cuntry The Returne of the Jury is Guilty

M[r] **John Walker** of Boston being bound by Recognisence to Appeare at this Court hath made his Apperance According to bond & is dismist

John Martin being Indicted for breach of his Maj[tty] Laws Called in Court Asked Guilty or Not Guilty pleads Not Guilty & putts himselfe upon tryall by god & y[e] Cuntry y[e] Returne & verdit of Jury is Not Guilty & is Cleared by procklamation paying fees

Robart Davis being found Guilty Acc[ess]ary of fellony by the Jury & Judgments given thare on the sentance of the Court is that y[e] sd Robart Davis pay twenty shillings to y[e] Genrll tresury or be forth with whipt on his Naked back with ten stripes & pay officers feese

The Court Desolved

At A Genrll Court of Tryall held for the Collony at Newport
the 3rd day of Septemb^{r} 1695

Caleb Carr Govr
Maj^{r} John Green D Govr
Benedict Arnold As^{t}
Samuell Cranston As^{t}
Jeames Barker As^{t}
Joseph Jenks As^{t}
Stephen Arnold As^{t}
Henry Brightman As^{t}
Giles Slocom As^{t}
Benj Smith As^{t}
William Gibson As^{t}
Jeffery Champlin As^{t}
Johnathan Hulmes Jus^{t}
Joseph Williams Jus^{t}
Wes^{t} Clarke Recd
Charles Tillinghast G Sarg^{t}
John Hulmes Tresuar
Epharim Turner Attorny

Grand Jury Ingaged
Jireh Bull foreman
Joseph Card
Thomas Gould
Thomas Brokes
Thomas Mallett
Thomas Wever
Sam^{ll} Davis
William Roades
John Rathbon
Benj Palmer
Thomas Langford
Johnathan Benitt

Jury of tryalls Engaged
Capt William Brinley foreman
Larance Turner
John Gould Junr
John Pepody
Joseph Barker
William Peckham
John Davis
Charles Dickinson
Jeames Rogers
Sam^{ll} Stibins
William Barker
Nicholas Easton

Anthony Shaw haveing Abused the Court the Court Sentenced him for his Misdemeaner to pay thirty shillings to ye Gen^{ll} tresuar & Charge of Court

John Warner being presented for Contempt of Authority pleads [*crossed out*: not] Guilty And Refers him selfe to be tride by the Juryes at ye bench The Sentance of the Court is that John Warner pay fourty Shillings in Court & offices fees

William Hack being Over to Court for breach of his Maj^{tty} pece Called in [122]
Court did not Appear but his Surties **Joseph Tisdall** & **John Godfrey** Appered: the Court for his neglect & Contempt se cause to Continue the bonds to ye next Court of Tryals ——

Daniell Williams Returned A grand Jury man for the town of Providence is find 13^{s}: 4^{d} **John Anggell** & **Richard Clemance** being Returned from sd town for ye Jury of tryalls & not Appearing is fined 13^{s}: 4^{d} Each

John Roads Grand Jury man for ye town of Warwick & **Jeames Briggs** of sd town for ye Jury of tryall not Appearing are fined 13^{s} 4^{d} Each

Joseph Mory of Jeames town being Returned A grand Jury man for sd town not Appearing is fined 13^{s}: 4^{d} The Court Desolved

At A Genrll Court of Tryalls held for the Collony
At Newport the 31st day of March 1696

Walter Clarke Govr
Majr John Green D Govr
Benj Arnold Ast
Capt Samll Cranston Ast
Capt Jeams Barkr Ast
Joseph Jenks Ast
Stephen Arnold Ast
Henry Brightman Ast
Giles Slocom Ast
William Gibson Ast
Capt Jeffery Champlin Ast
Capt Johnathan Holmes Just
Joseph Williams Just
West Clarke Recd
Thomas Townsend Shrif
John Pocock Attorny
John Hulmes Tresuar

Grand Jury Engaged
Capt John Stanton foreman
ffreegift Coggeshall
Thomas Brok
Richard Dun
Peleg Sherman
James Babcock
William Spencer
Henry Gardner
Andrew Willitt
Capt John Rogers
William Allin
George Sisson

Jury of Tryalls, Engd
Joseph Hull foreman
Thomas Wever
Charles Dyre
Jeames Brown
Will Burlington
Joseph Pemberton
John Weeden
Capt Danll Eldredg
John Crandall
Benj Spencer
Joseph Nicholoson
Gilbart Magjick

Danll Wilcock plt Against Capt **Will Southward** Deft in An Action of forceable Entry Damage five hundred pounds, the Case Called & by Consent of plt & Deft suspended to ye next Court.

Capt **Thomas Townsend** plt **Danell Eaton** Deft in An Action of trespass, the Case Called & by Consent of plt & Deft was suspended to ye next Court in Sepr.

Capt **Thomas Townsend** plt **William Hillard** Deft in An Action of trespass Suspended by Consent as aforesd.

Thomas Mallitt plt Against **Samuell Davis** Deft In An Action of Debt the Case Called the Deft pleads the Genrll Issue Committed to the Jury The verditt of the Jury wee find for ye Deft Coust of Court the verditt Accepted & ye bill of Cost Signed.

Nicholas Trott Esqr plt Against **Thomas Casse** & **Richard Durfie** Deft for none payment of One bill of Exchange Damage two hundred pounds The Action Called the Defts plead, the Genrll Issue the Case Committed to the Jury the verditt is wee find for the plt one hundred pounds three pounds Damage & Coust of Court The verditt Accepted: the Deft Enters A rehearing of ye Action to ye next Court of Tryall & have payd the Coast.

Richard Hancock plt by A writt of Ejectment Served on the tennants of Mr **William & Benj Brown** on Prudence Island Called in Court & the sd Hancock not having power to plead in the right of **Edmond & Margarett Willy** his wife in whose right hee sued the Court orders A nonsuit to ye Action.

Rebecka Coggeshall pl^t^ Against **Dan^ll^ Coggeshall** Deft in An Action of ye Case for non payment of A legacey given hir by hir husband **Joshua Coggeshall** deceased. The Case Called pleaded & Committed to ye Jury the Jury verditt is wee find for the pl^t^ hir Legacey given hir by hir husbands will & Cost of Court. The Verditt Accepted & Bill of Cost Signed ye Deft Enteres A nohearing & payd ye Cost

Robart Kelton being Called in Court & not Appearing Capt **Arther Venner** & **Will Randall** being bound for his Apperance the Court sentance is that ye bond is forfited for non Apperance.

Giddian Crofford Called in Court being under Recognizence no parson Appering to prsente hee is Cleared from his bonds paying fees

Joseph Latham is Cleared of his bonds paying ffees ye Court Desolved

At A Genrll Court of Tryall held for the Collony at Newport the first day of Sept^r^ *1696* [123]

Walter Clarke Govr
Maj^r^ John Green D Govr
Capt Sam^ll^ Cranston As^t^
Walter Nubary As^t^
Jeams Bark^r^ As^t^
Joseph Jenks As^t^
Stephen Arnold As^t^
Capt Joseph Sheffield As^t^
Giles Slocom As^t^
Benj Smith As^t^
Will Gibson As^t^
Jeffery Champlin As^t^
Johnathan Hulms Jus^t^
Joseph Williams Jus^t^
Will Champlin Jus^t^
Thomas Fry Jus^t^
West^t^ Clarke Recd
Thomas Townsend Shrif
John Pocock Gen^ll^ Attorny
John Hulmes Tresuar

Grand Jury Eng^d^
Capt Will Brinly foreman
Robart Carr
William Weden
Stephen Mumford
William Greenman
John Wipple
Giddian Freeborn
Georg Witman
Sam^ll^ Warden
John Lewis
John Rogers
Daniell Parce

Jury of Tryalls, Eng^d^
Capt Henry Tew foreman
Arnold Collings
Robart Little
Robart Tailor
Thomas Harris
Jobe Jenni
Henry Straitt
William Wanton
Alixander Gordon
George Deninson
Phillip Tillinghast
Daniell Coggeshall

A Rehearing upon An Action Depending Betwene **Nicholas Trott** Esqr pl^t^ **Thomas Casse** & **Richard Durfe** Deft upon the Rehearing the sd Durfie & Casse Appeares as pl^t^s the Case Committed to the Jury The verditt of the Jury wee find for Nicholas

Trott Def[t] one hundred pounds currant mony of New England three pence Damage & Cost of Cort The verdit Accepted & Judgment given

Thare being A bill of Indictment presented by **John Pocock** Gen[rll] Atturny to y[e] Grand Jury for Suspition that **Patrick Kane** & was the Cause of y[e] Deth of **Pall Stevens** the Grand Jury found A true bill the said **Patrick Caine** being Called for was brought to the barr by the Shriffe the bill of Indictment Reed unto him; hee holding his hand at the barr was asked Guilty or Not Guilty Answers not Guilty & Refers him Selfe upon tryall by god & the Cuntry The Verditt of the Jury is Wee find it Chancemedly by y[e] sd Patrick Kaine. Whareas **Patrick Kane** Glover being by the Jury of tryalls found Guilty of Chance Medly in the Deth of Pall Stevens Glov[r] Late of Newport whare by Law hee is Lyable to be Stigmtised And fined at the Discreshon of his Maj[tts] Judges as the Law in such Cases provides — The Sentance of this Court is that Patrick Kann shall be forthwith Branded on y[e] Right hand neare the thumb with the Letter **R** And all his goods forfited to his Maj[tty] And be Kept in Common Gole till till good Security be given to Authority in y[e] sume of one hundred pounds for his good behavour So Long as hee shall Continue in this Collony & pay officers ffees: Cap[t] Thomas Townsend Shriffe you are in his Maj[ttys] Name Requirrd to See this Sentance Executed forthwith at y[e] wiping post near y[e] Collony hous.

Mary Bason An Indian squaw being Charged by **Joseph Hicks** of Ports-mouth for fellony & shee oning guilty & sd it was by Instagation of **John Burdens** Negro **Jack** & mad it so Appear the sd Jack is Sentanced to be wipt on his Naked back with thirty nine Stripes & pay officers fees.

Samson Sherman being Returned by y[e] town of Portsmouth for grand Jury Man & Not Appering is fined 13[s] 6[d]

Francis Brayton & **John Albro** Jun[r] being Returned by sd town for Jury of tryall & not Appearing is fined 13[s] - 4[d] Each

The Court Desolved

[124]

At A Genrll Court of Tryall held for the Collony at
Newport the 30th of March 1697

Walter Clarke Govr
Maj John Green Dept
Capt Samll Cranston Ast
Walter Nubary Ast
Jeames Barker Ast
Joseph Jenks Ast
Stephen Arnold Ast
Joseph Sheffild Ast
Giles Slocom Ast
Benj Smith Ast
William Gibson Ast
Jeffery Champlin Ast
West Clarke Recd
Thomas Townsend Shrf
John Pocock Attorney
John Hulmes Tresur

Grand Jury Engagd
John Heath foreman
Thomas Cornell
William Allin
Stephen Mumford Snr
John Wood
Danll Wilcock
John Burdon
Israll Arnold
Henry hall
Rowland Robinson
Thomas Mallitt
Giddian freeborn

G Jury of tryalls Engd
John Rogers foreman
Isaac Martandall
Jireh Bull
John Baly
Stephen Mumford Jnr
Richard Clemance
Thomas Manchester
Tobias Brown
Robart Hugens
Thomas Durfee
Thomas Green
Edward Dyre

Christopher Allmey Junr Against Capt **Benj Church** Deft in An Action of Slander The Action Called Declaration & Answer Read thare proving Defalt in ye plts Declaration the Sence of ye Court thare be Anonsuitt

Henry Trasher Plt **Daniell Thurston** Deft In An Action of trespas Damage ten pounds The Case Called pleaded & Committed to the Jury the Juris verditt wee find for ye plt foure pounds Mony Damage & Cost of Court the verditt Accepted & bill of Cost Signed

Martha Lay Widdow plt Against **William Homsby** Deft In An Action of Breach of Covenant The Case pleaded And Committed to ye Jury the verditt of the Jury wee find for the plt Six pounds & three shilling debt & damage & Cost of Court the verditt Accepted

John Garrard plt Against **Peter Green** Deft In An Action of trespas upon the Case for with holding from ye plt Sertain Lands in the town of Warwick the Case pleaded & Committed to ye Jury the verdit wee find for ye deft two pence Damage And Cost of Corte the verditt Accepted

Zarubable Wascott Plt Against **Abraham Lockwood** of Warwick Deft in An Action of trespas upon ye Case for with holding & detaining from ye plt A sertain hous & Six Acres of Land Lying in the town of Warwick: the Issue Genrll the Case pleaded & Committed to the Jury the Juris verditt wee find for the plt the Six Acres of Land

Espetially Mentioned in ye Declaration & Caust of Court The verditt Acepted & bill of Cost Signed, John Pocock Attorney to Abraham Lockwood Enters A rehearing in the Case to ye Court of tryalls in Sepr next & hath payd ye Cost.

Mary Timberlake Junr Pl^t Against **Samuell Stebins** of Newport Def^t in An Action of ye Case for with holding from ye pl^t Sertain Lands in the town of Newport The Action Called pleaded & Commited to the Jury the verditt of the Jury is Wee find for the pl^t the Land sued for by Declaration & Cost of Court the verditt Accepted

An Action of trover Commenced by **Samuell Stebins** pl^t Against **Thomas Durfe** Junr Def^t. The Court for Some Reasons Sees Cause the Action Shall Abate

Robart Ayres being presented for working on ye first Day of the weeke & his Bill Read & demanded wheather guilty or not Guilty he possatifely den[y]ing to give his Answer which the Cort Judged to be Contempt Against ye Kings Authority for which the sd Robart Ayres is Sentansed to pay fourty Shillings in Mony to ye Gen^rll tresuar & officers fees.

Simon Parratt being presented for fencing part on the kings highway being Called in Court & Asked guilty or not Guilty pleads Not Guilty the presentment Committed to the Jury the Juris verditt is According to Evidence upon Record wee find Simon parrat Guilty of ye presentment: The Sentance of ye Court is that ye sd Simon Parratt Lay out the Land According to ye Record presented to ye Jury with in tenn days Otherwise the Sheriffe with his Ayde is to take ye fence down & ye Land to ye high way According to verditt & ye sd Parratt pay officers fees

The Court Desolved

[125]

At A Genrll Cort of Tryalls held at Newport ye 7th day of Sep^{t} 1697

Walter Clark Govr
Maj^{r} John Green D Go^{r}
Mr Sam^{ll} Cranston As^{t}
Capt Nath^{ll} Coddington As^{t}
Jeames Barker As^{t}
Joseph Jenks As^{t}
Stephen Arnold As^{t}
Joseph Sheffield As^{t}
Giles Slocom As^{t}
William Gibson As^{t}
Jeffery Champlin As^{t}
Wes^{t} Clarke Recd^{r}
Capt Thomas Townsend Sf
John Pocock Gen^{ll} Attorny
John Hulms Genl Tresur

Grand Jury Eng^{d}
Latham Clark foreman
John Davis
John Vaughan
Robart Ayres
Thomas Peckham
Thomas Rogers
Isaac Lawton
Jeames Lewis
John Thomas
Henry Tebbits
Thomas Hassard
Giles Parce

Jury of tryalls Eng^{d}
ffreegift Coggeshall foreman
John Gould
William Barker
William Weeden
John Rogers Junr
Thomas Sherman
Simon Smith
Jeames Babcock
Samson Battey
Henry Gardner
Micall Spencer
Joseph Gardner

Zerubable Wascott pl^{t} **Abaram Lockwood** def^{t} in A case of trespas upon a hearing procured by ye def^{t} where in ye deft is to pay costs for Jury &c The Action Called & pleaded & Committed to ye Jury the verditt of the Jury is wee find for Zorabable Wascott ye Six Acres of Land sued for Cost of Court & two pence Damage the verditt Accepted & bill of Cost Signed, **John Warner** Attorney for ye def^{t} having in Court payd the fees Allowed Enters An Appeall of the sd Action to be heard in the Gen^{r}ll Assembly to be held the Last wensday in Octob^{r} next Insuing & the sd Warner did in Court obledge himselfe in the sum of one hundred pounds to prosecute the sd Appeall as aforesd to Efect.

Joseph Hicks pl^{t} Against **Samuell Fairebanks** def^{t} in An Action of debt the Action Called & pleaded & Committed to ye Jury the Juris verditt is wee find for ye pl^{t} Seven pounds nine shillings & ten pence Cost of Corte And two pence Damage the verditt Accepted

Henry Tibbitts pl^{t} Against **Giles Parce** def^{t} in An Action of trespasse the case called pleaded & Committed to ye Jury the verditt is Wee find for the pl^{at} Cost of Court & two shillings Damage the verditt Accepted & bill of Cost signed. The def^{t} having payd the Cost in Court Enters A rehearing of the Case to ye next Court in March 1698

John Briggs of Kingstown pl^{t} Against **Josiah Jones** of So Kingstown def^{t} in An Action of trespas the Action Called & pleaded the Issue Gen^{r}ll & Committed to ye Jury the Juris verditt we find for ye pl^{t} Cost of Court & Eight Shilling Damage. After being by ye Court sent out three times the verditt Accepted & Bill of Cost Signed **Josiah Johnes** def^{t} having payd the Cost in Court Enters A Rehearing of the Case to ye Court of tryall in March 1698.

Nicholas Harris of ye town of Providence being bound over to Court for Contempt of Authority & being presented by ye Grand Jury A true bill pleads not guilty & upon plea[—] ye bill abates for [———] & he the sd Nicholas Harris Cleared by prock-lamation paying of fees —

Jeames An Indian & **Mary** his wife being indicted for felloniously taking ye goats of **Gabraell Jenings** pleads not guilty & come to tryall & was by the Jury found Guilty

The Sentance of the Court is that ye sd Jeames Indian & Mary his wife be Each of them whipt on their naked Backs with fifteen Lashes Each forth with at ye Comon whiping post & Returned to ye Gole till they or Either of pay unto Gaberall Jenings Seventeen pounds ten shilling & two pence & officers fees

The Court Desolved

[126]

At A Gen^{r}ll Court of tryalls held for his Maj^{tty} Collony of Rhoad Island And Providence Pla^{t} at Newport 29th of March 1698

Sam^{ll} Cranston Govr
John Green Dep^{ty} Govr
Nath^{ll} Coddington As^{t}
Robart Carr As^{t}
Jeames Barker As^{t}
Joseph Jenks As^{t}
Stephen Arnold As^{t}
Joseph Sheffild As^{t}
Giles Slocom As^{t}
Benj Smith As^{t}
William Gibson As^{t}
Jeffery Champlin As^{t}
Johnath Hulmes Jus^{t}
Joseph Williams Jus^{t}
John ffones Jus^{t}
Thomas ffry Jus^{t}
West^{n} Clarke Recd^{r}
Thomas Townsend Shreff
John Pocock Atty
John Hulmes Tresuar

Grand Jury Eng^{d}
Latham Clark foreman
Nicholas Easton
Thomas Wever
William Peckham
Benj Thare
Dan^{ll} Lawton
Joseph Rimington
Henry Tibbits
Phillip Long
John Rogers Junr
Dan^{ll} Thurston
John Paine

Jury of tryalls Eng^{d}

Benj Barton foreman
John Odlin Junr
Edward Smith
William Corey
Christopher Champlin
Peter Parker

Jeames Coggeshall
William Hawkings
William Arnold
Benjamin Green
Sam^ll^ Bennitt
Obadiah Coates

John Bridgs of Kingstown plt Against **Josiah Jones** Def^t^ upon A Rehearing the Action Called & pleaded & Committed to the Jury the Juris verditt Wee find for ye def^t^ Coust of Court & Eight Shillings & Six pence damage the verditt Accepted in Court

Sam^ll^ Stibbins pla^t^ **Thomas Durfey** Junr def^t^ In An Action of ye Case for Refusing to Deliver to ye pl^t^ A steer by ye Def^t^ Taken Damage ten pounds the Action Called thare being no Answer in ye Office by ye Def^t^ According to Law Nevertheless by consent of pl^t^ & def^ts^ with the Advice of the Court that ye Case com to plea & ye def^t^ putt his Answer in Court Which shall not be A presedent for ye future the Action pleaded & Committed to the Jury the Juris verditt is Wee find for the pl^t^ Cost of Court & foure pounds ten shillings damage The verditt Accepted & the bill of Cost Signed: the Def^t^ having payd the Cost Enters A Rehearing to ye Court of tryalls in Septr next.

Martha Lay Pl^t^: **William Hohnsby** Def^t^ in An Action of Brach of Covenant The Action Called pleaded & Committed to ye Jury the Jurys verditt, Wee find for ye pl^t^ Coust of Court & Breach of Covenant the verditt Accepted

Sam^ll^ ffones pl^t^: **John Spencer** Def^t^: The Action Called ye pl^t^ discontinues his Action.

Edmond Dolbear pl^t^ Against **Ebenezer Way** Def^t^ in An Action of Debt upon Acc. The Action Called pl^t^ appearing the Def^t^ not Appearing ye pl^t^ Enters A nihill dicett the Case Commtted to ye Jury to Inquire for damages the verditt of ye Jury is Wee find for ye pl^t^ twelve pounds Eight Shillings nine pence & Coust of Court & Six Shillings damage the verditt Accepted & bill of Cost signed

John Dolbear pl^t^ **Ebenezar Way** Def^t^ In An Action of Debt upon Account the Action Called ye pl^t^ Appearing the Def^t^ not Appearing the pl^t^ Enters A Nihill dicett the Action Committed to the Jury to Inquire for damages The Juris verditt is wee find for the plt five pounds five shillings & nine pence Cost of Cort & six shillings damage The verditt Accepted & Cost Assigned.

Jeames Green Pl^t^ **Jeames Samson** Def^t^ the Case Called the opinion of the Court for Defect in ye p^lt^ Declaration that ye Action Abate

Capt **ffrancis Foxcraft** pl^t^ **Phillip Phining** Def^t^ in An Action of debt upon Account the Action Called & pleaded Committed to ye Jury the Juris verditt wee find for ye pl^t^ one hundred & nine pounds two shillings & three pence Cost of Cort & three pounds damage the verditt Excepted

Joseph Bryer Pl^t^: **Thomas fox** Attorney to **John Tate** of Barbados Deft In An Action of debt upon Account The Case Called & Committed to ye Jury the verditt of the Jury is wee find for ye pla^t^ nine pounds nine shillings three pence halfe peny the Cost of Corte & five shillings Damage the verditt Accp^d^

John Stanton Pl^t^ **Ebenezer Way** Def^t^ in An Action of debt for hous rent the Def^t^ not Answering the Case Committed to ye Jury the Juris verditt wee find for ye plan^t^: Eight pounds three Shillings & seven pence & Cost of Court & six pence damage the verditt Accepted

[127] **Edmond Willy** & **Margrett** his wife & **Richard Hancock** & **Judeth** his wife Pl[t] Against **Jeames Sweatt** of Prudence Island Def[t] In An Action of the Case the Case Called & After A long debate before the Court thare being A Deferance betwene y[e] Declaration & Answer the Sence of y[e] Court is that whareas thare hath bene mistake boath by Pl[t] & Def[t] that y[e] Action Come to tryall — The Case pleaded & Committed to y[e] Jury the verditt Returned is wee finde for the Pla[t] title of Land & wright of possesion Sued for & ten pounds Damage & Cost of Court the Verditt Accepted & bill of Cost Signed the Def[t] having payd his Cost Enters a Rehearing to y[e] Court of tryalls in Septmb[r] next

Edmond Willy & **Margrett** his wife & **Richard Hancock** & **Judeth** his wife Pl[t] in An Action of the Case Against **Dan[ll] Parse** of Prudence Island Def the Case Called & Committed to y[e] Jury the Juris verditt Wee find for the plantifs title of Land & wright of possession Sued for ten pounds Damage & Cost of Court. The Verditt Accepted & bill of Cost Signed The Def[t] payd the Cost & Enters A Rehearing to y[e] Court of tryall in Septemb[r] next

Edmond Willy & **Margrett** his wife & **Richard Hancock** & **Judeth** his wife Pl[t] in An Action of the Case Against **Thomas Scranton** of Prudence Island Def[t] The Case Called pleaded & Committed to y[e] Jury the Juris verditt Wee finde for y[e] Pl[t] title of Land Right of possession sued for ten pounds Damage And Coust of Court The verditt Accepted & bill of Cost signed The Def[t] payd the Cost & Enters A Rehearing to y[e] Court of tryalls in Sep[tr] next

Edmond Willy & **Margrett** his wife & **Rich[d] Hancock** & **Judeth** his wife Pl[t] in An Action of the Case Against **Johnathan Hill** of Prudence Island Def[t] The Case Called pleaded & Committed to the Jury the Juris verditt Wee find for the Pl[t]: title of Land for Right of possession Sued for ten pounds Damage And Cost of Corte The verditt Accepted & bill of Cost Signed The Def[t] payd the Cost & Enters A rehearing to y[e] Court in Sep[t] next

Edmond Willy & **Margrett** his wife & **Rich[d] Hancock** & **Judeth** his wife Pl[t] in An Action of the Case Against **John Parse** Def[t] the Case Called and pleaded & Committed to y[e] Jury the Juris verditt Wee find for y[e] plantiff title of Land & Right of possestion sued for ten pounds Damage & Cost of Courte The verditt Accepted & bill of Cost Signed The def[t] having payd the Coste Enters A rehearing by y[e] Court of tryalls in Sep[tr] next

Thare being no Criminall Actions the Jury is Dismist & y[e] Court Desolved

At A Gen'll Court of tryalls held for the Collony at Newport
The Six day of Septemb' 1698

Maj' Sam'll Cranston Gov'	Grand Jury Eng'd
Maj' John Green Dep'y Gov'	John Blis foreman
Cap't Nath'll Coddington As't	Maj' Thomas Rogers
Cap't Robart Carr As't	Thomas Gould
Cap't Jeames Barker As't	Thomas Peckham
Cap't Richard Arnold As't	Joseph Bennet
Joseph Williams As't	Stephen Arnold Jn'
Cap't Joseph Sheffield As't	John Ward
Giles Slocom As't	John Manchester
Benj Smith As't	Job Green
Cap't John ffones As't	Jeames Babcock
Cap't Jeffery Champlin As't	Thomas Winterton
Wes't Clarke Recd	John Eldredg
Jireh Bull Shriffe	
John Pocock Attorny G'll	
John Hulmes G tresur	

Jury of tryall Eng'd

Jeremiah Smith fman	Edward Inman
John Vaughan	Samuell Wickam
Stephen Mumford	Joseph Pembelton
John Pepedy	Benony Sweatt
William Allin	Nicholas Easton
Rowland Robinson	John Rogers Jun'

The Court Called & Opened

Edmond Willy & Margrett his wife & **Richard Hancock & Judeth** his wife plantfs **Jeames Swete Dan'll Parce Thomas Cranston Johnathan Hill John Parce** of prudence Island Def'ts Called in Court on A rehearing in the Severall Cases by the plt Commenced Against y'e Defts [128]

Whareas at A Court of tryalls held at Newport for the Collony of Rhoad Island & providence plantations the Last tusday in March Last past Edward Willy & Margrett his wife & Rich'd Hancock & Judeth his wife in right of their sd wifes Commenced their Severall Actions Against the ten-nant in possestion of Maj' **William Brown** & **Benj-Brown** Esq'rs, their half part of prudence Island wharein the sd Willy & Hancock obtained verditts Against the sd tenants & Judgments of Court on sd verditts, And the Honrd Court then upon Motion granted the said tennants A Rehearing upon their Suffitient Bond for bringing on y'e sd Rehearing Which being Calld And the sd tennants Appearing in Cort this 6'th day of Sep'tr 1698 And the sd Hancock tho sollemly called not Appearing And the sd Willy by **Jeames Menzies** Gen'll his Attorny hearein Court Departing & receeding from his Case & plea Its tharefore considred By the Court that Judgment is Entred by Defalt Against sd Willy & sd Hancock & Margrett & Judeth their wifes And that all former verdict & verditts Judgment & Judgments in y'e sd Cases be quashed & Reversed as null & voide & this is the Judgment of this Court

Samuell Stibbins plt: on A Rehearing **Thomas Durfey** Junr Def^{t} The Case Called pleaded & Committed to ye Jury the Jurys verditt Wee find for the plt Cost of Court & foure pounds tenn shillings Damage The Verditt Accepted

Ebenezar Brenton of bristoll plt Against **Richard Burt** of Tanton Dft In An Action of Debt upon Account the Action Called pleaded & Committed to ye Jury the Jurys verditt Wee find for ye plt Eighteen pound, 9^{s} & 10^{d} as Appears by book Cost of Court & 2^{d} Damage ye verditt Accepted

John Hulmes pl^{t} Against **Solloman Curtis** of Bristoll Deft in An Action of debt by bond of thirty pounds the Action Called the Def^{t} ones the bond & Refers him Selfe to ye honrd Court for Judgment the Judgment of ye Court is that ye Def^{t} pay the Sume Sued for with Intrust at Six persent & Cost of Court

Thare being in Court A long Debate betwene **Jeames Babcock** of Westerly p^{lt} & **Erasmas Babbitt** of sd Westerly Deft In An Action of ye Case the Resolve of the Court is that ye pl^{t} shall mend som Defect in his Declaration & ye Case Com to plea the Issue Genrll & pleaded in Court the verditt of the Jury Wee finde for the pl^{t} & Cost of Court the verditt Accepted

Martha Lay pl^{t} Against **William Holmesby** Def^{t} in An Action of ye Case for breach of Covenant the Action Called pleaded And Committed to the Jury the verditt is wee for ye pl^{t} Cost of Courte & that ye Def^{t} shall Surrender ye goods by him taken from ye pl^{t}: the 5th of Apparell 1697 as by Evidence doth Appeare or the vallue of them & five pounds Damage the verditt Accepted

Thare being An Action of trespas & Ejectment Commenced by **ffrancis Brinley** pl^{t} Against **Charles Dyre** Def^{t} And thare being Along Debate in Court upon the Case & finding that thare was A former prosede by Charles Dyre present Def^{t} in the Court **of tryalls the** 7th of March 1694 whare hee obtained a verditt for the Land the Above sd francis Brinley Plan^{t} now Sueth for & Judgment in Said Court on Sd verditt And An Order for his possestion to ye Genrll Sargant **Charles Tillinghast** who possessed sd Dyre of sd Land which is Judged by this Court to be out of their Jurisdiction to Admitt of further Tryall thare being A law in ye Collony to the Contrary: Capt **John fones** As^{t} Enters his desent to ye Above sd oppinnion of ye Court

Christopher Almey pl^{t} Against **Joseph Chase** Wever Deft in An Action of trespas Damage thirty six pounds thare being A defect in ye declaration the Action Abates

Joseph Chase Wever pl^{t} Against **Christopher Almey** Deft the Case Called the Court see Cause that ye Action Abate

[129] **Edward Dyre** pl^{t} Against **Samuell Green** Deft in An Action of trespas upon ye Case the Action Called & thare being A defferance betwene the Ritte [writ] and Declaration the Court orders An Amendment & it Shall not be no bann to ye Action & ye Deft to have Liberty of A Replycation on the Immendation upon which Reply the Court See Cause that ye Action Abate

Thomas Townsend Late Shrife of the Collony pl^{t} Against **Thomas Durfe** Senr Def^{t} in An Action of ye Case for nonperformance of A bond or Obligation Debt & Damage fourty pounds The Action Called pl^{t} & Def^{t} Appearing the Def^{t} pleads ye Generl Issu not Guilty the Case pleaded & Committed to ye Jury the Jury verditt is wee find for the pla[t] Cost of Court & twenty pounds & six pence Damage the verditt Accepted & bill of Cost Signed the Def[t] having payd the Cost Enters A rehearing to the Court of tryalls in March next

Henry Cherry pl[t] **John Smith** Sadler Def[t] in An Action of Slander And Defamation the Issue Genrll the Action pleaded & Committed to y[e] Jury the verdit of Jury Wee find for y[e] pl[t] Cost of Court & Six Shillings Damage the Verditt Accepted

Edmond Dolbear & **John Dolbear** plantifs Against **Thomas Townsend** Late Shrif Def[t] the pl[ts] Declarations not being filed in time as the Law Required the deft Enters A nonsuitt to y[e] Actions

Joseph Hicks pl[t]: **Thomas Townsend** Late Shriffe Def[t] In An Action of the Case the Case Called & pleaded & Committed to y[e] Jury the Jurys verditt wee find for y[e] Deft Cost of Court the verditt Accepted

Presentments Called & y[e] Jury Impannaled on Crimminalls ——————

John Faning being presented for breach of his Maj[ty] peace Called in Court pleads not Guilty & Refers himSelfe to y[e] Jury The Juries verditt not guilty & hee Cleared by procklamation paying ffeese

William Chaplin being presented by the Grand Jury for Suspition of fellony Called in Court pleads not Guilty & Refers himselfe to the Jury the Jurys verditt is not Guilty

Isaac Ballord of Kings town being presented by the Kings Attorney for fellony by the Complaint of **John Carr** of Kings town being Called in Court the Bill Read to him pleads not Guilty & puts him Selfe upon y[e] Cuntry the verditt of the Jury is Guilty of y[e] Indictment —

Whareas Isaac Ballord was by the Jury found Guilty of his Indictment the Court See Cause to Suspende Sentance till the Court of tryall in March next & that hee in the Meanetime find good security in y[e] sume of twenty pounds for his Apperance at said Court & pay the presents fees due by Law

Coranall **Peleg Sanford** did in Open Court Obledge him Selfe in the Sume of twenty pounds that Isaack Ballard should appeare at y[e] next Court of tryall in March next

Daniell Wilcocks being Indicted for taking or fenceing A Highway in the town of Portsmouth prays that his hearing may be Suspended to the next Court of tryalls in March next which is by the Court granted

By Order of y[e] Court y[e] Shriffe brought in **Christophar Almey** his prison[r] who pleads for his son **Job Almey** being Also A prisoner & Could not Appeare & desires the Court not to take y[e] Advantage of his Sons not Appearing & hee would Abide y[e] Sentance of Each According to A warrant of Commitment to his Maj[tys] Comon Gole March 8th 1697 for A forse made on y[e] hous of **Joseph Chase** in the town of Portsmouth According to verditt of Jury found y[e] 8th day of March 1697.

The Court sentance is that you Christopher Almey pay A fine for sd Action to the King the Sume of five pounds & that your son Job Allmey allso pay five pounds as A fine to y[e] King for sd Action & that you boath remain prisoner in y[e] shrifs custody till y[e] fines be payd

Nathaniell An Indian being Indicted for wounding of **Gaberiell Ginnings** brought forth in Court pleads not guilty & puts himselfe upon ye Cuntry the Juries verditt is Guilty —

The Sentance of the Court is y^{t} ye sd Nath^{ll} Indian for breach of his Maj^{tt} peace pay ten groats & twenty pounds six shillings to Gabarell Ginings towards his one & Docters Charge 12^{d} for Cort Charges an to be a servant to ye sd Gaberell Jenings or his Assignes till sd sum Aforesd be payd & to be Remaine A prisoner till hee hath given good Security for ye same & pay prison fees

The Court Dissolved

[130] At A genrall Court of tryalls held at Newport for his Maj^{ttys} Collony of Rhoad Island & Providence Plants: ye 28th of March **1699**

Sam^{ll} Cranston Esqr Govr	Grand Jury
Maj^{r} John Green D: Govr	John Godfrey foreman
Capt Nath^{ll} Coddington As^{t}:	John Rogers Junr
Capt Robart Carr As^{t}:	Sam^{ll} Stapelton
Capt Jeames Barker As^{t}:	Thomas Harris
Capt Richard Arnold As^{t}:	William Corey
Capt Joseph Williams As^{t}:	Joseph Cook
Capt Joseph Shiffild As^{t}:	John Spencer
Mr Giles Slocomb As^{t}:	Joseph Runalls
Mr Benj~ Smith As^{t}:	Jeames Green
John Pocock G Atty	Hollon Curtis
West^{t} Clark Recd^{r}	Caleb Carr
Jireth Bull Shriffe	Robart Hicks

Jury of tryalls

Capt John Rogers foreman	John Coggeshall Junr
Thomas Gould	William Wanton
Thomas Wever	Richard Dune
William Peckham	Moses Lippett
Joseph Woodward	Edward Greenman
Joseph Nicholoson	Henry Straight

An Action of trespas on Ejectment Commensed **William Brenton Samuel Brenton & Jahleel Brenton** sons And Lawfull Children of **William Brenton** Late of Newport Marr^{r} & **Hannah** his wife Boath Deceased, By **Ebenezer Brenton** of bristoll their next friend Pl^{t} Against **Stephen Mumford** Sn^{r} & **Robart Ayres** Defts the Act Called in Court: the Defts plead for Issue not Guilty the Action pleaded & Committed to ye Jury: the verditt of the Jury wee find for the Deft & Coust of Court, the verditt Accepted & Cost Signed Apriell 17th **1699** Attorney for ye plts having payd the Costs of Court Enter A Rehearing of ye Abovesd Action by ye Court of Tryalls in Sep^{t} next -

Thare being An Action Commensed by **Benj Smith Israll Arnold John Rhoads & Olliver Carpenter** plts Against **Jobe Green** deft: & thare being A question by ye Deft of the power of the Lett^{r} of Attorney: Mr Benj~: Smith one of ye plats did in open

Court Ingage to stand by And Abide the Judgment of Court in sd Action if Cost & pay all Costs

Benj- Smith Israll Arnold John Rhoads & Oliver Carpento^{r} pla^{ts} in An Action of trespas the Action Called ye Def^{t} pleads Not Guilty as is sett forth in Declaration by ye pl^{t} The Case pleaded & Committed to ye Jury, The Juris verditt is wee find for ye Def^{t} Cost of Court The verditt Accepted & Cost Signed — —

Thomas Durfee Senr plt: Against **Thomas Townsend** Def^{t} on A Re-heareing the Case pleaded & Committed to ye Jury the verditt is wee find for ye Deft upon rehearing twenty pounds & two pence damage & Coust of Court

The Abovesd Thomas Durfe pl^{t} & Thomas Townsend Def^{t} did in Open Court owne that in Consideration of twenty shilling payd by ye pl^{t} to ye deft should be A finall Issue ye Above sd verditt & that all Cause of Action verditt & Judgments of Court are void & of no Efect & All differances Ended & Determined to this present Court

Joseph Hicks of Portsmouth Cooper pla^{t} Against **Thomas Townsend** Late Shrieff Def The Action Called & thare being A defect in ye declaration the Court Order ye Action Abate

John Dolbeare plt Against **Thomas Townsend** Late Shrieff Def^{t} in An Action of Escape. The Case Called ye plt Appeared ye Deft did not Appear the Case Committed to the Jury the verditt wee find for the pla^{t}: five pounds five shillings & nine pence debt & twell[ve] shillings & two pence damage & Courst of Court the verditt Accepted

Edmon Dolbeare pla^{t} Against **Thomas Townsend** Late Shriefe Def^{t} In An Action of Escape the Case Called ye pla^{t} Appeared: the Def^{t} did not Apeare & the Case Committed to ye Jury, the verditt wee find for ye plat twelve pounds Eight shillings nine pence debt: damage nine shillings & six pence & Cost of Court the Verditt Accepted

The Tryalls Ended & Crimonalls Called

Daniell Wilcocks of Portsmouth being presented by the grand Jury the Last Court for fencing in ye Common being brought to tryall this Court being Called to ye barr pleads not Guilty & puts him selfe on tryall by the Jury the Jurys verditt: not guilty, The prisoner Cleared by procklamation paying his fees [131]

Johnathan Barney being Indicted for suspition of shooting **Henry Cherry** wareby hee was killed Dead: Being brought forth to tryall held up his hand at ye Barr & pleaded Not Guilty of ye Charge & put him selfe upon the Jury for tryall the verditt of ye Jury was not Guilty, upon Which the prison^{r} was Cleared by procklamation paying his ffees The ffees payd & the prison^{r} Discharged — —

Robart Mondy being A prison^{r} in his Maj^{tty} Gole for suspition of Piracey & being by the Court Called for to be brought to ye Barr to Answer to A bill of Indictment found Against him, the Shrieffe Replying that the sd Monday had made his Escape from him & not to be found. The Attorny pleaded to ye bill & ye Court sent out ye Jury upon ye tryall who gave in their verditt that Robart Munday was guilty of Making Escape out of ye Shriffs Custody hee being Committed for piracey ye Court being Dissatisfied with ye verditt sent out ye Jury three times who gave ye same verditt —

The Sentance of ye Court is that the said Robart Munday hath forfited all his Monies gould plate coine & what soever other of his Estate is heare seized in Custody for the Kings use & ye Chargis Accruing on ye tryall &c

George Cuttler being presented by ye Grand Jury for susp of piricey & called in Court to ye barr pleads Not Guilty & Commits him Selfe upon tryall by God And the Cuntry, the Jurys verditt is Not Guilty, The Courts Order is George Cuttler shall have a hundred pounds of his mony that is in ye Govrs Custody deliverd him & the remaining part not to be delivered till ye fift of June next —

Richard Cornish being presented by ye Grand Jury for Suspition of Piricey & brough in Court to ye barr pleaded not Guilty & putt on tryall by god And the Cuntry the Juris verditt upon ye tryall is not Guilty. & cleared in Court by procklamation paying his fees the payd & ye prisoner Cleared —

Othaniell Trip of Kingstown having made his Apperance in Court is Cleared of his bonds —

Thomas Langford being Called in Court being bound Over for suspition of piricey & procklimation being made three times that if Any prson or parsons whatsoever Could give Evidence to ye Kings Justices In behalfe of his Maj^{tty} Against ye prisoner they may be heard & ye prisoner presented Accordingly but no pson Appearing hee is Cleared of his bonds —

Joseph Rogers called in Court being bound over for suspition of piricey & Procklamation being made three times that if Any prson or prsons whatsoever Could give Evidence to ye Kings Justices In behalfe of his Maj^{tty} Against ye prisoner they may be heard & ye prisoner presented Accordingly but no pson Appearing hee is Cleared of his bonds —

The Court Dessolved

[132] At A Genrll Court of tryalls held for his Maj^{tty} Collony of Rhoad Island & Providence Plan^{ts} at Newport 5th day of Septemb^{r} *1699*

Maj^{r} Samuell Cranston Govr	Grand Jury Engaged
Walter Clark As^{t}	Mr Latham Clarke
Capt Robart Carr As^{t}	Mr Jeames Coggeshall
Capt Jeames Barker As^{t}	Mr John Gould
Capt Joseph Sheffield As^{t}	Mr William Barker
	Mr Charles Dyre
	Mr Isaac Lawton
	Mr Dan^{ll} Lawton
	Mr Jobe Green
	Mr John Maxson Jr
	Mr Jeames Newton
	Mr Steven Hassard
	Mr Sam^{ll} Davis

Whareas thare was A rehearing Entred by **Will Brenton Sam^{ll} Brenton & Jahleel Brenton** sons & Lawfull Children of **William Brenton** Late of Newport on Rhoad Island Afore sd Mar^{er} Deceased & **Hannah** his wife by their Attorney **Jeames Menzies** ye 17th of Apriell **1699** the Action Called & the Jury Impanaled

William Stoddart foreman	Peter Barker
Joseph Card	John Easton J^{r}
Johnathan Bennitt	Thomas Harris
Adam Lawton	John Ward
Tobias Brown	Sampson Batty
Amos Stafford	William W[ood?]

William Brenton Sam^{ll} Brenton Jahleel Brenton Sons & Lawfull Children of **William Brenton** Late of Newport on Rhoad Island Afore Sd Marr^{er} & **Hannah** his wife Deceased: Doe by **Ebenezar Brenton** of Bristoll in ye province of ye Masathusetts bay in New England their next frinde being Sollemly Called in Open Court did not Appeare but made defalte tharefor it is Considered by the sd Court that ye sd William Sam^{ll} & Jahleel Brenton become Nonsuitte & that ye sd **Stephen Mumford & Robart Ayres** goe home with out day & that ye sd plantifs pay Costs to sd Stephen Mumford & Robart Ayres

William Stoughton of Boston Esqr Plantife Against **John Wilson** of Boston March^{t} Deft in An Action of Debt by Bond as Administ^{r} to y^{e} Estate of **Richd Wharton** of boston March^{t} deceased the Defendant owned the Bond And Confessed Judgment the principall & intrest of y^{e} Bond of 108$^{£}$ is Chancered to 192 pounds & Allowed of in Court with Costs

Samuell Sewell of Boston March Plantife Against **John Nelson** of sd Boston [*illegible*] Def In An Action of Debt by bond as Adm^{r} to y^{e} Estate of **Richd Wharton** of boston March^{t} deceased the Deft owned the bond sued for wharein Judgment was given for ye plant for ye principle & Intrest three Hundred twenty nine pounds Currant mony of New England Allowed in Court with Costs —

John Mico of Boston March^{t} Plan^{t} Against **John Nelson** of sd Boston March^{t} Def^{t} In An Action of Debt by bond as Administrat^{or} to ye Estate of **Richd Wharton** of boston March^{t} Deceased the Deft owned the bond sued for whare in Judgment was given for ye plan^{t} for principall & Intrest seventy eight pounds & Costs —

Jeames Willson pla: Against **Samuell Stibins** Butcher defendant in An Action of Debt by bill the Action Called & no defendant Appering it was Committed to ye Jury, the Juris verditt wee find for ye plantife five punds fifteen shillings & coste of Court ye verditt Accepted —

Capt **Thomas Townsend** Pla^{t} Against **Joseph Hicks** Def for unjust Mollistation the Case Called ye Deft not Apearing ye pla Enters A nihil dicett The Case Committed to ye Jury the Juris verditt wee finde for ye pla^{t} fifteen pounds Damage for unjust mollistation & Cost of Court the verditt Accepted —

Septemb^{r} 15th 1699 Joseph Hicks Def^{t} payd ye Cost of Court & Enters A rehearing to ye genrll Assembly in Octob^{r} next at Warwick

[133] **Thomas Bingham** plantife Against **Robart Wrightington** Def^{t} in An Action of Debt upon Account the Action Called ye Def^{t} not Appearing the Case Committed to ye Jury the verditt of ye Jury wee finde for ye pla. seven pounds seven shillings & Eleven pence & Coust of Court the verditt Accepted —

Cor^{ll} **Peleg Sanford** & Mr **Jahleel Brenton** Plantifs Against **John Carr** of Kings town Deft in An Action of trover & Conversion The Action being Called in Court three times ye Deft not Appearing the Case was Committed to ye Jury, the verditt of ye Jury is wee find for ye plantifs foure pounds damage & coste of Court the verditt Accepted

Nicholas Easton plt: Against **John Easton** son of **Peter Easton** Deft in An Action of detainure The Action Called & pleaded & Committed to ye Jury, the Juris verditt wee find for ye Defendant & Courst of Court the verditt Accepted —

John Wells of Kings town Pla^{t} Against **John Carr** of Kingstown Deft In An Action of debt the plan^{t} & deft Caled ye Case pleaded & Committed to the Jury, the Juris varditt is wee find for ye plan^{t} three pounds damage & Cost of Court the verditt Accepted

Thomas Peckham Junr Pla^{t} Against **Robart Wrightington** Deft in An Action of debt upon Account the Action Called & Committed to ye Jury, ye Juris verditt wee find for ye plan^{t} three pounds 15^{s} & 2^{d} & Cost of Court ye verditt Accepted —

Joseph Garratt otherwise by ye Indians called **Weequascook** Indian Sachem pla^{t} Against **Anguawas** alias **Ninnecraft** Sacham Def^{t} in An Action for with holding of certaine Lands from ye pla^{t} the pla^{t} & deft Called in Court & their Case pleaded & Commited to ye Jury the Jurys verditt wee finde for ye Defendant Cost of Court the verditt Accepted —

The Court Sated for trying of Crimanalls

Seasor Dawgo A prisson[r] being Indited for felloneiously taking of mony from **John Calverly** & brought to y[e] barr & Asked wheather guilty or not guilty of his Charge pleaded not guilty & put himselfe upon tryall by y[e] Jury the Jury Verditt is guilty
The Sentance of y[e] Court is that the said Seasor Dawgo be forth with whipt on his naked back at y[e] publick whiping post with fifteen stripes & to be returned to y[e] Gole & thare to remaine till hee pay six pounds mony to sd John Calverly butcher & officer's fees

Isrell Newton of Kingstown being Indicted for Contemp[t] of Authority & brought to y[e] barr pleads not Guilty & putt him selfe on y[e] Jury for tryall
The Jurys verditt is Guilty & the sentance of this Court is that the sd Isrell Newton shall pay a fine to y[e] King of five pounds mony forthwith to the Gen[r]ll tresuar of this Collony: Otherwise to suffer three month Imprisonment in his Maj[tt] Gole in Newport & allso pay two pounds eighteen shillings & foure pence for Exterordanary Charges as will Appeare by Account in the Shrieffs hands

Left **Jireth Bull** of Newport Late Shrieff of y[e] Collony being presented for breach of his Maj[tty] peace & brought to y[e] barr pleads not Guilty & putt him selfe on y[e] Jury for tryall the Jurys verditt Not Guilty & Cleered by procklamation —

Whareas **Isaac Ballord** of Kings town wever was at A gen[r]ll Court of tryalls held at Newport y[e] 6[th] of Septemb[r] 1678 presented by the kings attorney for fellony & by y[e] Grand Jury found A true bill the sd ballord being brought upon tryall pleads Not Guilty & putt him selfe on y[e] Jury for tryall y[e] Jurys verditt guilty of his Indictment, the Court upon som Consideration se cause to suspend sentence till the Court of tryalls in March next whare sd ballord Appeared but before sentance was given made his Escape this Court According to y[e] former verditt doe sentance the sd ballord to pay unto y[e] sd **John Carr** two fold for y[e] vallue of y[e] goods stolen & to be whiped on his naked back as sone as hee can be seised on by Authorety with in Any town in this Collony with fifteen stripes on his naked back & by y[e] Assistance or Justices Committed to y[e] Gole till y[e] sentance be fulfild & officers fees payd

The Court Desolved

[134]

At A Gen^{r}ll Court of tryalls held for his Maj^{tty} Collony of Rhoad Island & Providence Plantations at Newport ye 26th day of March *1700*

Sam^{ll} Cranston Esqr Govr
Maj^{r} John Green Dep^{t} Gen^{rl}
Mr Walter Clark As^{t}:
Capt Robt Carr As^{t}:
Capt Jeames Barke^{r} As^{t}:
Capt Richd Arnold As^{t}:
Mr Joseph Williams As^{t}:
Capt Joseph Sheffild As^{t}:
Mr Giles Slocom As^{t}:
Mr Benj Barton As^{t}:
Mr Joseph Hull As^{t}:
Capt Jeffery Champlin As^{t}:
Wes^{t} Clarke Recd^{r}
Mr John Hulmes Gen^{r}ll Tres^{r}
Mr John Pocock G^{r}ll Attorny
Mr Thomas Mallett Sherif

Grand Jury Engaged

Capt Christopher Almy fo-man
Capt Thomas Brooks
Mr William Allin
Mr Richard Dunn
Mr Giddion freeborne
Mr Henry Gardner
Mr Allixsander Huling
Mr John Thomas
Mr Robert Ayres
Mr John Brown
Mr Joseph Gardner
Mr Joseph Donell

Added to sd Jury
Mr Steven Mumford Jn^{r}
Mr Charles Dyre
Lef Nath^{ll} Shiffild
Mr Robart Hicks
Mr John Burden
Mr John Easton

Jury of Tryalls

Joseph Nickolson formn
Dan^{ll} Vaughan
George Cornell
Peleg Shearman Junr
John Davis
William Coo[k?]
John Weeden
John Mumford
Joseph Canderlin
Sam^{ll} Stapleton
John Easton Junr
Dan^{ll} Sebeare

Capt **Thomas Townsend** plant Against **Samuel Davis** cooper Def^{t} In An Action of Covenant by Lease for Rent the plant & Def^{t} Called the Action pleaded & putt to ye Jury the Jurys verditt wee find for ye Defendant Cost of Court the Verditt Accepted —

Mary Timberlake Widdow plantife Against **Henry Trasher** Defendant In An Action of ye Case for not p^{r}forming Covenant of Lease the Action Called. Plantife & Def^{t} Appearing the Case pleaded & Committed to ye Jury the Jurys verd^{tt} Being sent out three times wee find for y^{e} Def^{t} Coust of Court —

Nathaniell Croxford Plaintife Against **William Willson** of Boston Def^{t} the Case Called in Court the Def^{t} not Appearing the Case Committed to y^{e} Jury the verditt of the Jury wee find for y^{e} plantife the debt upon Account 7$^{£}$:2^{s}:2^{d} with Cost of Court & 20^{s} Damages The Verditt Accepted

Jeames Willson of Kingstown pla^{t}: Against **Edward Greenman** of sd Kingstown Def^{t} In An Action of trespasse for with holding from y^{e} pla^{t} sertaine Lands the action called pl^{t} & Def^{t} Appearing & pleaded & Committed to ye Jury the Jurys verditt wee finde Edward Greenman Def^{t} in possestion by Lease, the Court not sattisfide with ye verditt sent out ye Jury three times & brought ye same verditt

Richd Newland Plantife Against **George Cuttler** Def^{t} in An Action of Debt upon Account Debt & Damage thirty pounds the Case Called & Committed to ye Jury The Jury verditt wee find for ye Def^{t} Coust of Court. The verditt Accepted —

George Cuttler pla^{t} Against **Richd Newland** Def^{t} in An Action of Debt upon Account Debt & Damage Thirty pounds the Case Called & Committed to ye Jury the Jurys verditt wee find for ye Def^{t} Coust of Court the Verditt Accepted —

Action all Cases Ended: The Court for Tryall of Crimionalls

procklamation being made that If any pson or psons bound by recognisence or given bond to ye Kings Justices to prosecute in behalfe of his Maj^{tty} to Appeare in Court for now ye prisoners are upon tryall:

Joseph Pemberton being bound by Recognizence to this Court and Called in Court being Indicted for Contempte of his Maj^{tty}s Authority & brought to the barr the Jury Called over hee making no Exseptions Demanded Guilty or not Guilty pleads not Guilty & puts him selfe to tryall by god & ye Cuntry for tryall: the Jury After plea sent forth & bring in their verditt Guilty of Contempt of Authority —

The Sentance of this Court is y^{t} ye sd Joseph Pemberton for his Offence shall give A bond of twenty pounds to be of peacable & good behaviou^{r} to all his Maj^{tty}s Leach People with in this Gov^{r}ment till the next Gen^{r}ll Court of tryalls to be held for this Collony in Septemb^{r} next then & thare to make his Appearance to be discharged of his bonds if Nothing Appeare to ye Contrary & allso to pay all Costs & Charges that hath Accrued to ye goverment through his Afore sd Contempt & Remaine A prisoner till pformed— [135]

Edward Bliven of Westerly being bound to this Court & thare Indicted for Contempt of Authority & brought to ye barr & Demanded Guilty or Not Guilty of his Charge pleads Not Guilty & putts him selfe on ye Jury for tryalls, the Juris verditt is Guilty of Contempt of Athority, the sentance of ye Court for his Contempt is the same with Joseph Pembetons —

John Lewis of Westerly being bound to this Court & thare Indicted for Contempt of Authory & found Guilty by the Jury, is sentanced for his Contempt is the same with Joseph Pemberton —

William Earle being bound to this Court for Abusing ye Cunstable of the town of Portsmouth is found Guilty by the Jury for Abusing ye Cunstable & is sentenced to pay twelve shilling & officers ffees —

Margrett Blowre the wife of **Jeames Blower** of Newport being presented for Suspition of felloniously taking A peace of [—]omoad Silke from ye possestion of **Peter Treby** being brought to ye barr pleads not Guilty & puts hir selfe on god and the Cuntry for tryall. The Jury being sent out three times by the Court brings in their verditt not Guilty ye Court Accepts ye Verditt: & the sd Margrett Blowr was Cleared by procklamation

William Knowles of Kingstown being bound over to this Court: & procklamation made & thare no parson Appearing to prosecute is Cleared of his bonds —

Nathaniell Niells Junr being bound over to this Court & procklamation made as Aforesaid is Cleared of his bonds: **Robart Littfild** is Likewise Cleared of his bonds **Nath^{ll} Nieles** Senr **Sam^{ll} Eldredg Daniell & Thomas Cinnicott John Perry Benjamin Belsher John Beere & Robart Nickols** all being bound over to this Court & none to prosecute are Cleared of their bonds —

Whare as Mr **John Pocock** Kings Attorney hath given his Opinnion to this Court in behalfe of his Maj^{tty} Conserning one **Will Peas & Nath^{ll} Dyre** now prisoners who ware to Answer at sd Court to Som Crimes Alledged Against them that the sd Peas & Dyre are not Cognisable at sd Court for that ye Matto^{r} of fact Apearing against them was Done upon ye Seas thare fore falls with in ye Statute of ye 28th of Henry ye Eight & ye 15th Chapter & ought to be tryde by a spetiall Court of Oyre & Triminer [*sic*] According to An Act of this Collony made the 6th of May 1684

This Court taking ye premices into their Serious Consederation & upon mature debate of ye same doe see Just Grounds & Cause to suspent ye tryall of sd William Peas & Nath^{ll} Dyre at this Court & that they remaine Prisoners in ye Costady of ye Shrieff till thare be further Care taken by the Authority of this Collony for their tryall According to sd Statute & Law of ye Collony Afore Recited —

And it is farther Ordred that **Johnathan Bennett Thomas Michell Richd Newland & Charles Comes** shall be Continued under bonds till tryall as aforesd

The Court Desolved

[136]

At A Gen^rll Court of tryalls held for his Maj^{tty}s Collony of Rhoad Island & Providence plantations at Newport the 3 day of Septemb^r *1700*

Sam^{ll} Cranston Esq Govr
Walter Clarke D Govr
Capt Robart Carr As^t:
Mr Isaac Martandal As^t:
Mr Joseph Williams As^t:
Maj^r William Hopkings As^t:
Capt Joseph Sheffild As^t:
Mr Giles Slocom As^t:
Mr Benj Barton As^t:
Mr Benj: Smith As^t:
Capt Jeffery Champlin As^t:
Capt John Eldridg As^t:
Wes^t Clarke Recd^r
Thomas Mallitt Shrieff
John Rhoads Gen^rll Attorny
John Hulmes Gen^rll Tresua^r

Grand Jury Eng^d
Mr Nath^{ll} Bowdish foreman
Mr Joseph Card
Mr Peter Treby
Mr Thomas Peckham
Mr Jacob Mott
Mr John Rhoads
Mr Christopher Champlin
Mr Johnathan Mash
Capt Andrew Willitt
Mr George Whittman
Mr George Vaughan
Mr John Kinnion

Jury of tryalls

Capt John Rog^rs foreman
Sam^{ll} Thurston
John Coggeshall Junr
John Arnold
Jeames Dexter
Benj Sherman
Jeremiah Lawton
William Potter
Henry Godward
Thomas Mattison
Richd Higings
Hollon Curtis

Joseph Kent of Swansey & **Edward Ball** of Block Island Pla^t Against **Joshua Rayman** & **Mercey Rayman** his wife Def^t in An Action of ye Case for Detaining from ye pla^t severall goods belonging to **Peter George** & his wife boath of Block Island alis New Shorom Deceased The plt & deft called & the Jury Engaged on ye Case & the Answer of ye Defts being Imparfitt by reason of a mistake in the coppy of ye writt the sence of ye Court is that ye Deft putt in a new Answer in Court provided it be not for Abatment of ye progres & ye pla to make Replecation thare on which was Accordingly done & committed to ye Jury the Jurys verditt after being by ye Court sent out three times wee find for ye Defts Coust of Court

John Sheldon Pla^t **Mallachi Rhoads** Def^t the Action Called ye Declaration & Answer Read: the Court Sence is that ye Action is Not Leagally presented And shall Abate —

Samuell Davis cooper pla^t: **Daniell Campanell** Def^t In An Action of debt upon Account the Case pleaded & committed to ye Jury the Juris verditt Wee find for ye pla^t: Eight pounds fifteen shillings and Eight pence & 2d damage & Coust of Court, the verditt Accepted —

Septemb^{r} 6th the Court Opened for tryalls of Crimonalls

Lef Jeames Green
Edward Hoops
Joseph Dolliver Junr
Edward Green
John Whitman
Vallintine Whitman
John Green
Nich Utter Junr
Thomas Withers
Charles Perry
Robart Aylesworth
Dan^{ll} Erolt ye french Doctors son
Isrell Newton
Daniell Green
Ismaell Spinke

The Above sd persons being Indicted for Riators in the Narragansett Cuntry for Opposing the Shireffes Deputi in ye Execution of his Office —

Called in Court thare only Appeared Left **Jeames Green Joseph Dolliver** Junr **Edward Green John Whittman** & **Edward Hops** being Demanded wheather Guilty or Not Guilty of the Charge they stand Indicted for Left Jeames Green Joseph Dolliver Ed Green & John Whittman owned Guilty Leave themselves to ye Courts Judgment the Sentance of the Court is that **Jeames Green** for his offence shall pay unto ye Gen^{r}ll Tresuar of this Collony the sume of foure pounds current mony & **Joseph Dolliver** pay A fine of one pound currant mony to ye Gen^{r}ll Tresuar & **Edward Green** shall pay as Aforesd A fine of one pound mony And **John Whittman** pay as Afore sd the sume of tenn shillings mony And that the sd Persons Remaine prisoners in ye Custody of the Shrieffe till Every of them shall Ransume them selves by paying their fines as Aforesd — —

Whareas **Edward Hops** of Kingstown was by the Afore sd bill of Indictment for the Above sd Riotious Action & Resques the sd Hops pleaded not guilty & puts himselfe upon ye tryall by the Jury & the Jury finding him Guilty the sd hops is by the Court Sentenanced that hee shall have at ye publick whiping post well Layd on his bare back fifteen stripes with out hee can Ransom him selfe by paying the sume of two pounds currant mony to ye Gen^{r}ll Tresuar of this Collony at or before ye tenth of this Instant & in the meane time to Remaine A prisoner to his maj^{tty} in ye Custody of the Shrieff

[137] Whareas Left **Ladwick Ubdike** [*sic*] with his wife **Abigall** & his sister **Sarah Whiting alis Whithead** & **Sarah Whithead** daughter to ye afore sd Sarah &c ware Indicted & by Recognisance: he the sd Ladwick & Sarah Whitting alis Whitthead did appeare at ye Court of Tryalls held for his Maj^{tty} Collony of Rhoad Island & ye said bill of Indictment In behalfe of o^{r} Soveraine Lord the King Aleaging y^{t} hee ye sd Ladwick with his wife Abigall & sister Sarah Whitting alis Whithead with Sarah Whithead daughto^{r} to the sd Sarah did in A Riatious Manno^{r} Resque one **Isrell Newton** A prisone^{r} of his Maj^{tty} from ye Custody of **Sam^{ll} Davis** Spetiall Cunstable for his Maj^{tty} servis hee ye sd Ladwick for him selfe & wife & Sarah Whitting alis Whitthead sister to the Afore sd Ladwick Appearing & pleading to a bill for hirselfe & Daughto^{r} not guilty & putts them selves on tryall by the cuntry: the Jury finding the Persons Guilty, Tharefore the sentance of ye court is that ye sd **Ladwick Updick** shall pay for himselfe and defalt for nonApperance of his wife **Abigall** as aforesd to ye Gen^{r}ll tresury of this Collony the sume of five pounds currant mony, & it is the sentance of ye Court that ye sd **Sarah Whitting alis Whitthead** shall pay as aforesd the sum of thirty shillings cur-

rant mony & the Court taking in to Consideration that ye said Sarah daught^r to ye aforesd Sarah Whitthead being but A child be Acquitted And hee the sd Ladwick Updick with his sister Sarah Whitting alis Whitthead be kept in Custody of ye Shrieffe untill hee the sd Ladwick & Sarah shall Ransom them selves by paying the aforesd fines — —

Whereas **Vallintine Whittman John Green Nich Utter Junr Thomas Wither Charles Berry Robart Aylsworth Daniell Erolt** ye french Doctors son **Isrell Newton Ishmaell Spink** all of Kingstown ware by the above sd Bill of Indictment Indited with ye Afore sd **Jeames Greene** &ct & they not Appearing by vertue of a procklimation under the hand & seall of ye Honrd Govr granted by vertue of ye Acts of ye Gen^rll Assembly of this his Maj^tts Collony thare fore it is Adjudged & sentanenced by this Court that Nich Utter Junr Thomas Withers Charles Berry Robart Aylesworth Dan^ll Erolt ye french Doctors son Isrell Newton & Ishmael Spink doe pay ye sume of fourty shillings currant mony Each of them as by former Judgment will Appeare And it is Allso Adjudged & sentananced y^t sd Vallintine Whittman & Jeames Green upon ye submition of **George Whittman** & **Jeames Green** fathers of ye Afore sd Vallintine & John to this Court that they the sd Vallintine Whittman & John Green [*sic*] doe pay the sume of tenn shillings Apeace to be payd as Afore sd by Each of them selves In to ye Gen^rll tresuar of this Collony at or before ye 10th of Octob^r next Insuing & upon defalt or non payment According to ye time Afore sd Execution to goe forth from ye Recd^r to ye Shrieffe to seize their Estates or goods of Every ye aforesd parsons so neglecting & to make sale thare of According to Law & for want of their Estates to seize their psons & them to keepe in his Maj^tty Gole untill they shall ransom them selves by paying their fines &c —

And it is further ye Judgment & sentance of this Court that all Court charges & officers fees shall be payd out of ye fines & forfitures of ye Respective parsons sentanced at this Court & what Remaines to be putt into ye Gen^rll Tresury, And it is further Ordred that ye Charges of ye Court of Inquiry held at Kingstown Relating to ye rioters shall be payd out of ye fines of sd Rioters —

Whareas **Peter Erault Alis Pirrie Ayrault** french Docktor of Est Greenwich was bound by recognizence to this Court by vertue of A verditt of a Court & Jury of Enquiry held at Greenwich for A newsence & by him sd Docktor Committed in taking or fencing in ye kings highway in sd Greenwich, ye sd Dockter being by A grand Jury at this Court Indicted for A newsence Apperd in Court & pleading not guilty & putts him selfe upon ye Cuntry for his tryall the verditt of the Jury being ye sd Dockter was Guilty of A newsence It is tharefore ye Judgement & sentance of this Court that ye afore sd Dockter Peter Erolt Pirrie Ayroult shall Be the first day of Novemb^r next lay open ye sd highways by taking Away ye fences or other things that may Impeade ye passage of his Maj^tty subjects thare by horse or foot & that ye sd Dockter shall pay all Costs & Charges that hath Arisen by reason of fencing in sd highwayes & to Remaine his Maj^ttys prisoner in ye Custody of ye Shrieffe till payd, & it is further ye Judgment & sentance of this Court that if ye sd Dockter doe neglect or refuse to comply with ye Afore sd sentance by ye Afore sd time that then upon complainte from Any one in Authcrity in ye Afore said Town of Este greenwich to ye Govr or any two Assistance of this Collony that it shall be Lawfull for ye Govr or any two Ast as aforesd to grant forth his warrant to ye shrieff or his Deputy who shall take suffitient Aide with them if ocation Requires & Lay open ye sd highway & what charge shall thareby arise to be payd by ye Dockter —

Richard Greenell called in Court did not Appeare According to his bond & ye surties **Daniell Thurston & John Sanford** of Newport called to bring sd Greenell forth but neither Appered to discharge their bonds, nor Answer According to Law

The Court Desolved by procklamation

[138]

At A Gen^{r}ll Court of tryalls held at Newport the 25th of March *1701*

Sam Cranston Esqr Govr
Walter Clarke Dep^{ty} Gen^{r}l
Capt Robt Carr Ast:
Mr Isaac Martandall Ast:
Mr Joseph Williams Ast:
Maj^{r} William Hopkings Ast:
Capt Joseph Sheffild Ast:
Mr Benj Barton Ast:
Mr Benj Smith Ast:
Capt Jeffery Champlin Ast:
Ensign John Eldridg Ast:
Wes^{t} Clarke Recd^{r}
Tho Mallitt Shireff
John Rhoads Attorny G^{rll}
John Hulmes Gen^{r}ll Tresur

Grand Jury Engaged
Mr Latham Clark foreman
Capt Edward Pelham
Mr Thomas Gould
Mr William Allin
Mr Sam^{ll} Winsor
Mr Robart Bennitt
Mr John Corey
Mr John Lewis
Mr John Underwood
Mr Benj Spencer
M^{r} ffreegift Coggeshall
Mr William Phillips

Jury tryalls Eng^{d}:

Capt John Rog^{rs} forman
Steven Mumford Jn^{r}
William Randall
Joseph Whipple
Joseph Nichoson
Phillip Sharman
Adam Lawton
Jeremiah ffones
Gilbart Majick
Jeames Coggeshall
Thomas Brooks
John Paine (?)

Peter Ayralt french Docto^{r} pla^{t} in an action of debt **Samuell Davis** Coop^{r} Def^{t} the Action Called & ye Jury Impanaled the sence of ye Cort that ye Action Abate —

Garsham Waddall Pla^{t} in an Action of debt by bond **Nath^{ll} Dun** Def^{t} the Action Called & committed to ye Jury the Jurys verditt we find for ye pla^{t} seventeen pounds & eight shillings debt & damage & cost of court, ye court exsepts ye verditt & asignes cost —

Salvanas Scott of Providence pla^{t} Against **Joseph Latham** of sd Providence Def^{t} in An Action of trespas upon ye case ye Action called Declaration & Answer read ye Court see cause that ye Action Abate & ye Def^{t} allowed costs —

M^{r} **ffrancis Brinley** pla^{t} against **Seaborne Higings** Executrix & **Richd Higings** Exec^{r} Def^{t} of ye Last will & testament of **Epharim Higings** late of Newport deceased in An Action of ye Case for Account of sundry goods delivered sd Epharim in his life time the Deft pleading theire Evidence ware remote that ye Court would grant them An Imparlance to ye Court of tryall in Septembr next which was Granted —

Jeames Pepont & **Gabriell Barnone** Junr march [merchant] Plat against **Abraham Lewis** March Deft in An Action of ye Case for Better Security the Action Called & pleaded & Committed to ye Jury the Juris verditt wee find for ye Deft Cost of Court the verditt Accepted — —

Gabriell Barnone March [merchant] Against **Abraham Lewis** March Deft in An Action of ye Case for Better Security the Action called & committed to ye Jury the Juris verditt wee find for ye Deft Cost of Court: the plat in open Court Enters Arehearing of ye case in Septembr next — —

Jone Earle of Portsmouth plat Against Majr **John Albrow** of sd Portsmouth Deft in An Action of ye Case for not Laying out hir Equall Proportion of Lands with the rest of the Inhabitance of Portsmouth Damage one hundred & fifty pounds The Court upon ye debate being Imprfection & uncertantie in ye plt Declaration see cause the Action Abate

The Court Opened for Tryall of Crimonalls

[139] March 28 = 1701 Whareas **George Denison** & **Edward** & **Joseph Denison** his sons all of ye town of Westerly in the Collony of Rhoad Island & Providence Plantations having Appeared in Court to Answer ther former Commitent for fellony &c upon which the Court in Consideration of the Kings Evidences not being present: the Court see Cause to Continue the tryall of said psons untill ye next Court of tryalls to be holden at Newport on ye first tusday in Septembr next & doe order the Shrieff to take ye bodies of said Denisons into his costody & them safely keepe within ye Gole of Newport untill they be Delevered According to Law: upon Applycation by sd Joseph Denison & his Sons above named to this Court the Court have Allowed them to be bayled to Appeare at ye next Court as Above sd under ye paine of one thousand pounds & give bond for their Good Behaviour in the meane time

Ann Bryan being Indicted at this Court for ffelloniously taking or stealling out of ye hous of ye widdow **Rebecka Whipple** of ye town of Providence in this Collony the sume of foure pounds five shillings in mony shee ye sd Ann Bryan being brought to ye barr & hir Indictment Reade & holding up hir hand plads guilty & putt hir selfe upon ye Court Craving Mercey: The sentance of this Court is that ye sd Ann Bryan shall pay to ye widdow Rebecka Whipple According to ye Law of this Collony two fold & to Receive upon her Naked Back at ye publick whiping post in ye town of Newport fifteen Lashes or Stripes well Layd on with out shee forthwith ransom hir selfe by paying a fine of fourty shillings & to remaine a prisoner till this sentance be prformed & pay Officers ffees —

Whareas **Nathaniell Bowdish** Junr of Newport Weaver hath been Indicted at this Court for Commiting Buggery with a dog ye sd Bowdish holding up his hand at ye barr & his Indictment being Read to him & demanded wheather Guilty or not Guilty pleaded not Guilty & putt him selfe upon God & ye cuntry for tryall: the Jurys verditt that ye sd Bowdish was Guilty of an Attempt of Buggery with a doge the verditt being Accepted by this Court: doe sentance that ye sd Nathaniell Bowdish Junr shall for his

Attempt as Afore sd be forthwith branded on ye ball of his thumb on his right hand with a red hott Iron with the Letter **R** after which shall be tyed to a carts taile and at or neare ye town pound in ye town of Newport Recive ten stripes on his Naked back well Layd on & then shall follow ye carts taile till hee comes before the Collony hous then to recive ten stripes more upon his Naked back as afore sd & from thence shall follow sd carts taile till hee com before ye battrey in ye Afore sd town of Newport whare he shall recive ten stripes as Afore sd the Afore sd sentance being p^{r}formed ye sd Bowdish shall for three days ffollowing stand upon a stock neare ye Collony hous for ye space of one houre Each day with these words in Cappitall Letters fastned upon his brest (viz), heare I stand ffor Commiting the Most Horrid & Beastly Sin of Bugery or Sodomy with A dog: And allso shall find suffitient surties in ye sume of thirty pounds for his good behaviour for one yeare & a day after ye desolution of this Court

The Court Desolved by procklamation

[140]

At a Gen^{r}ll Court of tryalls held for ye Collony of
Rhoad Island & Providence Plan^{ts} at Newport
the 2th day of Sept^{r} *1701*

Sam^{ll} Cranston Esqr Govr
Walt^{r} Clark Depty Govr
Capt Robt Carr As^{t}
Capt Isaac Martandale As^{t}
Mr Joseph Williams As^{t}
Maj^{r} Will Hopkings As^{t}
Capt Joseph Shiffild As^{t}
Mr Benj Hall As^{t}
Mr Benj Barton As^{t}
Mr Benj Smith As^{t}
Mr Joseph Hull As^{t}
Capt Ed Greenman As^{t}
Wes^{t} Clark Recd^{r}
Tho Mallitt Shrieff
John Hulmes Gen^{r} Tres^{r}
John Pocock Gen^{r} Attorny

Grand Jury Engag^{d}
Capt Nich Carr foreman
Will Peckham
Sam^{ll} Thurston
Dan^{ll} Lawton
John Ward
Joseph Smith
Henry Hall Sn^{r}
Henry Tibbits
Joseph Case
Charles Haselton
Joseph ffry
Joshua Clarke

Peter Callamore & **Joseph Hinchman** of Situate plantifes Against **Joseph Healy** mar^{r} Def^{t} in an Action of ye Case damage fourty pounds currant mony ye Def^{t} having no Answer in ye office According to law ye pl^{t} Enters a nihildicet & the Jury was sent forth to Enquire ye damages the Juris verditt wee find for ye pl^{t} twenty six pound damage and cost of court fraight & all charges cleared ye verditt Exsepted Sep^{tr} 11: 1701 ye Def^{t} payd ye Cost of Court & Enter A rehearing to ye Court in March next ——

Daniell Wilcocks plantife Against **John Cuttler** Dockter Def^{t} in An Action of Debt for a sorrell hors called ye buck hors the Def^{t} having no Answer ye case committed to ye Jury to Inquire for damages ye Juris verditt wee find for ye pl^{at} his debt of Eight pounds Cost of Court & six pence Damage the verditt Accepted — August 13th 1701 The Deft having payd ye cost of court Enters A rehearing of ye Action to ye nex Court in March 1702

Samuell Dunn plt Against **Jireth Bull** Deft in an Action of debt by bond ye Deft having no Answer in ye office the Case committed to ye Jury to Enquire for damages the Jury verditt wee find for ye plt the forfiture of his Bond & Cost of Court. The Deft having in Court payd ye Cost of Court Enters his rehearing to ye Court of tryall in March next —

Jury of tryall Engd

John Rhoads foreman	John Potter
John Bayly	Robart Spencer
Will Coddington	Joseph Gardner
Jacob Clarke	Robt Ayres
John Sanford	Zachariah Roads
Nicholas Cottrell	Edward Smith

Joseph Sheffild attorney to ye major part of ye freemen & freeholders of ye town of Portsmouth plt Against **Will Earle** Deft in an Action of trespas upon ye case the case committed to ye Jury ye verditt wee find for ye plantife 2d damage & Cost of Court ye verditt Accepted

[141] Capt **Joseph Sheffild** attorney to Majr part of ye ffreemen & free holders of ye town of Portsmouth Plt Against **William Earle** of sd Portsmouth Deft In An Action of trespas upon ye Case Damage 10£ the Case Committed to ye Jury the verditt wee finde ffor ye plat & Coste of Court the verditt Accepted — Septembr 10th 1701 The Deft having payd ye Cost of Court in Boath the Afore sd Actions Enters a rehearing to ye Court of tryall in March next —

Zachariah Rhods plat in an Action of the Case for a ffraude &c **Stephen Arnold** Deft the Issue Genrll the Case pleaded & Committed to the Jury the verditt of ye Jury, wee ffind for the plant: the fraudelent deed to be Canseled & made voide & seven pounds Damage & Coste of Court: the verditt Accepted: The Deft having payd ye Cost of Court Enters A re-hearing to ye Court of tryalls in March next — —

The Court Opened ffor Tryall of Crimonalls

John Earle son of **William Earle** of Portsmouth being Indicted for making an Escape ffrom ye hands of Justis: brought to ye barr pleads not Guilty & putt him selfe upon tryall by the Jury the Juris verditt Guilty. The sentance of ye Court is that ye said John Earle pay fforthwith in court 13s : 4d & officers ffees —

John West son of **ffrancis West** of Kingstown According to his bonds made his Law full Appearance in Court —

Mary Wilbor Widdow of **Tho: Wilbor** Late of Portsmouth on Rhoad Island deceased upon hir Sollom Engagment in Open Court declared yt shee had a bastard Child begotten on hir body by **John Earle** of Portsmouth son of **Will Earle** which Child shee had in her Armes in Court upon which Affirmation ye Court sentance ye sd John Earle shall pay Each and Every weeke unto ye said Mary Wilbor one shilling & six pence in mony toward ye maintanance of sd Child untill hee shall come to ye Age of seven years

& give in Suffitient Bond of twenty pounds currant mony for y[e] pformance of sd sentance & Remaine a prison[r] till hee hath given bond as Afore sd & pay officers ffees—

Mary Wilbor afforesaid having Owned hir selfe in Open Court guilty of Committing ffornication with John Earle Afore sd whareby hee begott a Child on hir body the sentance of this Court is the said Mary Wilbo[r] pay unto y[e] Gen[r]ll tresuar of this Collony the sume of twenty six shilling & eight pence mony or be wipt on hir Naked Back at y[e] publick whiping post in Newport forth with with fifteen Lashes & pay officers fees.

Thom Mungo An Indian boy Servant to Cap[t] **Joseph Halis** now a prisoner in his Maj[tts] Gole being at this Court by the Kings Attorney Indicted for ffellony stealling a boat belonging to **Peter Treby** & y[e] bill being found by the Grand Jury a true bill y[e] sd Tom Mongo was brought to y[e] barr & Demanded wheather Guilty or not Guilty pleaded not Guilty & putts him selfe upon tryall by the Jury the Juris verditt being Guilty was three times sent out by y[e] Court & often reminded by the Judge of their Oaths in Observing Law & Evidence &c but y[e] Jury Confirming their first verditt: This Court doe thare fore in p[r]suance to y[e] Laws of this Collony sentance that y[e] sd Tom Mungo Indian boy shall Satisfie two fold & be forthwith whipt upon his Naked back fifteen Lashes at y[e] publick whiping post in y[e] town of Newport & to Remaine a prisoner till y[e] sentance be p[r]formed & pay officers fees —

Robart Belcher now a prisoner in his Maj[tts] Gole Appearing to this Court to be a vagrant hath made & declared Before this Authority severall notorious & wicked Lies & false hoods, this Court doe thare fore sentance y[e] sd Rob[t] Belchar shall be wipt at y[e] publick whiping post in y[e] town of Newport twenty one Lashes upon his Naked Back & Remaine a prison[r] untilll hee hath payd prison ffees —

The Court Desolved by procklamation

[142]

At a Gen^{r}ll Court of tryalls held for his Maj^{tts}s Collony of Rhoad Island & providence plantations &c at Newport the last Tusday in March *1702*

Maj^{r} Sam^{ll} Cranston Govr	Grand Jury Engaged
Walter Clarke de^{t} Govr	for Newport
Capt Robt Carr As^{t}	Mr Jeremiah Clarke forman
Maj^{r} Isaac Martandall As^{t}	Joseph Barker
Mr Joseph Williams As^{t}	John Green
Maj^{r} Wiliam Hopkings As^{t}	Jeremiah Weeden
Capt Joseph Sheffild As^{t}	for providence
Mr Benj Hall As^{t}	John Burden
Mr Benj Barton As^{t}	Jeremiah Smith
Mr Benj Smith As^{t}	Simion Smith
Mr Joseph Hull As^{t}	Sam^{ll} Warden
Capt Edward Green As^{t}	William Browning
Wes^{t} Clarke Recd^{r}	Will Brown
Tho Mallitt Shriff	Josiah Jones
John Hulmes G treasur^{r}	Joseph ffry
John Pocock G Attorney	

The Court opened by procklamaton for tryalls

Peter Callamore & **Joseph Hinchman** of Situate plan^{ts} upon A rehearing in an Action of ye Case Against **Joseph Halis** Marr^{r} Def^{t}

Jury of tryalls:

Nath^{ll} Dyre foreman	Joseph Gouldsmith
John Mumford	John Carder
Francis Carr	Tho Lillibridg
Will Collings	Tho Martin
Edward Smith	Walton Huling
Edward Sailes	George Cornell

The Case pleaded and Committed to ye Jury the Juris verditt wee find for Joseph Halis & Coust of Court the verditt Accepted & Judgment given.

Daniell Wilcocks Plaintif against **John Cuttler** of Boston Def^{t} upon A rehearing in an Action of debt for a hors Called ye buck hors the Case Committed to ye Jury: ye Juris verditt wee find for ye def^{t} Cost of Court ye verditt Accepted & Judgment given.

Samuell Dun Pla^{t} against **Jireh Bull** Def^{t} upon a rehearing in An Action of Debt by bond the Case Committed to ye Jury the verditt wee find for Sam^{ll} Dun ye fforfiture of ye bond Cost of Court & six pound damage the verditt Accepted & Judgment given.

Capt **Joseph Sheffild** Attorney to ye Majo^{r} part of ye ffreemen of the town of Portsmouth Pla^{t} against **William Earle** of sd Portsmouth Def^{t} In An Action of trespase upon ye Case on a Rehearing the Case Committed to ye Jury wee find for ye pla^{t} Cost of Court & 8^{d} damage ye verditt Accepted. Capt Joseph Sheffild Attorney to ye Majo^{r} part of ye ffreemen of the town of Portsmouth Pla^{t} in an Action of trespas [*interlined:* against Wm Earll] upon ye case on a Rehearing and the case committed to ye Jury wee find for ye pla^{t} Cost of Court & 4^{d} damag ye verd^{t} Accep^{td}.

Zachariah Rhoads plaᵗ Against **Stephen Arnold** of Pautixsett in the town of Providence Deft In An Action of fraudelent Dealling upon a rehearing the Case Committed to ye Jury the verditt of ye Jury wee find for ye plat the fraudelent deed to be Canseled & made voide twenty pounds damage and Cost of Court: the Deft having payd ye Cost & given bond of 800 pound in Court is Allowed his Appeall to ye Genrll Assembly in May next.

Resolved Waterman Plat Against **Thomas Whipple** Deft In An Action of [143] the Case for unjust Mollestation damag six pounds the Issue Genrll the case pleaded and committed to ye Jury the verditt Wee find for the plat five pounds damage & Cost of Court ye verditt Accepted & Judgment given.

Capt **Joseph Hallis** plat: Against **Peter Callamore** Deft in An Action of the Case Damage five hundred pounds the Case pleaded & Committed to ye Jury the verditt wee find for ye plat Cost of Court & six pence damage the verditt Accepted & Costs Assigned Petter Callamore Deft having payd the Costs Enteres A rehearing of ye Case to ye Court of tryall in Sepr next.

Samuel Davis Plat In An Action of Escape Against **Tho Mallitt** Sheriff Deft The Issue Genrll the Case pleaded & Committed to ye Jury the verditt wee find for ye plat ye Debt sued for which is Eight pounds ffifteen shillings & Eight pence Cost of Court & five Shillings Damage ye verditt Accepted & Cost Assigned the Deft having payd the cost Enteres A rehearing of sd Action to ye next Court in Sepr next.

The Court Opened for ye trying of Crimanalls &c

John Balcom of Providence being Indicted for Cutting of **Jeames bicks** cowes tayles & Allso for demollishing of a bridg in sd town in ye kings highway & being brought to ye barr pleaded Guilty & putt him Selfe upon ye bench for Mercy, the Court Justly Considering ye premices, and the notorious Actions of sd balcom Com[m]itted as Afore sd have Consider-ed his confession Have sentananced sd balcom to pay for his trancegrestion the sume of Eight pounds six shillings & Eight pence currant mony for ye Charge Expence & Damage done to ye sd bick to witt Expence And damages to ye sd Bick with ye Expence & Charges six pounds six pounds six shilling & Eight pence & ye Residue to make Restitution for ye Afore sd Damages And Also to pay A fine to his Majtt in to ye Genrl tresury for ye use of the Collony the sume of twenty shillings & to Remaine a prisoner in his Majtts gole in Newport till said sentance be truly payd & prformed to ye Shrieff for the uses Afore sd & pay Officers ffees And upon his Acquittance by paying the Afore sd sumes to give in good surty for his good behaviour untill the first tusday in Sept next —

Jeames Phillips of Providence being Indicted for Cutting of **Jeames Bicks** cows tailes & being brought to ye Barr pleaded not Guilty & putts him Selfe upon the Jury for tryall the Juris verditt Guilty the Court Justly Considering the premises & the Notorious Action of ye sd Jeames Phillips Committed as Afore sd have sentananced the sd Jeames to pay for his trancegretion sixteen pounds thirteen shillings & foure pence currant mony for ye Charges Expence & Damages done to the sd Bick to witt Expence & Charges 12 pound 13s & 4d & ye residue to make Recompense for sd Damages & Allso to pay A fine to his Majtts Into ye Genrll tresury for the use of ye

Collony the sume of 40^{s} & to Remaine a prisoner in his Maj^{tty} Gole in Newport till sentance of Court be truly payd & p^{r}formed to ye Shrieff for ye use Afore sd & pay officers fees & upon his p^{r}formance of the premises to give in good security in ye sume of thirty pounds for his good behaviou^{r} for one hole yeare after ye Desolution of this Court.

Henry Mory being Indicted for Demollishing A bridg in ye town of Providence pleaded not guilty & putts him Selfe upon tryall by the Jury the Jurys verditt not guilty: the Court having duly Considered ye premices see good Cause that the sd Henry Mory give in good Security by one Suffitient pson with him selfe in ye sume of thirty pounds to be of good behaviou^{r} to all his Maj^{tty} Leach people for one hole year & A day & to Remaine in his Maj^{tty} Gole till sd sentance be p^{r}formed —

Hasadiah Cumstock being Indicted for throwing of Stones in A Molitious manne^{r} at ye hous of **Jeames Bick** of Providence & bought to ye barr pleads not guilty & puts him selfe on ye Jury for tryall ye Juris verditt not Guilty upon Consideration the Court see good Cause y^{t} ye sd Hasadiah Cumstock give in good security by one suffitient pson with him selfe in ye sum of thirty pounds in mony for his good behaviou^{r} to all his Maj^{tts} Leach people for one hole year & remaine in ye Shrieff Custody till prformed.

[144] **Robin** An Indian Man being Indicted on suspition of Murdring of his wife or Squaw & brought to the barr pleaded Not Guilty & putt him Selfe upon tryall by the Jury but desired thare might bee three Indians putt on ye Jury which was Allowed by the Court the Jury being as followeth:

Nathaniel Dyre foreman	William Collings
John Mumford	Walton Huling
Edward Sailes	Tho Clarke
Thomas Martin	Indians
ffrancis Carr	Peter Monokick Henry of block Island
Joseph Goldsmith	Henry of block Island
	Toby Indian

The Case being pleaded by The attorney Gen^{r}ll and Committed to ye Jury the Juris verditt Guilty of Chance Meadly — The Sentance of this Court is that ye sd Robin Indian shall be forthwith branded on his right hand near the thumb with the Letter **R** & all his goods forfitted to his Maj^{tty} & to be keept in ye Common Gole till good security begiven to ye Authority for his good behavor in this Collony and pay officers ffees —

Roger Mory being bound by recognicence to this Court & Appeared is Cleared by procklimation paying officers fees —

Peter Callamore being bound over to this Court & Appeared is Cleared by procklamaton paying officers ffees —.

The Court dissolved

At a Gen^{r}ll Court of Tryalls Held at Newport the
ffirst day of Septemb^{r} *1702*

Maj^{r} Sam^{ll} Cranston Esqr Govr
Walter Clarke Dep^{t} Govr
Capt Robt Carr As^{t}
Maj^{r} Isaac Martand^{le} As^{t}
Mr Joseph Williams As^{t}
Maj^{r} William Hopkins As^{t}
Capt Joseph Sheffild As^{t}
Capt Robt Lawton As^{t}
Mr Benj Smith As^{t}
Mr Benj Barton As^{t}
Mr Joseph Hull As^{t}
Mr George Hasard As^{t}
West Clarke Recd^{r}
Tho Mallitt Shrieff
Lef John Hulmes G Atto^{ry}
Mr Nath^{ll} Dyre Gen^{rl} Attorney

Grand Jury Engd:
Mr Henry Brightman foreman
Mr Tho Rogers
Mr Peter Barker
Mr Dan^{ll} Vaughan
Mr John Easton ye second
Mr Abraham Anthony
Mr William Arnold
Mr Robart hannah
Mr John Sweatt
Capt Josiah Arnold
Mr John Thare
Mr Joseph Gouldsmith

The Court Adjorned by reason of the Govr of Bostons
Coming to town to the 3 Instant
The Court called & opened for tryalls

Sam^{ll} Davis Pla^{t} In An Action of Escape Against **Tho Mallitt** shrieff Def^{t} upon A Rehearing the Case Called the Jury Impanalled

Rowland Robinson foreman
Charles Dyre
Tho Lilly bridge
Joshua Coggeshall
John Gould
Rog^{r} burlingham
John Ward
Zuriell Hall
Reserved [*sic*] ffish
Elisha Coale
Sampson Batty
Joshu Clarke

The case Pleaded & Committed to ye Jury the verditt wee find for Samuel Davis the debt sued for & Cost of Court & foure pence Damage. [145]

Peter Callamore of Situate pla^{t} upon A rehearing in An Action of the Case Commenced Against him by Capt **Joseph Hallis** present Def^{t} at a Court of tryalls y^{e} Last tusday in March 1702 Damage 500$^{£}$ the Action Called And Committed to y^{e} Jury the verditt wee find for Peter Callamore the Revertion of former Judgment & Cost of Court the verditt Accepted &c.

John Easton Junr Son of John Easton Senr Pla^{t} Against **Samuell King** of Newport Baker Def^{t} In An Action of the Case for with holding from ye pl^{t} a hous & two Lotts of Land mortgaged to ye pla^{t} the Def^{t} not Appearing ye pla^{t} Enters A Nihildicett The Case Committed to ye Jury the verditt wee find for ye pla^{t} ye possession of ye Land & houses sued for According to mortgage & Cost of Court the verditt Accepted & Judgment Given —

Thare being an Action whare in ye Record^{r} is pla^{t} the Court doe order ye Attorney Gen^{r}ll to be Record^{r} in sd Action

Wes^{t} Clarke pla^{t} in An Action of ye Case in wright of his wife against **Henry Tew** late Maj^{r} of ye Island, for Not Maintaining & Keeping up A fence as he hath for Severall years past: the Answer having no Refferance to ye writt A nihildicett is Entred notwithstanding the nihildicett being Entred the pla^{t} Consents to Lose his costs & share on ye pla^{t} & Def^{t} Joynes Issue by Consent & Leave of ye Court the Case Committed to ye Jury their verditt is wee find for the Def^{t} & Cost of Court the Court Accepts ye verditt of ye pla^{t} Enter A rehearing to ye Court of tryalls in March next —

Thare being An Action Depending betwene **William Pasker** [Packer?] pla^{t} & Capt **John Meritt** Def^{t} being sick & could not Appeare & prays An Imparlance to ye next Court is granted —

It is ye Resoulfd of ye Court that ye Shireff take in to Custody the bodies of **Stephen Arnold** & **William Durfie** & them Safely keepe untill they give in Suffitient bond for their parsonall Apperance at ye next Gen^{r}ll Court of tryall in March next Insuing.

The Court Dessolved

[146]

At a Gen^{r}ll Court of tryalls held for her Maj^{sts} Collony of Rhoad Island And Providence plants at Newport ye 29th of March *1703*

Present:

Sam^{ll} Cranston Esqr Govr	Grand Jury Eng^{d}:
Walt^{r} Clarke Esqr Dep^{t} Govr	Capt William Brinley foreman
Capt Robt Carr As^{t}:	Mr Edward Smith
Maj^{r} Isaac Martindall As^{t}:	Mr William Allin
Capt Joseph Sheffild As^{t}:	Mr Will Barker
Capt Robt Lawton As^{t}:	Mr Peleg Roades
Mr Benj Smith As^{t}:	Mr Thomas Durffe Junr
Mr Joseph Hull As^{t}:	Mr Benj Sherman
Mr George Hassard As^{t}:	Mr Amos Stafford
Wes^{t} Clarke Rec^{dr}	Mr Edward Larking
Tho Mallett Shrieff	Mr Sam^{ll} Tift
John Hulmes Tresua^{r}	Mr John Potter
Nath^{ll} Dyre G Atto^{r}ny	Mr Tho Briggs

The Court Opened by procklimation for tryalls of Actionall Cases:

Jury of tryalls eng^{d}:

Capt Edward Pelham foreman	Will Carr
Robt Ayres	Alixand^{r} Gording
Will Hawkings Junr	Jonathan Bennitt
Will Randall	John Scott
Thomas Manchester	Ralph Chapman Junr
Joseph Nicholson	Tho Peckham Junr

Wes^{t} Clarke Pla^{t} Against Maj^{or} **Henry Tew** def^{t} upon A rehearing the Case delivered ye Jury the verditt of Jury is wee find for ye def^{t} cost of Court & ye Court accept ye verditt —

Capt **Timothy Clarke** of Boston Pla^{t} against Capt **William Brinley** def^{t} in An Action of trespas upon ye Cause the Case plead^{d} and Committed to ye Jury the verditt Wee find for ye pla^t twenty foure pounds, 13^s: 8^d debt & Coust of Court & 70^s damage The Court Accept ye verditt —

Thomas Cobb of Boston Pla^t Against **Jonathan Barney** Def^t In An Action of Debt debt and damage 25 pounds the Case pleaded & Committed to ye Jury the verditt wee find for ye pla^t ten pounds & Coust of Court & 12^d damage the verditt Accepted by ye Court — Apriell ye 6th 1703 the Def^t Enters A rehearing & hath Answered the Law in such Cases provided —

Mr **Benj Newbary** & **fflorance Marcartte** Pla^t against **ffrancis Pope** Def^t In An Action of Debt y^e Def^t putting in no Answer to y^e declaration y^e pla^{ts} Enter A nihill dicett & y^e Case Committed to y^e Jury the verditt Wee find for y^e pla^{ts} what Appeares due by Ballance of Acc^t, viz. the sume of 92$^£$=8^s=2^d & y^e sume of 178$^£$=11^s=8^d the whole Amounting to 263$^£$=19^s=10^d & Cost of Court & 12^d damage y^e Court Accepts y^e verditt —

John Earle of y^e town of Tivertown in y^e County of Bristoll in y^e province of y^e Masachusetts Bay in New England Pla^t Against **William Earle** of Portsmouth on Rhoad Island def^t In An Action of trespas & Ejectment for with holding & detaining Sundry Lands from ye pla^t ye def^t pleads in Issue hee leagally possesseth ye Lands sued for by ye pla^t & Committs ye Case to y^e Jury The Juris verditt wee find for y^e def^t Coust of Court y^e Court Accept y^e verditt —

Jonathan Sprage Pla^t **Jeames Bick** & **Elizabeth Bick** his wife Def^t In An Action of y^e Case upon An Assumsett the Case pleaded & Committed to y^e Jury y^e verditt wee find for y^e Pla^t 9$^£$=10^s & Coust of Courte y^e verditt Accepted, Apriell y^e 6th 1703 y^e Def^t payd y^e Cost & Enter A Rehearing to y^e next Court of tryalls in Septemb^r— —

Joseph Devell Pla^t Against **Peleg Smith** Def^t in An Action of trespass & Ejectment the Case pleaded & Committed to y^e Jury the verditt wee find for ye Def^t Corst of Court ye Court Accept ye verditt — [147]

Thare being a case commensed by Co^{ll} **Elisha Husinson** of Boston & Mr **John Saffin** of Bristoll Pla^t for them selves & assotiates purchasers of lands in Narrowgansett Cuntry against **Thomas Ayres** of sd Narragansett def^t and thare being a long debate in ye Court betwene Pla^t & def^t upon severall heads in ye declaration whare ye def^t pleads for an abatment of ye action the Court having considered ye premice see cause as it appeares to ye Court y^t ye lands with in fence claimed by the Pla^{t}s as sett forth in their declaration is not bounded as sett forth in sd declaration tharefore y^e judgment of y^e Court is y^t y^e action abate.

Zabdiell Baylston Pla^t against **John Cutto**^{r} def^t in an action of debt upon account the case committed to y^e jury the verditt wee find for y^e Pla^t 10$^£$ & cost of Court & 12^d damage the Court accepts y^e verditt

The Court of Oyre & terminer & Gen^{r}ll Gole Delivery Opened
the 3th of Apriell 1703

William Durfie being indicted for high misdemeaner & Breach of her Maj^{stis} peace & brought to y^{e} barr pleads not Guilty & puts him selfe upon god & ye Cuntry for tryall the Juris verditt not Guilty & ye sd Durfie Cleared by procklimation paying of fees —

Stephen Arnold of Patixsett in ye township of providence being Indicted for Committing a newsence by setting a fence Across a highway Leading to patixsett falls & brought to ye barr pleads not Guilty & putts him selfe upon ye Cuntry for tryalls The Juris verditt Guilty — The sentance of this Court is that ye sd Stephen Arnold keepe Open the highway & not fence it in Any more & for his Contempt pay a fine to her Maj^{sty} of ten pounds into ye Gen^{r}ll tresury for ye Collonis use & pay all offices fees & other Charges Amounting to foure pounds twelve shillings & Remaine a prisoner till this sentance be p^{r}formed —

Robart Munday Chirurgin being Indited for making his Escape out of hir Maj^{stis} Gole in ye town of Newport on Rhoad Island being Committed for suspition of pirecey & brought to ye barr pleads not Guilty & puts him selfe upon God & ye Cuntry The Juris verditt Not Guilty & Cleared by procklamation paying his fees —

James Bick of providence being Indicted for A froude & brought to ye Barr pleads not Guilty & puts him selfe upon ye Jury for tryall The Jury verditt Guilty: the sentance of ye Court is that ye sd James Bick pay a fine to her Maj^{stie} of forty shillings mony to ye Gen^{r}ll tresuar for ye Collonies use & pay offices fees & other Charges Amounting to foure pounds twelve shillings & Remaine A prisoner till sentance be p^{r}formed —

Ladwick Updicke And **Abigall** his wife being Indicted for Refusing to yeald obediance to ye Assistants Warrant being Called in Court pleaded to ye Joyn[*illegible*] of ye bill & ye Court upon Consederation thare of see cause to Quash ye bill — but upon Consideration of their Contempt of Authority being so hanious the Court see Cause to Continue them in bonds of thirty pounds to ye next Court of Gole Delevery in Septemb^{r} next then & thare to Answer what shall be presented Against them for sd Contempt —

Capt **Christopher Almey** tis ye sentance & Judgment of this Court that you remaine A prisoner untill you give in suffitient bond for your Appearance at ye next Genr^{ll} Court in Septemb^{r} next Insuing to Answer to such bills as shall be found Against you for threatning & Abusing you^{r} kinsman **Jobe Almey**.

It Appearing to this Court y^{t} **Hester Borne** ye wife of **John Borne** of Newport hatter hath taken upon her selfe to practice Chirirgany with in this Government not having good Judgment thare in the which if not prevented may prove prejuditiall to her Maj^{stes} subjects this Court doe tharefore Order that ye sd Hester Borne nor Any of her famaley for ye fuiture proseade in practiceing ye sd mistrey of Chirurganey with in this her Maj^{stis} Collony with out Licence from the Authority of ye Collony upon penalty of high Contempt —

William Exsena son of **Lawrance Exsena** of ye town of Newport on Rhoad [148]
Island being Indicted for murdring a french Boy one **ffrancis Noe** one of her Maj^{sts} prison^{r}s at Armes & brought to ye barr pleads not guilty & puts him selfe upon tryall

by God & ye Cuntry the Juris verditt Guilty of manslaughte^r, ye prisoner being Againe brought to ye barr & Asked why sentance should not be pronounced Against him According to Law: ye sd prisoner by his Counsiell prayed ye bennifitt of ye Clergey which was granted & According to law was by you p^rformed: the sentance of this Court is that you be returned to ye Gole from whence you came & thare to Remaine A prisoner till to Morrow being the 9th Instanteetwene ye hours of nine in ye morning & three in ye Afternoone then to be brought forth to ye publick whiping post in ye town of Newport then & there to be branded on ye bran[e?] of ye left thumb with ye Letter **M** & After this sentance is p^rformed to Remaine a [*sic*] for A year & A day: with out Suffitient Security given to ye Authrity as they shall require This is ye Sentance of this Court.

The Court Desolved

At a Gen^rll Court of Tryall Held at Newport for her Maj^{sties} Collony
of Rhoad Island & ye first tusday in Septemb^r
being ye 7th day of ye month in ye yeare ***1703***

Sam^{ll} Cranston Esqr Govr
Walter Clarke Esqr De^t Govr
Maj^r Henry Tew As^t
Maj^r Nath^{ll} Coddington As^t
Maj^r William Hopkings As^t
Mr Joseph Williams As^t
Capt Joseph Sheffild As^t
Mr Giles Slocom As^t
Mr Benj Smith As^t
Capt James Green As^t
Capt Jeffery Champlin As^t
Capt John Eldirge As^t
Wes^t Clarke Recd^r
Capt ffrancis Pope Shrieff
Mr William Hiscock Ts^r
Mr Nath^{ll} Dyre G Attorny

Grand Jury Eng^d:
Capt James Barker forman
Left^t Thomas Weever
Mr Bartholomew Hunt
Mr John Gould
Mr John Gould
Mr Samuell Stapelton
Mr John Sheldon
Mr Latham Clarke
Mr Dan^{ll} Lawton
Capt Joseph Danell
Mr Nath^{ll} Niles
Mr Tho Spencer
Hugh Stone
Tho Gould
Joseph Mory
Alixsand Huling
Tho Brooks

Jury of Tryalls Eng^d:

John Scott foreman
James Coggeshall
William Hawkings
William Randall
George Cornell
William Anthony
Tho Sherman
Sam^{ll} Gorton Junr
Henry Hall
James Willson
Caleb Carr
Joseph Weever

The Court Opened by procklimation for Tryall of Actionall Causes

Upon an Appeall by **Peter Brock** Appelant from A judgment Given Against him by two mag^{ts} in favou^{r} of **Sam^{ll} Davis** Appelee ye Appelant & Appelee called in Court ye Appele not Appearing Judgment was Given Against him for Defalt

Thomas Casey Appalant Against **William Gardner** Appele for Revers of A judg[ment] given Against Appelant in ye Justisses Court ye parties called in Court ye Appele not Appearing Judgment is Given Against ye Appele for Defalt —

Edward Purdy Appelant Against **Jeffery Champlin** Junr Appele from A Judgment given Against ye Appelant by ye Justisses in Kings town the Case Called boath partis Appearing ye Case pleaded & Committed to ye Jury the verditt wee find for ye Def^{t} ye former Judgment & Cost of Court ye Court Accepts ye verditt

Thomas Case appelant **Nath^{ll} Wellmer** appele from a judgment given against ye Pla^{t} in ye Justises Court ye partis called in Court Pla^{t} & def^{t} appearing & committed ye case to ye jury the verditt wee find ye confirmation of fformer judgment & cost of Court — ye Court accepts ye verditt.

Stephen Arnold & **Elisha Arnold** of pautixset Pla^{ts} Against **Zachariah** [149] **Rhoads** of sd patixsett def^{t} in An Action of Trespas the Action pleaded & Committed to ye Jury ye verditt wee find for ye Def^{t} Cost of Court, ye Court Accept ye verditt

Cor^{ll} **Elisha Hutchinson** of Boston & Mr **John Saffin** of bristoll Attorney to Maj^{r} **Humphrey Autherton** and Associates pla^{t}s against **Thomas Ayres** of Kings town Def^{t} ye Case Called in Court ye pla^{ts} pleading thare is no Legall Answer to ye Declaration Entred by ye Def^{t} hee omiting to Answer According to ye Law of ye Collony & practice of this Court having no referance to ye Date of ye writt nor Declaration in ye Defts Answer whare upon ye Court According to Law & practice of this Court doe Allow ye pla^{t} A nihill dicett — — — Afterwards pla^{t} & def^{t} by Consent Agree to Com to tryall ye Def^{t} pleading ye Gen^{r}ll Issue not guilty in manne^{r} And forme as it is sett forth in ye Declaration The Case pleaded & Comitted to ye Jury, John Scott foreman: Jeames Coggeshall Will Hawkings William Randall George Cornell, William Anthony, Thomas Shearman, Caleb Carr, Jonathan Bennitt, Robt Ayres, John Easton Jn^{r}, Gilbart Majack, the verditt Wee find for ye plantifes title of Land bounded in ye Declaration & Cost of Court — — The Def^{t} having payd ye Cost & Answered ye Law Enteres A rehearing to ye Court of tryall in March next —

Capt **Anthony Chickly** of Boston pla^{t} in an Action of trespas And Ejectment against **John Coggeshall** of Portsmouth Junr thare being no Issuable plea Entred by ye Def^{t} ye Pla^{t} Enters A nihill dicett & ye Jury sent forth to Inquire for Damages ye verditt wee find for ye pla^{t} 2^{d} Damage & Cost of Court ye Def^{t} prays A rehearing in Court to ye next Court of tryall in March next which was grantd hee Answering ye Law.

Joseph Mallison Pla^{t} In An Action of ye Case Damage two thousand pounds, Against **Nath^{ll} Willmer** March^{t} & **Joseph Palmer** Marr^{er} Def^{t}s ye Def^{t} plead in barr to ye Action & ye Court Considering thareon see Cause that ye Action Abate & Assigne ye Defs Cost of Court.

Thomas Martin Pla^{t} Against **Will ffanning** Def^{t} In An Action of ye Case Debt & Damage six pounds & Eleven shillings thare being no Answer to ye Action ye pla^{t}

Enters A nihil dicett the Case Committed to ye Jury ye verditt wee find for ye plat & Cost of Court ye Court Accepts ye verditt.

Humphrey Mosley [?] And **Thomas Nuttle** of London Plats In An Action of trespas & Ejectment Damage one thousand pounds Against **Elisha Cole** & **Stephen Northrop** of Kingstown Deft thare bing no Answer in ye office by ye Deft ye plat Enteres A nihill dicett & ye Jury sent forth the verditt wee find for ye plat 2d Damage & Cost of Court the verditt Accepted: the Defts Enter A rehearing to ye Court of Tryall in March next & hath Complyed with ye Law in such Cases.

Thomas Cobb of Boston Plat upon A rehearing Against **Jonathan Barney** & **Peter Marchall** Deft in An Action of debt debt & Damage twenty two pounds the Case pleaded & committed to ye Jury the verditt wee find for Jonathan barny Plat Cost of Court ye Court Accept ye verditt.

Thomas Casey Plat Against **Thomas Seares** Deft in An Action of debt upon Assumpsett Debt And Damage thirty pounds ten shillings the Case Called plat & deft Appearing the plat pleaded in barr to sd Action & ye Court Considering thareof see Just Cose that ye Action Abate & Assigne ye Deft Cost of Court.

Quintian Crafford plat Against **Thomas Casey** Deft In An Action of Debt & Damage nine pounds twelve shillings the Case Called & Committed to ye Jury the verditt wee find for ye Deft Cost of Court ye Court Accept ye verditt—

Thomas Casey plat as quarter Master to ye Company belonging to Capt **William Wanton** Against **Quintian Crofford** in An Action of debt debt & damage seventeen pounds foure shillings ye Deft by his Attorney pleads & Abatment to ye Action which ye Court upon Consideration Allowed & Assigned ye Deft Cost of Court

Thomas Casey plat **Richd Newland** Deft In An Action of Debt Debt & Damage nine pounds the Case Called pleaded & committed to ye Jury the verditt wee find for ye plat ye mony sued for & Cost of Court ye Court Accept ye verditt —

Robart Downing plat Capt **Peter Lawrence** & **Ralph Austing** Deft In An Action of the Case for one hole sheare of ye goods & prises taken by sd Capt Lawrance & Company Damage sixty pounds the Case Called & Committed to ye Jury ye verditt wee find for ye Defendants Cost of Court the verditt Accepted in Court

[150] **Samuell Pike** plat in An Action of Debt debt & Damage Eighteen pounds Against **George Lo[??]ison** Deft the Action Called, plat & Deft Appearing Issue Gined & ye Case Committed to ye Jury the verditt wee find for ye plat the mony sued for & Cost of Court the Court Accepts ye verditt

William Bright plat in An Action of Debt debt & Damage fourteen pounds Against **Robt Weeden** Deft The Action Called & Committed to ye Jury the verditt wee find for ye plat ye mony sued for & Cost of Court, ye Deft Enters A rehearing to ye Court of tryall in March next having payd ye Cost & Given bond According to Law —

Robart Weeden Plat in An Action of Debt Debt & Damage Sixty pounds Against **William Bright** Deft ye Action Called & Committed to ye Jury the verditt wee find for ye plat ye mony sued for in ye Declaration & Cost of Court ye Court Accepts the verditt ye Deft Enters A rehearing of ye Action to ye Court of tryall in March next having payd ye Cost & given bond According to Law

Robart Wrightington Pla^{t} **William Smitson, Joseph Veren, Richard Thomas** Def^{t} Each in An Action of Debt Debt & Damage Each three pounds fifteen shillings the pla^{t} & Defdants Called in Court Will Smitson not Appearing Judgment was Entred Against him for Defalt Joseph Veren & Richd Thomas Appering by their Attorney & pleads not Guilty the Case Committed to ye Jury The Juris verditt wee find for ye pla^{t} ye mony sued for in ye Declaration & Cost of Court ye Court Accepts ye verditt

John Easton Junr Son of **John Easton** Senr Pla^{t} In An Action of the Case for by past Rent of his farme Debt & Damage one hundred fiftie one pounds ten shillings Against **Isaac Ames** Def^{t} The Action Called & thare being no suffitient Answer According to Law ye Court grants ye pla^{t} A nihill dicett And ye Case Committed to ye Jury the Juris verditt wee find for ye pla^{t} the monies sued for & Cost of Court: ye Court Accepts ye verditt, the Def^{t} Enters A rehearing in Court payd ye Cost & gave bond According to Law to Reheare sd Action at March Court next Insuing —

Capt **John ffones** of Kingstown & **John Dolman** of East greenwitch Plan^{t} Against **William Dunken** Def^{t} in An Action of debt Debt & Damage fourteen pounds for by past rents The Case Called & Committed to ye Jury the verditt wee find for ye pla^{ts} ye mony sued for & Coust of Court ye Court Accept ye verditt —

Jonathan Sprage pla^{t} upon A rehearing **Jeames Bick** Def^{t} the Case Called & Committed to ye Jury the verditt wee find for Jonathan Spreag nine pounds ten shilings & Cost of Court: ye verditt Accepted Jeames Bick Appeall to ye Gen^{rll} Assembly to be held at Warwick in Octob^{r} next having Complyed with the Law in such Cases made and provided —

Peter Barbo^{r} of boston pla^{t} Against **Charles Packer** Def^{t} In An Action of Debt upon Account Debt & Damage thirty five pounds the Action Called & Committed to ye Jury the Juris verditt wee find for ye pla^{t} ye mony sued for & Cost of Court The Court Accepts ye verditt: —

Charles Packer Marr^{r} Pla^{t} Against **Ralph Austin** Quarter Master to ye Comp[an]y Belonging to Capt **Peter Lawrance** Def^{t} In An Action of ye Case for one hole Sheare of ye goods monies & prises taken by sd Capt Lawrance & Company the Case Called & Committed to ye Jury the verditt wee find for ye pla^{t} one hole shear & Cost of Court ye Court Accepts ye verditt —

The Court of Oyre & Terminer & Gen^{r}ll Gole Delivery Opned the 15th of Sep^{tr} *1703*

It is ye Sentance of this Court y^{t} ye Order of ye Assistance of Providence & Warwick shall stand & Abide in full forse Against **Thomas Hudson** ye reputed father of A Child begotten on ye body of **Sarah Hopkings** of sd Warwick & y^{t} ye sd Hudson be bound in A bond of 20 pound for his good behavou^{r} till next Court of tryalls & ye sume of fourty shillings or ye punnishment of fifteen Lashes sentananced by ye Aforesd Assistants is by this Court holy Remitted & made voide & that ye sd Thomas Hudson pay all Costs & Chargis & Remaine A prisoner in ye Shrieffs Custody till this Sentance be performed

[151] Itt is ye Sentance of this Court y^t^ **Abigall Curtis** for Committing of fornication shall be striped Naked from her wast upward & brought to ye publick whiping post in ye town of Warwick with in this Collony & thare to receive fifteen stripes upon her Naked Back or to pay A fine of fourty shilling in mony as ye Law Directs: & ye former Judgment of ye Assistance & Justisses of Warwick to stand in full forse & ye sd Assistants &c are to see this sentance p[er]formed with what Expedition may be & it is ye Sentance of ye Court that **Thomas Stafford** whome ye sd Abigall charges for Committing ye fact shall pay all Costs & Charges & give in bond of 20^£^ with two good securities for his good behavou^r^ till ye next Gen^r^ll Court of tryalls & to Remaine A prisoner till this Sentance be p^r^formed —

The Court Considering ye Charge of **Mehetible Wheaton** Against **William Arnold** of ye town ship of Warwick for Lying with her And gitting her with Child which she possitifly Declared in Court & allso had taken her Oath before Severall of ye Justisses on ye Maine Land on ye same upon which it is ye Sentance of this Court y^t^ Mehitable Wheaton for Commiting of fornication shall be striped Naked from her wast upward & brought to ye publick whiping post in ye town of Warwick with in this Collony & thare to Recive fifteen Stripes upon her naked Back or to pay A fine of fourty Shillings in Mony as ye Law Directs & William Arnold ye Reputed father of ye Child begotten on sd Mehi^tble^ Weeton shall pay unto ye Assistance or Justisses of ye town of Warwick or their successors in sd town for & toward ye maintanance of ye Child begotten as Afore sd 18^d^ p^r^ weeke for Each & Every weeke untill ye sd Child shall Attaine to ye Age of Six years & y^t^ him ye sd William Arnold pay all Cost & Charge of Court & be bound in A bond of 20^£^ for his good behavou^r^ to ye next Gen^rl^ Court of tryalls & Remaine A prisoner in ye Shrieffs Custody till this Sentance be p^r^formed —

Lef^t^ **Ladwick Updick** & his wife **Abigall** Cleared of their bonds by procklamation paying officers ffees —

Capt **Christopher Allmy** Cleared of his bonds by procklamation paying his fees

William Durfe Cleared of his bonds by procklamation paying his fees

The Court Desolved

[152]

At A Gen^{r}ll Court of Tryalls Held at NewPort for her Maj^{sties} Collony of Rhoad Island & Providence Plantations on ye Last tusday in March being ye 28th of sd Month *1704*

Sam^{ll} Cranston Esqr Govr
Walter Clarke D Govr
Maj^{r} Henry Tew As^{t}
Maj^{r} Nath^{ll} Codding[ton] As^{t}M^{r}
Maj^{r} Will Hopkings As^{t}
Mr Joseph Williams As^{t}
Capt Joseph Sheffild As^{t}
Mr Giles Slocom As^{t}
Mr Benj Smith As^{t}
Capt James Green As^{t}
Capt Jeffery Champlin As^{t}
Capt John Eldrid As^{t}
Wes^{t} Clarke Recd^{r}
Capt ffrancis Pope Shrieff
Mr Nath^{ll} Dyre G Att^{r}y
Mr Willm Hiscock G Tres^{r}

Grand Jury Eng^{d}
Joseph Nicholoson fman
Mr Jireh Bull
Joseph Cook
Mr Stukly Wascott
Mr Henry Gardner
[Capt *name crossed out*]
Thomas Broks
Mr Sam^{ll} Wickham
Mr Richd Higings
Mr John Headly
Mr Sam^{ll} Holmes
Mr Jonathan Barny
Mr Lawrance Turner

The Court Opened for ye tryall of Actionall Cases

An Action upon A rehearing Reheard by **John Coggeshall** of Ports[mouth] Against **Anthony Chickly** former Pla^{t} the Case pleaded & Committed to ye Jury,

Mr Rowland Robinson foreman
Will Collings
John Seger
John Stanton
Joseph frey
Joseph Anthony
John Dexto^{r}
Mallica Rhoads
John Carr
Ezekell Bull
George Stidman
Joseph holmes

The Juris Verditt wee find for ye pla^{t} which is upon A rehearing & Cost of Court The Verditt Accepted

An Action Reheard by **Isaac Ayres** now Pla^{t} Against **John Easton** Junr former Pla^{t} now Def^{t}: the Case Pleaded & Committed to the Jury ye verditt wee find for ye now Def^{t} & Cost of Court The verditt Accepted Isaac Ayres Appeales to ye Gen^{r}ll Assembly ye first wensday in May next having payd & given bond as ye Law Requires —

An Action Reheared by **Richard Newland** Now Pla^{t} Against **Thomas Casey** Junr formerly pla^{t} now Def^{t} The Case pleaded & Committed to ye Jury ye verditt wee find for ye Def^{t}: upon Rehearing one pound sixteen shillings & Cost of Court ye verditt Accepted —

Thomas Cobb of Boston Pla^{t} Against **Peter Marshall** of Newport Facto^{r} Def^{t} in An Action of debt: debt & damage twenty five pounds currant mony of New England the Case pleaded & Committed to the Jury the verditt wee find for ye pla^{t} ten pounds & Cost of Court the verditt Accepted ye Def^{t} Enters A rehearing to ye Court of tryalls in Septem^{br} next having payd ye Cost & given bond According to Law —

Daniell Wood Pla^{t} **William Earle** Def^{t} in An Action of trespas upon ye case Damage twelve pounds the Case pleaded & Committed to ye Jury ye verditt wee find for y^{e} pla^{t} & Cost of Court [Rehearing to September *crossed out*]

Thomas Stanbary Pla^{t} **Daniell Williams** Def^{t} the Case debated in Court y^{e} Court see Cause to Abate y^{e} Action —

Derrick Adolph Pla^{t} **Thomas Parker** Def^{t} in An Action of detinue Damage 20$^{£}$ y^{e} Action Called y^{e} Def^{t} pleads in barr the Court Considering y^{e} plea [153] see Cause to Abate y^{e} Action —

Jahleel Brenton Esqr Reciver of her Maj^{stis} tenth of Prizes Pla^{t} Against **Thomas Casey** Late quarter master to y^{e} Company formerly belonging to Capt William Wanton Commande^{r} of ye Briginteen Grayhound Def^{t} in An Action of trespas upon ye Case Damage three hundred pounds, ye Def^{t} pleads in Abatment of ye Action but the Oppinion of ye Court that ye Case be putt to ye Jury the Juris verditt wee find for ye pla^{t} fifty nine pounds four shillings & one peny due upon Acc^{t} & Cost of Court The verditt Accepted—

Richard Sherin of Boston Butcher pla^{t} A Gainst **Rowland Robinson** of Kingstown Def^{t} in An Action of debt & damage sixty pounds the Case pleaded & Committed to ye Jury wee find for the Def^{t} Cost of Court ye verditt Accepted —

Benj~ Green pla^{t} **Andrew Barton** Def^{t} in An Action of trespas upon y^{e} Case Damage twelve pounds y^{e} Case Committed to y^{e} Jury the verditt wee find for y^{e} Plan^{t} seven pounds Eight shillings one penny & Cost of Court the verditt Accepted —

Capt **Edward Pelham** Pla^{t} in An Action of trespas & Ejectment Damage 50$^{£}$ Against Capt **William Wanton** Def^{t} the Action Called in Court **Susanah Cornish** Coms into Court & saith y^{e} Def^{t} holds his possestion in her wright the Case pleaded & Committed to y^{e} Jury y^{e} verditt wee find for the pla^{t} y^{e} mortgage sued for & Cost of Court y^{e} verditt Accepted ye Def^{t} Entering A rehearing to ye Court of tryalls in Septr next having Answered the Law in Such Cases —

Peleg Chamberlin pla^{t} **Lawrance Clinton** Def^{t} in An Action of trespas & Ejectment for with holding from ye pla^{t} ye halfe of A hous & halfe A Lott Lying & being in ye town of Newport The Case Committed to ye Jurey ye verditt wee find for ye pla^{t} ye hous & Land sued for & Cost of Court the verditt Accepted ye Def^{t} Enters A rehearing to ye Court in Sepr next having Answered the Law in Such Cases —

Peter Barbe^{r} of Boston Pla^{t} Against **James Menzies** Gent^{n} Def^{t} in An Action of debt by bond Debt & Damage Debt & Damage fifty two pounds ye Case pleaded & Committed to ye Jury ye verditt wee find for ye pla^{t} & Cost of Court [*sum illegible*] ye verditt Accepted

Thomas Church of Bristol Pla^{t} Against **John Armestrong** Def^{t} in An Action of debt ye pla^{t} Appearing ye Def^{t} not Appearing ye pla^{t} Enters A nihildicett ye Case Committed to ye Jury wee find for ye pla^{t} ye bill sued for & Cost of Court ye verditt Accepted —

Richard Newland Pla^{t} **Thomas Casey** Junr Def^{t} in An Action of debt upon Assumsett ye Action putt to ye Jury ye verditt wee find for ye Def^{t} & Cost of Court — The verditt Accepted —

Thomas Durfee Junr Pla^{t} **James Menzis** Def^{t} in An Action of Debt by bill the Def^{t} Owned ye debt in Court & Confessed Judgment —

Thomas Casey Junr Pla^{t} **Richard Allin** Def^{t} ye pla^{t} & Def^{t} Called, ye Defend^{t} not Appering Judgment was Entred Against him for Defalt —

Dan^{ll} Coggeshall Pla^{t} **Thomas Peckham** Junr & **William Collings** Def^{t} In An Action of debt by bill ye Case Committed to ye Jury ye verditt wee find for ye pla^{t} ye Bill sued for & Cost of Court ye verditt Accepted —

Peter Marshall Appeland Against **Samuell Holmes** Appele from A Judgment Given by Hon^{rable} **Sam^{ll} Cranston** Govr & Capt **William Brinly** Justis of ye peace for ye Appele in ye sume of one pound & three shillings & charges The Case pleaded & Committed to ye Jury ye verditt wee find for ye Appelant upon An Appeall & Cost of Court ye verditt Accepted —

The Court Opened for ye tryall of Crimonalls

Daniell Williams Pla^{t} **Giddian Crofford** **Sam^{ll} Winsor** & **Nicholas Power** Def^{t} ye pla^{t} Complaines of ye Def^{t}s for A forsable Entry on ye pla^{t} Land & the parties by consent Enters in to A rule of Court to Com to tryalls & Abide the Judgment of Court & if pla^{t} or Def^{t}s be Cost to pay ye Cost of Court the Case Committed to ye Jury ye verditt Not Guilty thare fore wee find for the Defendants Charges & Cost of Court —
[154]

John Callender being Indicted for privattly Conniving Abetting & Accessary to A thefte Committed by one **peter hambleton** & Allso prevey to ye Conveying Away sd hambleton from ye hands of Justis, being brought to ye Barr & ye bill of Endictment Rede unto him & Demanded Wheather Guilty or Not Guilty pleads Not Guilty & puts him Selfe upon tryall to god & ye Cuntry, The Juris verditt Guilty, The sentance of Court is y^{t} ye sd John Callende^{r} doe pay A fine of five pounds to ye Gen^{r}ll tresury for his Trancegration & officers fees & to remaine A prisoner till sd sentance be p^{r}formed —

Peter An Indian being Apprehended & Comitted to her Maj^{sts} Gole for Endevouring to Committ A rape on ye Body of **Grace Lambert** A Young Woman & Bill found Against him by ye Grand Jury: And being Brought to ye barr pleads Not Guilty & puts him selfe upon ye Jury for tryall the verditt of Jury Guilty of Attempting A rape The Sentance of the Court is that ye sd Peter Indian be burnt on ye brane of his thumbe on ye right hand with ye Letter **R** & sold out of ye Cuntry by ye first Oppertunity by the Shrieffe & what & Indian shall be sold for shall be to Defray ye Charge of Imprisonment & other Charges that hee hath ocationed & to Remaine A prisoner in ye Custody of ye Shrieff till sold—

Whareas **James Bick** **Joseph Latham** & **John Page** are presented by the Grand Jury for fraudelently Asseming the name of **James Hides** & the Court Desire ye Assistance or Justisses of ye town of providence to Apprehend the Bodies of sd psons or As many of them as Can be found & Cause them to give in Suffitient bond to Appeare at ye next Gen^{rll} Court of tryalls to be held for sd Collony at Newport ye first Tusday in Septemb^{r} next Insuing & upon their Refusuall of Giving Such bond to be Committed to her Maj^{stys} Gole in the town of Newport to Answer to their presentment

The Court Desolved by procklamation

At A Gen^{r}ll Court of tryalls held at Newport for her Maj^{sties} Collony of Rhoad Island &c ye first tusday in Septemb^{r} 1704 being ye 5 day of sd Month — — — — — — — — —

Samll Cranston Esqr Govr
Walter Clarke Esqr D Govr
Maj^{r} Henry Tew — As^{t}
Maj^{r} Nath^{ll} Codding^{t} — As^{t}
Maj^{r} Will Hopkings — As^{t}
Mr Joseph Williams — As^{t}
Capt Jo: Sheffild — As^{t}
Mr Giles Slocom — As^{t}
Mr Job Green — As^{t}
Mr Richard Green — As^{t}
Capt Jeffery Champ~ — As^{t}
Capt John Eldrid — As^{t}
Wes^{t} Clarke Recd^{r}
Capt Nath^{ll} Sheffild G. Tresu^{r}
Capt Joseph Sheffild G. Atorney

Grand Jury Eng^{d}
Capt Andrew Willitt foreman
Tho. Peckham
Tho Burge
Robart Taylo^{r}
Joshua Coggeshall
Joseph Smith wever
John Ward
Sam^{ll} Sherman
John Rise
Isaac Tomson
Jeremiah Clarke
John Thomas
Pardon Tillinghast Junr
John Wanton
Capt Nicholas Carr

The Court Opened for tryalls

Andrew Barton Pla^{t} upon A rehearing **Benj Green** Def^{t} from the verditt of Jury And Judgment of Court of tryall the Last tusday in March 1704 pleaded & comited to ye Jury the verditt wee find for ye def^{t} upon A rehearing Cost of Court & 2*d* Damage the verditt Accepted ye pla Appealls to ye Assembly

Jury

William Allin foreman
Benj Thayre
John Sheldon
Jobe Almy
John Hill
Sampson batty
Ezekell bull
John Green
John Sanford
William Burington
John Rhoads
Thomas Mattison

Richard Sherrin pla^{t} upon A rehearing **Rowland Robinson** Def^{t} from A verditt of Jury & Judgment of Court of tryalls ye Last tusday in March 1704 the Case pleaded & Committed to ye Jury the verditt wee finde for ye Def^{t} & Cost of Court ye verditt Accepted, the pla^{t} Appealls to ye Assembly at providence ye Last wensday in Octob^{r} next & payd Cost —

[155] **Peter Marshall** Plantife upon A rehearing **Thomas Cobb** Def^{t} from A verditt of Jury & Judgment of A Court of tryalls ye Last tusday of March 1704 the Case pleaded & Commited to ye Jury the verditt wee find for ye Defend^{t} ten pounds And Cost of Court the verditt Accepted; the pla^{t} Enters An Appeall to ye Gen^{rll} Assembly at providence the Last wensday in Octob^{r} next Insuing & hath payd ye Cost —

Lawrence Clinton plat upon A rehearing **Peleg Chamberlin** Deft from A verditt of Jury & Judgment of Court of tryalls ye Last tusday in March 1704 the Case pleaded & Commited to ye Jury the verditt of Jury wee find for ye Deft And Confirmation of former Judgment & Cost of Court

John Albrow Junr of Portsmouth Plat Against **James Noise** of Westerly Deft In An Action of trespas & Ejectment Damage Eight hundred pounds Currant mony of New England The Case being Debated in Court the Court upon Consideration see Cause yt ye Action Abate & ye Deft Assigned his Costs.

Elisha Hutchinson of Boston And **John Saffin** of Bristoll boath of the province of ye Masachusetts bay in New England plats Agents for & In behalfe of ye heires & Others ye representatives of Major **Humphrey Aurerton** [*sic*] & Associates In An Action of trespas & Ejectment Damage two hundred pounds **Aron Jackwise** of Kings town Deft The Case being Debated in Court whare ye Defendt pleads in barr ye Court Considering ye reasons see Cause yt ye Action shall Com to tryall & ye Deft for Issue saith hee holds ye Lands sued for in right of her Majtie Ann Queen of England the Case pleaded & Committed to ye Jury ye verditt wee find for ye Deft & Cost of Court ye Court not sattisfide sente forth ye Jury three times who Returned ye same verditt.

Elisha Hutchinson of Boston & **John Saffin** of Bristoll in ye province of the Masathusett bay in New England Plats Agents for & in behalfe of ye heires And Others ye representatives of Major **humphrey Artherton** & Associates In An Action of trespas & Ejectment Damage two hundred pounds **John fones** of Kingstown Deft ye Case being Debated in Court whare ye Deft pleads in barr to ye Action ye Court Considering ye Reasons see Cause yt ye Action Come to tryall the Case pleaded & Commited to ye Jury the verditt of Jury wee find for the Deft & Cost of Court ye Court being Dissatisfide with ye verditt sent out ye Jury three times who Returned ye same verditt.

Thomas Green John Warner Samll Green & **Daniell Sunderland** plants In An Action of trespas Damage twenty pounds **Stephen Wilcocks** Deft the Action CAlled & Committed to ye Jury the verditt wee find for ye plats Cost of Court ye Deft Enters A rehearing to ye Court of tryall in March next & Payd Cost as ye Law provides.

William Britten plat in An Action of Debt by bond Debt & Damage 10£. **Thomas Starr** Deft ye Deft puting in No Answer ye plat Enters A nihil dicett & the Case Commited to ye Jury ye verditt wee find for ye plat ye forfiture of ye bond & Cost of Court ye verditt Accepted.

Derrick Adolph Plat **Thomas Parker** Deft in An Action of Detenue Damage twenty pounds ye Case pleaded & Commited to ye Jury the Juris verditt wee find for ye plat ye Doge if in being if not then six shillings & Cost of Court — the verditt Accepted.

John fones of Kingstown Son & heir of Capt **John fones** Decd & **Mary Dolman** of ye town of Est greenwitch Widdow & Administratrix of **John Dolman** Deceased Plantifs Against **William Duncon** Deft In An Action of trespas And Ejectment Damage 50£ the Court upon Consideration see Cause to Abate ye Action. -

Charles Dyre Appelant **John Rhoads** Appele & **Joseph fry** Appele from A Judgment Given Against ye Appelant by ye Honrd Govr & Major Nathll Coddington the Case pleaded & Commited to ye Jury the Juris verditt wee find for ye Defendants Cost of

Court ye verditt Accepted & A rehearing allowed ye Plat to ye next Court of tryalls in March next. — —

Upon y^e Request of Mr **Saffin** & for An Appeall for England in y^e Cases of Mr **Elisha Hutchinson** & Other his partners A Gainst **John fones** & **Aron Jaquis** the sence of y^e Court is that y^e pla^t ought to have A rehearing to Another Court before y^e Appeall be granted, The $Hon^r d$ Govr Enter his Desent Against y^e oppinion of y^e Court in y^t Case. — —

[156]

The Court Opened for y^e Tryall of Crimonalls

Joseph fry & **John Rhoads** being presented for Breach of Sabath on y^e first Day of y^e weake And Called to y^e barr the Bill Read unto them & Joseph fry Demanded of wheather Guilty or not Guilty owned Guilty & Refered him selfe to ye Bench John Rhoads being Demand Guilty or not Guilty pleads not Guilty & puts him Selfe upon ye Jury for tryall The Juris verditt Not Guilty of this presentment. —

Joseph Latham being indicted for Libeling Against **James Hides** being Brought to ye Barr & Demanded wheather Guilty or Not Guilty pleads Not Guilty & puts him Selfe upon ye Jury for tryalls the Juris verditt not Guilty.

Joseph Latham being Indicted for breach of her Maj^{sts} Gole in the town of Providence & being brought to ye barr & Demanded wheather Guilty or not Guilty pleads not Guilty & puts him Selfe upon ye Jury for tryalls the Juris verditt Guilty. —

Joseph Latham being Indicted for Libiling & Brought to ye barr the Bill read unto him & Demanded wheather Guilty or not Guilty of the Charge thare in Contained pleaded not Guilty & puts him Selfe upon y^e Jury for tryall The Juris verditt Not Guilty. —

Joseph Latham being brought to y^e Barr to Recive his sentance for Breach of her Maj^{sts} Gole in y^e town of providence The Judgment And Sentance of this Court is that Joseph Latham y^e $prison^{er}$ at y^e Barr being by y^e Jury of tryalls found Guilty as Afore Sd on y^e 5th of $Septemb^r$ 1704 shall pay A fine of thirty pounds Currant Silver mony of New England to y^e Gen^{rll} Treasuar of this Collony for y^e use of y^e Collony And Give Suffitient bond unto Her Maj^{stie} with two Suffitient Surties to the vallue of one hundred pounds as Afore Sd to be of peacable & good $behavou^r$ to all her Maj^{stis} Leach people with in this Collony for y^e tearme of one hole year And A day After y^e Desolution of this Court & to Remaine A prisoner In her Maj^{stis} Gole in y^e town of Newport till Every part of this Sentance be p^rformed & to pay all Charges & Officers fees. —

John Burden being bound over to this Court Appered thare being no Charge Came Against him is Cleared by procklamation paying officers fees

William Earle being bound Over to this Court Appered & thare being no Charge Came Against him is Cleared by procklimation paying offices fees

The Court of tryalls Desolved by procklamation

[*This concludes the transcription. Original Book A continues for about 150 further manuscript pages, to 1721 when county courts replaced the General Court of Trials.*]

APPENDIX

Records of the Court of Trials of the Town of Warwick
1659 - 1674

The records on the following pages are copied from a transcription made by Helen Capwell "from original records in the Library of George L. Shepley, Providence, R.I., 1922," and published as a pamphlet ca.1922 by The Shepley Press, Providence.

Records of the Court of Trials of the Town of Warwick 1659 - 1674

An action of the case concerninge acountes and debt entred by **John Geraerdy** Plantive against Lieftenant **Robert Waskote** Defendant damadge 300^{li} starling the 31 of January 1659

Jury men

Mr. Walter Todd foreman	Richard Carder
Mr Mathias Harvy	William Burton
Mr Anthony Loe	John Lippott, Se

The Issue is not guilty The verdict of the Jury is wee find for the plantive two hundred & fiftie poundes and cost of Court

A Review granted to Lieftenant Robert Waskote in the present Court this 7th of February 1659

An action of Trespase of the case entred by mr **John Greene** plantive against **Matthias Harvy** Deffendant, ye 13: of August 1660

Juerey men

Rich: Townesend forman	John: Lipode Senior
William Burton	John: Smith
Anthony: Looe	John Potter

The verdict of ye Juerey is, wee find for John Gereardy plantive Eighty one pounds, & cost of corte: This 22: of August 1660

Wee finde for Mr John Greene plantive six shillings & Eight pence: & Cost of Corte: ye verdict of ye Juerie, Juerie men Mr Looe Forman-James Sweete-William Burton: John Lipode Senny: John Smith John potter ye Issue is nott guiltie

ane action Entred by Francis Derby of Debt & Damage entred against Tho Relfe this 23 of August 1660

The ferdict of ye Juerie, George Lippott Giltie to ye Vallue of five pounds with cost of Corte Jueriemen Chosen this 23: August 1660

Rich Townesend forman	James Sweete
Wm Burton	Mr Bradly
John: Lipode senjr:	Tho: Stafford

Ye Ishshur not giltie

Ane action of debt dew by bills Entrid by Mr Holliman: against Peeter Busecott: This 9: of April 1661

At a Courte of trialles held in Warwicke the 4 of February: 1661: in his majesties name

An action of Trespas Entred by **James Greene** against **Thomas Staford** Senior Damag ten pounds Starling bearing Date the bearing datte ye 13th of January 1661

the Issue not guilty

Jurie men Chosen are

Thomas Relph forman	John-Sweet
William Burten	James-Sweet
John-Lipott Senior	Henry knowles

The verdit of the Jueri Wee finde for the Plantife fouer Poundes and Cost of the Courte Eigght pd peny

Judgement is Granted

An action of Tespas upon the Case Entred by Mr **Randall Houldon** against **Thomas Staford** Senior Damag Five pound

An nihell Dixit Entred by Mr Randall houldon against Thomas Staford Senior. The verdit of the Jury Wee Finde for the Plantife Eight bushells of Wheat and a peck of Wheate and For Dammag 01-10-0 and Cost of Courte Eight pd peny

Judgement is Granted

Juri men Chosen are

Thomas Relph foreman	John Sweet
William Burton	James Sweet
John Lippot Senior	Henry knowles

An action of trespase upon the Case Entred by Mr **Randall Houldon** against **Henry knowles** defendant Dammage Fouer pound

The Issue not giuly

Thomas Relph forman	James Sweet
John Lippott Senior	Thomas Greene
John Sweet	Thomas Bradly

The verdite of the Jury Wee find for the Defendant too pence Damage and Cost of Corte

Ordred By The Courte upon The entring of the verdite heaving sent forth the Judge three times that Mr John Smyth Deputy and Mr John Wickes Asisstant being the Courte Protest against the verdite Ordred by Courte upon Mr Randalls Houldon Requst that this Action bee Refered to the next Genrall Courte of Trialls to bee houldon at newport in march next for a farther Triall

An action of Dept upon ye Case entred by Mr **Randall Houldon** of warwicke against **Eliazer Collines** of ye sane Towne Dammage tenn pounds Starling bearing Date ye 26th: of march: 1662

Ye Partis beeing agreed ye action is withdrawne

an Action of Depte upon ye Case entred by Mr Elliazer Collines of warwicke against Henry knowles of y same Towne Damag Tenn pounds Starling--bearing date ye 29th of March: 1661:

Ye Partis beeing agreed ye action is withdrawne

an Action of ye Case Entred by **Francies Dorby** Inhabitant of ye Towne of warwicke against **henry knowles** Senior of ye same Towne bearing date ye 12 day of aprill 1662 Aprell ye 28 day 1662 Henry Knowles Defendant Entreth his demure untill ye next Courte to bee held ye 3d Cheuesday in august next in: 1662 ye partis beinge agred ye Actions is withdrawen:

An action of five pounds Damag Entred by **William Burton** and **Jeriamiah Wascott** of Warwick against Mr **John Greene** of ye same Towne bearing Date ye 10th of May: 1662

A non sheute ntrd by ye Defendant being yt it is not [- - - - *blurred* - - - - - - - -] to case Agust ye: 16: 1662:

An action of ye Case Entred By **James Greene** of ye towne of warwick against **Francis Hackklinton** Brick-macker for beter Security bearing Date ye 27th of July: 1662

The parties being agred ye Sheut is within drawen august ye: 18: 1662

At a Courte held in warwick in his majesties Name Charells ye second King of Great Britan france and Ireland and ye provinces ther to belonging ye 3rd of February 1662 an Action of ye Case for breach of Conevant Entred by James Greene against Francis Hacklinton both of this Towne of warwick Damage ten poundes Starling bearing Date of ye 18th of November 1662

an nihill Diset Entred by ye Plantife James Greene against francis hacklintin Defendant ye first Day of February: 1662

The petey Jeary are namly

Mr Edmund foreman Callverly	William Burton
Thomas Relph	Amos Wascott
John Lippott senior	John Sweett

The verditt of ye Jearey is Wee Find for ye Plantife Cost of Court and Seaven pounds Damage

Judgement is Granted

an Action of Dept and Damage Entred by **Laraunc Pinock** against **Francis Hackklinton** both of ye Towne of Warwick bearing Date ye 27 of July: 1662

an Action of trespas Entred by **francis Derby** against **John Lippott** Senior boeth of this Towne of Warwicke trespas twenty ponds bearing Date ye 8th of January 1662

The parties being agreed ye action is with drawn this 20th of January: 1662

an Action of ye Case Conserning trespas entred by James Greene of Warwick against John Lippott senior of ye same Towne bearing Date ye third of aprill Damadge fouer pounds Starling 1663

An action of the Case concerninge Trespasse entred by **John Greene** of Warwicke Generall Asistant Plantive against Mr **Mathias Harvy** of Warwicke Defendant this 29th of June 1663 Damage fifty pound Starlinge

August ye 18th 1663 booeth Parties beeing agreed the action is with Drawen

The 13th of Juley: 1663 The Towne Consell beeing mett to advics conserningye Triall of **Beniamin Smith Joseph Carpentner** and Mr **Henerey Reddarke Abiah Carpenter** of Patuxet Conserning A Riot & upon ye Request of ye Parties ye Towne Counsell Doe unanimousley Consent ye Magestrates may tranesfere ye matter to ye Generall Courte of Trialls

an Action of ye Case Concerning Trespas Entred by **Francies Dorbey** Plantife of ye Towne of warwicke against **William Resbey** of ye same Towne Defendant bearing Date ye 29th of Jeuley: 1663 Damadge Tin poundes

August ye 12th bouth partiyes beeing agred ye action is witth Drawen

an action Conserning Dept Entred by Mr **Wallter Todd** Inhabitat of this Towne of warwick against **Thomas Steanton** Inhabitant of ye same Towne Damadge ten poundes Starling bearing Date ye 4th of August: 1663 an nihill Diset Entred by ye Plantivf yt - - - - - - - ye defendant 14th of August 1663

at A Courte of Trialls held in his Maiesties Name ye 18th of august: 1663: The grand Juerey are namely Mr Wallter Todd forman Mr Mathias Harvie Christopher hauckherst Thomas Staford senior Sammuell Staford Henerey knowles ye names of ye pettey Jeurey are namely Mr Mathias Harvy forman William Burton John Sweet John Lippett Senior Christopher hauckeherst Thomas Braddley

ye verdit of ye Jeury Wee finde for ye plantivfe for Dept and Dammadge 2-14-05 and Cost of Courte

an action of ye Case Conserning trespas Entred by Mr **Thomas Greene** of warwick Plantiff aggainst **John Lippott** Senior of ye Same Town Defendant this 10th of august: 1663 Dammadge 20S August ye 18th: 1663: Ye parties beeing agred Ye action is with Drawne

Warwick August ye 18 Anno 1663

This presents witnes yt wheras **BenJamin Smith** and **Joseph Carpenter** of Pautuxsett was bound by Recognence to ye kinge to answer for a Crimmall acte Charged by Mr **John Greene** at this Courte of ye: 18th of august but by reason of ye suddene Death of Mr **John Smyth** Depeutey who had ye bond in his Custodey but now his papers beinge sharched the bond Cannot bee found wherfore ye Courte seeth Caues to dismiss them

an action of Defammation entred by **Jerimah Wastokoot** Inhabitant of warwick Plantife against Mr **Thomas Smyth** Inhabitant of Pautucket in warwick Damadge one hundred pound Starling bearing Date august ye 19th 1663 Ye parteys beeing agreed this 3d of October 1663 action is with Drawen an action of Defamation Entred by **Jerimiah Wastkoot** Inhabitant of This Towne of warwicke Plantife against **Elizabeth Scranton** of ye same Towne Defendant Dammadge on hundred pound Starling bearing Date ye 19th of august: 1663 a non shuet Entred by ye plantive ye First Day of November 1663

Juley ye 28th 1663 The names of ye Jurey men yt were Impaneled to mack enqurerey as a Coroneres Inquest Mr Mathias Harvy forman Mr Thomas Grene Thomas Relph William Burton John Lippott Senior Thomas Bradley William Resbey Rodger Burlingham Amos Wastkoot Richard Osboren francies Dorbey Jerimiah Wastkoott

This 29:th of Juley 1663

Wee which are Chosen one ye Juerie Conserning ye Death, of Mr **John Smyth** of ye Towne of warwick heave made a Diligent Sarch and Cannot Find yt any man or person is giltey of his Death but yt it is ye provident of God

An action of ye Case Conserning Trespas entred by Mr **John Greene** Genrall Asistant of warwick plantife against Mr **Mathias Harvy** Defendant of ye same Towne of this 15th of september 1663 Damadge fiftey Poundes Starling

an nihill Diesitt Entred by ye plantivfe agianst ye Defendant this 31 of October 1663

an action of ye case Conserning Dept Entred by Mr **Wallter Toadd** of warwicke against **John Colles** of ye same Towne Detpe and Damadge five poundes Starling bearing Date ye 18th of September: 1663

ye parties beeing booth agred ye action is with Drawen This 18th of Sentember 1663

an Action of ye Case Conserning Dept Entred by Mis **Anna Smyth** Inhabitant of ye Towne of warwicke against **Thomas Hedger** Senior Inhabitant of ye same Towne, Dept and Damadge tin poundes Starling bearing Date ye:18 of September 1663

Warwicke ye 3d of November 1663

At a Courte of Trialls held in warwicke his Maiesties Name

ye names of ye grand Juerey ar namley Mr Thomas Greene foreman Thomas Relph Thomas Bradley Richard Carder John Sweet John Lippot Senior

The pettey Jury are namely Mr Edmund Calverley for forman Richard Carder Thomas Relph John Sweet John Lippott Senior Rodger Burlingham

The action of ye Case Conserninge Trespass Dependinge betwixt Mr **John Greene** Plantive and Mr **Matthias harvy** Defendant beeing Called and a nihill Dicet beeing Entred in the ofice and William Carpenter macking Answer as Aturney to ye Defendant it beeing upon ye plantifes Request to ye Courte Demanded of him to show his warant of Aturney ye sayd Carpenter prodeuced a Leter of Aturney which he Afirmed was yt which Autherised him to bee Aturney to ye sayd Action whereupon ye Courte heavinge perused it and Caused it to be read found yt it gave him no Authoritey at all as Aturney to this Sheut where upon ye sayd Carpenter sayd hee had witnesse yt could Testifie yt ye Intent of ye Letter of Aturney was to Authoris him in this matter to which Answer was made yt ye Letter of Aturney Could not bee Enlarged by verball witnes but notwithstandinge ye sayd Carpenter prodeuced no witnesses neither desired leave of ye Courte to Stay whill hee could prodeuce any and Therfor ye Courte heave accordingley to Law Sent forth ye Jurey to bringe in a verdict Concerning ye Damadges ye Defendant Confessin ye Action by not apearing

The verdit of Ye Jeury

Wee Finde for the plantive Seaven pound Dammadge and Cost of Courte

Judgment is granted by ye Courte

Execution beeing given to ye Sargant his retarne is non east Inventes

Mr **Eliza Collines** entreth his traves Conserninge ye bill indeted by ye Grand Jeurey for fornication This 3d of November 1663

it beeing Demanded of Eliza Collines giulty or not giulty he answered not giulty he beeing Demanded by whom he would be trieyed he answered by God and ye Coantrey.

ye petey Jury ar namly Mr Stuckly Wascott foreman Rodger Burlingham henrey Reddack John horrud Christopher houckesherst Job Allmy ye verdit of ye Juery

Wee heave examined ye Testimonys and find Eliza Collines Giulty

Ordred by ye Courte yt Eliza Collinss hall pay forty shillings or sufer ye penalty of ye Lawe ortherwies provied in yt case as all so Cost of Courte

Ame Crowe acknowledging her Selfe guillty of ye Charge of Fornication layd agaienst her by ye Grand Juery referes her Selfe to ye mercey of ye bench for her ancear and Therfore it is Determined yt ye Sayd Ame Crowe Shall Pay fortey Shillinges to ye Towne Treasury upon Demand of ye Deputy and Asistant as allso Costes of Courte

An action of Dept and Damadge Entred by **franics Uslenton** Inhabitant whittin ye verg of this Towne of warwick against ye Estate of **Thomas Scranton** senior late Inhabitant of ye Same towne Dept and Damadge ten pound bearing Date ye 9th of november 1663

and Action of Dept and Damadge Entred by **Fraince Uslenton** Inhabitant whithin ye verg of this Towne of warwick **Elizabeth Scranton** Inhabitant of this ye same Towne Dept and Damaedg twenty pounds Starling bearing Date ye 9th of november: 1663

20th octobe 1666		
Mary holyman plantife	Atatchment	08-
Awashicoke Defendant	Debt & Damage	

6 novembe 1666		
Rich: Osboene plantife	an action of Debt	
franice Uslton Defendant	Debt & Damage	£06.--00.--00

warwicke ye 26th of December 1666

thomaes Walwin	An action of Defamation Entred by **Thomas Wallin** plantife against **Robert Collwell** Defendant Damages of £20 with Drawn ye 16 of febeuary 1666
Collins Elyza with Drawn	An Action of ye Case for breach of covenant Entred by Mr **Elyza Collins** plantife against **William Moor** Defendant both of Warwicke Dated ye 24 of January 1666: 67 to answer ye second Tusday in march next
Thomas humprey	**Thomas humphrey** plantife & **John Sweet** Defendant An action of Defamation Damages twenty pound
Osborn against ford	An Action of Debt Entred by **Rich Osborne** of warwike against **John ford** of ye Same £12 Debt & Damage estimable acording to Law ye Date of ye ritt is 28 of Janury 1666 wth Drawn ye 12 of february 1666
Mary Hollyman	An Atachment against **Awashcooke** for Debt Dated ye 20 day of october 1666: with drawen by **John Sweet**

An Action of Debt brought by By **rich: Osborne** plantife against Joh

Aprill the 17th 1667: atatchment or writt agst William Langly	**Richard Osborne** plantife **William Langley** Defendant in an arest or atatchment upon an Action of ye Case Damages £03-09

An Action of Debt Entred by **Jame Green** of warwicke against **Mr John an Indean** of nasakett Debt & Damage Eyghteen Shilling Currant pay Decembr ye 2d 1667 with Drawn ye

13th of Decembe 1667

Decbre: ye 14th 1667

An Action Entered by Mr **Jame Green** of of warwike against **Kokataweahkitt** an Indean for Debt, Debt & Damage £11 - 11 & 8

An Action of The Case touching Debt and accoumpts Entred ye 11th of January 1667 by Mr **Elyza Collins** of ye towne of warwicke plantife Against **John Smith** of ye towne of providence (mason) Defendant returnable ye second tusday in march next Ensuing ye Date heerof

with Drawen ye 22th of february 1667	An action of Debt upon bill Entred by **peeter buscoot** plantife against **jeremy Westcot** Defendant both of ye towne of warwicke in ye collony of road iland Debt & Damage 39s Dated ye 18th of January 1667 The cort will be ye 2d tusday in march next

John Throckemorton of providence plantiffe Entreth an action of ye Case for Debt, Debt & Damage five pound Cureant pay of this Collony against **John read** of warwicke Defendant Dated ye 24th of february 1667 with drawne

James Blakemore plantife **peeter Busecot** Defendant too answer ye 2d Tusday in march next at warwicke	an action of Slander Dated ye 15th of november 1669 Damage 20 pound this Action with drawne by a non shuitt no Declaration
Edward marshall plantife **george halsey** Defendant to answer ye 2d tusday in march next at wicke	An Action of Debt Debt & Damage Six pound 21 December 1669

moses mudge of patuxet plantife in an Action of ye case for Debt: Deb & Damages forty six shilling against **George Halsey** of pawtuxett Defendant: Entred ye 7th day of february 1669:70:

This action is withdrawne ye 14th Day of februarye 1669

An Action of ye Case Entred by **Joseph Jenckes** plantiffe against **Samuell Reape** Deffendant for Denying to accoumpt with ye plantiffe Damage £10: Curant pay of this Collony of road iland

Dated ye 15th of December 1671

withdrawne by the order of ye plantiff Sent by capt: greene ye 16 febr: 1671:72

An Action of ye Case for Debt Entred by **walter Todd** of warwicke plantiffe against **John wickes** Senior of ye Said Towne Deffendant Debt & Damage fower pound

Dated Ye nynth Day of february 1671:72

An action of ye case for Debt Entred by **John Gereardy** of warwicke plantife against **George palmer alias pamer** of petequonsett Defendant Debt & Damage tenn pound Starline

Dated ye 16th of february 1671:72

Withdrawne ye 17th by order of ye plantiffe they being agreed

An action Entred by Mr **Walter Tod** plantiffe against ye widdow of **Mastawasux** Debt & Damage of fower pound fower shilling Dated ye 2d of octobe 1672

An Action of Debt Entred by **John Gerreardy** Plantiffe Against **John an indean** Defendant whoe sometime was A Servat at **Stuckley Westcotts** house Debt & Damage twenty Shilling Currant pay of this Collony Dated ye 14th of november 1672

Elyza Collins plantife **Powan alias Powett** an indean Defendant An Action entred by ye plantife of Debt ye 11th of September 1674 Against the Defendant Debt & Damage Six pound Curant pay of ye Collony to be tryed at march Cort next after ye Date heerof ye 2d Tusday in march

8th of Octobr 1674	**Abell potter** plantiffe **John read** Defendant An Action Entred by ye plantife Debt & Damage £10 **Jeremiah westcott** warrant The Action was with Drawn they agreeing

First of January 74 A repleay taken out by **Jeremy westcot** bond being first given by hime of tenn pound to Answer **John Gareardy** in An Action of trespase about a Cow of Jeremy Westcott who eate some hay of John gereadys

John geready with Drays his suit ye same Day

Jo: Green agst
m :harvey

The Declaration of **John Greene** Plantive Inhabitant of the Towne of Warwicke against Mr **Mathias Harvy** Defendant Inhabitant of the Same Toune, in an action of Trespasse upon the Case bearinge Date the 13th of August 1660 is that the Defendant hath most InJuriously upheld his wife in pluckinge Downe the Plantives fence frontinge upon his mother Greenes lott which formerly hath been so longe posessed by the Plantives father Greene but is at present in the plantives posession The sayd fence formerly privately Demolished so that a man might rather have Imagined it to bee Indianes then English but this present wer publiq with a publiq acknowlegement of what was privately Done to the Plantives Damadge five pound

Starlinge for which cause the Plantive is forced to bringe this action to this honoured Court for Justice

By mee John Greene

Frances Doorby his indytment
against Hoyshak & wawisum

I **Frances Doorby** of Warwicke indyteth **Ahogshake & Wawisum** two Indeans Inhabitants in or about ye towne or township of warwicke in ye Collony of providence plantations in New england

For that upon ye 22th Day of may in ye yeer of our Lord 1662 ye Said Ahogshake & Wawisum ye Indeans above naimed Did set on fire ye Dwelling house of frances Doorby in ye nyght time, which did burne till ye said house was burned Downe to ye ground allso his Corne & goods was therin Destroyed which actt Done by Ahohogshake & Wawisum aforesd frances Doorby aforesd Doe avere to be a fellonious Act in them and therfore pray that they may Answer heer unto

Frances X Doorby
his marke

Doorby bound to his behavior

You **Francis Dorbe** acknowlege your selfe Indebted to the Comon weale of England the sume of Ten poundes to bee payd upon all Demaund the Condition of this obligation is such that if the above bounden francis Dorbe shall bee of a peaceable behaviour Towards all the states subiects untill the next Towne Court beinge to bee holden in this Towne of Warwicke the first Tuesday in November next ensuinge and here apeare and pay five pound for his Default if this Towne require it which tree voluntary engadgeth I say upon the performance of the promises payinge charges hee is to bee cleared and this obligation voyd Taken by mee John Greene Asistant this 4th of October 1659 his marke

Francis Dorbe

henry knowles Answer to mr houlden

The Answer of **henry Knowles** Defendant against Mr **Randall Houlden** Plantive to his Declaration bearing Date the 29th of January:1661:is not giulty of the trespas and therfor the writt to abate and and the Defendant to be Dismised with goodes & cost this 30th of January:1661:

Henry X knowles

Thomas bradly pla
peete Buzicott Defend

The Declaration of **Thomas Bradly** of the Towne of Warwicke Plantive against **Peter Buzicott** Senior blackesmith of the same towne of Warwicke in an action of

Slaunder bearinge Date the 3 of December 57 is that the Defendant hath most ignominiously slaundered the plantive, by Afirminge that the Plantive hath stole somewhat from him which forceth mee to bringe this action, to this honoured Court for Justice, and seinge that a mans good name is more worth than wealth, I cannot but charge him with one hundred pound Damadge, though it bee not sufficient recompense

Thomas Bradly

mr Greene & Mr Harvey

An answer by **Matthias Harvy** Defendant against Mr **John Greene** plantive, to his Declaration bearing Date ye 13 of August 1660, whereas ye plantive Doeth Declare yt the said Deffendant hath most In Juriously up held his wiffe in plucking Downe his fence to his Greate Damage, ye Said Matthias Harvy Defendant, Doeith Declare not giltie, yt neither he nor any aboute him, hath at any time plucked Downe or Removed any fence, of ye plantive, which stoode upon ye said plantives groend, or yt ever stoode one his fathers ground, and thare fore ye said Defendant, Doeth Declare, yt ye said plantive hath Dun him a greate wrong, therefor yt writ to abate, & ye Defendant to be Dismised by good Cost, this 15: of August 1660

by mee Richard Townesend
Auturney in the Case

INDEX TO NAMES

* indicates that the entry is for the person named as a juror or in a legal capacity (other than as a plaintiff or defendant)

INDEX TO PLACES AND SUBJECTS

Please note that the subject index is not exhaustive. Cases of debt have not been included unless they mention an item of special interest.